D1125079

A Centre of Wonders

For my dear friend, John.

James M. Lindman
[signature]

The Anatomy of Man's Body, as said to be governed by the Twelve Constellations.

♈ Aries, the head and Face.

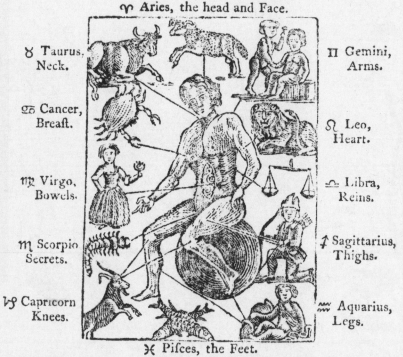

♉ Taurus, Neck.

♊ Gemini, Arms.

♋ Cancer, Breast.

♌ Leo, Heart.

♍ Virgo, Bowels.

♎ Libra, Reins.

♏ Scorpio Secrets.

♐ Sagittarius, Thighs.

♑ Capricorn Knees.

♒ Aquarius, Legs.

♓ Pisces, the Feet.

To know where the Sign is. First find the day of the month, and against it the sign or place of the moon, in the eighth column. Then finding the sign here, it shews the part of the body it is said to govern.

We have inserted the above, and the prognostics of the weather, according to the most approved methods; but think it proper to inform our readers, that, in this enlightened age, the learned put but little confidence in them.

A CENTRE *of* WONDERS

The Body in Early America

Edited by

JANET MOORE LINDMAN
and MICHELE LISE TARTER

Cornell University Press

ITHACA AND LONDON

Frontis: *The Man of Signs,* in *Poor Will's Almanack, For the Year of Our Lord, 1795,*
The Library Company of Philadelphia.

Copyright © 2001 by Cornell University

All rights reserved. Except for brief quotations in a review, this book, or parts thereof, must
not be reproduced in any form without permission in writing from the publisher. For information, address Cornell University Press, Sage House, 512 East State Street, Ithaca, New
York 14850.

First published 2001 by Cornell University Press
First printing, Cornell Paperbacks, 2001

Printed in the United States of America

Library of Congress Cataloging-in-Publication Data
A centre of wonders : the body in early America / edited by Janet Moore
Lindman and Michele Lise Tarter.
    p. cm.
  Includes bibliographical references and index.
  ISBN 0-8014-3601-X (cloth : alk. paper) — ISBN 0-8014-8739-0 (pbk.
: alk. paper)
    1. Body, Human—Social aspects—United States—History.   2. Body,
Human—Symbolic aspects—United States—History.   3. United
States—History.   4. United States—Social life and customs.   I.
Lindman, Janet Moore. II. Tarter, Michele Lise, 1960–   . III. Title.
  GT497.U6 C46 2001
  306.4—dc21   00-013068

Cornell University Press strives to use environmentally responsible suppliers and materials to
the fullest extent possible in the publishing of its books. Such materials include vegetable-
based, low-VOC inks and acid-free papers that are recycled, totally chlorine-free, or partly
composed of nonwood fibers. Books that bear the logo of the FSC (Forest Stewardship
Council) use paper taken from forests that have been inspected and certified as meeting the
highest standards for environmental and social responsibility. For further information, visit
our website at www.cornellpress.cornell.edu.

Cloth printing   10 9 8 7 6 5 4 3 2 1
Paperback printing   10 9 8 7 6 5 4 3 2 1

Contents

Acknowledgments   ix

"The earthly frame, a minute fabrick, a Centre of Wonders"   1
JANET MOORE LINDMAN AND MICHELE LISE TARTER

I. THE PERMEABILITY OF BODIES AND ENVIRONMENTS

Witchcraft, Bodily Affliction, and Domestic Space in
Seventeenth-Century New England   13
ROBERT BLAIR ST. GEORGE

Food, Assimilation, and the Malleability of the Human Body
in Early Virginia   29
TRUDY EDEN

"Civilized" Bodies and the "Savage" Environment
of Early New Plymouth   43
MARTHA L. FINCH

The Body Politic and the Body Somatic   61
JACQUELYN C. MILLER

II. DEMARCATIONS OF THE BODY

Murderous Uncleanness   77
KATHLEEN M. BROWN

"Clean of blood, without stain or mixture"   95
JENNIFER M. SPEAR

A "Doctrine of Signatures"   109
SUSAN M. STABILE

III. Bodies in Performance

Nursing Fathers and Brides of Christ   129
Elizabeth Maddock Dillon

Quaking in the Light   145
Michele Lise Tarter

"Antic Deportments and Indian Postures"   163
Alice Nash

The Body Baptist   177
Janet Moore Lindman

IV. Bodies in Discourse

Hannah Duston's Bodies   193
Teresa A. Toulouse

Body Language   211
Nancy Shoemaker

Emancipation and the Em-bodiment of "Race"   223
Joanne Pope Melish

The Problematics of Absence   237
Todd D. Smith

Selected Bibliography   255
Contributors   271
Index   275

Acknowledgments

A Centre of Wonders is the coming together of many disciplines, cultures, and voices. We would like to express our gratitude to the McNeil Center for Early American Studies at the University of Pennsylvania—and, in particular, Dr. Richard Dunn, the former director of the center, for his support of our scholarship. We would also like to acknowledge the community of scholars affiliated with the center who have encouraged and critiqued our work over the years. In addition, we thank the Omohundro Institute of Early American History and Culture at the College of William and Mary; at their first annual conference in 1995, we had the opportunity to meet many historians and literary scholars doing groundbreaking work on the subject of the body. It was at the institute's second annual conference that we began to conceptualize the framework of this book.

The title of this anthology comes from a manuscript letter of Dr. Benjamin Rush lodged in the Historical Society of Pennsylvania, and we are grateful for the society's permission to use this archival material. In addition, we appreciate the assistance of everyone at the Library Company of Philadelphia, including Jessy Randall and Phil Lapsansky, and most notably Jim Green, who shared with us the significance of the Man of Signs, which illustrates our book cover. We are equally grateful to our respective academic institutions for their generous support of our endeavor. Finally, and most significantly, we thank each of the writers in this book for their fine scholarly contributions to the ongoing cultural study of bodies in early America.

J. M. L. and M. L. T.

A Centre of Wonders

"The earthly frame, a minute fabrick, a Centre of Wonders"

An Introduction to Bodies in Early America

JANET MOORE LINDMAN AND MICHELE LISE TARTER

Images of bodies and bodily practices abound in early America: from spirit possession, Fasting Days, "buggery," "monstrous births," and infanticide to running the gauntlet, going "naked as a sign," flogging, bundling, and scalping. One popular icon of British North America was "the Anatomy," or Man of Signs, which appeared regularly in widely circulated almanacs. Illustrated as a European man sitting on a globe, his figure was encircled by the twelve zodiacal symbols, indicating the planetary effects on one's physiology.[1] This image placed the human form in vital relationship to the universe, with each constellation directly affecting a specific internal organ. Gemini, for example, was connected to the physiognomy of one's arms and shoulders; Libra, to the "reins and loins"; and Scorpio, to the "secrets." Accompanying the central motif was a chart detailing the phases of the moon and the body parts most vulnerable to lunar influence, thereby accentuating the perceived interconnectedness of human bodies to the stars. In such a context, the mortal frame was positioned as the center of an orderly and well-governed universe and was read as a microcosm, or "Anatomy," of the world.

This cultural artifact originated in medieval Europe and underwent myriad inscriptions in succeeding generations. In colonial America, it took a shape and force of its own, reflecting the convergence of religion and science in a malleable world of bodily encounters and cross-cultural intersections. The Man of Signs signified and was a signifier of somatic constructions; illuminated as a corpus in constant relation and revolution, it served as a center of providential and scientific wonders. As a product of the European imagination that became a symbol of the colonial process, the Anatomy thus provides multiple inroads for understanding the influence, impact, and significance of corporeality in early American contexts.

Capturing the many layers of corporeal connotations in eighteenth-century America, Dr. Benjamin Rush aptly described the body as "the earthly frame, a minute fabrick, a Centre of Wonders." This volume, drawing its title from Dr. Rush's passage, places bodies at the center of analysis to present them as physical entities and textual productions—as cloth woven with complex cultural meanings. Bodies are maps for reading the past through lived experience, metaphorical expression, and precepts of representation. They tell us about social rituals, food ways, dress codes, dance and movement, criminality, political conflict, religious ideology, warfare, gender roles, racial concepts, and formations of subjectivity and identity. Yet, as living, breathing, ingesting, performing entities, bodies afford a specificity of lived experience that has been devalued and all but erased in western philosophical traditions. Historian Lyndal Roper makes this point clear when she states: "Unless...we...can learn to admit the psychic and the corporeal, we shall never truly encounter the past."[2] Cultural reevaluation of the human frame reveals the historical importance of sentience and materiality in early American societies, and consequently leads us to a more complete story of the past.

Bodies are not only physical phenomena but also surfaces of inscription, loci of control, and transmitters of culture. They are never unmediated; they are related but not reducible to cultural concepts of differentiation, identity, status, and power. As Stallybrass and White assert, "The body cannot be thought separately from the social formation, the symbolic topography, and the constitution of the subject. The body is neither a purely natural given nor is it merely a textual metaphor, it is a privileged operator for the transcoding of these other areas."[3] Encompassing both the physical and the symbolic, it is, therefore, fully enmeshed in the social relations of power.

Bodies are always in the process of becoming; as open-ended categories, they are amendable to codes that restrict, contain, open, or expand them and the cultural and contextual interpretations of their corporeality. Culture shapes somatic experiences just as body codes and movements shape cultures. Whether forged by folk belief or scientific knowledge, the social construction of bodies reflects the need to create order from chaos; to delimit social hierarchies, gender roles, and sexual differences; to signify dominant religious and political ideas; and to set parameters of appropriate conduct, morality, and belief.[4]

The colonial project in the Americas initiated a set of relationships among some of the most diverse peoples in the world. Early contact among Native Americans, Europeans, and Africans was literally that—contact among different bodies, peoples, and cultures. The "discovery" of divergent societies, the "invasion" of foreigners into a settled land, and the "exchange" of bodies, diseases, technologies, and belief systems all constituted the Columbian enterprise. Understanding bodies in time and place is particularly revealing because the "discovery" of America ushered in a new period in human history. First, connecting the "old" world with the "new" touched off a chain reaction of cultural, economic, racial, and political conflicts and complexities that are still with us today. The Columbian Exchange introduced microbes, plants, and animals to both worlds at the same time it created settlements, institutions, alliances, and biracial and multiracial peoples. Second, sustained relationships among Native Americans, Europeans, and Africans occurred at a time when western concepts of bodies were undergoing dramatic change. These two developments created new foundations of knowledge and new relations of power that had lasting effect on both sides of the Atlantic.

An ideology of social hierarchy influenced early modern notions of race, whereby Europeans ascribed inferiority to those who were non-Christian and non-European. Though many early travelers to the Americas admired the "sturdy" and "well formed" bodies of Indians, they also criticized the indigenous peoples for their nakedness, shamelessness, and perceived licentiousness.[5] Conversely, Native Americans found these "strangers" puzzling and repulsive with eyes the color of the sky, hairy faces, and elaborate body coverings. The foreignness of Europeans was evident to the African Olaudah Equiano, who, while aboard a slave ship, feared that they—"those white men with horrible looks, red faces, and long hair"—would do nothing less than eat him.[6] On the other hand, as the slave trade developed and as Europeans had increasing contact with Africans, they advanced claims that "negroes" had "smaller brains" and "stronger, coarser nerves," which suited them well for their servile status in the Americas. Cultural subordination fused with racial inferiority as Europeans claimed that "white" people epitomized civilization, while those of darker complexion became equated with savagery.[7]

Race became a "natural" category based on the visual evidence of African and Indian bodies marked as "black" and "red," and, in the process, the body became what Robyn Wiegman calls "the origin of race truth." Europeans systemized this assumption by developing "scientific" theories, such as "polygenesis," to assert that phenotypic variance was due to the separate origins of the races. This theory gained political force as European society used it to justify brutal treatment of Africans and Indians. Racialized discourse served as a new weapon to codify and constrain human bodies based on a politics of difference.[8]

Gender also became an organizing principle of early contact in the Americas. Contemporary iconography often portrayed America as a Native American woman waiting to be "tamed" by a European man; pictured as a naked, dependent, "heathen" female, she was caricatured as the possession of Europe (the clothed, Christian male), who brought true religion, reason, and technology to her, a desirable yet vulnerable and uncultured "New World." Sexualizing and feminizing the landscape and its native peoples became part of the colonial project as the construction of gender took on renewed potency on the American continent.[9]

European discourses of gender underwent change with the application of scientific theory to power relations in the eighteenth century. New social and political ideologies stressed women's alterity, while emerging scientific theories shifted from a one-sex continuum to a binary two-sex model of human bodies. No longer historically defined according to Aristotelian theory as "inferior males," women were portrayed as essentially different from men. Emphasis on women's bodily difference from men was linked to a renewed ideology of domesticity that celebrated women's marital and maternal state. Still, the complementary nature of male/female relationships did not eradicate medical perceptions of the female corpus as weak and deficient or religious ideals of women as the daughters of Eve.

This new knowledge about corporeality and its subsequent discourses came from European science and philosophy. First, the Scientific Revolution redefined human physiology based on medical discoveries in the seventeenth and eighteenth centuries. Early modern science revised ancient and medieval concepts of human anatomy, and new information challenged Galen's longstanding theory of the body as a container of four humors that required balance to ensure good health and temperament. Scientific practices and technologies, such as dissection (to see the circulation of the blood) and microscopes (to view particles), allowed Europeans both a visual and visceral spectacle of the internal apparatus of the body. These scientific discoveries and revised frameworks were utilized to establish a hierarchy of social relations.[10]

Second, Enlightenment philosophy influenced "New World" concepts of the somatic by purporting a radical understanding of human society and identity. By privileging the mind over the body, European *philosophes* such as Descartes fabricated a hierarchical system that separated embodiment from reason. At the same time, they argued that only those who could control their physical and emotional passions could achieve self-mastery. The *philosophes* justified the creation of political and social discourses that were at once democratic and exclusive and based on "natural" capacities. Europeans celebrated "human" experience as the pinnacle of creation, while simultaneously limiting which bodies could have access to or be representative of power in a transatlantic world.[11]

The new meanings of bodily difference became evident in American versions of the Man of Signs.[12] In some, he stands tall; in others, he is hairy, or shaven, or his bowels are exposed; and, in one publication, he even appears androgynous with breasts. Eighteenth-century renditions of the Anatomy featured additional characters to represent the zodiac along with the traditional figures, reflecting hierarchical strategies that were being enforced in the sociopolitical world. An Anglo-American woman in colonial dress, for example, held an apple, or a flower, as the emblem of Virgo, sign for the Bowels; a Native American warrior with headdress, bow, and arrow, stood as Sagittarius, or the Thighs. Smaller in proportion to the man in the center, these constellations acknowledged the presence of new peoples and new bodies in North America while also placing them in subordination to the dominant symbol of the Anatomy.

Many bodies and many interpretations of bodies were coming together in the transitional world of cultural contact, conquest, and adaptation in early America. Inhabitants of the "New World" ascribed cultural meanings to corporeal variations based on race, gender, ethnicity, and status that eventually developed into concrete social categories. A 1729 imprint that used the Man of Signs succinctly verifies the fixity of racial identity and ethnic background by the eighteenth century, at the same time it secures the European male body as a central icon in this colonial context. Beneath the engraved image, the almanac editor acknowledged the public demand for this figure while he also promoted an essentialist view: "The Blackmoor may as eas'ly change his Skin/As men forsake the ways they'r brought up in;/Therefore, I've fet the Old Anatomy/Hoping to please my Country men thereby."[13]

By the end of the eighteenth century, the Anatomy had come to signify superstitious folk beliefs by many colonists who ridiculed its inclusion in almanacs. Printers retained the chart that documented the lunar cycle, denoting that audiences still acknowledged the effects of the cosmos on human life, but readers no longer accepted the mortal frame as a microcosm of the universe.[14] New images and constructs of corporeality emerged as "scientific" knowledge and enlightened philosophy defined and promoted bodily concepts based on "natural" differences, such as race and gender.

As an interdisciplinary project, *A Centre of Wonders* brings together scholars from different fields who contextualize and analyze bodies in early America through an array of critical approaches and themes. In multivalent and provocative readings of primary materials, many of these writers make innovative use of contemporary theorists as diverse as Elaine Scarry, Mary Douglas, Michel Foucault, Judith Butler, and Hélène Cixous. While some early Americanists have been reluctant to embrace the burgeoning field of cultural studies—and, in particular, to historicize and textualize bodies—this collection demonstrates the dynamic possibilities and promising results of interdisciplinary work. In no way do these essays compile a complete or definitive account of this subject; rather, their diverse methodologies and insights offer a starting point for an enhanced and sophisticated exchange of ideas.

In intratextual dialogues that reach across many historical time periods, topographies, and anatomies, these contributors examine societies from New England to Virginia, from Pennsylvania to Louisiana, spanning the years between 1600 and 1830. They advance our knowledge of bodies in time and place and demonstrate how particular cultures have made use of "the earthly frame." At times, the essayists approach the same primary materials from different viewpoints and reach quite distinct conclusions (Finch, Shoemaker); at others, they explicate histories from different perspectives, thereby complementing and advancing each other's cultural interpretations

(Brown, Toulouse). While this collection primarily explores the colonial experience of North America's eastern seaboard, its dialogue invites further research on embodiment that goes beyond a British colonial focus. Ultimately, this project not only calls for a sustained and dynamic practice of cross-disciplinary scholarship but also a redefinition of the parameters of early American studies.

Divided into four sections, the book distinguishes the most recent areas of interest and study on the body in early America. The first, entitled "The Permeability of Bodies and Environments," investigates the linkages between bodies and their environment, whether in the consumption of food, use of land, protection of houses, or management of epidemics. The second section, "Demarcations of the Body: Fluidity and Containment," addresses the creation of boundaries to constrict bodies within specific contexts and the intertwining relationship between fixed and fluid categories of corporeality. The nature of performativity is the focus of the third section, "Bodies in Performance: Corporeal Manifestations of Identity." The authors in this section consider the body as a site of performance and change, particularly in terms of gender and spirituality, prophecy and movement, and communal identity and otherness. The fourth and last section, "Bodies in Discourse: Race, Ideology and Public Rhetoric," examines the intersections of bodily constructs with social discourse and political ideology to produce new forms of status and domination.

There are salient, overarching themes about the body that emerge and link the articles together beyond the four designated sections of the book: these are correspondence, fixity, flux, and metaphor. First, the ancient theory of "correspondences," transplanted to the Americas with European migration, hypothesized connections existing between bodies and the wider world. This theme of correspondence is demonstrated in a number of essays (Eden, Finch, St. George, Stabile), including Jacquelyn C. Miller's discussion of the dialectic relationship between bodies, medicine, and government. As she argues, Benjamin Rush perceived the interrelations between science and politics when he contemplated the nature of disease and death in the yellow fever epidemics of the 1790s. Seeking curative methods for his dying patients, this statesman/physician also expressed anxiety and formed conclusions about the health of the body politic, the state of democracy, and the "constitution" of the recently formed national government.

Next, some of the writers explain how body constructs are used to institute fixity and control in specific communities (Brown, Lindman, Nash, Smith). Political power serves as a primary means to regulate bodies; whoever governs, controls, punishes, or owns others' bodies wields terrifying authority over the dependent, the captive, the convicted, and the enslaved. Thus, the cultural meanings projected onto bodies reflect a process of mapping: a political cartography that is demarcated by categories of difference, including race, gender, status, ethnicity, religion, and sexuality. Jennifer M. Spear contends, for example, that the blood cases of Spanish Louisiana, adjudicated by a legal hybrid of the old French *code noir* and the newly adopted Spanish law, illustrate the intricate selection process placed on those seeking entry into the upper class. This gatekeeping schema increasingly depended on a racialized understanding of bloodlines that was rooted in the French legal tradition but which gained new currency in an American setting.

In the act of restricting bodies, societies contain the perceived threats posed by those bodies that are labeled irregular—be they religious dissenters, criminals, or disorderly women. Social boundaries separating dirt and cleanliness, deviance and normalcy, heresy and orthodoxy all reinforce the fixity of somatic concepts. For example, Michele Lise Tarter recounts how Quaker women preachers traveling to New England perceived their activity as the inspiration of "divine light," while Puritans defined these outsiders as a contagion that warranted corporeal mutilation. Even when subversive, bodies can be used to mediate difference and maintain political power in times of great upheaval. As Teresa A. Toulouse carefully traces, Puritan society—besieged by an Indian war, a witchcraft craze, a charter crisis, and religious dissent at the end of the seventeenth century—appropriated one woman's body to make sense of a world gone astray. Hannah Duston's bodily transgression (murdering ten Indians to escape captivity) was framed as a heroic and redemptive act that served Cotton Mather's political agenda to revive the patriarchal family and the Puritan godly order.

Conversely, a third theme is the ways in which bodies can connote fluidity, flux, and change within a specific cultural context (Finch, Lindman, Nash). Trudy Eden asserts that those European colonists who "planted" their bodies in early America worried about the corporeal effects of environment, climate, air, and food. The fear of "going native"—of their physiology changing because they ate indigenous foods—established a new dimension of bodily surveillance. Fluidity in body concepts can also challenge fixed meanings of social difference, as in the case of race. Joanne Pope Melish analyzes how the instability of new somatic renditions, such as the belief that a "black" person's body could turn "white," transformed race into a mutable classification in the early nineteenth century. Yet, this variability instigated fear and anxiety that subsequently created new categories of racial containment, invoking the process once again.

Finally, some authors of this volume show how the body is often employed to symbolize the self, the other, and society (Brown, Smith, Stabile). As a metaphor, it creates connections between seemingly disparate things: in the Puritan context, Robert Blair St. George depicts how orderly houses reflect godly families which, in turn, represent the righteous communities of New England. Emblematic of explicit and implicit meanings, such metaphors reflect the ideological importance of the body to make sense of a "New World" undergoing dramatic cultural change. For instance, Nancy Shoemaker argues that skin color as a body metaphor and as a marker of cultural difference between Europeans and Indians came to dominate the racial discourse of early America. Metaphors also undergo change, as Elizabeth Maddock Dillon shows in seventeenth-century Puritan religion. "The bride of Christ" and "nursing father" metaphors lost their meaning for Puritan men as the two-sex model of bodily identity changed contemporary configurations of sex and gender.

Early America was a concatenation of corporeal encounters: "old" and "new" world beliefs and traditions were colliding and competing; diverse societies and peoples were coming together and changing; and new ideologies were developing and shaping this multifarious world. At every turn, bodily images and practices were being read, reinvented, adapted, and understood. As an "earthly frame," a "minute fabrick," and a "Centre of Wonders," the body was a source and center of interpretation, granted primary significance as an arbiter of social, cultural, and political power. In richly nuanced and complex readings of viscera and text, this anthology proffers an equally multivalent exploration of early American bodies in cultural interchange, converging in historical flesh and bone.

Notes

1. For more information on this image, see Marion Barber Stowell, *Early American Almanacs: The Colonial Weekday Bible* (New York: Burt Franklin, 1977), 19–25; Keith Thomas, *Religion and the Decline of Magic* (New York: Cambridge University Press, 1971), 196–297, and Peter Eisenstadt, "Almanacs and the Disenchantment of Early America," *Pennsylvania History: A Journal of Mid-Atlantic Studies* 65 (spring 1998): 148, 156.

2. Lyndal Roper, *Oedipus and the Devil: Witchcraft, Sexuality, and Religion in Early Modern Europe* (New York: Routledge, 1994), 27.

3. Peter Stallybrass and Allon White, *The Politics and Poetics of Transgression* (Ithaca, N.Y.: Cornell University Press, 1986), 192. Also see Roy Porter, "History of the Body," in Peter Burke, ed., *New Perspectives on Historical Writing* (College Station, Pa.: Pennsylvania State University Press, 1991), 206–32. Scholars in various fields have contributed to this work including Michel Foucault, *The History of Sexuality*, trans. by Robert Hurley (New York: Vintage Books, 1990); Michel Foucault, *Discipline and Punish: The Birth of the Prison*, trans. by Alan Sheridan (New York: Pantheon Books, 1977); M. M. Bakhtin, *Rabelais and His World*, trans. H. Iswolsky (Cambridge, Mass.: MIT Press, 1968); Pierre Bourdieu, *Distinction: A Social Critique of the Judgment of Taste*, trans. R. Nice (Cambridge, Mass.: Harvard University Press, 1984); Norbert Elias, *The Civilizing Process*, trans. by E. Jephcott, vol. 1 and 2 (New York: Pantheon, 1982, 1983); Mary Douglas, *Purity and Danger: An Analysis of Concepts of Pollution and Taboo* (New York: Praeger, 1966); and Clifford Geertz, *An Interpretation of Cultures: Selected Essays* (New York: Basic Books, 1973).

4. Feminist scholars have also written extensively on the body. For a sample of this work, see Judith Butler, *Bodies That Matter: The Discursive Limits of Sex* (New York: Routledge, 1993); Elizabeth Grosz, *Volatile Bodies: Toward a Corporeal Feminism* (Bloomington: Indiana University Press, 1994); Susan Bordo, *Unbearable Weight: Feminism, Western Culture, and the Body* (Berkeley: University of California Press, 1993); Zillah Eisenstein, *The Female Body and the Law* (Berkeley: University of California Press, 1989); Luce

Irigaray, *This Sex Which Is Not One,* trans. Catherine Porter with Carolyn Burke (Ithaca, N.Y.: Cornell University Press, 1989), and Janet Price and Margrit Shildrick, eds., *Feminist Theory and the Body: A Reader* (New York: Routledge, 1999).

5. See Fernando Colon, *The Life of Admiral Christopher Columbus By His Son Ferdinand,* trans. Benjamin Keen (New Brunswick, N.J.: Rutgers University Press, 1959).

6. See James Axtell, *The Invasion Within: The Contest of Cultures in Colonial North America* (New York: Oxford University Press, 1985); *The Interesting Narrative of the Life of Olaudah Equiano, Written by Himself,* ed. Robert J. Allison (Boston: Bedford Books, 1995), 54.

7. See Thomas Laqueur, *Making Sex: Body and Gender from the Greeks to Freud* (Cambridge: Harvard University Press, 1990), 150–55; and Jennifer Morgan, "'Some Could Suckle Over Their Shoulder': Male Travelers, Female Bodies, and the Gendering of Racial Ideology, 1500–1700," *William and Mary Quarterly* (January 1997): 167–92.

8. See Robyn Wiegman, *American Anatomies: Theorizing Race and Gender* (Durham, N.C.: Duke University Press, 1995), 27–28. Also see Emmanuel Chukwudi Eze, ed., *Race and the Enlightenment: A Reader* (Cambridge, Mass.: Blackwell Publishers, 1997), 5.

9. Kathleen M. Brown, *Good Wives, Nasty Wenches and Anxious Patriarchs: Gender, Race, and Power in Colonial Virginia* (Chapel Hill: University of North Carolina Press, 1996), 54–58, discusses the use of gender (and gendered language) as a primary category that shaped colonial encounters in British North America.

10. Lester S. King, *The Medical World of the Eighteenth Century* (Chicago: University of Chicago Press, 1958); Ludmilla Jordanova, *Sexual Visions: Images of Gender in Science and Medicine Between the Eighteenth and the Twentieth Centuries* (Madison: University of Wisconsin, 1989); and Londa Schiebinger, *Nature's Body: Gender in the Making of Modern Science* (Boston: Beacon Press, 1993).

11. Peter A. Schouls, *Descartes: The Enlightenment* (Montréal: McGill-Queen's University Press, 1989), 148. Also see Roy Porter, *The Enlightenment* (Atlantic Highlands, N.J.: Humanities Press International, 1990) and Dorinda Outram, *The Enlightenment* (New York: Cambridge University Press, 1995).

12. With the first printing press of Massachusetts in 1639, the Man of Signs became a regular feature of almanacs, which served as a standard channel for information in Anglo-American society. By the mid-eighteenth century, there were more than fifty different almanacs printed in the colonies, and at least three-quarters of these reproduced this symbol; in fact, printers indicated that their almanacs would not sell if they failed to include this archetype. See Eisenstadt, 151–53.

13. This imprint appears on the back cover of *Pennsylvania History* 65 (spring 1998), in relation to Eisenstadt's study.

14. Eisenstadt, 156.

I

THE PERMEABILITY OF BODIES
AND ENVIRONMENTS

Nova Svecja seu Pensylvania in America Descriptio, from Tomas Campanius Holm, *Kort Beskrifning om Provincien Nya Swerige Uti America, Som Nu fortjden af The Engelske Kallas Pensylvania,* The Historical Society of Pennsylvania (call no. 702 C186).

Witchcraft, Bodily Affliction, and Domestic Space in Seventeenth-Century New England

Robert Blair St. George

In 1658 a bolt of lightning tore into John Phillips's house in Marsh-field, Massachusetts. When the smoke thinned and the smell of brimstone abated, Phillips was discovered "dead on the hearth ... without any motion of life." Piled beside his burned and broken body were fragments of his burned and broken house:

> Many bricks of the chi[m]ney were beaten downe the principle Rafters split the battens & lineing next [to] the chi[m]ney in the chamber broken, one of the maine posts of the house into which the summer was framed torn in to shivers & great part of it carried severall rod from the house, the dore where the ball of fire came downe Just before the s^d Phillips was broken downe, out of the girts or sumer afores^d being a dry oake was peices wonderfully taken.

Incidents of invasion, affliction, or supernatural assault—from lightning, hail, or "lithobolia" (strange episodes in which stones were mysteriously hurled at the roofs and sides of houses)—occurred throughout the seventeenth century and continued well into the eighteenth. Yet above all, assaults on the bodies and houses of ordinary people were a central feature of witchcraft. As such scholars as John P. Demos, David D. Hall, and Carol F. Karlsen have demonstrated, those accused of practicing witchcraft were typically (but not invariably) female, old, unmarried or widowed, or were individual women whose independent control of real property made them the focus of distrust, animosity, and hostility in their communities.[1]

From individuals pushed to the dangerous margins of the body social came forces that both contorted and inverted bourgeois embodiment. The drama

13

of misshapen figures is most developed in stories about possession, when witches, acting for Satan, took symbolic control of someone's body and recast it in a malefic image. From entering the actual bodies of victims, it was a short step in metaphor for a witch or demon to enter their houses and reek havoc at similar bodily points, and it is on this precise "analogie" of bodies and houses that this chapter concentrates. In Newbury, Massachusetts, in 1679, for example, William Morse claimed that flying sticks and stones barraged his house's roof, that furniture danced in midair, and that the locked front door proved useless. "We heard a grete noyes of A hoge in the house," Morse recalled, "and I aros and found a grete hoge in the huse and the dore being shut I opened the dore the hoge running vilently out." He grew more anxious when his shoemaking tools disappeared from a windowsill, only to come flying down the chimney in disarray moments later. The chimney malfunctioned badly, with other objects coming down and into the house as often as they went up and out.[2]

Similar events occurred in 1682 at George Walton's house in Portsmouth, New Hampshire. Pelted by rocks from every conceivable direction, the structure was the target of a "stone-throwing devil." Here, too, there was a distinctly topsy-turvy quality to what transpired, as objects assumed the active role of persons. Chairs began to dance in midair, and to disappear and reappear at will. A cheese jumped from its press and crumbled on the floor. Several cocks of hay somehow levitated off the ground and settled in nearby trees. As at Morse's, objects that belonged on tables refused to stay put. Note, however, where and exactly what went wrong. A gate was ripped off its hinges. Stones came into "the Entry or Porch of the House." Glass windows shattered without apparent cause. A spit flew up the chimney, came back down, and was then thrown "by an invisible hand" out a window.[3]

Investigations of witchcraft in seventeenth-century New England have succeeded in relating specific cases or entire outbreaks to such issues as community tension, economic faction, inequalities of gender and wealth, the complex popular beliefs sustained by lay Puritans as they struggled to accommodate both "superstition" and doctrinal reform, and the social psychology of aging and its attendant marginalization. But little work has focused on the symbolic textual work accomplished in the depositions and other narratives that appeared as part of judicial proceedings. As the strange incidents at the houses of Phillips, Morse, and Walton suggest, one symbolic connection was frequently repeated and thus stands out as crucial to the relationship of witchcraft, bodies, and domestic space: the metaphoric equivalency drawn between the dwelling house and the human body, between architecture and the extended range of meanings attached to the concept of embodiment. As will be shown in this chapter, witches attacked houses because these structures of wood, brick, and stone were material metaphors of the human body; because of the extended meanings of the body, the house references malefic assaults against the family unit (the "little commonwealth," or dynastic body), the church (Christ's body), government (the political body), and community order (the social body). The problematics of gender and social authority cut through each of these layers referenced in metaphoric compression by the dwelling house. Houses had piercings, openings, places where the interior realm of protected people and protected goods came into contact with the exterior world of chance, risk, power, and forces both seen and unseen. Houses were implicated in the play of meanings in seventeenth-century New England culture precisely because they were the recognized spatial domain of women, individuals seeking ways to redress the patriarchal structure of law and property that contained their actions, that limited their lives. House-body metaphoric play attains its most precise equivalency in witchcraft narratives.

Of course, sources that address the analogous correspondence of architecture and anatomy are relatively easy to come across. They include the Bible (especially Paul's letters to the Corinthians), metaphysical poetry written in old and New England, and sermons, diaries, and early modern architectural treatises. Seventeenth-century English writers, for example, seized on the metaphor to describe the skeletal aspects of houses. John Donne observed how "The rafters of my body, bone/Being still with you, the Muscle, Sinew, and Veine,/Which tile this house, will come again." Robert Herrick added that the "body is the Soules poore house, or home/Whose Ribs the Laths are, and whose Flesh the Loame." The "loame" or plaster that Herrick describes was the flesh that covered up the carcass of the house. Joseph Moxon defined a "Carcass" as "the Skeleton of an House, before it is Lath'd and Plastered." And Richard Neve, borrowing Moxon's diction for his own treatise on house construction in 1703, defined the carcass as "The Timber-work (as it were the Skeleton) of a House, before it is Lathed or Plaister'd." New England poets typically stressed the transient qualities of the skeleton and its temporal covering of flesh. Anne Bradstreet viewed her aging body as "my Clay house mouldring away." Edward Taylor stated that "I but an Earthen Vessell bee," "a Mudwall tent, whose Matters are/Dead Elements, which mixt make dirty trade." As parts of an architectural skeleton, the particular names for the different framing members of a New England timber house also suggest bodily discipline: post head, collar, shoulder, hip, "prick post," and foot. In sum, the materiality of a house and its accompanying language—its timbers, tiles, laths, and bricks—ideally functioned as signs of Christ's perfect body, and as a corresponding model of a "loving" social order. Seeking help through prayer, Taylor used architectural imagery to articulate the common theme of self-abasement: "I'm but a Flesh and Blood bag: Oh! do thou/Sill, Plate, Ridge, Rib, and Rafter me with Grace."[4]

Beyond the metaphoric treatment of the skeleton (i.e., the timber frame), the analogies that tie the body's limbs, organs, and features to architectural models are remarkably exact from the late sixteenth century through the early eighteenth (see accompanying figure). Although it finally confirms a

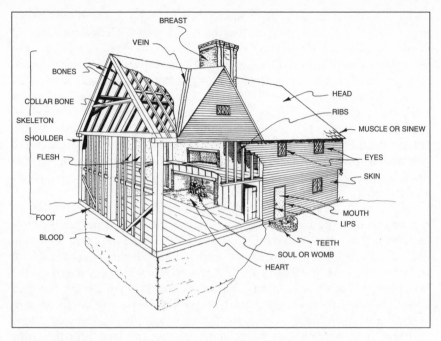

The following labels appear on the drawing: BREAST, VEIN, BONES, COLLAR BONE, SKELETON, SHOULDER, FLESH, FOOT, BLOOD, HEAD, RIBS, MUSCLE OR SINEW, EYES, SKIN, MOUTH, LIPS, TEETH, SOUL OR WOMB, HEART

The Human House and Its Parts in Seventeenth-Century New England. Drawing by Robert Blair St. George.

prevailing hierarchic and male concept of the body, the most agile play in bodily metaphor appears in Robert Underwood's *A New Anatomie. Wherein the Body of a Man is very fit and aptly (two wayes) compared: 1 To a Household. 2 To a Citie.* For our purposes, Underwood's poem is useful because it juxtaposes an impressive array of architectural spaces and functions with marginal notations that state exactly what bodily member is being referenced. When the house-body analogies it presents are collated and compared with the plan of a typical English postmedieval house, the image that results offers a detailed representation of the human figure in material substance.[5]

The cross passage or screen in the house corresponds to the waist that connects the lower body to the upper; it is a passage between the two bodies that one enters through the front door or mouth. Turning into the lower body, one enters the kitchen, defined by Underwood as the "place from the Groines to the Midrife." Here are various vessels or bowels—perhaps hogsheads or tubs—full of food "which long there, did not stay," but was sent quickly "*Gutters, Holes,* and *Channels*" out of the house. In the margin Underwood states that gutters and holes refer to "The Yard & the Fundament" (penis and anus), which allow polluted waters and solids to pass through the end of the house into a channel cut in the ground. Also in the kitchen are several objects representing abdominal organs. "A Pott hunge boyling there" represents the stomach. Under the stomach, instead of a fire, "a Fountain did appeare," representing the liver. Underwood's treatment of the kitchen as the "lower" body contains several key body parts, including ones that suggest the gender of his metaphoric house: the bowels, urine, penis, anus, stomach, kidneys (with collick and stone), liver, blood, and gall bladder.

From the body's lower end, Underwood then moves to the hall, "devided from the *Kitchen* with a / Thinne and slender wall." Normally a room used both for meals and for gatherings around a central floor hearth, the hall contains two vital organs. The heart is a seat, "like unto / a Throne of Maiestie: / Or to a Chair of Estate." This heart-throne, "in colour somewhat redd," is the social heart of the family and the preferred position of the patriarch. And "About this roiall Seate" was a bellows-like "thing in substance light"—the lungs—which ventilated the heart ("Hale in the cool and tender air") and which, if stopped, then "the seate and all the house, / do presently decay." In the upper end of the house-body, Underwood's language grows more specific. A room "over head is seelde with Bone like Ivorie," a layer of bone he likens to the skull. The brain itself is represented by a bed, which "(in Pallet wise) doth lie upon the floore." The metaphoric linkage of bed and brain seems logical: dreams and portents occurring during sleep took on qualities of prophecy and revelation, and sleep was commonly conceived as a time of dangerous vulnerability to invisible forces. From the bed arose the brain's Wit: "It is his common guise, / Much company for to frequent, / and in his tabletalke, / To argue there of many thinges, / to make his *Clapper* walke."

The clapper figures the house's tongue and was most frequently a term used to describe a talkative person's tongue. "That Clapper of the Divell," one author explained in the late 1630s, is "the tongue of a scould." In early modern England and New England, scolds were often perceived as troublesome women, whose fondness for gossip and rumor could both set neighbors "by the ears" with partial truths and cause the maintenance of family discipline to be difficult at best. Minister Thomas Adams spoke for many men when he stated that "woman, for the most part, hath the glibbest tongue.... She calls her tongue her defensive weapon, [but] a firebrand in a frantic hand doth less mischief." Scolds spoke in a variety of styles, from "murmuring," "slighting," and "affronting" to "reviling" and "railing" in a high-pitched shriek; the noisiness of a scold's tongue perhaps reminded weary listeners of the clapper of a bell. The clapper suggests how important it was for a household's "head" to ensure proper "government of the tongue" among lesser bodily members: women, servants, and children.[6]

As I have already suggested, house-body analogies as playful as those described by Underwood appeared in early New England in the dense metaphors of poetry by Edward Taylor and Anne Bradstreet, of sermons by the Mathers, and in the terse entries of Samuel Sewall's diary. Taylor, for example, referred to the windows of a house as "the Chrystall Casements of the Eyes," and equated a cupola to "my brain pan turrit." A brief sample of house-body analogies from seventeenth-century New England sources demonstrates their clear derivation and variation from English tradition: the roof is the head, laths the ribs, plaster the flesh, clapboards the skin, windows the eyes, door the mouth, threshold the lips, door lintel the tongue, hearth the heart, and the fire the soul and womb.

That early New England houses metaphorically extended a woman's heart, womb, and soul to the hearth and fire argues the house was an arena of female authority. But why should this have been the case in New England more than in England itself? One reason might be that Puritan patriarchs were in fact more "feminine" than their English counterparts. While engaged in lives that saw power mediated through the church, government, and commerce, men at the same time invoked the integration of a feminine role in which men, as "brides" of Christ, sat down at communion, as at a marriage feast, to celebrate their roles as "handmaidens" of the Lord. Ministers, surely committed to the defense of patriarchy, likened themselves to women's breasts, from which their congregations "may receive the sincere milk of the Word"; they urged their flocks to "suckle at the breasts of both Testaments." Perhaps from a psychological perspective, as David Leverenz has argued, Puritan men were thus both authoritarian and submissive, individuals who at once denied inner conflicts over having been "spoiled" and "feminized" in childhood, and found in "feminine" emotional dependence a sense of personal affirmation; "female imagery provided a transformational vocabulary satisfying desires for dependence while denying ambivalence in fantasies of regressive union."[7]

Surely such metaphors served to naturalize dramatic differences in the relative position and power of men and women in early New England society. Male property owners no doubt realized that women granted control over domestic affairs would be "deputy husbands" and wield that authority in service of the corporate estate. The appropriation by Puritan patriarchs of feminizing discourse therefore worked to build an identification with the submissiveness of women; the politics of identification shaped across gender lines do not indicate any real integration of a feminized role on the part of men, despite the language involved. Indeed, the language of men being "brides" actually strengthened, in a subtle manner, their control over women, and allows us to see in the human house one arena in which gender politics were debated.[8]

The problem for patriarchs was clear: how to naturalize the house as a hierarchic body that could effectively contain and limit the social position of women while simultaneously granting them some authority within the household. One technique lay in the design of the New England "saltbox" house itself. It was an architectural strategy that announced the sanctity of the nuclear family and so ordered space that the family's "head" could maintain an idealized surveillance over the dependent members of his body. The front of the house presented an image of order and control to the public way. In New

England a public face of order was essential to maintaining family government and gender relations; one legal source, *The Surveyor's Dialogue,*
phrased the question precisely in 1607: "And is not every Mannor a little
common wealth, whereof the Tenants are the members, the land the body,
and the Lord the head?" Transplanting the organic language of republican
political theory to family discipline, husbands were "heads" of the household's body, and wife and children its lower extremities. The exterior order
of the house provided architectural proof of patriarchal discipline. With its
window/eyes, door/mouth, roof/brain visible from the street, the human
house provided a male model of society, but one that could incorporate
within its gendered figure elements usually conceived as female.[9]

Take, for example, the most visible and expensive element of any house-
body, the chimney. When some houses were built in the first generation of
settlement, this "female" feature was incorporated and figured as a specifically male emblem. In Maine in 1634, John Winter affirmed that "I have built
a house heare at Richmon Island that is 40 foote in length & 18 foot broad
within the sides, besides the Chimnay & the Chimnay is large with an oven
in each end of *him,* & *he* is so large that we Can place our Chittle [kettle]
within the Clavell [lintel] pece. We can brew & bake and boyle our Cyttell
all at once in *him* with the help of another house that I have built under the
side of our house." Yet the central place of women in the household's interior body gains support from the metaphoric correspondence of elements relating to the chimney: the hearth and fire to the heart, womb, and soul of the
house. Women worked constantly at the hearth, tending fires and performing the many tasks associated with their heat: cooking food, processing soap,
dying cloth, rendering offal from a late November slaughter. Each move at
the hearth called for adjustment to crane, jack, pot, trivit, draft, kindling,
coal. As one proverb of the period put it, "A woman can never go to the
hearth without tampering with it," for in tending the flame she symbolically
tended the soul of the house. Edward Taylor made the connection in worry-
ing over the state of his soul:

> My Fireless Flame! What Chilly Love, and Cold?
> In measure Small! In Manner Chilly! See.
> Lord blow the Coal: Thy Love Enflame in mee.

He asked God to put new life in his soul, and directed God's aid to his hearth:

> But oh! if thou one Sparke of heavenly fire
> Wilt but drop on my hearth; its holy flame
> Will burn my trash up.

Seventeenth-century women associated fire and ovens, emblems of the soul,
with pregnancy. A belief in early modern England held that a woman might

be impregnated by fire if spark or cinder burned her apron above the knee. Cotton Mather even prescribed a prayer for women to repeat during labor: "Therefore now let it please thee to Bless the House of thy Hand-Maid." Finally, the chimney was commonly conceived in early New England as the "breast" of the dwelling, symbolically dressed in a covering "mantle."[10]

While exterior facades announced a patriarch's faith in prescriptive norms and his incorporative or "feminizing" strategies—strategies with a hegemonic dimension—rear lean-tos and back doors ensured that women, domestic servants, and informal backyard visits would remain hidden. As the saltbox house plan incorporated the kitchen, formerly placed at the house's "lower end," and relocated it at the rear, it sustained the image of family self-discipline only by demoting women, cooking, and kitchen conduct from the "lower" but publicly visible end to the socially invisible "backside" of the domestic body. By the turn of the eighteenth century, however, kitchens located in rear lean-tos were the norm throughout New England. The incorporation of the woman's principal work domain into the body of the hierarchic house signaled a new form of gender enclosure and segregation that placed women and children even further under the watchful eye of the husband/father; the actual timing of this spatial segregation is difficult to determine. As Cotton Mather observed in 1725, women "ly very much Conceal'd from the World, and may be called *The Hidden Ones*," especially in rural towns.[11] The change was already underway by the late 1680s and suggests that an attempt to maintain surveillance over women through architectural means may have come in response to narratives that described women—in the role of aged hag, widow, controller of property, and witch— as piercing, assaulting, and symbolically subverting the hierarchic order of the social world that contained them.

The material world spun out of control at the houses of John Phillips, William Morse, and George Walton. Body parts contorted. Chairs flew around rooms. Animals passed through locked doors. In still other cases, barns burned where no fire was visible, and entire houses blew down in gusts of angry, providential wind. Phillips, Morse, and Walton concluded their houses were bewitched, and for good reason. In folk tales in old and New England, witches often attacked houses at their weak points or bodily openings. They entered and left houses by chimneys (breasts), slipped miraculously through keyholes (related to the tongue), and passed nonchalantly through doors (mouths) and windows (eyes) well secured by terrified homeowners. As "piercings" in the thin membrane that separated the world of interior artifice from the dangerous exterior universe of entropic nature and divine affliction, these focal points also served as passages between the visible and invisible worlds. Witches attacked the points of bodily vulnerability in the house—the breast or heart, mouth, and eyes—that defeated the premature enclosure and complete regulation of the upright body. As Robert West has observed, "[T]he simple popular conception was that demons entered the body through its orifices, ordinarily with bewitched or unblessed food, or, if to a devotee, perhaps through the ignoble parts."[12]

Witchcraft narratives make bodily piercing, assault, and subversion of hierarchy a key trope of their symbolic force. In New Haven, in 1655, three young girls heard a witch making a "great fumbling at the chamber door." Doors and windows were preferred targets. According to Joseph Marsh of Hartford, when young Elizabeth Kelley saw Goodwife Ayres invisibly enter her house, she screamed, "There she comes over the mat." In Stratford, Connecticut, in 1692, accusations made against Hugh Scotia included that "he also sayd ye devell opened ye dore of eben booths hous made it fly open and ye gate fly open." That same year a Salem man recalled that when his son was ill in 1680, as Bridget Bishop "Came oftener to the hous he grew wors & wors: as he would be standing at the door would fall out & bruis his fase upon a great Step Stone as if he had been thrust out bye an invisible hand."[13]

Narratives often represent windows (eyes) as more vulnerable than doors (mouths). In the 1656 case against Eunice Cole in Hampton, New Hampshire, two local women heard "something scrape across the boards of the windowe." Joseph Safford of Salem claimed that Bridget Bishop's familiars escaped through a window too small for the witch herself. "Rising erly in the morning and kindling a fir in the other Room," Safford recalled:

> mi wife shricked out I presently Ran into the Room wher my wife was and as soon as ever I opened the dore my [wife] said ther be the evill one take tham wherupon I Replyed whar are thay I will take them if I can shee said you wil not tek them and then sprang out of the bed herselfe and went to the window and said thar they went out thay wer both biger than she and thay went out ther but she could not.

In an interrogation of Mary Lacey in July 1692, the Salem court asked how she had gotten into Timothy Swan's bedchamber. "W'ch way did you gett in?" they asked. "The Divel helped us in at the window," she answered.[14]

Finally, witches were associated with the chimney of the house-body and its "opening" at the hearth. Elizabeth Knapp of Groton claimed in 1671 that the devil had urged her to murder family members, neighbors, and her own children, "especially the youngest—tempting her to throw it into the fire, on the hearth, into the oven." In Connecticut Abraham Fitch claimed that Elizabeth Clawson came into his chamber invisibly one night in 1692: "I saw a light abut the bignes of my too hands glance along the sommer of the house to the harth ward, and afterwards I sawe it noe more." That same year in Salem, Eleazar Keyser saw strange apparitions in his chimney. "Being in my own house, in a Roome without any Light," he explained,

> [I] did see very strange things appear in the Chimney. I suppose a dozen of them. w'ch seemed to mee to be something like Jelly that used to be in the water and

quaver with a strainge Motion, and then quickly disappeared soone after which I did see a light up in the chimney aboute the bigness of my hand some thing above the bar w'ch quivered & shaked, and seemed to have a Motion upward upon Which I called the Mayd, and she looking up into the Chimney saw the same, and my wife looking up could not see any thing, soe I did and doe very Certainly Concider it was some diabolicall apperition.[15]

Although narratives suggest that doors (mouths), windows (eyes), and chimneys and hearths (heart/breast/womb/soul) were attacked most often, other parts of the house proved equally vulnerable to witches. Hannah Perley of Salem stated that Elizabeth How "appared to her throug[h] a crevic of the clabourds" (metaphorically meaning a cut in the skin). Mary Brown of Reading deposed against Sarah Cole of Lynn, charging, "my self and children have often heard lik the throwing of stone against the house and the creatures crying like catts upon the Roffe of the house." This could be done directly—by flying in a window, for example—or it could be accomplished through the use of image-magic: small dolls or "poppets" the witch could secrete in the hidden places of her own house-body, often in small corners or small "holes." While helping in 1685 to "take downe the Cellar wall of The Owld house" in Salem where Bridget Bishop had once lived, John Blye and his son William found "in holes of the s'd owld wall Belonging to the s'd sellar found Severall popitts made up of Raggs And hoggs Brusells w'th headles pins in Them, w'th the points out ward."[16]

   With a world of demons, witches, and portentous fires announcing God's wrath and threatening their bodies, people took various steps to minimize risk of deformity and death. The most obvious was to attack or disembody the witch herself through countermagic. But witches reputedly had superhuman strength and were not easy to challenge. Direct evidence of countermagical strategies is scattered unevenly and demands caution in interpretation. Much has been written about the "magic guarding" of the house in western culture—meaning attempts to use things like amulets, salt, shoes, and pieces of iron to guard against malefic assaults—but much of it is antiquarian, fragmentary, and beyond arguing that houses somehow needed "protection," lacks interpretive cohesion. However, if we look at these techniques from the perspective of the house-body metaphor, the scraps of documentation make a new kind of sense. Vulnerable points or piercings needed protection through medical, religious, and architectural means. Spirits attacked the same orifices where disease and sin collect, and they were as worrisome to ministers and magistrates as to carpenters and yeoman farmers. Anyone's house could become a theater of divine affliction and magical force. The same fears that drove individuals to value the protection of church ordinances drove them to guard symbolically the house that represented the family's body.[17]

   To guard against arbitrary disaster, people carefully planned the time when they built their houses: by the season, the position of the moon, the schedule of holy days, and, perhaps for a wealthy individual planning a large or ostentatious house, the stability of local class relations. In 1692, just as he was serving as a judge in the Salem witchcraft trials, Samuel Sewall consulted his minister, Samuel Willard, to ascertain that the moment was right to build a new house. Willard must have calmed his apprehensions, for construction moved apace. Once moved in, Sewall and his family held a private fast to offer thanks for their new lodgings: "Mr. Willard begins with Prayer, and preaches from 2 Chron. 34. from Luke 1, 50, and then concludes with prayer ... I appointed this day to ask God ... [to] bless us in our new house." Yet doubt crept into Sewall's mind when the structure was "violated" at its most vulnerable points during a storm in 1695.

> Mr. Cotton Mather dined with us, and was with me in the new Kitchen when this was; He had just been mentioning that more Ministers Houses than others proportionably had been smitten with Lightening; enquiring what the meaning of God should be in it. Many Hail-Stones broke throw the Glass and flew to the middle of the Room or farther ... I got Mr. Mather to pray with us after this awfull Providence; He told God He had broken the brittle part of our houses, and prayd that we might be ready for the time when our Clay-Tabernacles should be broken.

Three years later, in a pious reversal of the "poppet's" image-magic, Sewall placed cherubim heads at the gates to his property, believing they would endow the house with protective forces.[18]

Various objects were thought to have protective powers in safeguarding a house, but only a few material remains are well documented. Some New England husbandmen buried objects in the cellar and chimney walls of their structures as construction proceeded. Dedham's John Farrington laid a spoon up in his cellar wall, apparently convinced that the implement's presence in his foundation might symbolically "feed" his house and give it added strength. Shoes were also concealed behind walls, above windows, under floors, in roofs, and in chimney stacks. Although they are one aspect of the symbolic "dressing" of the house, in vernacular practice, boots and shoes had also been used to conjure and contain the devil, and when placed in walls near windows, doors, or under hearths, they might trap an evil spirit as it tried to enter.[19] As gestures that strengthened, guarded, and blessed the house-body, each of these otherwise obscure features affirmed the house as a living being, a "thing" with personified attributes, a fetishized material presence in New England communities.

Throughout England in the sixteenth and seventeenth centuries, people buried small "witch bottles" under their thresholds or hearths or laid them up in the wattle-and-daub work over the door a witch was most likely to enter. Some bottles were glass and filled with colored threads, bones, hair, nail parings, and even cloth hearts pierced with pins; these were buried beneath the hearth to protect against witches who might come down the chimney. When placed in the ground inverted and filled with cloth hearts, sharp metal implements, and the urine, hair, and nail parings of a bewitched person, the bulbous shapes of these bottles were believed to simulate bladders that would give the witch sympathetic abdominal spasms and ultimately cause death.[20] If not buried beneath the hearth, witch bottles were associated in some way with the chimney, since they were intended to prevent witches from entering the house. After a series of stone-throwing attacks that focused on the door, windows, clapboards, and roof, a group of Quakers in George Walton's Portsmouth house promptly "did set on the Fire a Pot with Urine, and crooked Pins in it, with [the] design to have it boil, and by that means to give Punishment to the Witch, or Wizard (that might be the wicked Procurer or Contriver of this Stone Affliction) and take off their own, as they had been advised." In 1692 Roger Toothaker, a Billerica physician, described how his daughter had killed a witch using a similar technique. Her method was simple and again focused on the chimney area. She "gott some of ye afflicted persons urine and put it into an Earthen pott and stopt said pott very close and putt said pott *into* a hott oven, and stopt up said oven and ye next morning said *childe* was dead." Still others, especially colonists from England's northern and western counties, may have carved their chimney posts with designs that would prevent a witch from crossing the threshold, lined their chimneys with salt-glazed bricks, or put salt in small niches built into a chimney jamb because they believed that salt could ward off demons and purify the house.[21]

Rocks may have rained down from heaven, ripping roofs and riling tempers. Hogs may have stepped miraculously across thresholds. Salt may have kept spirits, unable to step across its charmed barrier and make *malificium*, at bay in a chimney. Yet these unusual events helped seventeenth-century people focus on a central existential problem: how could one tie together the myriad material details of everyday life in such a way as to reveal the latent connections between quotidian experience and the larger, more elusive formations of gender, kinship, church, and state? Mapping the body onto an inanimate object—the house—allowed them to consider their own lives in relation to social structure and politics. Having reviewed the relationships between gender and the control of architectural space in colonial New England, it now seems clear that steps taken to purify one's house were at the same time steps to protect one's body as the locus of subject position and also as an emblem that at once implied the overlapping logics of family, government, and the anticipated perfection of eternal life. The house was a central metaphor in early New England precisely because these meanings reverberated through its material fabric, and because it thus provided the possibilities for counter-metaphoric work of the sort that witchcraft narratives make apparent. The house-body thus also counter-imaged the subversion of family order, church government, and republican ideology; it was a symbolic vessel, a "mudwall tent" in which piercings mattered as much as walls, in which objects might dance at will and defeat any insistence on domestic order, and in which women assumed control of an economic sphere within the larger constraints of patriarchal ideology.

Notes

This essay is based upon the discussion of bodies and buildings in Robert Blair St. George, *Conversing By Signs: Poetics of Implication in Colonial New England Culture* (Chapel Hill: University of North Carolina Press, 1998), 115–204.

1. Quoted from Nathaniel B. Shurtleff, *Thunder & Lightning and Deaths at Marsh-field in 1658 & 1666* (Boston: privately printed, 1850), 18. In 1706 lightning struck the house of Vigilans Fisher in Dedham, and bricks were "beat off the Chimney ... and one of the Spars of the House split from the chimney down-wards to the Plate, and from thence taking the Post of the fore door" (*Boston Newsletter*, June 10–17, 1706). See John P. Demos, *Entertaining Satan: Witchcraft and the Culture of Early New England* (New York: Oxford University Press, 1982); David D. Hall, *Worlds of Wonder, Days of Judgment: Popular Religious Beliefs in Early New England* (New York: Alfred A. Knopf, 1989), 71–116; and Carol F. Karlsen, *The Devil in the Shape of a Woman: Witchcraft in Colonial New England* (New York: W. W. Norton, 1987), 77–116.

2. *Records and Files of the Quarterly Courts of Essex County, Massachusetts,* ed. George Francis Dow, 9 vols. (Salem: Essex Institute, 1912–1975), 7:355–56, 358. William Morse's original testimony is printed in Abner Morse, *Memorial of the Morses; Containing the History of Seven Puritans of the Name of Morse and Morss* (Boston: Coolidge & Wiley, 1850), unpag. appendix. The Morse case is described in detail in Demos, *Entertaining Satan,* 132–52.

3. R[ichard]. C[hamberlain]., *Lithobolia: or, the Stone-Throwing Devil* (London, 1698), reprinted in *Narratives of the Witchcraft Cases, 1648–1706,* ed. George Lincoln Burr (New York: Barnes & Noble, 1914), 62–64.

4. St. George, *Conversing with Signs,* 141–45. *The Complete Poetry of John Donne,* ed. John T. Shawcrosse (Garden City, N.Y.: Anchor, 1967), 111; *The Complete Poetry of Robert Herrick,* ed. J. Max Patrick (New York: W. W. Norton, 1968), 367 (H-865: "The Body"). Joseph Moxon, *Mechanical Exercises, or the Doctrine of Handy-Works,* ed. Benno M. Forman (London, 1703; reprint, New York: Prager, 1970), 152–66, s.v. "carcass," "hips." According to Richard Neve, *The City and Countrey Purchaser and Builder's Dictionary* (London, 1703), 96, loame is a type of mud used in plastering walls and therefore appropriate to the idea of one's body being a "house of clay." Bradstreet, "As Weary Pilgrim, Now at Rest," in *The Puritans,* ed. Perry Miller and Thomas H. Johnson, 2 vols. (New York: Harper and Row, 1963), 2:579; *The Poems of Edward Taylor,* ed. Donald E. Stanford (New Haven: Yale University Press, 1977), 48–49, 172, 218–19.

5. The section that follows is drawn from Robert Underwood, *A New Anatomie. Wherein the Body of a Man is very fit and aptly (two wayes) compared: 1 To a Household. 2 To a Citie* (London, 1605).

6. *Oxford English Dictionary,* cf. "clapper," citing Henry Shirley, *The Martyr'd Souldier, a Tragedy* (London, 1638); Underwood, *A New Anatomie,* 15. Thomas Adams, "The Taming of the Tongue," in *The Works of Thomas Adams,* ed. James Angus, 3 vols. (Edinburgh, 1861–1862), 3:17. On the dangers of the tongue, and its association with the danger and "passions" of women, see Robert Blair St. George, "'Heated Speech' and Literacy in Seventeenth-Century New England," in David Grayson Allen and David D. Hall,

eds., *Seventeenth-Century New England* (Boston: Colonial Society of Massachusetts, 1984), 275–322; Mary Beth Norton, "Gender and Defamation in Seventeenth-Century Maryland," *William and Mary Quarterly* 44 (1987): 3–39; and Clara Ann Bowler, "Carted Whores and White Shrouded Apologies," *Virginia Magazine of History and Biography* 85 (1977): 411–26.

7. On "Brides of Christ," see essay by Elizabeth Maddock Dillon in this volume. Also see David Leverenz, *The Language of Puritan Feeling: An Exploration in Literature, Psychology, and Social History* (New Brunswick, N.J.: Rutgers University Press, 1980), 142–44; Allan I. Ludwig, *Graven Images: New England Stonecarving and Its Symbols, 1650–1815* (Middletown, Conn.: Wesleyan University Press, 1966), 155–68; and Richard Godbeer, "'Love Raptures': Marital, Romantic, and Erotic Images of Jesus Christ in Puritan New England, 1670–1730," *New England Quarterly* 68: 3 (September 1995): 355–84.

8. On this point generally, see discussions in Elizabeth Reis, *Damned Women: Sinners and Witches in Puritan New England* (Ithaca, N.Y.: Cornell University Press, 1997); and Amanda Porterfield, *Female Piety in Puritan New England: The Emergence of Religious Humanism* (New York: Oxford University Press, 1992).

9. John Norden, *The Surveyor's Dialogue* (London, 1607), sig. E2.

10. *Poems of Edward Taylor,* 5, 157. Cotton Mather, *Elizabeth in her Holy Retirement: An Essay to Prepare a Pious Woman for her Lying In* (Boston, 1710), 25. Quoted in *The Trelawney Papers,* ed. James Phinney Baxter, *Documentary History of the State of Maine,* vol. 3 (Portland, Maine, 1884), 31–32 (emphasis added). Donne also conceived of the soul in terms of fire, and wrote of "the flame/Of thy brave Soule, that shot such heat and light/ ... and made our darkness bright" (*Complete Poetry of John Donne,* ed. Shawcrosse, 32). E. Estyn Evans, *Irish Folk Ways* (New York: Devin-Adair, 1957), 58–59, discusses the Irish folk belief that the soul of the house exists in the flame at the hearth and that "the soul goes out of the people of the house" when the fire dies; "when the smoke dies out of a house, it does soon be falling down."

11. Cotton Mather, *El Shaddai: A Brief Essay ... Produced by the Death of Mrs. Katharin Willard* (Boston, 1725), 21. On the separation of front and back zones in English houses by the late seventeenth century, see Eric Mercer, *English Vernacular Houses* (London: Royal Commission on Historical Monuments, 1975), 73–75.

12. Robert Hunter West, *Invisible World: A Study of Pneumatology in Elizabethan Drama* (Athens: University of Georgia Press, 1939), 28; see also George Ewart Evans, *The Pattern Under the Plough: Aspects of the Folk-Life of East Anglia* (London: Faber and Faber, 1966), 79–80.

13. *New Haven Town Records 1649–1662,* ed. Franklin B. Dexter (New Haven, Conn.: Yale University Press, 1917), 1:251; testimony of Joseph Marsh, in Charles J. Hoadly, "Some Early Post-Mortem Examinations in New England," in *Proceedings of the Connecticut Medical Society, 1892* (Bridgeport: Buckingham and Brewer, 1892), 213; John M. Taylor, *The Witchcraft Delusion in Colonial Connecticut, 1647–1697* (Hartford, 1908; reprint, New York: Burt Franklin, 1971), 118–19; *The Salem Witchcraft Papers: Verbatim Transcripts of the Legal Documents of the Salem Witchcraft Outbreak of 1692,* ed. Paul Boyer and Stephen Nissenbaum, 3 vols. (New York: Da Capo Press, 1977), 1:97.

14. Massachusetts State Archives, vol. 135 ("Witches," 1656–1750), deposition 1, verso; *Salem Witchcraft Papers,* 2:452, 526.

15. Quoted in Demos, *Entertaining Satan,* 103; Taylor, *The Witchcraft Delusion,* 107; *Salem Witchcraft Papers,* 1:177. See also the account of William Beale of Marblehead, who claimed in August 1692 to have seen the "shade" of mariner Philip English near his chim-

ney: "Where I lay in my bed which was layed low & neire unto the fire towards the nor-
ward parte of the roome I beeing broade Awake I then saw up on the south jaame of that
Chimny A dark shade w'ch covered the jaam of that chimney aforesayed from the under
floore to the upper floore & alsoe a dar[k]ness more then it was beefore in the southerne
part of the house & alsoe in the middllee of the darkness in the shade uppon the jaame of
the chimny aforesayd I beeheld somethinge of the forme or shape of A man" (*Salem Witchcraft Papers,* 1:317).

16. *Salem Witchcraft Papers,* 1:101, 225; 2:448. For compiled references to "poppets"
from the 1692 Salem trials, see Richard Godbeer, *The Devil's Dominion: Magic and Religion in Early New England* (Cambridge, U.K.: Cambridge University Press, 1992), 38–40.

17. On the role of church ordinances as a form of family "protection," see the comment in David Hall, "Toward a History of Popular Religion in Early New England,"
William and Mary Quarterly 3d ser., 41: 1 (January 1984): 54.

18. *The Diary of Samuel Sewall,* ed. M. Halsey Thomas, 2 vols. (New York: Farrar,
Giroux & Straus, 1973), 1:287, 330, 337, 400; see also Hall, *Worlds of Wonder,* 217–18,
following Exodus 25:18–22.

19. See the compilations of such discoveries in J. M. Swann, "Shoes Concealed in Buildings," *Northampton Museum and Arts Gallery Journal* 6 (December 1969): 8–21.

20. On London examples of witch bottles, see Catherine Maloney, "A Witch-Bottle
from Dukes Place, Aldgate," *Transactions of the London & Middles Archaeological Society* 31 (1980): 157–59, and examples cited in Ralph Merrifield, "The Use of Bellarmines
as Witch-Bottles," *Guildhall Miscellany* 3 (1953): 3–15. For an example uncovered from
the site of the ca. 1699 meetinghouse that preceded the Brattle Square Church of 1773 in
Boston, see "A Greybeard Jug at Fenway Court," in *Fenway Court* (Boston: Isabella
Stewart Gardner Museum, 1981), 26–27.

21. C[hamberlain]., *Lithobolia,* in Burr, *Narratives of the Witchcraft Cases,* 74; *Records
of Salem Witchcraft, Copied from the Original Documents,* ed. W. Elliot Woodward, 2
vols. (Roxbury: printed for the author, 1864), 2:26–27. For other instances of "urinary
experiments," see Godbeer, *Devil's Dominion,* 44–46. On the use of witch bottles, Bellarmines, and bones in East Anglia and nearby Cambridgeshire, see Evans, *Pattern Under
the Plough,* 32–33, 57–58, 74–82, esp. 77: "In one of the grey-beard jars discovered in Ip-
swich ... there was a cloth heart with pins stuck in it among the following objects: sharp-
ened splinters of wood, brass studs, nails, hair, glass chips, and a much-rusted table fork
without a handle." See the contents of a witch bottle now in the Norwich Castle Museum,
illustrated in Ivor Nöel Hume, "German stoneware bellarmines—an introduction," *An-
tiques* 74: 5 (November 1958): 441, fig. 6. For a witch bottle recently discovered by ar-
chaeologists in Essington, Pennsylvania, dating probably from ca. 1748, see M. J. Becker,
"An American Witch Bottle," *Archaeology* 33: 2 (March–April 1980): 19–23 (with illustration of contents, including pins, bird bones, and a pot shard). On witch posts in
seventeenth-century English houses, see Mary Nattrass, "Witch Posts," *Gwerin* 3: 5 (June
1962): 254–67, and R. H. Hayes and J. G. Rutter, "Cruck-Framed Buildings in Ryedale
and Eskdale," *Scarborough and District Archaeological Society Research Report,* no. 8
(1972): 87–95.

Food, Assimilation, and the Malleability of the Human Body in Early Virginia

Trudy Eden

> For since the substances of all animals are in perpetual flux, the whole body
> will be thus destroyed and dispersed, unless other similar substances be
> supplied to replace what has flowed away.
>
> Galen, *Hygiene*

Scholars of embodiment explore the multitude of ways in which individuals shape their bodies as forms of self-identification in response to external influences, a process that Chris Schilling has described as an ongoing construction project in which the body is a malleable "entity in the process of becoming." Sociologists and anthropologists have begun to question the role of food in realizing such communication in contemporary societies. According to Deborah Lupton, management of the body through diet can manipulate appearance to achieve multiple social meanings, among which are control and stability in a highly uncertain, postmodern world. Claude Fischler has concluded that all foods have meaning within their particular cultural, culinary systems. They give an identity to the eater through what he terms "incorporation," the presentation of food through the mouth to the body for transubstantiation into flesh. By means of this process, humans establish their affinity with people who eat similarly and their difference from those who do not. Fischler also has elaborated on what Paul Rozin describes as the "omnivore's paradox." Because humans are omnivores, they are free to substitute a wide range of edible substances in their diets when they desire or when circumstances demand. However, such freedom is fraught with danger because of a great incertitude about the transformative effects of unknown foods on the body.[1]

29

These studies leave the impression that concerns about the many contingencies of life, the plasticity of the body, and its response to manipulation through diet—particularly how foods alter the body and the social implications of those changes—are a phenomenon of postmodern life. In fact, they are not. They have existed in western society for millennia, albeit at times elusively. In early America, these considerations became more important when English men and women migrated to the Chesapeake region of North America, an environment lacking in traditional English foodstuffs, and faced a radical dietary change. It was an adaptation that many didn't make because they perceived that consumption of the Amerindian diet would produce undesirable physical, mental, and moral changes. It would eradicate their Englishness. Whereas before 1607 Englishness was a status that everyone born and living on the island enjoyed freely and equally, after that year among the English peoples who moved to different climates it became an acquired asset. Like other more tangible valuable possessions, those people in the upper ranks of the fledgling Chesapeake society reserved for themselves the foods that guaranteed their ethnic integrity, and those in the lower orders either starved or accepted a possible change of identity.

The quote from Galen given at the beginning of this chapter describes what was a fact of life in the ancient western European world and remains one today. The body, in order to live, must repair its worn-out parts and replace its dead ones. It does so in a process known as assimilation. Ancient philosophers often interchanged the term with "nutrition," the means by which the body attracted, retained, and converted all useful foods and expelled impotent or harmful wastes. Galen termed assimilation an "artistic process" because he believed an innate drive to forestall chaos and preserve individual identity in an environment of constant flux directed the body's purposeful selection of appropriate foods. The Hippocratic treatise, "Nutriment," asserted that no one needed to be taught what to eat because natural instinct served as a guide. Similarly, Aristotle styled this process a psychic power, the presence of which defined life.[2]

The body selected elementally suitable foods. Most ancient philosophers believed that the four elements of earth, air, fire, and water composed the entire universe. The individual form of any organism, in other words its unique identity, depended on its internal ratio of these elements, which fluctuated continually and accounted for all changes in life such as aging and disease, as well as other physical, psychological, and emotional human experiences.

Assimilation occurred with violence and resistance. Aristotle posited that some "active principle of growth" residing in all parts of the body "laid hold" of food that could potentially become flesh and retained it until conversion took place. Galen agreed. He wrote that each body part attracted nutriment to it, "devoured" all of the useful fluids to the point of satisfaction, forced those fluids to adhere, and finally assimilated them.[3] The process was adversarial rather than unilateral because all foods exerted some effect on the body, even if slight. A diet that did not vary and supplied the same elemental combinations evoked no physical alteration. However, if it differed in quality from the customary, the body evidenced the transformation readily or over time, depending on the degree of dietary change. Assimilation, then, was not the value-neutral exchange of chemicals we regard it to be today. Rather, it resembled a negotiated and potentially hostile takeover in which the body altered and assimilated food, and the food, in turn, produced change within the body.[4]

This ancient theory remained vital in the early modern period. Most writers of contemporary popular dietaries relied heavily on it although they did not explicate it to their readers. Rather, it remained an assumption on which they reiterated dietary advice on manipulating the temperament, the essential indicator of a person's mental, moral, and physical status.[5] These guidebooks to the human condition instructed readers how to determine the nature of their own temperaments and consequently those of others through astute observance of external physical characteristics.[6]

According to these texts, each of the four elements in the human body possessed a corresponding quality: air was dry; water, wet; earth, cold; and fire, hot. One or two of these qualities predominated in every person in the form of entities called the humors. The temperament reflected the ratio of the humors and dietitians described four basic types: melancholic (combined cold and dry qualities), choleric (hot and dry), sanguine (hot and moist), and phlegmatic (cold and moist). A person's external bodily signs such as skin color, temperature, physical appearance, and bodily habits such as agility or quickness signified his or her temperament, which, in turn, indicated his or her inner character.[7] For example, Thomas Elyot informed his readers that a body exhibiting a sanguine temperament looked white and ruddy and displayed plenty of hair, often tinted red. It tended toward fleshiness and possessed large veins and a great and full pulse. Even though the sanguine person had a short temper, T. W. Master believed temperament to be the "Prince of all Temperatures" because the persons fortunate enough to have it were steadfast, brave, and spoke with wit and eloquence. To all writers, a balanced sanguine temperament most nearly approximated perfection because it represented the perfect combination of heat and moisture.[8]

Temperamental evaluation occurred on personal, ethnic, and regional levels. Although the English exhibited all four temperament types, when considered as a group, they were phlegmatic because they lived in a cold, damp climate and ate the flora and fauna that grew there. Early modern Europeans thought that the environment influenced all organic life and that noticeable similarities occurred among peoples, animals, and plants that lived within the same region and consequently breathed the same air, drank the same water, and nourished themselves with the other organic forms that did so. They acknowledged that smaller regional environments existed within larger ones and recognized the consequences for humans. Therefore, they classified the English temperamentally as part of the larger group of northern Euro-peans, distinguishing them from southern Europeans, yet believed that both groups shared tempermental likenesses that differentiated them from Asians and North Americans or any other group that resided in a dissimilar geo-graphical area.

The least desirable of the four temperaments, the melancholic, contrasted sharply with the sanguine. Master described it as "the most unfortunate" be-cause its elemental qualities of cold and dryness were the very antithesis of the heat and moisture needed for life. Leaden and lumpish, the melancholic person seemed "Dead before the appointed time of death." The English readily determined a melancholy temperament by a sad or grim countenance; a yellow, earthy-brown, or black visage; a lean, hard body and skin; and a slow pace. Melancholic persons tended towards anger, stubbornness, and churlishness. In extreme cases melancholy incited furious fits or madness. Yet, moderate endowments of its qualities could cause sharp wits, an ability to learn quickly, and inventiveness.[9]

These texts presented a body that was malleable, subject to internal and external change through six influences known as the nonnaturals: food, en-vironment, exercise, sleep, excretion and repletion, and the passions. Al-though each affected the internal humoral balance, most authorities believed food and the environment to be the most powerful.[10] This concept of the malleability of the body was the belief in perpetual flux expressed by Galen and others. The Renaissance authors presented such incredible flexibility in a positive rather than a negative light. Instead of portraying the human body as helpless in the face of chaotic universal forces, they depicted it as raw ma-terial to be sculpted using those same forces as tools. If the highly desirable sanguine temperament resulted from a balance of heat and moisture, then a person not possessing that balance could achieve it by eating (and assimilat-ing) foods that counteracted his or her natural temperament. To continue with the examples given above, a cold and dry melancholic temperament would require substantial additions of hot and moist foods to effect a change. The already sanguine temperament could be maintained with foods of a simi-lar humoral quality.[11]

The English classified all foods accordingly. For example, beef, goat, hare, boar, salt flesh, salt fish, coleworts, all legumes except white peas, coarse brown bread, and old cheese promoted melancholy.[12] They highly regarded foods that exhibited a balance of heat and moisture, like sugar, because their elemental quality so closely resembled that of the sanguine person and thus of the perfect human body. Quality was a loaded term in this time period. Although technically it signified the degree of intrinsic heat and moisture within a food, it did not escape social and economic construction and pos-sessed other meanings. By 1600, dietitians stressed that the substance or de-gree of refinement of a food as well as its elemental quality affected a per-son's appearance and character. In the vocabulary of Norbert Elias and

Mikhail Bakhtin, refined foods made "civilized" bodies and gross foods made "grotesque" ones.[13] Dense or heavy foods that most stomachs digested with difficulty—such as hard cheese, beans, rice, all whole grains, unleavened breads, and potages—fell into the latter category. The dietaries stated that the people who consumed them were slow, stupid, and crass. Foods of a light or subtle substance—such as the flesh of young animals, young fowl, wine, leavened bread made of pure wheat, and fresh eggs and milk—produced refined bodies.[14] In England, the "gross" foods constituted standard fare for the middling to lower classes, while the "refined" foods appeared most frequently on the tables of the well-to-do.

Most societies distribute food among their members along their established social hierarchies and as the foregoing paragraphs suggest, the English were no different.[15] Localism powerfully informed English food practices. The English, like all Europeans, believed that their Englishness derived from the ingestion of English foods and exposure to the English climate. Deprived of those foods, they would lose their English identity. Just as a house built with brick and repaired with straw would cease to be the same dwelling, so, too, an English person nurtured on English foods and sustained with non-English foods would no longer be English. As long as English men and women remained on their island, this aspect of their nutritional beliefs did not cause concern. In the Chesapeake this localism surfaced. The scarcity of traditional English foods and the abundance of American foods, particularly Indian corn, shifted the criteria of the valuation of foods and the bodies they produced from "coarse" and "refined" to "English" and "Indian." However, the distribution of those foods played out the same way over the social hierarchy. People of higher status claimed English foods, by money or force. Their social inferiors either accepted Indian foods and the consequences of their changed diet or starved.

Early descriptive literature of the Chesapeake illustrates the pervasiveness of this belief. Before and during the early colonial occupation, English writers often compared the habitable qualities of the area to an earthly paradise. Such qualities included mild climate, natural fecundity, peace, and an abundant if not luxuriant food supply—all of which, commentators believed, guaranteed health and longevity to its inhabitants.[16] These early narratives vary widely in their provenance and degree of overstatement. Their significance lies in the fact that all writers believed in the importance of the kinds and qualities of foods available in the Chesapeake to devote considerable amounts of attention to them.

Most authors divided edible Virginia into fruits, fish, flesh, and fowl. They wrote of forests dense with mammals, skies blackened by passing flocks, and rivers in which the multitudes of fish overflowed the banks. Turkeys, sturgeon, and deer especially impressed observers because of their size, numbers, and ready availability. Berries covered the forest floor, while grapes, melons, nuts, and fruit hung abundantly from the trees.[17]

Maize (often referred to as "Turkey wheat" or "Guinea wheat") impressed early observers even more because of its apparently easy cultivation, short growing time, and almost unbelievable yields. John Smith reported that each planted maize kernel yielded anywhere from six hundred to fifteen hundred more. Thomas Hariot felt the increase could be up to two thousandfold. Not only were yields high, but two crops could be raised in the same season because of the short time it took the plants to reach maturity. Hariot believed that one man could grow enough maize to feed himself for twelve months by planting a patch of ground one hundred yards square. He estimated that the labor time for the entire growing season would be less than twenty-four hours.[18]

The theme of abundant variety accommodated the practicalities of assimilation. First, abundance assured that sustenance would always be available to assimilate. Not even the time and effort required to gather food, or the minimal cost, would interfere with the food supply. Second, variety guaranteed that all body parts would receive the exact substances they needed to repair their losses. Third, and not coincidentally, the kinds of foods the writers noted held an elevated status among the English. With the exception of maize, they were the foods of the wealthy. As such, they held a promise of self-improvement for all people who did not consume them regularly.

In the early seventeenth century, most of the English population would not have eaten the foods promoted by the tracts on the Chesapeake. The English cultivated fruits of all kinds, including many imported from Europe and the Americas. However, their popularity and affordability below the upper classes is doubtful. Because they were expensive even when in season, relatively few people ate them. Raspberries recently grew there, as had red and black currants, which the seventeenth-century English believed to be gooseberries. Melons and cucumbers, like raspberries, did not grace common gardens. Only "great personages" consumed melons. Although strawberries grew in the woods in England, they were small and not comparable to those expensive varieties cultivated in the gardens of the well-to-do.[19]

Much of the population ate fish, at least on the weekly abstinence days, and of course, some types of fish cost more than others. Sturgeon, one of the three fish reserved for royal usage, was not only expensive but also scarce. Although officials in Tudor and Stuart England relaxed game laws so that all could take game, deer remained an exception. The rich preferred venison, a food of such high status that recipes for counterfeit venison could be found in contemporary cookery books. Squirrel was also a dish for the wealthy. These items may have been found at local town markets, but their cost would have been prohibitive for most English people. By the seventeenth century, domestic fowl, and presumably wild as well, became another expensive foodstuff. The presence of poultry at one's table signified upward mobility. Turkeys gained in popularity and started to replace the peacocks, swans, bustards, and herons of the Renaissance English diet.[20]

Famines occurred in England in the sixteenth century. During the first half of the seventeenth century, England's economy was depressed, food prices were high, and some foods scarce. The common laborer's diet consisted of bread, beef, cheese, and beer.[21] Stories of the foods available to anyone for little or no labor or money must have been very enticing to those people experiencing such difficulties.

It is not surprising that the earliest account of the natives who regularly ate the foods described above portrayed them as royalty. It elided the categories of "Indian" and "refined." Theodore de Bry's prints, based on John White's illustrations and Thomas Hariot's descriptions appended to the 1590 edition of Hariot's *Briefe and True Report of the New Found Land of Virginia,* depict an array of lords, princes, and princesses and give great detail about their external demeanor and comportment. White posed his subjects in classical Greek style reminiscent of ancient sculptures of gods and goddesses, each appearing stunningly healthy. De Bry clearly wanted to convey the message that the Amerindian peoples differed only minimally from the English. He even compared them to the Picts, the ancient ancestors of the English.[22]

This image of a godlike existence in the midst of a bountiful forest did not match up with the experience of the early settlers, many of whom died from disease and starvation. Historians have formulated several theories why. The colonists lacked the practical experience to live off nature. They succumbed to "New World" diseases, and they suffered from Old World diseases brought with them or developed from the unsanitary conditions on their trans-Atlantic ships. They were lazy, lacked discipline, and may have had different ideas about labor. Finally, they may have suffered from the psychological effects of starvation such as anorexia and indifference.[23]

Another cause of the tragedy of the early years is the contemporary beliefs about assimilation. The colonists may have resisted eating on a daily basis the wild or cultivated Amerindian foods because they believed that their bodies would assimilate them and they would experience unwanted physical, mental, and moral changes. Several sources support this theory. John Smith's works published years after the early settlement offer three. First, Smith did not confirm de Bry's appraisal. Although the Virginia natives impressed him with their height, straight stature, comely proportions, and superb agility, he also observed that they were brown skinned, crafty, quick of apprehension, and ingenious although quick tempered, malicious, and fearful.[24] This description closely approximated the melancholic temperament, the least desired of all temperaments. It did not convey the image of refinement or royalty.

In another text Smith commented that the natives experienced marked bodily changes as their diet altered from season to season. They ate fish, turkeys, and squirrels in March and April and switched to acorns, walnuts, and fish (with occasional beasts, crabs, oysters, tortoises, and berries) in May and early June. From June through August they ate roots, berries, fish, and green corn. Wrote Smith, "It is strange to see how their bodies alter with their diet, even as the deare and wilde beastes they seeme fat and leane, strong and weak."[25] Smith's comment refers to more than the size or weight of native bodies. In his world, a lean body indicated a choleric temperament because the heat of the body burned up foods before it could extract their nourishment. A fat body, which lacked enough heat to digest foods efficiently, signified a cold and moist, or phlegmatic, temperament. In these passages Smith depicted native bodies as under the stressful influence of the chaotic state of the natural world. They were, in Galen's words, in perpetual flux, their identity dependent on their constantly shifting food supply.

Second, in the beginning of the settlement, the Virginia Company, apparently assuming its colony's natural produce to be exactly the same as England's, planned for the colonists to live off the forests to some extent. When it communicated as much to John Smith, he replied, "Though there be fish in the Sea, foules in the ayre, and Beasts in the woods, their bounds are so large, they so wilde, and we so weak and ignorant we cannot much trouble them." A key factor lies in Smith's words, "they so wilde." "Wild" in England referred to animals that lived in a forest owned by the king or the gentry and surrounded by English habitations. They were connected with English civilization on several levels. Smith's words suggest foods with qualities very different from the fare in England. There, the aristocracy and the wealthy ate the "wild" foods of their forests like deer, turkey, and sturgeon but they hardly looked like the Amerindian king Powhatan or the princes of his tribe, notwithstanding John White's classical portrayal of them. Native Americans did not limit their diet to those species familiar to the English. They consumed most of the animals living in the forest including skunk, porcupine, opossum, and hawks. Englishmen, such as Thomas Hariot, described Native Americans as "savage," due to their diets, and believed that over time consumption of the same foods would alter their English bodies accordingly.[26]

At one point in the early months of the settlement, when the Amerindians either refused to trade with the English or had no maize with which to trade, Smith commanded the colonists to forage in the forest. They replied that they would not eat "savage trash." Whether Smith agreed with the colonists on this point is not clear. He was a practical man who chose life over death and told his men that if they could get the food past their mouths, their stomachs would digest it. Of course, that may have been what the colonists feared.

Other survivors of the early settlement offered further support to this theory. A narrative written by Jamestown residents Thomas Studly and Anas Todkill indicates the colonists only believed that they had a sufficiency of food after an English supply ship arrived and they possessed a stock of oats, meal, and wheat. In other words, food to them meant English food. When shortages occurred and the opportunity arose, the colonists preferred to purchase pilfered ships' biscuits from the sailors of visiting vessels in exchange for "money, saxefras, furres, or love" rather than to eat a native diet.[27]

The colonists' refusal to consume Amerindian foods included maize. From the beginning of settlement, the Virginia Company of London intended to establish English plants. The company's instructions to its first group of settlers in 1607 advised them to plant their own seeds immediately, an act they successfully accomplished soon after their arrival. By the following June the crop had grown to be the height of a man.[28] In the spring of the following year, the colonists cleared forests to cultivate more acres. Although John Smith instituted the first attempts to plant maize at that time, he met with resistance from the colonists, many of whom wished the crop would fail. Historian Philip Bruce surmised it was because they wanted to return to England. It could have been because they did not want to eat it, and would have rather seen that cleared land used to grow more English grains. After Smith left the colony in 1609, the colonists neglected their maize and consumed their livestock instead.[29]

Contemporary beliefs about maize did not sanction it as human food. Many people thought it toxic. John Gerard's popular *Herball,* first published in the sixteenth century, instructed its readers that although the "barbarous Indians" who knew no better and were "constrained to make a vertue of necessitie" ate it and believed it a good food, maize provided little to no nourishment and made bread as hard as sea biscuits (hard tack). It was "of hard and evill" digestion and "a more convenient food for swine than for men."[30] Nearly one hundred years later, John Parkinson's herbal stated that eating too much of it would "engender grosse blood," meaning it would make one "physically, mentally, and spiritually coarse and unrefined."[31] Diego Sarmiento de Acuña, the Spanish ambassador to the court of James I, wrote to Philip III, the king of Spain, in 1613 that the majority of the English colonists in Virginia suffered because they had maize, a little fish to eat and water to drink, which was "contrary to the nature of the English."[32] John Hammond in his later account of Virginia and Maryland, "Leah and Rachel," agreed. He, too, explained the high death rates in the Chesapeake by "the want of such diet as best agreed with our English natures."[33] That the consumption of native foods caused drastic transformation may have been the unwritten rationale in another letter to Philip III from Pedro de Zuñiga, Sarmiento de Acuña's predecessor. He informed the Spanish king that several of the English who had been "put among" the natives had themselves become "savages."[34]

Finally, Sir Thomas Gates's laws, enacted in 1610 to control the excessive behavior of the colonists, illustrate what the colonists wanted for food. Among the statutes prohibiting crimes such as sodomy, adultery, and theft were sections that regulated the food consumption of the colonists. One prohibited mariners from selling English ships' provisions to any "Landman" for a price higher than those prices set by the colony and fixed on the main masts of all harboring ships. Anyone, regardless of his quality or condition, who without permission from Gates killed any domesticated animal, either his own or that of another, could be sentenced to death. A third law punished with death anyone caught robbing any garden of a root, herb, or flower; or destroying any garden, robbing a vineyard or picking grapes, or stealing wheat.[35] These laws laid down the highest of penalties for the killing of domestic *English* animals and cultivated *English* vegetables and fruits. They set no price on the abundant wildlife, or on maize, another indicator that at least some of the colonists would not eat it.

Finally, sources show how the distribution of "English" and "Indian" foods occurred within and between existing social groups. The former, whether regarded as "coarse" or "refined," became high-status foods claimed by some persons over their social inferiors. For example, the rank-and-file veteran colonists made distinctions between themselves and new recruits. The Virginia Company supplied all new colonists with a year's worth of English meal and legumes; however, when they arrived at the colony, the receiving colonists took away those provisions and gave them maize instead.

Furthermore, men who possessed political authority set themselves apart from the common colonists. They reserved the best English provisions, such as meats, wheat, and vegetables, for themselves. At times they also took the common provisions. Just before Samuel Argall arrived to govern the colony of Virginia in 1617, the colony had experienced a brief prosperity and he took control of eighty cows, eighty-eight goats, and a company garden that fed the entire community and yielded a profit of three hundred pounds. At the end of his two-year term, agricultural production had dwindled to practically nothing and only six goats remained. On his arrival back in London, Argall had to defend himself against charges of eating all of the food himself or, perhaps, showing favoritism in distributing it to others. It was a procedure the Virginia Company officials had conducted ten years before, that time for Edward Maria Wingfield whose council members accused him of refusing to share his chicken and beer with them and giving them bad corn to eat instead. They "tried" and "convicted" him, locked him in a boat on the river, and reported the incident to company officials in London. At his London hearing, Wingfield claimed his accusers actually ate the chickens that he raised on his own efforts and that he only showed favoritism when one of his men was seriously ill by allowing him to receive a pint of peas cooked with pork.[36]

Another theory for the starvation at Jamestown, then, is that the colonists believed they would, at the very least, have to continue to eat English foods in order to retain their English identity. So powerful was this understanding that some chose starvation over the possibility of becoming Amerindian.[37] From the very beginning, the settlers of Virginia went to great pains to transplant their culinary culture and become self-sufficient in terms of English food. They did not simply ease themselves into the forests and adopt the diet that allegedly made the natives such fine physical specimens. At a great expense of time, labor, and money, they cut down ancient forests, removed massive stumps, and created fields accessible to their plows and draught animals. They planted English seeds and transported English livestock. Once they succeeded at those efforts, they still imported great amounts of English foodstuffs to satisfy their requirements.

Those needs went beyond simple hunger. In a world that accepted constant and chaotic bodily change as a daily event, food served as the instrument of control. In a world that tied the physical body tightly to the mental, moral, and spiritual person, food served as a primary arbiter of identity. In the Chesapeake's incoherent and threatening forests, English food promised the colonists stability in a highly uncertain world, and an unbroken affinity with the families and other English people they left at home.

Notes

I thank the Virginia Historical Society and the College of Physicians of Philadelphia for supporting the research necessary for this essay.

1. Chris Schilling, *The Body and Social Theory* (London: Sage Publications, 1993), 4–8; Deborah Lupton, *Food, the Body, and the Self* (London: Sage Publications, 1996), 15–19; Claude Fischler, "Food, Self, and Identity," *Social Science Information* 19 (1980): 937–53; Paul Rozin, "The Selection of Foods by Rats, Humans, and Other Animals," *Advances in the Study of Behavior* 6 (1976): 21–76. See also Lynn Harbottle, "Fast Food/Spoiled Identity: Iranian Migrants in the British Catering Trade," in Pat Caplan, ed., *Food, Health, Identity* (London: Routledge, 1997), 97–110.

2. Galen, *On the Natural Faculties,* trans. Arthur John Brock (New York: G. P. Putnam's Sons, 1916), 33, 39; Hippocrates, "Nutriment," in *Hippocrates,* trans. W. H. S. Jones (Cambridge, Mass.: Harvard University Press, 1962), 345; Galen, "Mixtures," in *Selected Works,* trans. P. N. Singer (Oxford, U.K.: Oxford University Press, 1997), 270; Robert Montraville Green, *A Translation of Galen's Hygiene* (Springfield, Ill.: Charles C. Thomas, 1951), 7.

3. Aristotle, "On the Soul," in *The Complete Works of Aristotle,* ed. Jonathan Barnes (Princeton, N.J.: Princeton University Press, 1984), 659, 661–63, and "On Generation and Corruption," in *Complete Works,* 526; Green, *Galen's Hygiene,* 7; Galen, "The Soul's Dependence on the Body," in *Selected Works,* 169, and *Natural Faculties,* 251, 307.

4. To quote Galen, "[W]henever two bodies meet and engage over a considerable period of time in mutual conflict in relation to their alterations it is inevitable that each of them acts and is acted upon. It may be that, if the period of conflict is a short one, the body which comes to be dominated does have some effect on that which comes to dominate, but this effect is so small as to be imperceptible." Galen, "Mixtures," 280. See also Galen, *Natural Faculties,* 195; and Galen, "Soul's Dependence," 169.

5. The theory, also known as the complexion theory, constituted the "workhorse" of medical diagnosis and treatment of disease. See Nancy Siraisi, *Medieval and Early Renaissance Medicine* (Chicago: University of Chicago Press, 1990), 78–152.

6. Many authors published dietaries in Renaissance England. Elaine O'Hara-May, *Elizabethan Dyetary of Health* (Lawrence, Kan.: Coronado Press, 1977), and Kenneth Albala, "Dietary Regime in the Renaissance" (Ph.D. dissertation, Columbia University,

1993), are the two contemporary analyses of these texts. Most achieved a middle ground between the extremely complex ancient theories preserved in Latin medical texts, and the lyrical aphorisms of *The Regimen Sanitatis,* a straightforward poem of health advice believed to have been written for Robert, duke of Normandy, in the late eleventh century by physicians at the famed medical school in Salerno, Italy. The latter was still popular in the early seventeenth century and many extant seventeenth-century Virginia inventories list Thom Paynell's translation, published first in London in 1597 and again in 1633. John Ordronaux, *Code of Health of the School of Salernum* (Philadelphia: J. B. Lippincott, 1871), 27–32; and Wyndham Blanton, *Medicine in Virginia in the Seventeenth Century* (Richmond, Va.: The William Byrd Press, 1930), 95.

7. O'Hara-May, *Elizabethan Dyetary,* 49–58, 138–47; Siraisi, *Renaissance Medicine,* 101–106; Albala, "Dietary Regime," 45–50. Three primary sources that devoted considerable detail to the temperament are Levinus Lemnius, *Touchstone of the Complexions* (London, 1576); Thomas Elyot, *Castel of Helth* (London, 1541), and T. W. Master, *The Optick Glass of Humors* (London, 1663).

8. Elyot, *Castel,* 2–3; Master, *Optick,* 110–18; Lemnius, *Touchstone,* 88–106; Paynell, *Regimen Sanitatis,* 141–43.

9. Choleric temperaments appeared yellow or red and belied an inflammatory nature prone to argument. White complexions usually accompanied phlegmatic temperaments. People who displayed them were believed to be slow, fat, and lack courage. Master, *Optick Glasse,* 125–27, 130; Elyot, *Castel,* 12; Lemnius, *Touchstone,* 146–47; and Paynell, *Regimen Sanitatis,* 145.

10. See Martha L. Finch's essay in this volume on the perception of environmental influences on the bodies of New England colonists.

11. Authors varied in their belief of just how far diet could stretch a body. For example, Levinus Lemnius advised that a complete transformation from one temperament to another was possible. Like all authors, he believed the sanguine temperament to be the most desirable and offered his readers a multiple-page description of its attributes. Lemnius, *Touchstone.* Other authors did not refute Lemnius's liberal stance; they were just less explicit.

12. Elyot, *Castel,* 12.

13. Norbert Elias, *The Civilizing Process,* vol. 1, *The History of Manners* (Oxford: Basil Blackwell, 1978); and Mikhail Bakhtin, *Rabelais and His World,* trans. H. Iswolsky (Bloomington: Indiana University Press, 1984), 303–367.

14. Elyot, *Castel,* 101; O'Hara-May, *Dyetary,* 109–10; Albala, "Regime," 87–95.

15. For a cross-cultural analysis of food distribution within societies, see Jack Goody, *Cooking, Cuisine, Class* (Cambridge, U.K.: Cambridge University Press, 1994).

16. Charles L. Sanford, *The Quest for Paradise* (Urbana: University of Illinois Press, 1961), 10.

17. Nathaniel Shrigley, "A True Relation of Virginia and Mary-Land," in Peter Force, comp., *Tracts and Other Papers, Relating Principally to the Origin, Settlement, and Progress of the Colonies in North America* (Washington, D.C.: William Q. Force, 1844), vol. 3, no. 6, 4–5; Thomas Hariot, *A Briefe and True Report of the New Found Land of Virginia* (Frankfurt: Theodore de Bry, 1590; reprint, Readex Microprint Corporation, 1966), 19–20; Philip Barbour, ed., *The Complete Works of Captain John Smith* (Chapel Hill: University of North Carolina Press, 1986), 1: 151–56; Edward Williams, "Virginia: More Especially the South Part Thereof, Richly and Truly Valued," in Force, *Tracts,* vol. 3, no. 11, 12, 21–3; His Majesties Counseil for Virginia, "A Declaration of the State of the Colonie and Affaires in Virginia," in Force, *Tracts,* vol. 3, no. 5, 22; Alexander Whitaker, "Virginia's Natural Bounty," in Louis B. Wright, ed., *The Elizabethans' America*

(Cambridge: Harvard University Press, 1965), 222; and Andrew White, "An Account of the Colony of the Lord Baron Baltamore, 1633," in Clayton Colman Hall, ed., *Narratives of Early Maryland 1633–1684* (New York: Charles Scribner's Sons, 1910), 5–10.

18. Hariot, *True Report*, 14–15; Smith, "Map," 157. See also His Maiestie's Counseil, "Declaration," 12; and Whitaker, "Natural Beauty," 223.

19. J. C. Drummond and Anne Wilbraham, *The Englishman's Food* (London: Jonathan Cape, 1958), 110–11, 343; C. Anne Wilson, *Food and Drink in Great Britain* (Chicago: Chicago Academy, 1991), 341–42.

20. Wilson, *Food and Drink*, 35, 46–47, 83–84, 108–10, 129. The other two royal fish were whales and porpoises, neither of which appear frequently in early descriptions of Virginia.

21. Drummond and Wilbraham, *Englishman's Food*, 98–99.

22. Hariot, *Briefe and True Report*, n.p.

23. Edmund S. Morgan, *American Freedom, American Slavery* (New York: W. W. Norton, 1975), 70–91; Edmund S. Morgan, "The Labor Problem at Jamestown," *American Historical Review* 76 (1971): 595–611; Carl Bridenbaugh, *Jamestown 1544–1699* (New York: Oxford University Press, 1980), 45–60; Carville V. Earle, "Environment, Disease, and Mortality in Early Virginia," in Thad W. Tate and David L. Ammerman, eds., *The Chesapeake in the Seventeenth Century* (Williamsburg: University of North Carolina Press, 1979), 96–125; Wyndham B. Blanton, "Epidemics, Real and Imaginary, and Other Factors Influencing Seventeenth-Century Virginia's Population," *Bulletin of the History of Medicine* 31 (1957): 54–62; and Karen Ordahl Kupperman, "Apathy and Death in Early Jamestown," *Journal of American History* 66 (1979): 24–40.

24. Barbour, *Works of Captain John Smith*, vol. 2, 114.

25. Ibid., vol. 2, 264–65, 162–63.

26. Ibid., vol. 1, 202–3.

27. Ibid., vol. 1, 209–10.

28. The colonists planted a field previously cleared and used by the natives. Reports assessed it to be only about four acres, which may be why the Virginia Company received complaints of starvation written the following September. Alexander Brown, *The Genesis of the United States* (New York: Russell & Russell, 1964), 83, 166–67. John Smith's later account claimed that the colonists had plenty of food, most of which they acquired from the Amerindians. Philip Alexander Bruce, *Economic History of Virginia in the Seventeenth Century* (New York: Macmillan and Co., 1896), 195.

29. Bruce, *Economic History*, 196, 198, 202.

30. John Gerard, *Gerard's Herball* (1636; reprint, London: Gerald Howe, 1927), 25–26.

31. John Parkinson, *Theatrum Botanicum* (London, 1640) as quoted in John J. Finan, *Maize in the Great Herbals* (Waltham, Mass.: Chronica Botanica Company, 1950), 167–68.

32. Brown, *Genesis*, 660.

33. Brown, *Genesis*, 660; John Hammond, "Leah and Rachel, or The Two Fruitful Sisters Virginia and Mary-Land," in Force, *Tracts,* vol. 3, no. 14, 10.

34. Brown, *Genesis*, 572. Spanish colonists in Mexico in the eighteenth and nineteenth centuries also had reservations about the consequences of the consumption of maize, and like the English, used it to make class distinctions. See Jeffrey M. Pilcher, *¡Que Viven Los Tamales!: Food and the Making of Mexican National Identity* (Albuquerque: University of New Mexico Press, 1998).

35. Sir Thomas Gates, "Articles, Lawes, and Orders, Divine, Politique, and Martiall for the Colony in Virginea," in Force, *Tracts,* vol. 3, no. 2, 14, 16.

36. Edward Neill, *History of the Virginia Company of London* (Albany, N.Y.: Joel Munsell, 1869), 19–21, 180, 237.

37. The "you are what you eat" philosophy still played an important role in social philosophy as late as the early twentieth century. Professional home economists working in large cities on the eastern coast of the United States told immigrant women that they and their families would not be American until they ate American foods and offered them instruction in nutrition and cookery to assist their culinary and cultural assimilation. Harvey Levenstein, *Revolution at the Table* (New York: Oxford University Press, 1988), 104–5.

"Civilized" Bodies and the "Savage" Environment of Early New Plymouth

Martha L. Finch

On a cold day in November 1620, when the English Separatists aboard the *Mayflower* first set eyes on Cape Cod after a grueling transatlantic voyage, "they fell upon their knees and blessed the God of Heaven" for their safe arrival in the "New World." Having endured two months of stormy ocean passage during which most had become ill and one man had died, they were immensely thankful to be again able "to set their feet on the firm and stable earth, their proper element." Although they sensed that this foreign "wilderness" must finally be their proper element, its "hideous and desolate" appearance was discouraging. With "no friends to welcome them nor inns to entertain or refresh their weatherbeaten bodies," the settlers imagined New England gazing on them with its "weatherbeaten face." The Separatists saw themselves, chilled and exhausted, reflected in the land's gray winter visage. To turn away from that face engendered no hope, for "if they looked behind them, there was the mighty ocean," barring them "from all the civil parts of the world." Before them lay a frighteningly "savage" land full of the unfamiliar and unknown—"woods and thickets," "wild beasts," and "savage and brutish men"—which the settlers would have to face. They set themselves to carving out "a place of habitation."[1]

William Bradford's version of the birth of Plymouth Colony, from which the above is taken, was written ten years after these events occurred, and it presents the Separatists' initial experiences of New England in a particular way for a particular purpose. Bradford intended his history to emphasize the dangers of "this wilderness" and the advances the English settlers and their God had made on it since those meager and tenuous beginnings. An earlier document, *A Relation or Iournall of the beginning and proceedings of the English Plantation setled at Plimoth in New England,* written within a year or two of their landing, provides a more immediate, complex, and ambivalent rendering of the events. The *Relation* offers little in the way of rhetorical gloss, instead presenting the Separatists' first days in America as intensely physical, thoroughly sensuous, and active. The initial sighting of the New England coastline "much comforted us, especially seeing so goodly a land, and wooded to the brink of the sea. It caused us to rejoice together." After anchoring in the "pleasant bay," they "relieved [them]selves with wood and water, and refreshed [their] people." Unable to catch fish for fresh food, they found and ate fat mussels, which unfortunately made both sailors and passengers extremely sick, causing them "to cast and scour [vomit and have diarrhea], but we were soon well again."[2]

In the following days and weeks, the English actively engaged the land in numerous ways. They repeatedly waded three-quarters of a mile through freezing surf in order to reach shore, "which caused many to get colds and coughs." A reconnoitering party discovered "excellent black earth," woods that were open and easily traversed (due to regular burnings by local Indians, they later discovered), and juniper, "which smelled very sweet and strong and of which we burnt." Meanwhile, "our women" went on shore "to wash, as they had great need." Another party of sixteen heavily armed men set out to penetrate further inland and find a site on which to settle. During this three-day expedition through the forest, they saw Indians, who ran away as the English men followed them (although, during a later excursion, arrows and musket shots would be vigorously exchanged). In their pursuit of the Indians, the party "marched through boughs and bushes ... which tore our very armor to pieces," and thirst drove them to drink "our first New England water with as much delight as ever we drunk drink in all our lives."[3] They discovered Indian graves and winter stores of maize buried in the ground, and they loaded themselves with as much corn as they could carry, given that they were also "laden" with heavy armor. They grew fatigued walking in sand along the shoreline and so moved inland again, finding cultivated land, strawberry plants, walnut trees, and canoes.

On the third day, as they turned back toward their ship, they lost their way in the woods. Bradford, who was walking in the rear of their single file line, was caught by a leg and jerked into the air by "a very pretty device, made with a rope of [the Indians'] own making and having a noose as artificially made as any roper in England can make, and as like ours as can be." His companions presumably released Bradford, and they finally "marched" their way out of the woods and returned to the ship.[4] Within days, colder weather set in, which, coupled with inadequate food supplies, constant drenching from the surf, and the rigorous labor required to investigate the coastline and inland reaches for a place on which to settle for the winter, caused many members of the English party to become ill. Those physically able determined to take advantage of the cleared and cultivated site of a deserted Indian village, Patuxet, and set about constructing shelters there.[5] By spring, nearly half of the original party of 102 members had died; however, although they knew they were "but strangers as yet at Patuxet," the survivors found themselves adapting to the new environment, learning native land cultivation and fishing practices from Tisquantum, whom the English also called Squanto, the only surviving member of the original Patuxet.[6]

The English Separatists had been urban artisans during their twelve-year tenure in the Netherlands, and they were remarkably unprepared for the harsh realities of the New England winter. Confronted with a multitude of unfamiliar but often exhilarating experiences and the perceived and real dangers of "skulking" Indians, wolves, cold weather, disorientation in the woods, lack of nourishment, unfamiliar food, and sickness, the settlers' narratives of their first months in New England track a visceral, thoroughly embodied interaction with the wilderness—its terrain, climate, and inhabitants, both human and nonhuman. The struggle for survival took place in the immediate contact between human and environment, and those dialectical moments generated alterations in English bodies and the New England landscape. Extensive and sophisticated scholarship on seventeenth-century New England has investigated the rhetorical interpretations of the landscape as "wilderness" and "garden" and their influence on the development of ideologies about America and Americans, conflicts between Indian and European land use, and English commodification of the land and its resources.[7] This chapter draws on these histories for some of its interpretations of the historical material. However, as a whole, these works have focused little attention on the physiological interactions between environment and bodies and how English settlers understood that exchange. Moreover, none have considered how particular historical human bodies were constructed through their contact with the New England environment.

The exchange between body and environment is always saturated with particular cultural concerns, expectations, and interpretations. Puritan images of New England as both "wilderness" and "garden" provided religiocultural metaphors for what the Puritans believed to be the transformation of untamed, chaotic, raw environment into civilized, ordered, productive farms and villages.[8] The polarized categories of wilderness and garden might be transposed into other familiar dichotomies: nature and culture, wild and civilized, space and place. Collapsing these dichotomies involves focusing on lived experience, investigating how human beings go about organizing the world, turning unstructured, frightening space into familiar, meaningful place. The polarized metaphors of wilderness and garden that came to define seventeenth-century ideological constructions of the New England countryside conflated in the actual physical experience of material exchange with environmental elements. According to social theorist Bryan S. Turner, the human body is "simultaneously an environment (part of nature) and a medium of the self (part of culture). The body is crucially at the conjuncture of human labour on nature ... and thus critically at the conjuncture of the human species between the natural order of the world and the cultural ordering of the world."[9]

The Separatists brought with them to America two cultural understandings about their physical relationship to the environment that existed in some tension with each other and yet functioned together to produce certain kinds of rhetoric and activities in New England. These two were derived from the Hippocratic and Galenic physiology of the humors and from a Calvinist theology of the body as it was adapted by English Puritan ministers and John Robinson, the Separatist pastor who had remained in Leiden. From these theologians the Plymouth settlers had inherited an emphasis on "godly industry," which they understood to be hard physical labor to convert the savage wilderness into a civilized landscape. The transformation of this land into a garden by English bodies was pursued according to a central cultural motif for the colonial period that permeated how Europeans understood their physical relationship to American land—the motif of possession. The Separatists voyaged to America with the intention of "planting" themselves there: laboring on the land and ordering it according to English Calvinist notions of godly civilization and exploiting its natural resources for profit.[10] During those first months, however, the wilderness threatened to possess them, physically and psychologically—to consume them, in a sense—as members of their party died: Mary Allerton gave birth to a stillborn boy, Bradford's wife Dorothy fell or, in despair, jumped overboard and drowned while the *Mayflower* was anchored in Provincetown Harbor; and one after another was overcome by scurvy or influenza. Environmental elements unfamiliar to English bodies weakened by the ocean crossing were blamed; reflecting on this moment in Plymouth's history, William Wood observed in 1634 that "the searching sharpness of that purer climate creeping in at the crannies of their crazed bodies caused death and sickness."[11]

Wood's view that the "purer climate" of New England could insinuate itself into human bodies reflected standard seventeenth-century notions about human physiology and the body's relationship to its environment. Pre-Cartesian English bodies in the early seventeenth century were constructed according to an ancient model that provided the unconscious and conscious structuring for all physiological experience and interpretation of that experience. The human being was understood to be a complex moral and organic entity composed of fluids and particles, the humors and spirits—in constant flux and flow. The four humors and their related personality temperaments corresponded to the four elements—earth, air, water, and fire—which in turn provided all raw matter with forms and properties—heat, moisture, cold, and dryness. Because the human body was composed of the same elements and qualities as all other material things, the boundaries between soul, body, and environment were unstable and permeable; there was, as Rhys Isaac has noted, a "unity between the environment and the intimate self." Through the exchange between elemental, humoral, and spiritual qualities, human physiology and moral character were understood to be continuously and directly influenced and altered by climate, weather, seasonal variations, temperature, air, and food. At the same time, the kind and amount of exercise or idleness one pursued, including physical labor within a particular environment, determined one's bodily and moral health. Close attention, then, was paid to one's relationship to the environment, including that which entered into and was excreted from the body and the body's activities.[12]

Recent theorizing, as well, has produced an understanding of the human body as permeable. That a surrounding environment can "creep into" one's body is echoed by environmental theorist Arnold Berleant, who offers a dynamic model of the human body, not unlike that of the humoral body of the seventeenth century, a body that is continuously influenced by its physical surroundings, ingesting and exploiting its environment and in turn being received into and shaped by it.[13] Throughout the first half of the seventeenth century in Plymouth Colony, this activity of mutual receiving and ingesting, or consuming, played out in an energetic dialectic whose immediate site of exchange was the human body. The notion of *body* and the term *consumption* are employed here in a number of interrelated ways, both literally and metaphorically. At the most immediate physiological level, English people ate wilderness foods and inhaled wilderness air. They believed that these elements could in turn cause ill health and even death—there was the very real threat of being physically destroyed or consumed by New England resources. But human bodies are never merely physical objects; they are invested with layers of cultural significance and meanings that determine how particular bodies are understood to function physiologically and how they should relate to their environments. The colonists believed that living in a new land would inevitably cause their bodies and souls to change and take on qualities of that environment; without vigilance, they could, in fact, become wild creatures, their English godliness consumed by the environment and replaced with a "savage" character. Part of that vigilance required them to impose, with their bodies, their own English sense of order on the wilderness, particularly by industriously working to clear trees, build fences, roads, and houses, and cultivate fields.

"Civilizing" the wilderness helped to ensure that its "savage" influence would be held in check, while healthy labor promoted a moral character. The Separatists' vigorous plantation-building in Plymouth Colony was energized by a Calvinist theology of the body, modified by Puritans like William Ames and by John Robinson. The goals of Ames's "practical theology," which had influenced Robinson's ideas, was "eupraxia," or proper conduct; visible actions gave God's will concrete existence in the world.[14] A humorally based concern that bodies and souls might be perilously influenced by their surroundings was countered by the belief that rigorous activity in the world as a true sign of chosenness by God could overcome the undesirable effects of one's environment. The threat that the environment posed to the Puritans' physical and moral selves might be contained by imposing on the landscape English models of "habitation." Throughout the seventeenth century, progressively more land came into English possession, and natural resources—furs, fish, trees—were "commodified," as William Cronon has noted.[15] Both land and resources were altered or, in fact, consumed.

The New England environment confronted the Separatists with an inescapable material presence. On one hand, it threatened to absorb them, body and soul, and yet, on the other hand, it offered them the potential of increased health and material gain through the ingestion, to recall Berleant's term, of New England air, foodstuffs, land, and resources. In fact, in the very act of consuming the land, the settlers would feel themselves being consumed by it. With the malleable and industrious body as the site of mutual exchange between the physical New England environment and cultural expectations about that environment, both sides of this dialectic—consuming and being consumed—are important to investigate in detail in order to understand how particular kinds of historical human bodies were generated through their interactions with the New England wilderness.

In the context of the first side of the dialectical exchange, the Plymouth settlers experienced the potential of New England to consume them physically and morally. In a humoral economy, physical and spiritual health depended on a balance or harmony between one's constitution and the surrounding environment, and numerous travel writers recognized European fears about the effects a foreign "New World" climate and natural resources might have on bodily and moral well-being. The exchange of qualities between human and environment created the potential danger to English people who might sicken and die or become morally altered by the wilderness—taking on its "savage" qualities—before they were able to impose their own alterations on the landscape.[16] Thus, promotional writers assured their readers that New England was "a most excellent place, both for health and fertility." Puritan Francis Higginson, for example, organized his description of New England according to the four elements because, he asserted, "the life and wel-fare of euerie Creature here below ... doth by the most wise ordering of Gods prouidence, depend next vnto himself, vpon the temperature and disposition of the foure Elements, Earth, Water, Aire, and Fire," and he endeavored to prove "that there is hardly a more healthfull place to be found in the world that agreeth better with our English Bodyes." Higginson argued that New England's climate, in fact, was healthier for English bodies than was England itself: "many that haue been weake and sickly in old *England,* by comming hither haue been thoroughly healed and growne healthful and strong." Thomas Morton found New England to be superior to England— its soil more fertile, air healthier, wildlife more fecund, winds less violent, and rain more moderate. For William Wood, the country was colder in the winter and in summer "hotter than is suitable to an ordinary English constitution," and yet "both men and women keep their natural complexions ... fresh and ruddy" and "not very many [are] troubled with inflammations or such diseases as are increased by too much heat."[17]

New England appeared to offer an agreeable setting for a transplantation of the "English vine." However, for a Puritan sensibility, the fear persisted that settlers might become contaminated by a "savage" land and subsumed by a foreign environment that had produced humans no more civilized or regenerate than the "wild Indians." Bradford recorded that the Separatists had worried that "the change of air, diet and drinking of water would infect their bodies with sore sicknesses and grievous diseases," and he imagined in graphic detail tortures the "savage people, who are cruel, barbarous and most treacherous" might inflict on vulnerable English bodies.[18] Although Bradford's worst fears concerning the Indians did not come to pass, the settlers' first years in New England did present numerous difficulties that kept the question open as to which side—savage or civilized—would eventually consume the other. For the Separatists and their traveling companions "compacted together" on the *Mayflower,* as for all who made the ocean crossing in the early decades of the seventeenth century, the voyage was fraught with the discomforts of close quarters and seasickness and the dangers of more serious illness. The settlers arrived with lowered resistance to disease, which, for the *Mayflower* group, was compounded by the fact that they arrived during the winter months with poor food supplies and no shelter from the elements, occasioning the deaths of many of them.[19]

Seen as more seriously crucial than physiological illness and death, however, was the danger of persons' souls becoming corrupted by the "savage wilderness," for the humoral conception of the human being meant that environment, body, and moral soul interpenetrated in a continuous exchange of qualities. John Canup has clearly delineated the threat the wilderness posed to Puritans in their construction of sin. Inordinately degenerate bodily practices seemed to be "somehow a natural consequence of transplantation into a wilderness environment." For example, a crop of multiple sexual sins—incest, sodomy, and bestiality—flourished in Plymouth in 1642. Bradford struggled with the possibility that, although their community had been planted by "religious men ... and they came for religion's sake," the environment could undermine their best intentions and nurture seeds of wickedness that bore fruit in English bodies. Not relishing the notion that "Satan hath more power in these heathen lands, as some have thought," Bradford preferred to imagine that "the Devil may carry a greater spite against the churches of Christ and the gospel here, by how much the more they endeavour to preserve holiness and purity amongst them." In other words, Bradford believed that if Satan truly held sway in New England, "any transplantation of civility and Christianity" would be "frustrate[d]" and their project ultimately doomed. But even if the wilderness were not, finally, Satan's domain, the body of Saints must watch its members closely, lest "one wicked person may infect many" and sin—always simultaneously moral and physical—thrive in the heathen soil.[20]

Fearing the physical and spiritual threats posed by uncontrolled interaction with the environment, Plymouth's leaders worked to enclose and contain their community—and the community's bodies—by palisading their town and attempting to limit expansion beyond its confines. Settlers discovered, however, that New England actually offered an exceptionally healthy and prosperous climate for English bodies, which drew them out of the settled village of New Plymouth. As they implemented native methods of cultivation and ate indigenous foodstuffs, integrating both with familiar English husbandry practices and plants, the Plymouth colonists thrived. They lived longer and with more "physical vigor," according to John Demos, than their English counterparts, and some believed that women were more fertile and produced more twins because of the healthful and agreeable climate. Separatist Edward Winslow attested that, when compared with "other parts of America, I cannot conceive of any to agree better with the constitution of the English, not being oppressed with extremity of heat, nor nipped by biting cold; by which means, blessed be God, we enjoy our health, notwithstanding those difficulties we have undergone, in such a measure as would have been admired if we had lived in England with the like means."[21]

Looking back on their first years in New England, Bradford marveled at the colonists' ability to thrive in the face of adversity. It was, he argued, *because* they had experienced many "enemies to health," such as "change of air, famine or unwholesome food, much drinking of water, sorrows and troubles," all of which were normally "causes of many diseases, consumers of natural vigour and the bodies of men, and shorteners of life," that God had upheld them and caused them to prosper. "It is not by good and dainty fare, by peace and rest and heart's ease in enjoying contentments and good things of this world only that preserves health and prolongs life," he asserted. Bradford experienced the pervasive anxiety among colonists concerning their rejection of England and emigration to New England, which they attempted to justify through a rhetoric that mingled ideas about the health and moral benefits of living in America. Bradford held up rigorous life in New England as superior to the civilized world of those who still languished in England. Others agreed with him, arguing that "if men desire to have a people degenerate speedily, and corrupt their mindes and bodies too ... let them secke [*sic*] a rich soile, that brings in much with little labour; but if they desire that Piety and godlinesse should prosper, ... let them choose a Countrey such as this."[22]

Over time, Bradford and others who remained in Plymouth found themselves thoroughly invested in New England, given over to what they construed as the sometimes threatening but always invigorating actions of the land's climate and natural resources on their physical and moral beings. As their bodies absorbed local knowledge and resources, they were, in turn, absorbed by them, their physiological, mental, and moral structures, they believed, fundamentally altered from those they had been in England or Holland. As Bradford argued, thriving in the wilderness, rejecting its savagery but acquiring the godly character it could instill, required hard physical labor and a determination to withstand difficulties in the "weatherbeaten face" of adversity. Successfully working the land and gaining a visceral sense of its character motivated most colonists to push beyond their initial fears of the dangerous power this new place might exert on them. Despite the intentions of their original leaders, within the first few years Plymouth's settlers began to move outside their palisaded town into the country, claiming more land for themselves.

The Plymouth colonists' move into the New England frontier, consuming its land and resources, presents the other side of the dialectical exchange of consumption between English culture and New England environment that took place at the level of the human body. While in Leiden, the Separatist congregation had felt themselves being driven out of their original and adopted homelands of England and the Netherlands for cultural and religious reasons, and they were determined to "transplant" themselves onto American soil. They worried that their children were growing up without an English identity, and they wanted the opportunity to pursue freely their particular understanding of godly worship. They hoped to advance the gospel of Christ "in those remote parts of the world" or at least be "stepping-stones unto others for the performing of so great a work."[23] But beneath their cultural concerns and religious rhetoric lay another motivation at least as powerful, if not more so—"the consumption of space."[24] Like the founders of the Massachusetts Bay Colony who would arrive ten years later, the Plymouth settlers saw New England and its much advertised natural resources as a land provided by God for the furtherance of worldly enterprise. Robert Cushman, one of New Plymouth's investors, argued, as would John Winthrop and John Cotton a few years later, for the settlers' legal rights to the land. James I, Cushman pointed out, had claimed English possession of the territory of New England by royal decree because it was perceived to be "a vast and empty chaos," "spacious and void"—a "wilderness." Adopting this justification, Bradford had argued that America was a "vast and unpeopled countr[y] ... devoid of all civil inhabitants, where there are only savage and brutish men which range up and down, little otherwise than the wild beasts of the same."[25] It would be dependent on English settlers, by rigorous labor and "godly industry," to plant themselves in this "empty" land in order to transform what they perceived to be a savage wilderness into a cultivated garden.

The survival of the first English settlers at Plymouth depended on their imposition of a particular cultural order on the natural environment. As they stepped off the *Mayflower* into a "New World," the Separatists' bodies penetrated that world, carrying with them familiar models for orienting themselves in the unfamiliar surroundings. Encountering threats to their bodies' integrity—tainted mussels, suspicious Indians, an animal snare, freezing rain, unmapped forests—the *Mayflower* passengers set about structuring the natural environment. They immediately erected crude temporary shelters, and within the first year had measured out their town and begun work on houses, gardens, and meeting house-fort, enclosing themselves within a protective palisade. The layout of structures, fences, and fields in familiar English patterns physically oriented colonists in the environment and clearly delineated "civilized" from "savage" space, fortifying their sense of well-being, safety, and order.[26]

Towns and individual homesteads were limited in size by physiological constraints—that is, the time it took to walk from buildings to fields or from village to village. Early in the colony's history, farmers knew their land well by walking it daily. Having descended from yeoman farming families in England, it seems likely that the first settlers were able to develop a visceral sense of the climate, the change of seasons, and how to work the land, as Demos has claimed.[27] An intimate physical relationship with the environment evolved as farmers "husbanded" the land: men felt and smelled the soil; toiled to plow, plant, and harvest their fields; and learned to read the weather. Like a human body itself, the land was "broken" and "dressed," the wilderness domesticated. Women worked their gardens of English vegetables and herbs, and their families ingested the fruits of their labor and of the soil. While Indian corn, squash, and beans, as well as American fish and game, were staples during the first years of settlement, transforming the land involved the transplantation of English fruits, vegetables, grains, grasses, and livestock, which consumed more and more land, replacing indigenous plants and animals. A dynamic melding of English culture and New England nature occurred as the settlers' roots took hold in the soil.[28] Experiences multiplied into a familiar, tangible sense of place, so that a year later Edward Winslow could exult in Plymouth's accomplishments in fishing, hunting, and Indian relations and their knowledge of wild fruits and shellfish and write, "We ... walk as peaceably and safely in the wood as in the highways in England."[29]

And yet, Winslow further noted, "the country wanteth only industrious men to employ, for it would grieve your hearts if, as I, you had seen so many miles together by goodly rivers uninhabited."[30] The crux of possession for the settlers lay in bodily habitation of the land—the building of permanent houses and fences, the cultivation of property. Unlike the Indians, who roamed the land like the "wild beasts of the forest," the Separatists were to plant themselves and labor industriously there. The Plymouth leaders brought with them a vastly different understanding of the human-environment relationship, and thus a different construction of the human body than that held by the native inhabitants.[31] Despite the crucial support provided by Massasoit and Tisquantum in the first years of settlement, Cushman claimed that the native inhabitants lacked "industry" and had neither "skill [n]or faculty to use either the land or the commodities of it," and so it was an "undressed country," "marred for want of manuring, gathering, ordering, etc."[32] According to English law, land was considered empty and available if it were not cultivated and harvested in a particular Anglo-European pattern of land "improvement" that entailed enclosing property with fences, building permanent structures, and plowing fields, planting them with English crops.[33] For the English at Plymouth, this principle was energized by their pastor John Robinson's theology of eupraxia, which played out in a polemic against "idleness" and an advocation of industrious labor. God, according to Robinson, had determined that "man" must "labor ... in dressing the garden; and ... eat bread by the sweat of his brow.... Art and industry must supply nature's defects." While "labor brings strength to the body, and vigour to the mind," idleness, on the other hand, "brings bodily poverty" and "mischiefs."[34] Mixing Robinson's Calvinist theology with accepted humoral understandings regarding "exercise" and "idleness," Plymouth colonists believed that to fulfill the purposes for which God had called his people into America required hard physical labor—a body that was rigorously disciplined to reap the fruits of the earth by toil and sweat—which, in turn, would produce morally superior human beings. In December 1621 Cushman advised against those coming who "look after great riches, ease, pleasures, dainties, and jollity in this world," for "the country is yet raw; the land untilled; the cities not builded; the cattle not settled. We are compassed about with a helpless and idle people, the natives of the country."[35]

Bradford's and Cushman's understandings of the Indians as uncivilized, incompetent, and indolent derived from European constructions of "civilized" and "savage," which were in large part grounded in differing conceptions of utilization of the environment. Native modes of living on the land involved moving their villages to various sites in a regular pattern throughout the year, according to fish and game migrations and the growing season; these practices, according to English law, denied the Indians right of property possession. Male Indian bodies were seen as disorderly, savage, and lazy because they "ranged the forests" for fish and game, while women performed the horticultural labors.[36] For the Separatists, the ideal New England body was one not dissipated with sensory pleasures and a frivolous hunting lifestyle, such as that lived by Indian men (and European gentry); it was, certainly, vulnerable but also rigorously "planted" in the soil, civilized by the hard labors performed there, and therefore entitled to exclusive ownership of it. During the "Great Migration" of 1630–1640, new homesteads and towns multiplied within and outside of Plymouth Colony, as English settlers penetrated further westward into the frontier, expanding their territorial possessions. Native inhabitants, however, were often unwilling to watch their own uses of the environment be subsumed by English activities. As physical contact between the Pequots and Puritan settlers increased in Connecticut, the native inhabitants complained that the English were "overspread[ing] their country, and ... depriv[ing] them thereof." The massacre of the Pequots in 1637 by English and

Narragansett men violently enacted a central tension between radically different understandings of physical existence. For the English, it was a tension between savage and civilized bodies and their conflicting understandings of the human-environment relationship. Violence that consumed a certain kind of human body was considered necessary to "empty" the area of its "savage" element and open up new land for "civilized" settlement.[37]

The increasing dispersal of Plymouth settlers into the wilderness, however, worried William Bradford. The "appetite for land" drove people to invest in properties that they were no longer able to traverse in a day's walk or to cultivate and plant. As fields near the town of New Plymouth became overused and depleted—consumed, in fact—people kept their houses in town but moved themselves onto outlying properties. In 1633, members of the General Court worried that the town "is like to be dispeopled" and agreed to require individuals to give up their homes in town if they were not going to inhabit them, so that others could live there. Property must be physically and permanently inhabited, "for the maintenance and strength of society." The law, however, did not stop the flow of people out of town and into new territory, and, in 1644, Bradford lamented that the church at New Plymouth was "like an ancient mother grown old and forsaken of her children, though not in their affections yet in regard of their bodily presence and personal helpfulness."[38] Despite the original argument that to tame the "savage land" required planting oneself in the soil and working it with hard physical labor, the population throughout all of New England was extremely fluid and transient. Even for Bradford, the metaphorical and practical consumption of the environment proved too enticing to resist. Despite his initial fears of the harmful effects of New England air, soil, and water on English bodies, Bradford later rhapsodized about the wilderness delights spread before the hungry Saints:

> And now with plenty their poor souls were fed,
> with better food than wheat, or angels' bread; ...
> "Eat, O my friends, (saith Christ) and drink freely,
> Here's wine and milk, and all sweet spicery; ...
> I myself for you have this banquet made...
> In this wilderness."[39]

One hundred thirty-five years after William Bradford penned his paean to the savory feast God had prepared for his people in the wilderness, St. John de Crèvecoeur wrote in a similar vein, exulting in the marvelous, albeit dangerous, power of the New England environment to engender a radically new kind of human being—the American farmer. Whereas "in Europe," Crèvecoeur argued, future Americans "were as so many useless plants, wanting vegetative mould and refreshing showers," in New England, "by the power of transplantation, like all other plants they have taken root and flourished! ... The goodness and flavour of the fruit proceeds from the peculiar soil and exposition in which [people] grow," he continued. "We are nothing but what we derive from the air we breathe [and] the climate we inhabit." Thus, for Crèvecoeur, those who settled on the land and cleared, fenced, and tilled it, transplanting the best qualities of Europe into the fecund soil of America, produced the most admirable kind of human being. These were not the "bad people"—Euroamericans whose tempers were altered by the "wild meat" of the forest and who were enticed to discard the plough and become unruly hunters like the "barbarous Indians"—but "well-clad," "fat," "useful citizens," whose labors had translated a "hitherto barbarous country into a fine, fertile, well-regulated district."[40]

This new kind of human being whom Crèvecoeur believed he had discovered in America had been born in the early seventeenth century in Plymouth Colony. New England had threatened to consume those who first stepped off the *Mayflower,* confronting the Separatists with a body-environment relationship fraught with danger. Leery of the physical and moral threat presented by contact with New England, settlers were nonetheless drawn to the land. Humoral understandings of the body's permeability to its material surroundings produced bodies that were vulnerable, malleable, and adaptable. Living in New England did seem to alter the colonists' physiologies, as they became healthier and more fertile than those who remained in England, and their senses developed a visceral knowledge of the environment and how to manipulate it. Physiological changes were understood to be linked to alterations in their moral constitutions, which might absorb the savagery of the wilderness. But the settlers argued that hard labor on the land, as John Robinson had promoted, and confrontations with its elements generated greater "godliness." Actively imposing their industrious bodies on the natural environment, inhabiting and anglicizing it in familiar ways, they altered it according to particular notions of "civilized" culture. Believing theirs to be civilized bodies, the colonists generated a civilized environment and a body-environment relationship that may have been experienced as more harmonious and yet remained laden with the struggle to subdue the frontier. As the century progressed, American goals to tame the "wilderness" would continue to be based on the New English precedent for consuming the land and its resources and bringing "civilization" to more and more of the continent. Yet, even in the late eighteenth century, Crèvecoeur believed that the "savage" American environment still threatened to consume the unwary. The seventeenth-century interchange between English culture and New England nature produced an Euro-American human body both vigorous and vulnerable, both consuming and consumed.

Notes

1. William Bradford, *Of Plymouth Plantation, 1620–1647,* ed. Samuel Eliot Morison (New York: Alfred A. Knopf, 1994), 61–62, 25, 64.

2. *A Relation or Iournall of the beginning and proceedings of the English Plantation setled at Plimoth in New England* (London, 1622), in *Mourt's Relation: A Journal of the Pilgrims at Plymouth,* ed. Dwight B. Heath (Bedford, Mass.: Applewood Books, 1963), 15–16.

3. English travelers to America were suspicious of drinking the water they found there, unsure of its effects on their bodies and character (see below).

4. *A Relation,* 19–24, 35–37; Bradford, *Of Plymouth Plantation,* 64–66, 69.

5. The settlers learned the name of the former Wampanoag village, whose inhabitants had died four years earlier from disease, from Samoset, who first visited them in March 1621 (*A Relation,* 51; Bradford, *Of Plymouth Plantation,* 79–80). On the decimation of the New England native population due to disease, see Francis Jennings, *The Invasion of America: Indians, Colonialism, and the Cant of Conquest* (New York: W. W. Norton, 1975/1976), 15–31.

6. *A Relation,* 55, 58, 61; Bradford, *Of Plymouth Plantation,* 77–79, 81, 447; Eugene Aubrey Stratton, *Plymouth Colony: Its History and People, 1620–1691* (Salt Lake City, Utah: Ancestry Publishing, 1986), 21.

7. See, e.g., Roderick Nash, *Wilderness and the American Mind,* 3rd ed. (New Haven, Conn.: Yale University Press, 1982); Peter N. Carroll, *Puritanism and the Wilderness: The Intellectual Significance of the New England Frontier, 1629–1700* (New York: Columbia University Press, 1969); William Cronon, *Changes in the Land: Indians, Colonists, and the Ecology of New England* (New York: Hill and Wang, 1983); John Frederick Martin, *Profits in the Wilderness: Entrepreneurship and the Founding of New England Towns in the Seventeenth Century* (Chapel Hill: University of North Carolina Press, 1991); Jennings, *Invasion of America;* James Axtell, *The Invasion Within: The Contest of Cultures in Colonial North America* (New York: Oxford University Press, 1985); Ann Kibbey, *The Interpretation of Material Shapes in Puritanism: A Study of Rhetoric, Prejudice, and Violence* (Cambridge, U.K.: Cambridge University Press, 1986); Andrew Delbanco, *The Puritan Ordeal* (Cambridge, Mass.: Harvard University Press, 1989); John Canup, *Out of the Wilderness: The Emergence of an American Identity in Colonial New England* (Middletown, Conn.: Wesleyan University Press, 1990); Myra Jehlen, *American Incarnation: The Individual, The Nation, and the Continent* (Cambridge, Mass.: Harvard University Press, 1986). Of these, I have found Canup's focus on "the threat that the physical and human environments of America seemed to pose for the transplanted English culture" (3) most helpful in my own analysis of the Separatists' views of the New England wilderness as dangerous and "consuming."

8. See, e.g., Karen Ordahl Kupperman, "Climate and Mastery of the Wilderness in Seventeenth-Century New England," in David D. Hall and David Grayson Allen, eds., *Seventeenth-Century New England* (Boston: The Colonial Society of Massachusetts, 1984), 19–20; Martin, *Profits in the Wilderness,* 113–17; Cecilia Tichi, *New World, New Earth: Environmental Reform in American Literature from the Puritans through Whitman* (New Haven, Conn.: Yale University Press, 1979), 47–54; Yi-Fu Tuan, *Landscapes of Fear* (New York: Pantheon Books, 1979), 55.

9. Bryan S. Turner, *The Body and Society: Explorations in Social Theory,* 2nd ed. (London: Sage, 1996), 66, 230. For the body's role in the human undertaking of ordering unfamiliar "space" into ordered "place," see Edward S. Casey, *The Fate of Place: A Philosophical History* (Berkeley: University of California Press, 1997), 202–42; Yi-Fu Tuan, *Space and Place: The Perspective of Experience* (Minneapolis: University of Minnesota, 1977), 43–50; Jonathan Z. Smith, *To Take Place: Toward Theory in Ritual* (Chicago: University of Chicago Press, 1987), 24–46; J. Douglas Porteous, *Landscapes of the Mind: Worlds of Sense and Metaphor* (Toronto: University of Toronto Press, 1990), 70.

10. See Stephen Greenblatt, *Marvelous Possessions: The Wonder of the New World* (Chicago: University of Chicago Press, 1991).

11. *A Relation,* 41; Bradford, *Of Plymouth Plantation,* xxiv; George D. Langdon Jr., *Pilgrim Colony: A History of New Plymouth, 1620–1691* (New Haven, Conn.: Yale University Press, 1966), 12; William Wood, *New England's Prospect,* ed. Alden T. Vaughan (Amherst: University of Massachusetts Press, 1977), 28.

12. E. Ruth Harvey, *The Inward Wits: Psychological Theory in the Middle Ages and the Renaissance* (London: The Warburg Institute, 1975); Karen Ordahl Kupperman, "Fear of Hot Climates in the Anglo-American Colonial Experience," *William and Mary Quarterly* 41 (1984): 213–14; Clarence J. Glacken, *Traces on the Rhodian Shore: Nature and Culture in Western Thought from Ancient Times to the End of the Eighteenth Century* (Berkeley: University of California Press, 1967), 8–12, 80–88; Rhys Isaac, *The Transformation of Virginia, 1740–1790* (Chapel Hill: University of North Carolina Press, 1982), 51; Robert Burton, *The Anatomy of Melancholy* (1621), ed. Floyd Dell (London: George Routledge and Sons, 1931), 128–48, 188–217. For a recent analysis of conflicting interpretations of the influence of the environment on human bodies and the early construction of racial categories in colonial Spanish America, see Jorge Canizares Esguerra, "New World, New Stars: Patriotic Astrology and the Invention of Indian and Creole Bodies in Colonial Spanish America, 1600–1650," *The American Historical Review* 104 (1999): 33–68. As well as determining the relationship between body, environment, and health, the humors influenced gender distinctions, which were based upon humoral characteristics—women's bodies tended to be cold and moist, men's were hot and dry—rather than on physiological structures; see Anthony Fletcher, *Gender, Sex, and Subordination in England, 1500–1800* (New Haven, Conn.: Yale University Press, 1995), 33–36; Thomas Laqueur, *Making Sex: Body and Gender from the Greeks to Freud* (Cambridge, Mass.: Harvard University Press, 1990), 63–113. See Trudy Eden's article in this volume for further description and analysis of the humoral philosophy.

13. Berleant writes, "Bodies are not static objects with fixed and permanent boundaries. They are dynamic and fluid, receiving and acting, ingesting and expressing, engaged in a dynamic transaction with the field they inhabit.... The very spaces we inhabit are appropriated as a commodity to be as fully exploited as legally allowed.... The very forms our bodies take are themselves the product of ... environment" (*Living in the Landscape: Toward an Aesthetics of Environment* [Lawrence: University of Kansas Press, 1997], 106).

14. William Ames, *The Marrow of Sacred Divinity* (London, 1623; reprint, in *The Marrow of Theology: William Ames, 1576–1633,* trans. and ed. John D. Eusden [Durham, N.C.: Labyrinth Press, 1983]), 232–36; Perry Miller, *The New England Mind: The Seventeenth Century* (Cambridge, Mass.: Belknap Press, 1982), 164–65.

15. Cronon, *Changes in the Land,* 159–70.

16. European discoveries and explorations of the Americas increased the awareness of the immediate impact that the human body and its environment exerted on each other. Clarence J. Glacken has noted that ancient humoral theories of the environment's influence on the body, so potent during the medieval and Renaissance periods, became even more applicable and thus influential in unfamiliar lands, while the capacity for humans to modify their environments became more obvious in "what many considered virgin lands unchanged since the creation" (*Traces on the Rhodian Shore,* 358, 460–97).

17. Kupperman, "Climate and Mastery of the Wilderness," 13; Canup, *Out of the Wilderness,* 8–28; John Smith, *A Description of New England* (London, 1616) in *Works,* ed. Edward Arber, 2 vols. (Westminster: Archibald Constable, 1895), 1:13; Francis Higginson, *New-Englands Plantation* (London, 1630), 5, 9; Thomas Morton, *New English Canaan* (London, 1632), 64; Wood, *New England's Prospect,* 32.

18. Canup, *Out of the Wilderness,* 5, 10; Bradford, *Of Plymouth Plantation,* 26. Bradford noted that the Plymouth group originally intended to plant themselves in northern Virginia, in fact, rather than further south, because they knew that "such hot countries are subject to grievous diseases and many noisome impediments which other more temperate places are freer from, and would not so well agree with our English bodies" (28).

19. Bradford, *Of Plymouth Plantation,* 58, 77–79, 84; Robert Blair St. George, " 'Set Thine House in Order': The Domestication of the Yeomanry in Seventeenth-Century New England," in *New England Begins: The Seventeenth Century,* vol. 2, *Mentality and Environment* (Boston: Museum of Fine Arts, 1982), 180. On the rigors of seventeenth-century transatlantic voyages, see David Cressy, *Coming Over: Migration and Communication between England and New England in the Seventeenth Century* (Cambridge, U.K.: Cambridge University Press, 1987), 144–77.

20. Canup, *Out of the Wilderness,* 29–54; Bradford, *Of Plymouth Plantation,* 316–22.

21. St. George, " 'Set Thine House in Order,' " 180; John Demos, "Notes on Life in Plymouth Colony," *William and Mary Quarterly* 22 (1965): 271; Kupperman, "Climate and Mastery of the Wilderness," 16–17; Edward Winslow, "Winslow's Relation," in *Chronicles of the Pilgrim Fathers of the Colony of Plymouth, 1602–1625,* ed. Alexander Young (New York: Da Capo Press, 1971), 369–70.

22. Bradford, *Of Plymouth Plantation,* 328–29; *The Planters Plea* (1630), in *Tracts and Other Papers,* ed. Peter Force, vol. 2, n. 3 (Gloucester, Mass.: Peter Smith, 1963), 18. Andrew Delbanco has detailed the tensions that colonists felt concerning their renouncing England for New England and their use of "medical and theological notions about purification" to construct "America as a place of cure" (*Puritan Ordeal,* 83–84).

23. Bradford, *Of Plymouth Plantation,* 23–24.

24. Jonathan Beecher Field, " 'Peculiar Manuerance': Puritans, Indians, and the Rhetoric of Agriculture, 1629–1654," in *Plants and People,* ed. Peter Benes, The Dublin Seminar for New England Folklife, Annual Proceedings, 1995 (Boston: Boston University, 1996), 22.

25. Bradford, *Of Plymouth Plantation,* 25.

26. *A Relation,* 41–44, 48; Bradford, *Of Plymouth Plantation,* 72, 76, 85, 94, 111; Edward Winslow, "A Letter Sent From New England" (1621), in *Mourt's Relation,* 81–86; Edward Winslow, "Good Newes from New England" (1624), in *Chronicles of the Pilgrim Fathers,* 295; John Pory, Emmanuel Altham, and Isaack de Rasieres, *Letters,* in *Three Visitors to Early Plymouth,* ed. Sydney V. James Jr. (Plymouth: Plimoth Plantation, 1963), 11, 24, 76.

27. Darrett B. Rutman, *Husbandmen of Plymouth: Farms and Villages in the Old Colony, 1620–1692* (Boston: Beacon Press, 1967), 4; John Demos, *A Little Commonwealth: Family Life in Plymouth Colony* (London: Oxford University Press, 1970), 13–14.

28. John R. Stilgoe, *Common Landscape of America, 1580 to 1845* (New Haven, Conn.: Yale University Press, 1982), 12–17, 141; St. George, " 'Set Thine House in Order,' " 161–62; Field, " 'Peculiar Manuerance,' " 12–24; Daniel A. Romani Jr., " 'Our *English Clover-grass* sowen thrives very well': The Importation of English Grasses and Forages into Seventeenth-Century New England," in *Plants and People,* ed. Peter Benes, The Dublin Seminar for New England Folklife, Annual Proceedings, 1995 (Boston: Boston University, 1996), 25–37; Peter W. Cook, "Domestic Livestock of Massachusetts Bay, 1620–1725," in *The Farm,* ed. Peter Benes, The Dublin Seminar for New England Folklife, Annual Proceedings, 1986 (Boston: Boston University Press, 1988), 109–25; Michel de Certeau, *The Practice of Everyday Life,* trans. Steven Rendall (Berkeley: University of California Press, 1984), 92–93, 117–18.

29. Winslow, "A Letter," 83–85.

30. Ibid., 84.

31. William Cronon's work clearly delineates the ecological ramifications of the differences in Indian and English interactions with the New England environment. For an analysis of the use of body metaphors in European and Indian cross-cultural communication, see Nancy Shoemaker's article in this volume.

32. Bradford, *Of Plymouth Plantation,* 23–25; R[obert] C[ushman], "Reasons and Considerations touching the lawfulness of removing out of England into the parts of America" (1622), in *Mourt's Relation,* 91–92. Cf. John Winthrop, "General Considerations for the Plantation in New-England; with an Answer to Several Objections," in *Chronicles of the First Planters of the Colony of Massachusetts Bay, from 1623 to 1636,* ed. Alexander Young (Boston: Little and Brown, 1846), 271–72; John Cotton, "God's Promise to His Plantations" (London: Old South Leaflets, 3, no. 53, 1630; reprint, Boston: Directors of the Old South Work, n.d.), 1–16.

33. See, e.g., David Grayson Allen, "*Vacuum Domicilum:* The Social and Cultural Landscape of Seventeenth-Century New England," in *New England Begins: The Seventeenth Century,* vol. 1, *Introduction: Migration and Settlement* (Boston: Museum of Fine Arts, 1982); Jennings, *The Invasion of America,* 82–83.

34. John Robinson, *New Essays; or, Observations Divine and Moral* (1628) in *The Works of John Robinson* (Boston: Doctrinal Tract and Book Society, 1851), 113–16.

35. Robert Cushman, "Cushman's Discourse," in *Chronicles of the Pilgrim Fathers of the Colony of Plymouth, 1602–1625,* ed. Alexander Young (Boston: Little and Brown, 1841), 256, 265. Regarding humoral notions of the influence of exercise and idleness on one's physical and moral health, Robert Burton wrote that exercise, in moderation, was good for "the preservation of the body," while idleness was "the bane of body and mind, the nurse of naughtiness, stepmother of discipline, the chief author of all mischief, one of the seven deadly sins, and a sole cause of this and many other maladies, the devil's cushion" (210).

36. Peter A. Thomas, "Contrastive Subsistence Strategies and Land Use as Factors for Understanding Indian-White Relations in New England," *Ethnohistory* 23 (1976): 1–18; Kathleen J. Bragdon, *Native People of Southern New England, 1500–1650* (Norman: University of Oklahoma Press, 1996), 14–20, 102–29; Cronon, *Changes in the Land,* 54–58.

37. Bradford, *Of Plymouth Plantation,* 294–97; Jennings, *The Invasion of America,* 202–27; Cotton, "God's Promise to His Plantations," 5–6. See also Kibbey, *The Interpretation of Material Shapes in Puritanism,* 92–105.

38. Nathaniel B. Shurtleff, ed., *Records of the Colony of New Plymouth in New England,* 12 vols. (Boston: William White, 1855–61), 1:17, 11:18; Bradford, *Of Plymouth Plantation,* 252–54, 315, 334; Martin, *Profits in the Wilderness,* 120–21.

39. William Bradford, "A Descriptive and Historical Account of New England in Verse," in "Governor Bradford's Letter Book," Massachusetts Historical Society, *Collections* 3 (1794): 79.

40. J. Hector St. John de Crèvecoeur, *Letters from an American Farmer and Sketches of Eighteenth-Century America,* ed. Albert E. Stone (New York: Penguin Books, 1981), 66–105, quotes from pp. 69, 71, 76–77, 94.

The Body Politic and the Body Somatic

Benjamin Rush's Fear of Social Disorder and His Treatment for Yellow Fever

JACQUELYN C. MILLER

In October 1793, during Philadelphia's fifth major outbreak of yellow fever in a turbulent century, Benjamin Rush and his students attended hundreds of diseased victims. Using the method of treatment Rush had devised in the preceding weeks, they aggressively purged and bled their patients in the hope of facilitating a cure. As Rush related in his published account the following year, the therapeutic efforts of one of his students, Edward Fisher, involved drawing over a hundred ounces of blood, during ten bleedings, from a Mr. Gribble, a cedar cooper in Front Street; from Mr. George, a carter from Ninth Street, he took about the same amount in only five bleedings; from Mr. Peter Mierken he bled one hundred and fourteen ounces in five days, the relatively larger quantity a reflection of his patient's weight; and Mr. Toy, a blacksmith near Dock Street, "was eight times bled in the course of seven days." Rush pronounced that all these men had survived the disease and were "this day living and healthy, instances of the efficacy of copious blood-letting, and of the intrepidity and judgement of their young physician." Furthermore, Rush contended, this daring spirit on the part of many of the city's medical practitioners assured that "[n]ot less than 600 of the inhabitants of Philadelphia probably owe their lives to purging and bleeding."[1]

The inhabitants of Philadelphia, and indeed the entire country, felt Rush's influence not only in the medical sphere, of course, but in the political as well. In particular, Rush's political involvement was felt in his capacity as a signer of the Declaration of Independence, a tireless worker in the formation of state and federal constitutions, a social reformer, and an author of numerous political treatises. In this chapter, I will argue that these two spheres of interest and activity—the medical and the political—coalesced in Rush's life and

61

thought, and that the particular methods he developed to deal with disorders in the somatic dimension of late-eighteenth-century American life reflect his simultaneous concern with maintaining the political health of the new American nation.[2] Rush believed that order and tranquility in the body politic depended on the existence of a well-balanced republic; analogously, his idea of a healthy body also emphasized the need for equilibrium, which was to be maintained through a combination of dietary, hygienic, environmental, physical, and medical means. Thus, just as Rush anticipated that frequent elections would release the social and political tension built up among competing factions within the political body, so he expected that purging and bleeding would remove the surplus of stimulus from the physical system and would relieve the vascular pressures that resulted when the body was in a diseased state. To gain a fuller understanding of the origins of these impulses in Rush's thinking and actions, it is necessary to examine briefly the medical milieu from which he emerged.

Rush, like many of his contemporaries, was very interested in questions relating to the nature of human life and its passing states of health and disease. Human life, according to Rush, was "perfect animal life," the "flawless combination of motion, sensation and thought." The "human body," Rush believed, "contains so many marks of ineffable wisdom, power, and goodness in its construction, that it would be an act of impiety to enter upon the considerations of its functions, without doing homage to its divine architect." Despite Rush's assumption of a divine Creator as the originator of life, he followed the trend of eighteenth-century scholars by arguing that the functions of the soul, though not the soul itself, were united to the body. These functions, which included the processes of growth and nutrition, the power to respond to stimuli, and mental activity, all "remained within the province of physiology."[3] Consequently, Rush believed that physical, moral, and political ailments were all parts of the same whole, and were legitimate concerns of the medical profession.

Given this framework, the important questions that Rush and some of his contemporaries sought to answer were what brought human life into action and what caused it to falter. According to Rush's Edinburgh professor, William Cullen, it was the physiological tone of the nervous system that was responsible for health and disease. For example, Cullen regarded nervous energy as the source of life and believed that a fever was "a spasm of the extreme arteries" caused by the condition of the brain. Furthermore, the appearance of a fever denoted that a state of debility would follow. He often used bleeding and purging cautiously to help relax this constriction, though not in the early stages of fever. Building on these ideas, Cullen's student John Brown argued that there were two fundamental states of disease, rather than just one state of debility as Cullen had proposed. One of these states of disease, according to Brown, was the result of too much nervous stimulation, the other the consequence of too little, thus calling for either depleting or stimulating remedies. Rush's innovation, which he developed during the 1793 epidemic, was to reduce Brown's system of two disease states to just one—the state of "morbid excitement," proposing that the one "proximate" cause of all diseases was a state of excessive excitability or spasm in the blood vessels, particularly the arteries, in various parts of the body. For Rush, then, the logical treatment in all cases of illness would be bleeding and purging, which, within his theoretical framework, was done not to balance bodily fluids but to reduce vascular tension mechanically.[4] This new "heroic" treatment for yellow fever was both influenced by and contributed to Rush's new theory of disease.

Rush's infamous regimen of mercurial purging and profuse bloodletting did not go unchallenged in his day, but merely continued a pattern of controversy that began during the early days of the epidemic over disease causation and treatment.[5] His therapy for yellow fever emerged from his investigative efforts to find a means to alleviate the pain and despair of his suffering patients during the early weeks of the 1793 epidemic, a search that led him to Dr. John Mitchell's report of his treatment for the acute putrid fevers that beset Virginia in 1741. Mitchell, who gave his patients strong purges, even when their pulse rate was so low that he could hardly feel it, proposed that evacuations were necessary to bring the fever "to a perfect crisis, and solution." Mitchell's account resonated forcefully with Rush's tendency to view physicians as masters, not servants, of nature, and lent support to his faith in the potential of humans to understand and combat disease. Rush's discovery of Mitchell's treatment gave him the courage to develop his own bold cure of purging and bloodletting, advocating in extreme cases the loss of up to four-fifths of the blood in the body.[6] Prominent among Rush's many contemporary critics were those physicians and laypersons who found the use of stimulants such as quinine bark, wine, and cold baths more to their liking. Despite this competition in terms of treatment, however, Rush's aggressive approach to treating disease, known as "heroic therapeutics," eventually became very widespread in the early decades of the nineteenth century, particularly in the South and West, but declined in popularity by mid-century.[7] Rush's radical new theory of disease and his equally iconoclastic cure were, in part, the result of his sense of helplessness in coping with such a dramatic crisis as the 1793 epidemic. His theories and therapeutics, however, were carried out in a much broader social context, which I will examine in the remainder of this chapter. His writings, in fact, clearly reveal his conviction that more than his patients' lives and his professional reputation were at stake. Rush felt certain that his "miracle" treatment had profound implications for the American body politic, as well.

By the 1790s Philadelphia's most controversial physician was very troubled over the well-being and ultimate survival of the fledgling American nation; consequently, his distress over unhealthy constitutions went beyond the physical domain to encompass the political and moral arenas. As a concerned citizen of the new republic, Rush had been actively and passionately engaged in a number of political battles regarding the creation of both state and federal constitutions, and as a member of Philadelphia's burgeoning middle class, he had a vital interest in healing the city's moral ailments. Rush's medical treatments in the postwar era were thus infused with important political meanings and class overtones as a result of his growing fear of "pestilences" in realms other than the somatic, including plagues of "mob" violence, dangerous democratic impulses, intemperance, and vice.[8]

The American Revolution was the paramount experience of Rush's life, particularly since he saw it not only as a war for political independence, but also as an ongoing revolutionary process of social and moral reform. In light of Rush's broad view of the Revolution, it is not surprising that important links exist between his medical ideas and his reform efforts. Rush's regimen of aggressive bloodletting and intense purging makes the most sense, therefore, when understood not only as a remedy for yellow fever, but also as a means of controlling the passions of the body politic. I contend that Rush's treatment should be envisioned in part as his attempt to avert a second American military and social conflagration, a conflict he dreaded might lead to a Reign of Terror comparable to the one underway in France. Rush's tendency, then, to view his treatment for yellow fever in broader political terms was part of a dialectical process involving three factors—his consistent use of medical language to conceptualize his political views and, vice versa, his belief that changes in forms of government could alter the physical disposition of the citizenry, and his formulation of a unitary theory of disease.

Rush's medical and political writings dramatically illustrate the great extent to which he saw the body politic and the body natural as inextricably intertwined.[9] His practice of attributing a double meaning—medical and political—to words like *constitution* was extended to a variety of other medical phrases.[10] Early in the war against Britain, Rush, in an effort to keep his wife's spirits up, concluded one of his letters to her with the words: "All is for the best, and all will end well. Our city must undergo a purgation." He made a similar comment to John Adams about the same time, saying that "it will require one or two more campaigns to purge away the monarchical impurity we contracted by laying too long upon the lap of Great Britain." On another occasion, Rush expressed his dislike of Tories by saying that he hoped they would take up with General Howe's army so that the "continent in the meanwhile will be purged of those rascals whose idleness or perfidy have brought most of our present calamities upon us."[11]

Rush also criticized members of the patriot cause and expressed his concern over the health of the new country in medical terms. Disparaging George Washington's military abilities in a famous letter to Patrick Henry, Rush expressed his frustration over the general state of the country's health by remarking that "[America's] counsels [are] weak, and partial remedies applied constantly for universal diseases." Throughout the war Rush's mood was in constant flux, vacillating between a sense of pessimism and optimism, depending on the direction of events. He based his positive outlook, in part, on his medical experiences. "I have sometimes seen a sick man recover under all the disadvantages of ignorant physicians, a negligent nurse, bad diet, and unsuitable medicines, owing entirely to the strength of his constitution." This knowledge, then, "encourages me to hope well of my country. Her stamina are sound notwithstanding she has been these two years in the hands of quacks. The goodness of her constitution alone will save her from the feebleness and ignorance of her counsels and arms."[12] As a patriot and as a physician, therefore, Rush's constitutional interests were always two-dimensional and his continuous employment of medical metaphors to discuss political topics, which were always infused with intense moral significance, demonstrates quite clearly how closely these two worlds meshed in his everyday reflections.

A closer examination of Rush's writings reveals, however, a second factor that supports my view that his treatment for yellow fever served his broader political concerns, particularly his belief that the organization of social and political systems affected the health of the people who populated those systems.[13] He argued before the American Philosophical Society on February 4, 1774, for example, that "the abolition of the feudal system in Europe, by introducing freedom, introduced at the same time agriculture; which by multiplying the fruits of the earth, lessened the consumption of animal food, and thus put a stop to [leprosy, elephantiasis, scurvy, venereal disease, plica polonica, smallpox, and the plague]." In Rush's estimation an awareness of the interdependence of political slavery and particular diseases that deform and debase the human body could only serve as a powerful motive "to enhance the blessings of liberty [and] to trace its effects in eradicating such loathsome and destructive disorders."[14] His tendency, however, to see a correlation between the health of the populace and the form of government they lived under continued through the rest of his life, though he sometimes had to revise the evidence he presented to prove his argument. In his 1791 manuscript containing his lectures on animal life, Rush contended that "[i]n no part of the world is animal life, as far as it respects the human species, in a more perfect state, than in France, Britain, Ireland, and the United States," adding that "[t]here is an indissoluble union between moral, political, and physical good." Eight years later, in his published version of these lectures, he excluded France and Ireland from his list of "perfect states," reflecting in all likelihood his disillusionment with the French Revolution and his response to the Irish Rebellion of 1798.[15] Given the political turmoil in these two countries, neither provided an environment conducive to the good health of its citizens. And in Rush's view the newly formed United States was not faring much better.

Very soon after the thirteen colonies had declared their independence from England, Rush began to worry about ramifications of what he saw as an excess of liberty among some members of the patriot cause. Rush was not a reluctant revolutionary, but he was a social conservative who preferred that social change proceed in a controlled and orderly fashion. On the adoption of the new state constitution of Pennsylvania, Rush found the ideas of fellow, but more radical, "friends of liberty" too "much upon the democratical order" for his taste. Consequently, he came to think that the political separation from Britain might not in itself "fix the constitution of America forever," and that once set free, the tide of revolutionary spirit was going to be difficult to control. His primary concern was that "liberty is apt to degenerate into licentiousness as power is to become arbitrary." Revealing his growing belief in the necessity of controlling the lower orders in the political realm, Rush also argued that "restraints are as necessary in the former [licentiousness] as the latter case [power]." Rush's tendency to emphasize a middle path is also apparent in his correspondence with John Adams a few years later, when he asserted that the perfection of government consisted in "providing restraints against the tyranny of rulers on the one hand and the licentiousness of the people on the other."[16] And one way to assure that this equilibrium was maintained and that health reigned in the body politic was, according to Rush, to institute a proper constitution with checks and balances. But as the local political conflicts of the late 1770s proved, there was little agreement over what a "proper constitution" entailed.

For Rush, the Pennsylvania Constitution came to symbolize a consequence of the struggle for independence that he had not anticipated—the increased interest and involvement of people who had previously played a less direct role in the political process. He was forced to acknowledge their presence time and time again, not only as a result of the controversies that continued to surround the creation of state and federal governments, but also by other actions that the common folk took in order to make their voices heard. Rush did not welcome their participation. Instead, his class biases were exhibited when he interpreted their involvement as potentially dangerous. For example, in his response to the news of the Fort Wilson Riot, Rush argued that the event was proof that "Poor Pennsylvania" had degenerated from a democracy to a mobocracy and had become "the most miserable spot upon the surface of the globe."[17] According to historian Robert Brunhouse, the afternoon battle that occurred at the house of former Congressman James Wilson on October 4, 1779, between a group of poor militiamen and several "gentlemen" who were ostensibly guarding the property, was "the highwater mark of radical democracy in Pennsylvania during the revolutionary period." This incident, which resulted in an estimated six or seven deaths and more than twice that number wounded, began as a demonstration by soldiers who protested having to shoulder an unequal share of the war's military and economic burdens.[18] Rush's sympathies clearly lay with the "gentlemen" under attack. He preferred that members of the lower classes not discuss politics at all, remarking once that the less that servants argued over political subjects the better, as "such disputes, especially among ignorant people, generally confirm prejudices and increase obstinacy."[19] Underlying this elitist view of politics was a definite fear that popular politics would encourage social disorder and violence, thus harming the health of the body politic.

Rush eventually observed a more direct cause-and-effect relationship between the political and somatic spheres. In 1787 he anticipated that the new federal Constitution, "like a new continental wagon," would "overset our state dung cart with all its dirty contents," and, therefore, provide the perfect vehicle for "traveling fast into order and national happiness." It became increasingly clear, however, that new governments in and of themselves would not bring about the social stability and harmony he so desired. Rush contended that the minds of the citizens of the United States were wholly unprepared for peace in 1783, noting that, as a result, the military and political events of the American Revolution had set in motion a number of mental diseases. "The excess of the passion for liberty, inflamed by the successful issue of the war, produced, in many people opinions and conduct which could not be removed by reason nor restrained by government." He adds that "[f]or a while, they threatened to render abortive the goodness of heaven to the United States, in delivering them from the evils of slavery and war." Instead, "the extensive influence which these opinions had upon the understandings, passions and morals of many of the citizens of the United States" produced a "species of insanity" that Rush named *Anarchia*. *Anarchia* was accompanied by another mental illness that he labeled *Revolutiana*. Rush viewed this last malady as a state of hypochondriasis that struck only those who were enemies of the Revolution, and ascribed their deaths "to the neglect with which they were treated by their ancient friends, who had adhered to the government of the United States."[20] He was not speaking metaphorically here but considered these political diseases actual clinical conditions that could be treated like any physical malady.

Of course, Rush had never rested his hopes totally on the creation of a particular political system. He had long had a twofold interest in matters of a constitutional nature. As a physician he had always been concerned with the well-being of the physical body, despite the fact that much of his energy in the 1780s was focused on the health of political constitutions. The tables were turned, however, in the 1790s when Rush directed his attention more decidedly toward the treatment of biological and moral constitutions. At that point, the social struggles of the previous decade caused him to imbue disease, medical therapeutics, and his patients' bodies with multifaceted political significance.

Throughout the Revolutionary era, Rush continued to support elite rule and to view the lower classes as being under the power of their passions. Based on Aristotelian political thinking and the Enlightenment idea that reason was associated with propertied men who, as a result, were the natural leaders of public affairs, Rush took this notion to a new level. In a lecture on "Diseases of the Passions" that he gave at the University of Pennsylvania sometime before 1792, he argued that "the human mind may be compared to the British government." According to Rush:

> The Will is the King; the Understanding, the House of Lords; the Passions, the House of Commons; the Moral Faculty, the Court of Westminster; and the Conscience, the High Court of Chancery. To this last are all appeals made, it is above all Law and answerable only to the Supreme Being. As the Government can be well conducted only when these five powers harmonize with each other, so the Mind can alone act equably and right when the Harmony of its Powers is perfect.

Considering Rush's tendency to link unleashed passions with the nonruling classes, it is not surprising that he considered their representatives in the House of Commons "the most turbulent and most liable to disturbance and corruption of any part of the British Government," and "in the same manner are the Passions most liable to be misled and become turbulent." Rush's analysis, then, implicitly connected the passions with the masses through their elected officials, and the will, the conscience, the moral sense, and reason with the elite members of society. He recognized, however, that "notwithstanding all, the Passions are an important part of the Mind, and are not without their use."[21] But even this backhanded compliment carried with it an insult, given that Rush judged the masses to be of little worth in and of themselves. They became valuable only when they were useful to the ruling classes. The masses, then, according to Rush, could make a contribution to society, but only if their passions were controlled in order to bring them into harmony with their superiors.

At this point Rush still had faith that the government formed by the Constitution of 1787 was the correct one. Despite certain setbacks, Rush had high expectations regarding the physical health of the country, continued to believe that "passions produce fewer diseases in a republic than in a monarchy," and that in time "the effects of the political passions upon health and life will be still less perceptible in our country."[22] All he wanted was to remove the obstacles that would allow the government to function properly. Consequently, Rush turned his attention to one of the major hindrances to the country's health—the presence of immoral behavior.

Rush tried to determine how he, as a physician, could do his part to rid the country of vice. The morals of others had long concerned Rush, and as early as 1774 he had wondered whether one might discover a regimen, or a medicine, that would "improve, or alter the diseased state of the moral faculty?" In 1786 he gave a presentation before the American Philosophical Society on the effects of physical factors on moral behavior, which he humbly described as a "feeble effort to increase the quantity of virtue in our republic." At this time he argued that vice, like disease, could be affected by a variety of physical causes, including the use of spirituous liquors. Three years later, in an attempt to reach an even larger audience, he presented a graphic representation of this process in his "Moral and Physical Thermometer." Other than a brief comment that medicines could improve morals, Rush's essay on the moral faculty contained little explicit information on how they were to be used.[23] Despite this absence, some evidence exists that Rush did attempt to treat vice medically beginning in the late eighties.

Rush and Dr. Samuel P. Griffitts joined efforts in 1786 to establish a free medical clinic for the poor in Philadelphia, the first such institution in the United States. According to Rush, the Dispensary, as it was called, along with the city's recently created Humane Society, stood as "lasting monuments of the humanity of the *present* citizens of Philadelphia." In addition, Rush believed that the morals of the poor "are of more consequence to society than their health or lives." His impetus to provide free medical care to the poor went beyond a mere desire to attend to their physical ailments and extended to what he perceived as their moral debilities as well. For instance, Rush explicitly noted that he and his colleagues "applied the principles of mechanics to morals, for in what other way would so great a weight of evil have been removed by so small a force," though his writings are silent on the exact treatment they used.[24] Rush's own words regarding vice and therapeutics nevertheless signifies that he had linked his social, political, and medical concerns in ways that went beyond the merely metaphorical.

Rush contended in his discussion of the moral faculty that disease, like other physical conditions, could also have a negative effect on one's ability to choose between good and evil. While he believed that fevers and madness most frequently disposed one to vice, he also thought that hysteria and hypochondriasis, as well as other states of the body "accompanied with preternatural irritability, sensibility, torpor, stupor, or mobility of the nervous system," could contribute to immoral behavior. Because the moral faculty in these situations was impaired as the result of disease, Rush suggested a medical regimen consisting of exercise, a cold bath, and a change in climate. He was much more confident, however, that "religious melancholy and madness, in all their variety of species, yield with more facility to medicine, than simply to polemical discourses, or to casuistical advice."[25] Clearly then, by the 1790s Rush had expanded the physician's purview to cover the realms of moral and mental illness, diseases that Rush believed had increased as a result of the larger political and social struggles of the Revolutionary era.

The third factor that supports my argument regarding the political significance of Rush's treatment for yellow fever was connected to his development in 1793 of a theory of disease that emphasized the unitary nature of physical disorder. As discussed earlier, Rush argued that not just fevers but all illness was "a form of morbid excitement" produced by an overstimulation of the whole system. According to Rush, if all ailments were caused by "capillary tension," then there was only one disease in the world.[26] This focus on overstimulation and excitement reflected Rush's preoccupation with the excesses of the members of the body politic that resulted from the events surrounding the American Revolution. And by thinking of all physical illness as essentially the same, he created a medically based intellectual framework that he would use to encompass moral, mental, and political maladies as well. Though Rush did not devise his unitary theory of disease until 1793, his comment to John Montgomery a decade earlier to "remember anodynes, not blisters, are the proper remedies for Pennsylvania in the present stage of her disorder" reveals a longstanding tendency to promote a therapy that would calm, rather than heat up, any disorder within the body politic.[27]

Rush's assumptions concerning issues of health and disease suggest that he devised his regimen of aggressive bloodletting and intense purging not only as a method of treating yellow fever but also as a means of controlling the passions of the body politic. When it became clear to Rush in the 1790s that balanced political constitutions and recurrent elections had failed to achieve their appropriate ends, he apparently took matters even further into his own hands. His belief that all diseases were a type of fever, the product of capillary stress, and thus necessitated depleting remedies, guaranteed, in his mind, that large numbers of overstimulated bodies could eventually be calmed through a regimen of bleeding and purging.[28] Thus blood would be shed in America as in France, but in the former case the indiscriminate flowing of blood unleashed by the French Reign of Terror would be replaced by a set of controlled conditions in which bloodletting would be practiced under the close supervision of a trained expert and only on the diseased elements of the political body.

During the 1790s Rush never openly linked the social-political and medical dimensions of his purging and bleeding regimen, but he did so several years later. Writing to John Adams in 1806, Rush proposed that "the remedies for a yellow fever would do wonders with the heads of the men who now move our world. Ten and ten (as our doses of calomel and jalap were called in 1793) would be a substitute for a fistula in the bowels of Bonaparte." Furthermore, Rush argued, "bleeding would probably lessen the rage for altering the Constitution of Pennsylvania in the leaders of the party who are now contending for that measure." In short, he believed that there was "a great field opened for new means of curing moral and political maladies." Rush continued to view the world of politics through the mind of a physician and to address medical concerns in light of their impact on the body politic. It is not surprising, then, that in addition to its purpose as a medical regimen, Rush's controversial treatment for yellow fever was also a technique to control the passions of the country's inhabitants, particularly the lower classes.[29] By the time of the yellow fever epidemic of 1793, Rush believed that if those members of society who constituted an arm, a leg, or the belly of the body politic were pacified, the masses would no longer attempt to usurp the functions of the governing head. Achieving command over the passions would result in a healthy body politic where people of all classes, colors, and creeds could live together in virtuous accord. Rush's effort to achieve his utopian dream, however, not only put his medical reputation in jeopardy, but also reveals his strong social conservatism.

Others who shared Rush's conservatism also appreciated the larger political implications of his aggressive measures to quiet the fevers of his patients. It is interesting that one of the most lucid statements regarding the necessity of such an approach came from Connecticut, the place Rush singled out years earlier as one of the healthiest regions "upon the surface of the globe," because of its long history of republican government.[30] Ardent Connecticut Federalist and Congregationalist minister Timothy Dwight advanced a very different image of his native land in 1794. Writing Oliver Wolcott in June of that year, Dwight bemoaned "the present turbulent state of politics" in Connecticut, "when every wicked exertion is used to inflame the human breast, by unkindling the worst of the passions." This situation, however, could be relieved, Dwight contended, if "every good man" endeavored "to confine it [the fire] within as narrow limits as possible." Evidently Dwight's advice was not heeded to his satisfaction, since he informed Wolcott the following October that "the hell of democracy has opened upon us in this state lately." And, he warned, if the "*yellow-fever* of politics" was not allayed by the following winter, the steady people of New England would be forced "to use Doctor Rush's remedies."[31] Perhaps George Washington's decision to send troops to western Pennsylvania to suppress the "whiskey rebels" that same year can be seen as just such a preventive political antidote.

Although Rush's writings do not include an explicit statement on the connection between political upheaval and epidemic disease in 1793, his assumption that moral, political, and physical health were thoroughly interdependent would have led him to such a conclusion. His use of political metaphors when speaking of the body and medical and disease images when discussing politics, his belief that changes in forms of government would modify the physical disposition of the body politic, and his unitary theory of disease were all factors in the broader political implications of his treatment for yellow fever. Since Rush not only contemplated applying medical remedies to moral disorders but had actually attempted to execute such a reform program, it is reasonable to think that his efforts to treat yellow fever in 1793 had a significance beyond the traditionally medical sphere. Rush's remedy for the fever thus makes more sense if examined in light of his intense yearning for social harmony and his concomitant anxiety over the continuing existence of political factions and social fragmentation. And his insistence that the yellow fever had chased all other diseases from the city, making it a "monarchical disorder," can be viewed as an effort to unite Philadelphians once again to oppose a common enemy in the ongoing American Revolution.

Notes

A previous version of this chapter appeared as "Passions and Politics: The Multiple Meanings of Benjamin Rush's Treatment for Yellow Fever" in J. Worth Estes and Billy G. Smith, eds., *A Melancholy Scene of Devastation: The Public Response to the 1793 Philadelphia Yellow Fever Epidemic* (Canton, Mass.: Science History Publications, 1997), 79–95.

1. Benjamin Rush, *An Account of the Bilious Remitting Yellow Fever, as it Appeared in the City of Philadelphia, in the Year 1793* (Philadelphia: Thomas Dobson, 1794), 271, 319.

2. In this regard I am contributing to the recent body of work that documents linkages between the political and medical arenas during the eighteenth century. See, for instance, Thomas Laqueur, *Making Sex: Body and Gender from the Greeks to Freud* (Cambridge, Mass.: Harvard University Press, 1990); and Londa Schiebinger, *Nature's Body: Gender in the Making of Modern Science* (Boston: Beacon Press, 1993). For a thorough guide to writings by and about Rush and his various endeavors, see Claire G. Fox, Gordon L. Miller, and Jacquelyn C. Miller, comps., *Benjamin Rush, M.D.: A Bibliographic Guide* (Westport, Conn.: Greenwood Press, 1996).

3. Eric T. Carlson et al., *Benjamin Rush's Lectures on the Mind* (Philadelphia: American Philosophical Society, 1981), 52, 67; and Benjamin Rush, *Three Lectures Upon Animal Life, Delivered in the University of Pennsylvania* (Philadelphia: Printed by Budd and Bartram, for Thomas Dobson, 1799), 2–5, 78–83. These published lectures were derived from actual lectures Rush gave at the University of Pennsylvania; the earliest known manuscript version dates from 1791.

4. For a more detailed discussion of Cullen, Brown, and Rush's theories of disease, see R. H. Shryock, *Medicine and Society in America: 1660–1860* (Ithaca, N.Y.: Cornell University Press, 1960), 68–72; and Eric T. Carlson and Meribeth M. Simpson, "The Definition of Mental Illness: Benjamin Rush (1745–1813)," *American Journal of Psychiatry* 121 (1964): 211.

5. Philadelphia physicians also argued over the questions of where the dreaded yellow fever originated and how it was transmitted. For a detailed account of the personalities and controversies associated with each of these issues, as well as an examination of Rush's willingness to challenge established medical authority, see J. H. Powell, *Bring Out Your Dead: The Great Plague of Yellow Fever in Philadelphia in 1793* (Philadelphia: University of Pennsylvania Press, 1949; reprinted, New York: Time Incorporated, 1965), 12–43.

6. Rush, *Account*, 197, 200–204, 271; Rush to John R. B. Rodgers, Oct. 3, 1793, in L. H. Butterfield, ed., *Letters of Benjamin Rush*, 2 vols. (Princeton, N.J.: Princeton University Press, 1951), 2:695–96. For a discussion of Rush's view of the role of the physician, see Carl Binger, *Revolutionary Doctor: Benjamin Rush, 1746–1813* (New York: W. W. Norton, 1966), 228–29. In addition, for a discussion both of Rush's fervent belief in the simplicity of the underlying principles and laws of medicine and science and of his confidence that human society could be improved by applying mechanics to all sorts of human ills, see Henry F. May, *The Enlightenment in America* (New York: Oxford University Press, 1976), 153–76, 208.

7. For accounts of the contemporary debates about Rush's treatment, see Powell, *Bring Out Your Dead*, 76–132; William S. Middleton, "The Yellow Fever Epidemic of 1793 in Philadelphia," *Annals of Medical History* 10 (1928): 441–44; Joseph McFarland, "The Epidemic of Yellow Fever in Philadelphia in 1793 and Its Influence Upon Dr. Benjamin Rush," *Medical Life* 36 (1929): 480–96; and Martin S. Pernick, "Politics, Parties, and Pestilence: Epidemic Yellow Fever in Philadelphia and the Rise of the First Party System,"

William and Mary Quarterly 29 (1972): 573–76. Concerning the impact of Rush's "heroic therapeutics," see Robert B. Sullivan, "Sanguine Practices: A Historical and Historiographic Reconsideration of Heroic Therapy in the Age of Rush," *Bulletin of the History of Medicine* 68 (1994): 211–34; Alex Berman, "The Heroic Approach in Nineteenth Century Therapeutics," *Bulletin of the Society of Hospital Pharmacists* (Sept.–Oct. 1954): 321–27; Charles Rosenberg, "The Therapeutic Revolution: Medicine, Meaning, and Social Change in 19th-Century America," in *Sickness and Health in America: Readings in the History of Medicine and Public Health,* 2nd ed., rev., ed. Judith Walzer Leavitt and Ronald L. Numbers (Madison: University of Wisconsin Press, 1985), 46–48; and Joseph Ioor Waring, "The Influence of Benjamin Rush on the Practice of Bleeding in South Carolina," *Bulletin of the History of Medicine* 35 (1961): 230–37.

8. For an analysis of Rush's involvement in the development of the United States penitentiary system from a similar perspective, see Thomas L. Dumm, *Democracy and Punishment: Disciplinary Origins of the United States* (Madison: University of Wisconsin Press, 1987), 87–112.

9. Peter Gay has written about the role that medicine played in the "recovery of nerve" in relation to several major European Enlightenment figures. He demonstrates that the *philosophes* wholly believed that progress in one sphere of life would initiate progress in others. Gay, *The Enlightenment: An Interpretation,* 2 vols. (New York: Knopf, 1969), 2:12–23, 25.

10. For an examination of the eighteenth-century dual meanings of the word *constitution,* see Robert Lawson-Peebles, *Landscape and Written Expression in Revolutionary America: The World Turned Upside Down* (Cambridge, U.K.: Cambridge University Press, 1988), 76. For an excellent discussion of how the use of metaphors and analogies not only reflects the ways in which individuals have attempted to come to terms with the world around them—the strategies through which the unfamiliar experiences of life are made more familiar—but how they also play a creative role in shaping human perceptions, and by extension, human behavior, see George Lakoff and Mark Johnson, *Metaphors We Live By* (Chicago: University of Chicago Press, 1980).

11. Rush to Julia Rush, April 14, 1777, *Letters,* 1:138; Rush to John Adams, Aug. 8, 1777, *Letters,* 1:152; and Rush to Julia Rush, [Sept. 18], 1776, *Letters,* 1:113.

12. Rush to Patrick Henry, Jan. 12, 1778, *Letters,* 1:182–83; and Rush to John Adams, Jan. 22, 1778, *Letters,* 1:191–92.

13. In the opinion of medical historian George Rosen, Rush, along with Thomas Jefferson, presented the most precisely stated views on the topic of physical and political health. Rosen, "Political Order and Human Health in Jeffersonian Thought," *Bulletin of the History of Medicine* 26 (1952): 32–44.

14. Rush, "An Inquiry into the Natural History of Medicine Among the Indians of North-America, and a Comparative View of Their Diseases and Remedies, with Those of Civilized Nations," *Medical Inquiries and Observations,* 2nd Amer. ed., 4 vols. (Philadelphia: Thomas Dobson, 1794), 1:9–77; quotes from pp. 24–25. I am building my argument on Robert Lawson-Peebles's observation that Rush saw a cause and effect relationship between the political disturbances and epidemic disease during the 1790s. Lawson-Peebles, however, stopped his analysis short by saying that "yet, even with an apparently clear diagnosis of his country's ills, Rush had not been able to minister to it." *Landscape,* 98.

15. Carlson, *Rush's Lectures on the Mind,* 66, 162.

16. Rush to Charles Lee, Oct. 24, 1779, *Letters,* 1:244; Rush, "On Patriotism," *Pennsylvania Journal,* Oct. 20, 1773; Rush to Anthony Wayne, Sept. 24, 1776, *Letters,* 1:114–15; and Rush to John Adams, Oct. 12, 1779, *Letters,* 1:240.

17. Rush to Charles Lee, Oct. 24, 1779, *Letters,* 1:243–44.

18. Robert L. Brunhouse, *The Counter-Revolution in Pennsylvania, 1776–1790* (Harrisburg: Pennsylvania Historical Commission, 1942), 75.

19. Rush to Julia Rush, April 14, 1777, *Letters,* 1:138.

20. Rush to Timothy Pickering, Aug. 30, 1787, *Letters,* 1:438; Rush to Richard Price, June 2, 1787, *Letters,* 1:418; and Rush, "An Account of the Influence of the Military and Political Events of the American Revolution Upon the Human Body," *Medical Inquiries and Observations,* 1:263–78; quote on p. 277. For a discussion of Rush's definition of mental illness, see Carlson and Simpson, "The Definition of Mental Illness," 209–14.

21. Manfred J. Waserman, "Benjamin Rush on Government and the Harmony and Derangement of the Mind," *Journal of the History of Ideas* 33 (1972): 639–40.

22. Rush to John Adams, June 15, 1789, *Letters,* 1:517.

23. Rush to Granville Sharp, July 9, 1774, John A. Woods, ed., "The Correspondence of Benjamin Rush and Granville Sharp, 1773–1809," *Journal of American Studies* 1 (1967): 8; and Rush, *An Oration, Delivered Before the American Philosophical Society, Held in Philadelphia on the 27th of February 1786; Containing an Enquiry into the Influence of Physical Causes upon the Moral Faculty* (Philadelphia: Charles Cist, 1786), 27, 39–40. The "Moral and Physical Thermometer" is reprinted in *Letters,* 1:facing page 512.

24. Rush to Jeremy Belknap, Jan. 8, 1788, *Letters,* 1:448.

25. Rush, *Oration,* 20, 34.

26. Shryock, *Medicine and Society in America,* 69–70; and Carlson and Simpson, "The Definition of Mental Illness," 211.

27. Rush to John Montgomery, July 4, 1783, *Letters,* 1:305.

28. Rush, *Account,* 271, 319.

29. Rush to John Adams, Nov. 25, 1806, *Letters,* 2:935; and Rush, *Account,* 329–30. According to several observers, including Rush, the epidemic of 1793 was particularly "destructive among the poor." See Matthew Carey, *A Short Account of the Malignant Fever, Lately Prevalent in Philadelphia,* 4th ed. (Philadelphia: Matthew Carey, Jan. 16, 1794), 61; Abraham Shoemaker, *Poulson's Town and Country Almanac* (Philadelphia: Zacheriah Poulson, 1794), [n.p.]; and Rush to Elias Boudinot, Sept. 25, 1793, *Letters,* 2:681.

30. Rush, *Three Lectures Upon Animal Life,* 62.

31. Timothy Dwight to Oliver Wolcott Jr., June 3 and Oct. 26, 1794, Oliver Wolcott Jr. Papers, vol. 13, nos. 32 and 41, The Connecticut Historical Society (I used the microfilm edition [Reel 3] housed at the David Library, Washington Crossing, Pennsylvania).

II

DEMARCATIONS OF THE BODY: FLUIDITY AND CONTAINMENT

Effigies of a Maid All Hairy, & an Infant that was born Black, by the Imagi-nation of the parents, from *Aristotle's Compleat Master-Piece*, The Library Company of Philadelphia.

Murderous Uncleanness

The Body of the Female Infanticide in Puritan New England

KATHLEEN M. BROWN

Zech.13.1 *There shall be a Fountain Opened for Sin, and for Uncleanness.* Your *Sin* has been *Uncleanness,* Repeated *Uncleanness,* Impudent *Uncleanness,* Murderous *Uncleanness:* You must, like the *Leper,* Cry out, *Unclean! Unclean!*

Cotton Mather, Warnings from the Dead (1693)

On June 8, 1693, Puritan minister Cotton Mather used the occasion of a public execution to deliver a dramatic lecture on the fatal consequences of uncleanness. As he noted in his diary, he had long wanted to preach on this topic: "I had often wished for an Opportunity, to bear my Testimonies, against the Sins of *Uncleanness,* wherein so many of my Generacon do pollute themselves," he wrote. Rather than pursue the opportunity, however, Mather let Providence do its work. "Their Execution, was ordered to have been, upon the Lecture of another; but by a very strange Providence, without any Seeking of *mine,* or any Respect to mee, (that I know of) the order for their *Execution* was altered and it fell on *my Lecture Day.*" Fortified both by his own desire to speak and the backing of Providence, Mather exhorted "one of the greatest Assemblies, ever known in these parts of the World," on the evils of uncleanness. Gathered to witness the executions of two women for infanticide, the crowd heard the thirty-year-old Mather deliver one of his most dramatic and commercially successful sermons. "The Sermon was immediately printed; with another, which I had formerly uttered on the like Occasion; (entitled, *Warnings from the Dead*)," Mather recorded proudly in his diary, "and it was greedily bought up; I hope, to the Attainment of the Ends, which I had so long desired. T'was afterwards reprinted at London."[1]

Mather's diatribe against sexual uncleanness and the publishing opportunity it spawned were occasioned by the executions of a twenty-eight-year-old white woman, Elizabeth Emerson, and an unnamed "Black Fellow-Sufferer," who was listed in other records as Elisabeth or Elisabeth Negro. Barely mentioning that a second woman also awaited the hangman's noose, Mather focused his comments on Emerson, incorporating her gallows statement into *Warnings from the Dead* and subsequent publications. Convicted of killing her illegitimate twins in 1691, Emerson sealed her fate by attempting to hide the evidence; she stuffed the bodies into a cloth bag and then buried them behind the house she shared with her parents. Over two years elapsed between the crime and Mather's lecture on uncleanness, which Emerson listened to in its entirety before processing to the gallows and her death.

Emerson's crime marked an important shift in the legal prosecution of infanticide. Going to trial just six months before the outbreak of witchcraft accusations at Salem, Emerson may have made slow progress to the gallows because the colony was busy hanging witches in 1692. Her execution came just a month after the last of the Salem imprisoned were reprieved and released by Governor Phips. Yet Emerson's crime could not be said to have gone unnoticed. The sensational nature of her case provoked Massachusetts legislators to change the law under which infanticide was prosecuted at a time when many laws in the colony were being revised under the colony's new charter of 1691. Adopting a 1624 English statute, Massachusetts no longer implicitly defined infanticide as a species of common law murder. Under the provisions of the new law, the mere concealment of a birth of a dead illegitimate child became sufficient evidence for convicting the mother of infanticide. Although formal reception of this law took four years and another sensational case, the impact on conviction rates was striking: only one of ten accused under the guidelines of the 1624 law was acquitted during the 1690s, giving that decade both the highest rate and highest total number of infanticide convictions between 1670 and 1780. After 1730, as a more sentimental view of motherhood took hold and as white women of means were less likely to be prosecuted for sexual offenses, juries became increasingly reluctant to convict women of infanticide under the 1624 statute. This trend distinguished the final decade of the seventeenth century in Massachusetts as the least forgiving of mothers who killed their illegitimate infants.[2]

The publication of Mather's sermon also marked the beginning of a new pattern. Other ministers had previously published on the subject of uncleanness, most notably Samuel Danforth, who used the occasion of a seventeen-year-old man's execution for sodomy to denounce all types of illicit sexual activities in *Cry of Sodom* (1674). But Mather gave this denunciation a new target, which apparently resonated with his fellow ministers and their readers. According to a noted historian of crime literature, *Warn-*

ings from the Dead was the first of five books published during the 1690s and devoted to the cases of women executed for infanticide. In this context, Mather's choice of Emerson's execution to publicize his message about uncleanness seems to be of more than ordinary significance. Emerson's alleged double infanticide not only provoked a legal redefinition but sparked a wave of publications in which readers followed convicted women to the hangman's noose. The body of the female infanticide thus became an emblem of the colony's uncleanness and the means by which ministers could attempt to reclaim authority that had become tarnished by their complicity in the Salem proceedings. For Cotton Mather, who had prominently professed his belief in witchcraft before the proceedings and only reluctantly and belatedly spoken out against them, the opportunity to occupy the moral high ground must have been irresistible.[3]

Mather's sermon employed hyperbolic language connecting sin with death, topics that were already so emotionally fraught in Puritan New England that they hardly needed amplification. Expanding on Job 36.14 ("They dy in Youth, and their Life is among the Unclean"), Mather identified uncleanness as not just an evil prerequisite for, but a *cause* of premature death. "*An Early and a Woful* **Death**, *is the Fruit of an Unclean and a Wicked* **Life**," he warned, citing death and infertility as two of the punishments God visited on the unclean.

Mather distinguished two different meanings for "unclean." Used generically, the term described many kinds of wickedness. "All our Sinfulness," Mather noted, "is call'd *A Filthiness of Flesh & Spirit.*" Attempting to explain the aptness of the filth-sin metaphor, he reasoned, "a man that Lives in Sin against the God that made him, is denominated in Job 15.16. *An Abominable and Filthy man*. Why? Because the most Loathsome, Dirty, Nasty Object in the World, is not so Distastful unto us, as all *Wickedness* is unto our God, who is, *Not a God that hath pleasure in Wickedness.*" Mather allowed his listeners to imagine the "Nasty Object" for themselves, hoping perhaps to underline God's revulsion at human sinfulness.

Generic wickedness paled in comparison to the sexual uncleanness Mather believed afflicted many "young people" in the 1690s. "There is One peculiar sort of *Wickedness,* which the Term of **Uncleanness** is more strictly put upon," he observed; "tis the Violation of that *Chastity,* which is Enjoyned upon us, by the Seventh Commandment." Sexual sinfulness was a particularly odious form of uncleanness "because of a Special *Filthiness,* and *Ugliness,* which this Vice is attended with." Indeed, sexual uncleanness was so vile and contaminating that even public condemnations of it threatened to compromise further the already corrupt nature of humankind. "Such is the Wretchedness of the Corruption, in man, that it is hardly safe so much as to mention [uncleanness] in his Hearing," Mather explained. Rather than speak the unspeakable, Mather noted the biblical convention whereby sexual uncleanness could be designated by its opposite: "The word for, *The Unclean,* is *The Holy;* because tis not easy to find any word Convenient and Emphatical Enough, to set out the detestable *Unholiness, that is in such Uncleanness."* Offering an elegant illustration of anthropologist Mary Douglas's contention that categories of purity and pollution mark social locations beyond the bounds of ordinary society where the defiled can become, as well as oppose, the pure, Mather's acknowledgment of the alchemical relation between the unclean and the holy became part of the justification of his own lengthy discussion of uncleanness.[4]

Sexual uncleanness might have been unspeakably wicked, but Mather appears to have had little difficulty speaking about it. In this he followed the example of Samuel Danforth, whose vivid comparisons of sexual sin to filth he occasionally borrowed. He departed from Danforth, however, in cataloguing sexual sins hierarchically, noting the increasing degree of uncleanness that each represented. "Cursed *Self-Pollution"* was "usually the first pit of *Uncleanness,"* he noted, followed by "Odious *Fornication,* which is a further Step, of that *Uncleanness,* whereunto the Raging Lusts of men do carry them." Next came the "Inexpressible *Uncleannesses"* of *"Inordinate Affection"* in marriage, which sometimes grew into *"Adultery."* The defiling sin of incest was yet another expression of uncleanness, wicked for its disruption of family government. Mather found the vileness of sodomy and buggery "horrible to be Spoken!" but not too horrible for a lengthy digression, complete with an illustrative case of bestiality in New England. To this list of *"Acts* of *Uncleanness,"* Mather appended unclean thoughts and words as forms of wickedness prohibited by both the Bible and "Natural *Reason* and *Conscience* in man." Although not bodily acts like fornication, *"Looking upon a Woman to Lust after her"* and *"Filthiness & Foolish Talking"* merited censure because they could lead to more terrible sins. The sexual nature of such thoughts and words, however, was what led to their classification among the filthiest of sins.[5]

Although the distinctly Puritan worldview of Mather's sermon should not be dismissed, the New England minister invoked concepts of cleanliness and filth that were common currency throughout the English-speaking world. Settlers used terms synonymous with "unclean" to describe a variety of individuals, behaviors, and conditions they deemed undesirable, unhealthy, or dangerous. Often, as Mather's sermon illustrates, these terms appeared in discussions of moral and spiritual matters to communicate the power of sin to pollute or corrupt an individual's relationship with God. Mather's description of sin as "filth" was common not only in early modern sermon literature, where one might expect it, but in early colonial courtrooms, where justices employed the language of England's ecclesiastical courts to describe moral crimes. Less frequently, early Americans used the terms *clean* and *dirty* to express concerns about the healthfulness of the urban environment or to comment on personal cleanliness. Often they conflated the tidiness of the household with cleanliness of person, especially of women: clean clothing, combed hair, clean hands and face, sweet breath, and white teeth might be extolled along with snowy bed linens, polished kitchen implements, and newly scoured floors.[6]

To modern eyes, the cleanliness language of the colonial period appears mainly to consist of metaphors that bear little relation to the twentieth-century focus on hygienic bodies. Although many of these metaphors originated in older traditions of washing the body—never strong in England and long lost by the seventeenth century—others referred to smelly organic filth, for example, corpses or excrement, traditionally associated with death and disease. Metaphors about sin polluting the soul the way filth polluted or sickened the body remained vital in part because of continuities in ideas about filth, even as many cleanliness metaphors lost their connection to actual cleanliness practices. References to purity or filth in early modern religious discourse thus appear to float free from the anchor of "real" bodies. Yet, as a reading of Mather's sermon suggests, twentieth-century distinctions between metaphors and "real" bodies might obscure more than they illuminate in a world in which people believed that magic and Providence as well as so-called "natural" causes like contagions, miasmas, and humoral imbalances determined the health of the body. The very words with which Mather condemned sin as filth—for example, "nasty"—occupied both the moral and material realms, making it difficult to distinguish between the two. For Puritans, the lost practices behind metaphors about cleansing the soul were at least partially recovered in the concept of a body whose spiritual and physical afflictions were linked and expressive of divine will. Beliefs in the power of Christ's blood to wash away a sinner's iniquity created a new reality for the saints, providing them with an anchor for concepts of cleanliness.[7]

Throughout the colonial period, sexual wrongdoing produced the most emotionally charged public language about cleanliness. Illicit sex inspired inflamed rhetoric not simply because it was an odious and potentially expensive sin for the community but because it combined immorality with bodily filth, resulting in a physically embodied and expressed uncleanness as well as a moral uncleanness. No other sin—theft, fraud, false witness, covetousness, pride, or envy—inspired Puritan ministers to such high-pitched rhetoric about filth and pollution. Even gluttony and murder, which were also sins of the body, did not provoke such excited sermonizing. This contrast was especially apparent in Cotton Mather's *Pillars of Salt* (1699), a compendium of confessions by condemned evil-doers that included Elizabeth Emerson's statement.[8]

Mather's *Warnings from the Dead* offers a glimpse of a fervently Protestant early modern body, in which proscribed sexual acts were loathsome not simply because they sullied the purity of the soul, but because of their location in the "lower" regions of the body, strongly associated with organic filth.[9] The unclean body described by Mather was physically as well as spiritually afflicted, succumbing to disease and death as a consequence of God's wrath over its sinfulness. In a world in which disease might be providentially caused or cured, "filthy" sexual practices straddled moral and medical approaches to the body. Executions of female criminals like Elizabeth Emerson allowed ministers to minimize the abstraction in the metaphor of the unclean body and to explain graphically the danger sinners posed to the Puritan social body.[10]

A fuller appreciation of Mather's sermon requires that we examine the Emerson infanticide case more closely and consider both the filth-avoidance practices of early New England and Mather's own efforts to combine providential and medical views of the body. Mather's insistence that the health of the body reflected God's will reveals his continuing commitment to the ideal of a godly Puritan community and his interest in protecting his own tarnished ministerial authority. Yet, as a member of the prestigious Royal Society in London, Mather was also familiar with seventeenth-century medicine and well connected to transatlantic scientific circles. His discussion of a providential body, brought to its death by its own uncleanness, was not so much a rejection of the natural philosophy and scientific thinking that were beginning to attract the attention of elite Bostonians, but a means of salvaging providentialism by grounding it more in the health and materiality of bodies.[11]

Invoking these potent categories, men like Mather asserted their authority to comment on the larger social order as well as on the behavior of their parishioners, even as their own ministerial influence suffered a decline at the century's end. The new colonial charter, which limited Puritan political and cultural influence, the post-Salem renunciation of spectral evidence, and new skepticism about interpreting the workings of Providence all contributed to this decline and to the marginalization of men like Mather, who had been one of the loudest proponents of beliefs in witchcraft and Providence. Indeed, Mather's awareness of his own waning influence may have been a prime reason for the high pitch of his rhetoric and his focus on topics about which there was little controversy: sexual sin and filth.

As Mary Douglas has noted, concepts of pollution and purity define social boundaries and hierarchies as well as delimit rules for the conduct of daily life. Social, cultural, and even political authority often include the power to define cleanliness and filth for the rest of one's society. Emerson's grievous crime and subsequent execution provided Mather with a near-perfect opportunity to unite his view of the providential body with contemporary concepts of uncleanness and to use both to diagnose the ills of Puritan society. When we situate Mather's text in terms of the public execution that inspired it, Emerson's uncleanness becomes Puritan uncleanness; the unclean body of the female infanticide becomes the unclean social body. Containing her crime with potent rhetoric about uncleanness and a logical flow chart of sin, Mather revealed his own struggle to purge Puritan society—and perhaps himself—of corruption and to reassert his authority to define moral cleanliness and filth.[12]

In her final confession, Elizabeth Emerson identified her "Haughty and Stubborn Spirit" as the reason for her disobedience to her parents and her first step down the path to the gallows. Born in 1665, the fifth of Michael and Hannah Webster Emerson's fifteen children, Elizabeth seems to have been punished severely at an early age for her recalcitrance. Her father's appearance in Essex County Court in 1676 to answer charges that he beat his daughter excessively is suggestive of the clash between the stubborn eleven-year-old and her violence-prone father. According to her gallows statement, disobedience led to keeping bad company, which paved the way to uncleanness. Emerson's illicit sexual behavior became public knowledge in April 1686, when she gave birth to her first illegitimate child.[13]

Following her initial transgression, Emerson seems to have been watched closely by both her parents and her neighbors. Several times during the spring of 1691, as her daughter grew heavier, Hannah Emerson asked her bluntly whether she was with child, but Elizabeth admitted nothing.[14] She later confessed to being fearful of killing her mother with the news of her pregnancy. This fear, she claimed, also motivated her to give birth silently on the trundle bed at the foot of her parents' bed early in the morning of May 8. Never once calling out for help, Emerson left the twin infants amidst the bedclothes. Her claim that neither baby cried was her main evidence of their stillbirth and of her own innocence of infanticide. Michael and Hannah Emerson corroborated their daughter's account of the babies' silence, claiming that they slept through the ordeal and noticed nothing amiss when they arose early that morning.[15]

Sharp-eyed neighbors, who might have been counting the months since Emerson's first dizzy spell at public meeting or carefully noting her size, could have become alarmed by her failure to emerge from the house on May 8. They also might have been tipped off by Samuel Lad, the married man whom Emerson later identified as the father and the only person she told about her pregnancy. When the group of two men and four women came to the Emerson household during the time of the public meeting on Sunday, May 10, they found Emerson washing dishes but, in her own words, feeling "unwell." While the women took Emerson into another room to search her for signs of recent childbirth, the men headed for a place in the yard where they suspected she might have buried an infant. That they identified the burial site immediately suggests someone may have seen Emerson working in the yard shortly before their arrival. Not one, but two dead infants, contained in a cloth bag, rewarded the searchers' efforts.[16]

The next day, the four women, "tow of us being Midwifes and the other tow acquainted amongs women" examined the bodies. All the women believed that the babies had been born alive "att thear full time." Three of the four women claimed that one baby had its hand clasped around its umbilical cord, which was wrapped around its neck. All four women noted that the second baby's cord was wrapped around its thigh. The women were unsure what this meant about the means of death, although the three who had seen the clasped hand believed this ruled out a stillbirth. Unable to find definitive signs of murder on the bodies of the infants, the women agreed that Emerson was guilty of wrongdoing: "[W]e do certainly believe yt ye Childeren perished for want of help & Caer att time of travell."[17]

For twenty-four hours, Emerson refused to identify the father of her children and insisted that no one, not even her parents, knew of her pregnancy, delivery, or efforts to hide the bodies. On May 11, however, she named Samuel Lad. That Emerson confidently claimed Lad and "no body el[se]" to be the father suggests she had only one sexual partner at the time of conception. Lad appears to have visited with Emerson the night before her delivery and probably knew of his lover's pregnancy. Michael and Hannah Emerson claimed complete ignorance not only of their daughter's condition, but also of the birth on the morning of May 8 and the burial two days later. Apparently wanting desperately to believe her daughter's denials, Hannah continued to ignore signs of advanced pregnancy until told of the infanticides when she returned from meeting.[18]

A sensational double infanticide committed by a sexually notorious white woman gave the youthful and ambitious Mather the opportunity he craved in the aftermath of the Salem witch trials. Emerson's progression from bad company to bastardy and infanticide presented a powerful lesson in the etiology of uncleanness. Gradually consuming the body and soul of a woman who had enjoyed the privileges of religious instruction, uncleanness numbed her to her own wickedness and the certainty of divine retribution, hastening her along the path to her death.

Beyond speaking publicly about unspeakable acts of wickedness—a waiver of taboos that defined his ministerial privilege and authority—Mather hoped to diagnose the source of New England's moral corruption. Again, Emerson was the perfect foil for this task. Unlike the vast majority of women convicted of infanticide, who tended to be poor, in servitude, African or Indian, Emerson was white and the daughter of churchgoing, if not reputable, Puritans. Only with difficulty could a witness to her execution construe her as distant "other" or "outsider" to the godly community. Mather hardly needed to spell out the implication. Indeed, he seems to have assumed that his listeners would understand it; Emerson's sinful corruption was a specimen of the corruption *within* the Puritan body that would eventually kill it if it was not purged.

If godly people failed to excise corruption from the social body, Mather warned, divine curses would strip that body of its young men:

What Multitudes among us, do we see *Dy in Youth!* This Land is making the *Lamentation* that was made by the Church of old, *The Lord ha's called an Assembly against me, to Crush my Young men.* How many Scores of *Young men* have sometimes been lost from one Little Town, within two of three Years, by the Disastrous *Plagues* and *Wars* that have been upon us! ... Unto us may our God say, as He said unto *Israel* of old, *Your Young men have I Slain.*

The reasons for the decimation of young men seemed clear to Mather: "Methinks, the *Wickedness,* & Especially the *Uncleanness* too rise among our Young People, should be acknowledged, among the Causes of these Calamities." As a consequence of losing its male members, New England would be rendered weak and feminized: "So little *Joy* indeed ha's our God in our Young People, that He is every day saying over them, *Indians, Do you come; Frenchmen do you come; Fevers, do you come; & cut off as many of those young People, as come in your way!*"[19]

Although Mather admitted that New England's troubles could have emanated from the "Beastly Baseness" of "*Old* people," who seemed to be pious but might actually be "the most *Wanton Satyrs* in Secret places," he quickly returned his attention to young people whom he believed to be the worst offenders. "If all the *Young People,* that have many ways, *Polluted themselves, from their Youth up,* were turned out of our Assemblies," he speculated, "we should have Thin Assemblies Left!" This comment clearly reflected competing anxieties about the impure condition of the churches and Mather's own worries about his irrelevance to members of his own generation. He identified the "two ... most ungrateful Seasons, that *Young People* take to multiply those their Diabolical *Pollutions,*" as "the Close of *Sabbath,*" and the "Joy of the *Harvest.*" Emerson's example again hovered behind the words, as the twins were likely conceived during the harvest of 1690. "Instead of being improved in *Thankfulness* to God," Mather reproved, young people used these times of year to spread "*Uncleanness* through the Land."[20]

Interpreting Emerson's crime as an example of the rising tide of uncleanness among all "young people," Mather was remarkably restrained about denouncing the special dangers of female uncleanness. Most of his warnings were aimed at both men and women, although he singled out young men as the victims of the punishments God sent to smite the social body. That Emerson's execution inspired the sermon, however, and that the vast majority of people hung for uncleanness were female (the exceptions being men condemned to death for adultery or bestiality) skewed Mather's message about the plague of uncleanness sweeping the land.

Fulminating about uncleanness at the executions of unchaste women was a noncontroversial way for ministers to assume the moral high ground in the aftermath of the debacle at Salem. As there were few executions of male sexual offenders at the end of the seventeenth century, male uncleanness rarely became such a public spectacle; nor would it have resonated so deeply with Puritans, who were convinced that women had a special vulnerability to diabolical temptations and sins of the flesh.[21]

Mather was not the only minister to seize this opportunity during the 1690s, nor was this his last chance to preach on this subject—although arguably his rhetoric reached its most fevered pitch at Emerson's execution. The executions of Sarah Threeneedles and Sarah Smith both afforded him similar opportunities. Reverend John Williams of Deerfield also preached at the execution of Smith, quickly publishing his sermon *Warnings to the Unclean* (1698). In addition to the thousands of spectators who flocked to these two executions, the stories of Threeneedles's and Smith's unclean lives reached untold numbers of readers through Mather's *Pillars of Salt,* where they joined the confession of Elizabeth Emerson to demonstrate how uncleanness would bring early death and, ultimately, the demise of the Puritan community. Clearly, there was no shortage of people interested in hearing or reading this message.[22]

Metaphors about uncleanness conjured different mental images in the seventeenth century than they do today in the postgerm-theory, postcleanliness-revolution twenty-first century. Mather's listeners would not have considered the unbathed body necessarily to be an unclean body. Most would not have thought of a live body when Mather asked them to imagine nastiness and filth: excrement and rotting corpses were the literary conventions for indicating dangerous pollution. But the conjunction of Mather's sermon with Emerson's execution for infanticide—a crime of the flesh that included sexual intercourse, pregnancy, birth, and the burial of infant corpses—would have made it difficult for listeners *not* to think of bodies. Seventeenth-century ideas about personal cleanliness and the metaphoric emphasis on polluting sexual sins, exemplified in this case by a condemned woman, brought together ideas about female sexuality, sin, the body, and death in ways that made the female body the standard for most kinds of bodily and social corruption.

During the seventeenth century, most Europeans embraced what we might call a "linen-centered" standard for personal cleanliness. Beliefs that the skin transpired noxious matter that collected on its surface and that friction, rather than bathing, was the most effective way to remove the filth, encouraged a focus on clean clothes rather than on the bodies the clothing covered. Early modern clothing reflected this view of bodily filth. Linen shifts or chemises, worn by men and women next to the skin, were the most numerous garments in any late-seventeenth-century wardrobe and the ones most likely to be washed. Clothes layered on top of the chemise were made of wool, leather, or other such materials and were rarely laundered. When dirt became visible on these outer garments, they might be brushed or spotted and hung out to air but they would not have been washed regularly.[23]

Like chemises, bed linens were seen as repositories of bodily filth that included the sweat emitted by the skin and bodily fluids like menstrual blood and semen. It was not uncommon for early modern travelers to comment on the cleanliness of sheets, noting the color ("brown with perspiration" or "white") and the presence of vermin. It was also not uncommon for women to reserve special linens for use during childbirth. These coverings for bedding and the garments worn by the birthing woman and her infant had great emotional significance and were often passed down from mother to daughter. When they were newly made or purchased for a particular birth, they might also be invoked as a legal defense against infanticide under English law in cases where a child subsequently died. But they were also ritually significant in that they protected bedding used in ordinary life from the bodily fluids produced during childbirth. Those fluids were filthy only when, as Mary Douglas has noted, they were "matter out of place." Although a stained set of childbirth linens was not dirty when used at a birth, the bloody material produced at birth would have been deemed filthy if it remained on the everyday bed linens.[24]

In this linen-centered economy of cleanliness, Puritan ministerial garb was the ultimate emblem of moral and literal purity. Set off dramatically by his black coat, the minister's distinctive display of white linen marked him as not only a man of God but also a gentleman. He wore this linen around his neck, overlaid by a long white collar, known as a falling band or a Geneva Band. The material for this ministerial collar was always pure white, although it might be either opaque or sheer.[25] It is likely that Cotton Mather delivered his sermon on uncleanness wearing the occupational garb that marked him as a clean man, in both a moral and literal sense. It was expected that a minister would provide an example of moral cleanliness but, if he hoped to preside over wealthy and cosmopolitan congregations like those in late-seventeenth-century Boston, he also needed to effect the image of a gentleman. In an age before bathing, no gentleman wearing white linen at the neck could neglect to change it regularly, for a collar worn for too many days would display his skin's effusions to the world. No minister would have considered it politic to reveal so much of the grotesque body he was hoping to hide and that he was exhorting his congregation to discipline.[26]

Several details of Emerson's case, which likely became public during the trial in September 1691, resonated with these seventeenth-century concerns about filth avoidance. First, the fact that Emerson was confronted with her crime while washing the dishes, moments after burying her dead infants, would have seemed a gruesome irony to Puritans: with metaphoric blood dripping from her hands, Emerson continued with her domestic routine like any good wife, except that it was the Sabbath, she had never been married, and she had just finished hiding the bodies of her two dead infants. Second, the fact that her interrogators questioned her while she was on the very bed in which she had given birth—the same bed that her parents allegedly stumbled by, unaware that anything was wrong—would have raised an obvious question for any New England woman who had witnessed a birth; what had Emerson done with the soiled childbed linens, which would surely have revealed her secret to her household? Had she hidden or buried them, knowing that it would be impossible to wash them covertly? Or had she simply continued to sleep on linens saturated with blood and amniotic fluid? Any seventeenth-century person with doubts about Michael and Hannah Emerson's innocence would have thought skeptically about the sight and smell of blood on the bed linens. They might also have wondered whether Emerson continued to sleep on such radically soiled bedding on the nights following the birth. No one seems to have asked whether Emerson, who had concealed her pregnancy from her own mother, had taken the trouble to borrow special childbirth linens.[27]

Finally, there is the gesture of sewing a cloth bag for the infants before burying them. Most of Emerson's English-speaking contemporaries would have seen a similarity between her action and traditions of wrapping the corpse in white linen or cloth before burial. Although storing the bodies in a bag would have made it easier for Emerson to hide and move the bodies, convenience does not appear to have been her only motive. Rather, it seems that she sewed the bag *after* she hid the babies in the chamber chest and as she was preparing to place their bodies in the ground. Allegedly willing to let the infants die of neglect, Emerson honored taboos about placing unprotected corpses directly in the soil. Her own adherence to filth avoidance thus makes an unexpected appearance in a crime that Mather depicted as the epitome of uncleanness.

Securely positioned on an unassailable moral high road, Mather confidently traced the connections between filth and its multiple associations, including disease, death, brutish behavior, poverty, sterility, and the fires of lust. This range of topics gave him great latitude to speak about the troubles plaguing Puritan society in the early 1690s. He also demonstrated that, even in the aftermath of Salem, he was unwilling to give up providentialism or the denunciation of Satan's works. Filth provided a safe way to point the finger at the Devil in Puritan society with the full backing of natural philosophy. No one except the Devil and his minions would contradict Mather and claim to love filth—unless, of course, he was suffering from a mental derangement, the emerging Enlightenment explanation for antisocial behavior.[28]

In addition to connecting uncleanness with early death—the dominant theme of the sermon—Mather commented extensively on the relationship between uncleanness and the health of the body. Uncleanness, he noted "will bloodily Disturb the Frame of our Bodies, and Exhaust and Poison the Spirits, in our Bodies, until an Incurable *Consumption* at Last, shall cut us down, *Out of Time.*" Many diseases traced their origins to uncleanness, he claimed, including "Gouts, Cramps, Palseyes, and Scorbutick Taints, upon the whole Mass within us." Sketching a disease etiology that reflected workings of Providence through the natural world, he added, "Yea, There is a Grievous Disease that sometimes Invades *Horses,* and because that *Men* do now so much Play the *Bruit,* that very Grievous Disease, is in a disguise come upon *Men* also, to Chastise their Bruitishness." Uncleanness not only caused disease, according to Mather, but was something to avoid as if it were disease. Listing reading as one of the antidotes to a persistent unclean spirit, Mather urged the congregation to "shun all obscaene Books, as you would the Rags that had the *Plague* about them."[29]

Uncleanness also broke down the distinctions between humankind and brute animals, with fearful consequences for a person's relationship with God, in whose image "he" was created. Noting how terrible it was for God-like man to "Smutty His Picture with all the *Superfluities of Naughtiness,*" Mather imagined a scene in which "it should be said, *There is a man, that is a Beast? There's a man Wallowing like a Dog, & like a Swine, in the most base Uncleanness!*" In imagery redolent with Puritan hatred of Quakers, Mather also compared unclean people to "*Unclean Goats,* Quaking and Shaking, before the Tribunal of the Lord Jesus Christ, as they shall at the Last Day." "Hav[ing] done Bruitish Things with their *Bodies* in this World," he predicted, "they shall therefore be Raised with *Ugly Bodies* in the World to come."[30]

Contradicting a passage from Proverbs in which uncleanness becomes the means for the poor to gain a piece of bread, Mather sketched a different relation between wealth and uncleanness. "It is commonly by *Fulness of Bread,* that persons do Pamper themselves into *Uncleanness,*" he observed, but "by *Uncleanness* they come to be Scarce worth a *Piece of Bread,* when they go off the Stage." Ruining men's estates and laying their "*Honour* in the Dust," uncleanness would inevitably lead to bitter poverty and loss of reputation.[31]

Their prosperity taken from them, Mather's unclean also:

leave the World, with the Humiliation of seeing *None;* or … but a *Poor* Posterity rising after them. Tis a frequent Thing, for that Great Blessing of Children, to be *Deny'd* where the Guilt of much *Uncleanness* is Lying on the Soul.... Or, if Children are not always *Deny'd,* yet they are often *Cursed,* where much *Uncleanness* is cleaving to the Family.

If children did survive, he observed, they were likely to be cursed with sickness or destined to fight their own losing battle with uncleanness. Thus the sins of the fathers would be visited upon their sons.[32]

Sexual uncleanness appeared in Mather's text as the burning fires of lust, which might be met by God's own punishing "*Everlasting Fire*" on the judgment day. Citing Proverbs 6.17, "*Can a man take fire in his Bosome, and his Cloaths not be burnt,*" Mather condemned young people for taking unclean persons into their company. Ultimately, the fires of lust would destroy without purifying, he warned: "Be not such a *Beast* as to run into the Fire; *A Companion of such Fools will be destroyed.*"[33]

Never far beneath the surface of Mather's rhetoric about filth, the Devil was the ultimate source of uncleanness and the purveyor of filth. Far from being reticent about the active presence of the Devil in New England, Mather used filth metaphors to talk extensively about evils inspired by Satan. "The *Unclean* have Gratify'd the *Devil,* who is a *Foul-Fiend,* in their Filthinesses," he alliterated. "For this cause, the Judgment of God upon them, will be, *Depart, ye Cursed, with the Devil and his Angels.*" Uncleanness also transformed the human body from the temple of the Holy Ghost to the "*Hog-sties* of the Devil," a phrase that Mather borrowed directly from Danforth's *The Cry of Sodom*. The young people Mather identified as being most guilty of sexual wrongdoing luxuriated in "Diabolical *Pollutions,*" which Mather hoped they would identify with the fate of the condemned woman and subsequently reject.[34]

For consolation, Mather offered his listeners several preventive measures for avoiding uncleanness and seeking repentance. In addition to prayer, fasting, and industrious activity, Mather recommended that an individual struggling with an unclean spirit might try singing hymns. Such a remedy not only offered distracting thoughts for the mind, but also set the tempted body to pious activity. In a specific plea to Emerson to repent, Mather also recommended "vomiting" sins in confession, an act of bodily expulsion that purged uncleanness like so much bodily corruption, and shedding melting tears to wash the feet of her savior.[35]

In the absence of lengthy or revealing diary entries, it is dangerous to speculate about Mather's personal connection to his sermon other than to note that it gratified his professional ambitions. What did his comments about uncleanness and early death reflect about his perception of his own body and his family life? Diary entries describing his regime of fasting and prayer when impure thoughts or doubts assailed him suggest that Mather believed the embodied nature of uncleanness merited an embodied response. In this regard, he appears to have practiced what he preached.[36]

We can also gather Mather's sense of his own mortal frame from the dissonance between his diary and sermon personae. Although in his diary, Mather identified himself as part of the generation whose uncleanness was bringing plagues upon New England, in his sermon he assumed the distant role of a community elder disgusted by the excesses of "young people." This is classic jeremiad, and should not surprise us, but we should note Mather's *private* inclusion of himself among the generation of youthful sinners.

Mather's interpretation of a family tragedy may help further illuminate his own relation to providentialism, uncleanness, and guilt over his role at Salem. Just two months before delivering the sermon, Mather suffered a personal tragedy that he had initially interpreted as being a consequence of witchcraft. This tragedy, like the crime of Elizabeth Emerson, incorporated infant death and bodily corruption, but Mather appears to have fixed on only one possible interpretation of the workings of Providence, at least in the pages of his diary. Young Increase Mather, named for Mather's illustrious father, was born without a rectum, and died a slow, agonizing death. Mather attributed the deformity to a fright his wife Abigail had experienced during pregnancy over a threat made by a witch. But as the providentialism of his own sermon suggests, he might easily have interpreted his son's death as a divine punishment for the sins of a father who had played such an important role in the witchcraft persecutions that wracked the colony. Seen in this light, the execution sermon appears as an effort not only to regain the moral high ground by condemning that which was by nature abhorrent, but to protect himself from the disturbing possibility that his son's death from an inability to expel uncleanness might have been God's curse for Mather's complicity in the sins of New England.[37]

Four years after delivering Emerson's execution sermon, Mather had the opportunity to comment on the behavior of yet another Emerson sister. Hannah Emerson Duston, the eldest of the Emerson children, effected a dramatic and much publicized escape from Indian captors in 1697. Taken from her Haverhill home less than a week after giving birth to her twelfth child, Duston was forced to march to New Hampshire before she decided to give Providence a helping hand. Using an Indian hatchet and with the help of a fellow captive, she killed ten Indians, including two women and six children, taking their scalps to prove her deed. In a curious twist of fate, her companion in escape was Mary Neff, the woman who had examined Emerson's dead infants but claimed not to have seen the tiny hand clutching the umbilical cord.[38] Transforming the family reputation for unjust violence into righteous vengeance, Mather's Duston also transformed the symbolic connections between the female body and the Puritan social body. Purifying, protecting, and revenging, Duston's deed overshadowed the acts of her younger sister. In Duston, the weak woman who found the courage to do what corrupt and effeminate men could not, Mather found the answer to Emerson, the embodiment of New England's corruption and the reason for its effeminacy. Washing away the sins of her sister and, indeed, nearly all historical memory of her, Hannah Duston became yet another example of the wonderful workings of Providence and of Mather's authority to interpret it.

Mather's compendium of execution confessions, *Pillars of Salt,* appeared soon after the Duston sermon. Along with Williams's *Warnings to the Unclean,* this work capped a decade in which the body of the white female infanticide assumed enormous symbolic value for Puritan ministers and the spectators who attended or read about the executions. By the 1720s, Mather, his fellow ministers, and many New England courts were beginning to embrace a different concept of female bodies and sensibility, one that emphasized innate piety and maternal tenderness. In *Elizabeth in her Holy Retirement* (1710), Mather argued that these two qualities were linked, with the dangers and pains of labor motivating women's superior piety. Seventeenth-century notions of innate female moral depravity and bodily corruption did not disappear with the rise of this new view of womanhood, however, but continued to justify public punishments of women of color and their white servant counterparts. With uncleanness inhering in their racial identities and poverty as well as in their histories of illicit sex and infanticide, the condemned women of the eighteenth century were increasingly depicted as deviant outsiders whose criminality made their excision from the social body necessary. In hindsight, Mather's passionate condemnations of uncleanness at the Emerson execution appear as a rearguard effort to redeem the grotesque white female body through the power of ministerial authority even as that body had already begun its long journey to privacy and gentility.[39]

Notes

The author thanks Sheila Brown and Elizabeth Bouvier for assistance with the research for this chapter and Thomas Doughton, Wayne Franklin, Lucia Knoles, Abby Schrader, Walt Woodward, and the two anonymous readers for their comments on the text. Research and writing of the chapter were supported by the American Antiquarian Society Mellon Postdoctoral Fellowship.

1. Worthington Chauncey Ford, ed., *Diary of Cotton Mather*, 2 vols. (New York: F. Ungar, 1957), 1:164–65.

2. Peter C. Hoffer and N. E. H. Hull, *Murdering Mothers: Infanticide in England and New England, 1558–1803* (New York: New York University, 1984), 20, 33–40. See also Cornelia Hughes Dayton, *Women Before the Bar: Gender, Law, and Society in Connecticut, 1639–1789* (Chapel Hill: University of North Carolina Press, 1995), 207–15, especially 210–11, for the cluster of infanticide cases in Connecticut in the 1750s.

3. Samuel Danforth, *The Cry of Sodom Enquired Into; Upon Occasion of the Arraignment and Condemnation of Benjamin Goad, for his Prodigious Villany, together with A Solemn Exhortation to Tremble at Gods Judgements, and to Abandon Youthful Lusts* (Cambridge, 1674); Daniel A. Cohen, *Pillars of Salt, Monuments of Grace: New England Crime Literature and the Origins of American Popular Culture, 1674–1800* (New York: Oxford University Press, 1993), 55.

4. Mary Douglas, *Purity and Danger: An Analysis of the Concepts of Pollution and Taboo* (New York: Praeger, 1966), 159–79.

5. Peter Stallybrass and Allon White, *The Politics and Poetics of Transgression* (Ithaca, N.Y.: Cornell University Press, 1986), 108–9. Danforth, *The Cry of Sodom Enquired Into;* Cohen, *Pillars of Salt,* 55.

6. County courts from Massachusetts to the Chesapeake described the illicit sexual unions of Anglo-colonial men and women as "foul," "abominable," "filthy," and "odious." Those found guilty of sexual misdeeds might be sentenced to be ritually cleansed of their sins by donning a white sheet and carrying a white taper as they begged the forgiveness of the parish.

7. For Renaissance manners, see Giovanni Della Casa, *Galateo: Renaissance Treatise on Manners,* 3rd ed. rev. (Toronto: Centre for Reformation and Renaissance Studies, 1994). For changing cleanliness practices and ideals, see Georges Vigarello, *Concepts of Cleanliness: Changing Attitudes in France since the Middle Ages* (New York: Cambridge University Press, 1988); Alain Corbain, *The Foul and the Fragrant: Odor and the French Social Imagination* (Cambridge, Mass.: Harvard University Press, 1986). For Puritan ideas about magic, epidemiology, and healing, see also Richard Godbeer, *The Devil's Dominion: Magic and Religion in Early New England* (New York: Cambridge University Press, 1992); Patricia Ann Watson, *The Angelical Conjunction: The Preacher-Physicians of Colonial New England* (Knoxville: University of Tennessee, 1991). I am indebted to Wayne Franklin for pointing out that words like *nasty* applied to both moral and material filth.

8. Cotton Mather, *Pillars of Salt* (Boston, 1699). For the market in published execution sermons and confessions, see Daniel E. Williams, *Pillars of Salt: An Anthology of Early American Criminal Narratives* (Madison, Wis.: Madison House Publications, 1993), and Cohen, *Pillars of Salt*. Cohen describes Mather's *Pillars of Salt* as "the most ambitious piece of crime literature to appear in New England up to that time" (55). Many of the excerpts from this text were incorporated into his massive *Magnalia Christi Americana* (London, 1702), where Emerson continued to represent uncleanness.

9. Mikhail Bakhtin, *Rabelais and His World,* trans. Hélène Iswolsky (Bloomington: Indiana University Press, 1984), 368–436; Stallybrass and White, *Politics and Poetics of Transgression,* 108–9, 144–45.

10. On the purging of the social body through rituals like executions, see David D. Hall, *Worlds of Wonder, Days of Judgment: Popular Religious Belief in Early New England* (New York: Knopf, 1989), 168–96.

11. Michael P. Winship, *Seers of God: Puritan Providentialism in the Restoration and Early Enlightenment* (Baltimore: Johns Hopkins University Press, 1996). Hall, *Worlds of Wonder,* 196–97, notes the similarity of rituals for curing the social body and the physical body.

12. See Douglas, *Purity and Danger,* 130; Susan Sontag, *Illness as Metaphor* (New York: Farrar, Straus, & Giroux, 1977), 71, for her examination of disease metaphors as vehement ways of discussing social disorder and evil; Kenneth Silverman, *The Life and Times of Cotton Mather* (New York: Harper & Row, 1984), 55–137; and Hall, *Worlds of Wonder,* 181, for his claim that the clergy made themselves central to the public theater of executions.

13. Laurel Thatcher Ulrich, *Good Wives: Image and Reality in the Lives of Women in Northern New England, 1650–1750* (New York: Knopf, 1980), 198; *Vital Records of Haverhill, Massachusetts, to the end of the year 1849,* 2 vols. (Salem, Mass., 1993), 1:113. This child appears to have been living in the Emerson household with her unmarried mother at the time of the double infanticide. See Suffolk County Court Records, file #2636, p. 93, for the reference to the first child "which was standing by."

14. Examination of Hannah, the wife of Michael Emerson, May 11, 1691, Suffolk County Court Records, file #2636.

15. Interrogation of Elizabeth Emerson, September 25, 1691, Suffolk County Court Records, file #2636.

16. Suffolk County Court Records, file #2636, May 10, 1691, 93.

17. Report of the female examiners, May 11, 1691, Suffolk County Court Records, file #2636.

18. Suffolk County Court Records, file #2636, May 11, 1691.

19. Mather, *Warnings from the Dead,* 56–57.

20. Ibid., 58–59.

21. Carol Karlsen, *The Devil in the Shape of a Woman: Witchcraft in Colonial New England* (New York: Norton, 1987); Elizabeth Reis, *Damned Women: Sinners and Witches in Puritan New England* (Ithaca, N.Y.: Cornell University Press, 1997).

22. John Williams, *Warnings to the Unclean: In a Discourse from Rev. XXI.8* (Boston, 1698); Mather, *Pillars of Salt,* 99–102; Edwin Powers, *Crime and Punishment in Early Massachusetts, 1620–1692: A Documentary History* (Boston: Beacon Press, 1966), 287–94. I am indebted to Thomas Doughton for pointing out the large crowds that attended Threeneedles's execution.

23. Vigarello, *Concepts of Cleanliness,* 17, 41–52, 58–77. See also Marjorie Hicks, *Clothing for Ladies and Gentlemen of Higher and Lower Standing* (Washington, D.C.: Smithsonian Institution, 1976); William Byrd, *Histories of the Dividing Line betwixt*

Virginia and North Carolina, ed. William K. Boyd (New York: Dover Publications, 1967), 77, for a woman's offer to wash his linen.

24. Ulrich, *Good Wives*, 126; Douglas, *Purity and Danger*, 35, 40; Byrd, *Histories of the Dividing Line*, 317. I am indebted to Thomas Doughton for reminding me of the "linen defense"; on this point, see Hoffer and Hull, *Murdering Mothers*, 68–69.

25. See Ulrich, *Good Wives*, 184–85, 196–201; Paul Boyer et al., eds., *Notable American Women*, 3 vols. (Cambridge, Mass.: Harvard University Press, 1971), 1:535–36.

26. Michel Foucault, *The Care of the Self*, vol. 3, *The History of Sexuality* (New York: Vintage Books, 1988); Norbert Elias, *The Civilizing Process*, trans. Edmund Jephcott (Oxford: Basil Blackwell, 1978); Bakhtin, *Rabelais and His World*; see also Winship, *Seers of God*, 94–95, for Mather's desire to be seen as a gentleman.

27. The "linen defense," noted in a 1673 English case by Hoffer and Hull, seems not to have applied here (*Murdering Mothers*, 68–69).

28. Winship, *Seers of God*, 99–100.

29. Mather, *Warnings from the Dead*, 46–47, 66.

30. Ibid., 52, 53.

31. Ibid., 49.

32. Ibid., 50–51. My language in this paragraph reflects my sense that Mather was thinking specifically about the patrilineal transmission of sin.

33. Ibid., 53, 67.

34. Ibid., 48, 53, 59.

35. Ibid., 64, 73, 75–76.

36. Mather, *Diary*, 1:187, 189.

37. Ibid., 1:162.

38. For a fresh treatment of Mather's use of Hannah Duston, see Teresa A. Toulouse's article in this collection. Ulrich, *Good Wives*, 184–85, 196–201; Paul Boyer et al., *Notable American Women*, 1:535–36.

39. Ulrich, *Good Wives*, 196; Cohen, *Pillars of Salt* , 117; Hoffer and Hull, *Murdering Mothers*, 47–48; Dayton, *Women Before the Bar*, 207–15.

"Clean of blood, without stain or mixture"

Blood, Race, and Sexuality in Spanish Louisiana

JENNIFER M. SPEAR

In 1776, Margarita Wiltz, declaring that it would be "convenient to her to have information given on the purity of her blood," initiated the first *limpieza de sangre,* or purity of blood, case to occur in Spanish Louisiana. The impetus for filing this suit was her impending marriage to Jacinto Panis. Because Panis was an officer in the Spanish military, Spanish law required Wiltz to demonstrate that she was either a member of the nobility or that her family was of untainted blood.[1] However, Louisiana's young and relatively fluid "New World" social order posed problems to those families who wished to have their social standing acknowledged. The social structure of New Orleans was still under construction, boundaries of social organization were unclear, and, in the transition from French to Spanish control, there were questions about who were the legitimate elite. Initiating a *limpieza de sangre* case was one avenue to public acknowledgment of a family's purity and status. While Wiltz and the other *limpieza de sangre* petitioners had particular material or legal reasons for initiating these cases,[2] my interest lies in what they used these cases to do: through their declarations of *limpieza de sangre,* these petitioners attempted to articulate what elite status meant. By holding that a particular bodily fluid—blood—embodied that status, petitioners contributed to a process of racialization in which cultural differences were naturalized and considered inheritable. They relied on both an older notion of race as lineage or line of descent, especially descent from nobility, but also on a newer, emerging biophysical conception of race that distinguished those of *sangre limpia,* or pure (European) blood, from all others, a concept central in the emergence of biological racism.[3]

95

Blood, as Michel Foucault has argued, can be a powerful metaphor for identity, especially when bounding one identity from another. In *The History of Sexuality*, Foucault argues that, in the eighteenth and nineteenth centuries, the "symbolics of blood" represented an aristocratic hegemonic order that was giving way to a bourgeois order revolving around the "analytics of sexuality." In aristocratic societies that depended on "systems of alliance, the political forms of the sovereign, the differentiation into orders and castes, and the value of descent lines ... blood constituted one of the fundamental values."[4] Yet, while the aristocratic symbolics of blood was losing its power in Europe, the power of blood as a marker of identity was increasing, especially in the slave societies of the Americas. As such a marker, it cannot be separated from issues of sexuality, as it was through reproductive sexual relationships that blood was "mixed" and the boundaries blurred. The *limpieza de sangre* cases in late-eighteenth-century New Orleans can be seen as defensive reactions by members of an insecure elite to a perceived increase in the blurring of social boundaries. In this chapter, after describing the general context out of which they emerged, several *limpieza de sangre* cases will be analyzed. These illustrate how social and cultural qualities, such as honor, legitimacy, conduct, respectability, and reputation, were embodied in the language of blood and thus became racialized.

First colonized by the French in 1699, Louisiana became part of the Spanish empire in the 1760s.[5] Although those of French descent remained the majority of Euro-Louisianans and Spanish governors promised to uphold existing French law, the transition from French to Spanish governance led to what one Louisiana historian has characterized as a system that was "partly French, partly Spanish, but not wholly either one or the other."[6] One aspect of this hybrid legal system was the informal introduction of the Spanish concept of *limpieza de sangre*. To exclude Jews and Muslims, including those who had converted to Catholicism, from holding "positions of confidence and preeminence," individual religious and secular institutions began enacting *limpieza de sangre* statutes in mid-fifteenth-century Spain. In the language of the statutes, a personal or familial history of practicing a non-Christian faith became an inheritable, ineffaceable stain upon one's blood. When the Spanish established colonies in the Americas, they imported the concept to legitimate a new colonial hierarchy, one that was based on categories of race rather than religion, which, in turn, transformed *limpieza de sangre* into a principle of racial exclusion.[7] In Spanish Louisiana, some Euro-Louisianans took advantage of the availability of this metropolitan concept and used it to articulate their own local understandings of racial exclusion, in the process defining what they believed it meant to be "white."

Between 1776 and 1796, when these cases occurred, those defined as "white" became a minority in New Orleans. The censuses of 1778 and 1791 show that the total population grew from 3,059 to 4,816 during this time, but the proportion of the population labeled *blanco* declined from 51 percent to 43 percent. The number of those recorded as free people of color more than doubled (from 353 to 862), while their percentage of the New Orleans population increased from 12 to 18 percent; and the slave population as a percentage of the total remained almost static. At the same time, those defined as *sang mêlé*, or "mixed blood" (which included *mulatos, quaterons,* and *mestizos*—labels that themselves relied on calculations of blood), distinguished in both censuses from the *noirs,* or blacks, formed the fastest growing segment of the population, almost doubling in thirteen years, from 418 in 1778 to 879 in 1791.[8] In addition to people who literally blurred the boundaries between white and black, entries in the notarial and sacramental records indicate occurrences of what Patricia Seed has termed "racial variability."[9] In a typical example of this variability, one woman, Clara Lopez de la Peña, was variously referred to as a *mulata,* a *mestiza,* and a *quaterona,* while in the baptism records of most of her children, she and her children were not marked by a racial designation, indicating their acceptance as "white" (at least by the recording priest).[10]

The Spanish government did not let this blurring of social boundaries go uncontested. In 1786, Governor Miró attempted to establish a color line through the use of clothing and ornaments as visual markers of "race." He prohibited *mulatas* and *quateronas libres* from wearing feathers or jewels in their hair; he ordered them to comb their hair flat, cover their heads with handkerchiefs, and avoid "extravagant luxury in their dressing," claiming it was "already excessive." The Cabildo, New Orleans' city council, also tried to construct a social color line, continually issuing prohibitions against taverns serving a heterogeneous clientele, which included free and enslaved Indians, European and Euro-American soldiers, free people of color, and Afro-Louisianan slaves, but apparently to no avail. Similarly, the Cabildo had trouble in prohibiting Euro-Louisianan men from attending the Saturday night dances held for free people of color.[11]

The color line was most clearly, and yet still not completely, defined in the prohibitions against *métissage.*[12] When Alejandro O'Reilly established Spanish authority in Louisiana in 1769, he issued a proclamation reenacting the French Code Noir of 1724, which included a prohibition against marriages between whites and blacks, both free and enslaved.[13] However, during the Spanish era, it was possible to petition for a dispensation against this prohibition and at least one such dispensation was granted in 1769 to Jean Paillet, a Euro-Louisianan, and Catherine Villeray, the daughter of Charlotte, a *mulata libre.* While the record of their marriage has not survived, the baptism records of four of their children are entered in the baptism registry known as the "Book of White Persons Only" where they are identified as legitimate, confirming a married state between Paillet and Villeray.[14]

It is possible that priests performed such marriages without recording them in the registers or, conversely, recorded the marriages but not the socioracial label of the bride. In 1797, the Sisters of the Ursuline Convent debated "whether they were willing to admit to the day school for instruction and within the convent as half boarders the *Mulaticas* [young mulatto woman] who were applying for this arrangement." They decided "unanimously" against such a proposal but noted that they would continue to accept "the legitimate daughters whose fathers were white and mothers *quateronas* as they have been received until now."[15]

While *métissage* in the form of marriage was rare, though not nonexistent, nonmarital *métissage* clearly was not uncommon. Although it had existed since the beginning of European colonization of Louisiana, nonmarital *métissage* appears to have increased both in prevalence and in acceptance during the last quarter of the eighteenth century. Religious and secular officials complained about the prevalence of extramarital and interracial relationships and also expressed a virulent hatred of the offspring of these relationships. Governor Miró decreed that he would "punish with all severity of the law all those who live in concubinage." He also declared that he would not tolerate "the idleness of *mulatas* and *quateronas libres*" who subsisted on "licentious lives" and "carnal pleasures." In 1795, Bishop Luis Peñalver y Cárdenas complained that "most of the married and unmarried men ... lived in concubinage and some fathers even obtained mistresses for their sons." In a letter to another Spanish official who had a long-standing relationship with a woman of color, military governor Caso Calvo complained that "every day the white folks, all the inhabitants and even the nobles, forgetting their principles, shamelessly and improperly mix with the colored women." These relationships, he went on to say, created "an issue who constantly vituperates and condemns their ancestors" and were "the true cause and beginning of all insubordination." New Orleans resident Luis Chevalier de Beaurepos refuted *mulata libre* Magdalena Canella's claim of ownership of a disputed slave, asserting that her "only proof ... rests on the sworn word of some *mulatas*, libertines like herself."[16] As anthropologist Verena Stolcke has argued for the Spanish American colonies in general, "Mulattos, mestizos, and other mixed categories in particular were objects of disgrace. They inspired deep distrust because," as *sang mêlé*, "they made racial barriers uncertain, placing in doubt or actively threatening the emerging racial hierarchy."[17]

Yet not all Euro-Louisianans were critical of *métissage* nor were they as hostile toward the *sang mêlé*. According to Pierre Clément de Laussat, the French official responsible for Louisiana during its retrocession from Spain to France and then its sale to the United States, *mulatas* and *quateronas libres* were "in great demand" and "much sought after" by Euro-Louisianan men who were frightened of the "burdens of family life" or "wearied by the monotony of the company of their wives." Laussat himself seems to have been unconcerned with *métissage* and the *sang mêlé*, casually noting in his diary that one particular dinner host "had ten mulatto children." According to Bishop Luis, this acceptance of *métissage* and its offspring certainly included the men who participated in them who, he wrote, do "not blush at carrying the illegitimate issue they have by [these relationships] to be recorded in the parochial registries as their natural children."[18]

An examination of baptismal records supports Bishop Luis's contention and also shows a growing acceptance of these relationships and their off-spring over the late eighteenth century. In the 1750s and 1760s, the phrase "of an unknown father" became more and more common in the baptism entries of nonwhite children, especially those in which the child was described as a *mulata* when her mother was a *negra*.[19] Occasionally, the priest would record the father as an "unknown white father" but most often whiteness went unmarked. By the 1780s and 1790s, however, it became more common for white fathers to be acknowledged as such. In 1782, Nicolas Rousseau appeared at the baptism of his son Pedro, labeled a *mulato libre,* as indicated by his signature in the registry. The recording priest noted that Luis Hazeur de Sonne and Josef Tribuño appeared at the baptisms of their children (both described as *quaterons* while their mothers were labeled *mulatas*) with the phrase "with the natural Father."[20]

Some relationships can be guessed at by reading between the lines of manumission records which, in general, tend to be silent on the question of relationships between the owner and the manumitted slaves. In my sample of manumissions from the years 1778 and 1791, I found only one record (out of 117) in which the manumitter explicitly stated that he was the father of the slaves to be manumitted and he was a *mulato libre.* There is, however, a certain profile of manumission, which would seem to indicate some kind of close relationship between the manumitter and the manumitted. In 1791, for instance, Don Martin Robin emancipated his *negra* slave Maria Rosa, aged twenty, and her three-year-old *mulata* daughter Eloisa, "for the much love and fondness I have for them." Although this phrase appears in many manumission records (including those in which the owner has also been motivated by a cash payment), acts that freed a woman and her children in which the child's racial designation indicates a white father, like that of Maria Rosa and her daughter, could very well be an owner manumitting his lover and their children. Others manumitted children but not their mothers, such as Claudio Gaudeau who freed three children aged nine through twelve, for "the good services that I have received from their mother and for the much love and care that I have" for the children even though he continued to enslave their mother.[21] Gaudeau's failure to manumit the mother is not necessarily an indication that he was not the father of her children as, according to historian Gwendolyn Midlo Hall, "men had a tendency to emancipate their children more rapidly than their concubines, in order to better keep the latter under their control."[22]

Unlike the manumission records, Euro-Louisianan men did sometimes recognize their nonwhite children in their wills. Andrés Juen acknowledged three natural children, aged twenty-two to twenty-five, all by different women, in his will written in 1784. Having no legitimate descendants, he left one thousand pesos to one child and two thousand pesos to the other two, noting that one deserved this inheritance "for her special care of him and the paternal love he professes for her."[23] While Euro-Louisianan men do not seem to have rushed to take advantage of the relatively more liberal Spanish policy on *métissage* marriage, they did take advantage of Spanish policy that allowed them to transform their natural children, who were ineligible to inherit, into legitimate heirs by a simple acknowledgment in the presence of a notary.[24]

As we can see from Juen's donations to his children, Euro-Louisianan men of wealth were not adverse to relationships with women of color. Neither were men of status, including at least one high-ranking Spanish official, Nicolas Maria Vidal, the Spanish military legal counselor and lieutenant governor in the 1790s. Vidal had at least two children with *mulata* Eufrosina Hinard—Carolina Maria Salome born in 1793 and Maria Josefa de las Mercedes born in 1795—who were not acknowledged as such in their baptism records, which described them as the children of Hinard and a "father unknown." However, in his will, Vidal acknowledged both Carolina and Maria as his natural children by Hinard, along with two other daughters he had had in Cartagena; one with a *mulata libre,* the other with a *negra libre.* Vidal named these four daughters or their respective mothers as his "only and universal heirs."[25]

In part because wealthy and prominent men like Juen and Vidal recognized the children they had with women of color and bequeathed property to them, the last quarter of the eighteenth century saw the emergence of what historian Kimberly Hanger has tentatively called a free black "elite," "although [it was] not [yet] on the scale of the *gens de couleur* of Saint-Domingue in the same period or of the large free black property holders" in antebellum Louisiana.[26] While still clearly occupying a subordinate position within New Orleans social hierarchy, the emergence of this black "elite" made determining one's social status a complicated equation of wealth, occupation, kinship, and color. And, while most of the families involved in the *limpieza de sangre* cases were already in positions of social and official prominence, they used their petitions to legitimize their social standing, and, in doing so, asserted that the possession of untainted blood, or a pure "white" lineage, was a necessary qualification for such status.[27]

Each of the eight cases initiated between 1776 and 1796 follows the same general pattern. Included in the documentation are certified copies of their baptisms and those of their parents as testimony to their legitimacy, as well as testimonials from several witnesses. In her petition, Margarita Wiltz laid out the questions to which her witnesses responded. They were asked whether or not they knew her as "the legitimate daughter of the lawful marriage of Juan Luis Wiltz and of Maria Dohl and that they had her during their marriage which they contracted according to the rites of the Church and that they nursed and fed her in their home and family and called her daughter and she called them parents?" The following two questions asked for the same information about her parents. The fourth question asked the witnesses to testify that "she, her parents and grandparents and the rest of her ancestors, both paternal and maternal, are old Christians, pure of all bad races of Moors, Jews, Mulattos and Indians, and that they are not recently converted, nor have they been prosecuted for infamies or crimes, nor made to do penance, but on the contrary have always enjoyed a good reputation for their habits and purity of blood." The fifth and final question asked the witnesses to describe the general rumor and reputation of Wiltz and her family.[28]

Lineage, and the legitimacy of that lineage, was the first issue to be established and demonstrates that *limpieza de sangre* petitioners were concerned with delineating status distinctions through blood, beginning a process that would "fix" cultural characteristics as natural and innate to particular groups of people. Legitimacy in and of itself conferred "great honor and advantage," and only legitimate children could receive holy orders from the church and secular honors, or inherit from their parents. In addition, a family's *limpieza de sangre* could only be guaranteed through legitimate, church or state-sanctioned, class and racial endogamous marriages.[29] Witnesses, just as Josef Martinez testifying for Juan Diego Riado, stated that they knew the petitioner to be "the legitimate [child] of the legitimate marriage" of the petitioner's parents. But being born of a lawful marriage was not enough. Martinez also swore that Juan Diego had been "educated, fed, and recognized as [a legitimate son]" by his parents. Or as Pedro de La Ronde asserted, his parents "called [him] their son and [he] called them [his] parents."[30]

The fact that children are born into a lineage through women meant that the responsibility for maintaining pure blood lines weighed more heavily on women's shoulders than men's. When Martin Palao petitioned the king for permission to marry Martina Josefa Prieto y Laronde, he enclosed documents and testimonials proving that she was fourteen, the legitimate daughter of Juan Prieto and Teresa Josefa Laronde, "of honest character ... [and] noble birth" as well as pure of blood, and had a dowry of three thousand pesos in silver. As the prospective groom, Palao underwent much less scrutiny, as he enclosed only one document: a copy of his baptism record proving that he was twenty-nine and had indeed been baptized.[31] Inasmuch as the notion of blood within *limpieza de sangre* was the symbolic carrier of social and racial qualities, the maintenance of racial categories were, as Tessie Liu has written, "predicated upon control of women and sexuality."[32]

In the Spanish American colonies, honor was an important concept that, according to historian Ann Twinam, "served as an overarching complex of ideas, attitudes, and values that set the ideal standards for elite behavior" at the same time that it "was the ethos which rationalized the existence of the colonial hierarchy."[33] Honor, however, operated differently for men and women. In the first place, men could attain honor through, for instance, military heroics, while women were generally held responsible for maintaining honor: for them it was something that could be lost but not won. In addition, honor was closely connected to sexual propriety, particularly for women of status whose families sought to enhance their social position. Because, in Stolcke's words, "social position [was] attributed to inherent, natural, racial, and therefore hereditary qualities, the elite's control of the procreative capacity of their women [was] essential for them to preserve their social preeminence."[34] Consequently, any sexual misbehavior by an elite woman would not only bring dishonor on herself but also on her family and her future descendants. Men's sexual misbehavior, on the other hand, might reflect on themselves but rarely influenced the honor of an entire lineage; that is, their dishonorable behavior was individualized in a way that women's was not.

But, for these petitioners and for their witnesses, blood symbolized more than the legitimacy of one's lineage, the absence of sexual misconduct, and familial honor. Occupation and conduct, reputation and respectability, faith, and, most importantly, an inchoate conception of race also were embodied in blood. Adelaida d'Estrehan's ancestors had held "distinguished employment[s]," such as that of her grandfather who was a Chevalier of the Order of St. Louis, a "distinction that is conceded to Noble persons alone." Similarly, Carlos Favre Daunoy's father was, at the time of his petition, serving as a judge—an appointment given only to "those subjects of [the] most eminence." Wiltz's family had always been employed in "what persons of quality distinguish themselves," while Wiltz herself had always engaged "in virtuous works." One of the Prieto witnesses testified that "the occupations of this family have always been respectable [and] he has not heard or known of any inferior position they have held." Conduct was also seen as demonstrative of the quality of one's blood. Another petitioner asked his witnesses to testify that his parents were "honorable [and] of honorable conduct" and that he did not frequent taverns or other "indecorous public places."[35]

Religion, while losing its centrality in defining *limpieza de sangre,* maintained a place in doing so. Testifying for his niece, Diego Prieto declared that her paternal ancestors were "of Old Christian faith ... [not] of any new converted doctrine." Nor, he added, had they ever "been punished by the Holy Tribunal or the inquisition." Every petitioner had at least one witness who testified that the petitioner's ancestors were "old Christians ... not recently converted." Moors and Jews were still considered impure, as the petitioners' families were asserted to be "clean of all stain of ... jews and Moors."[36] The fact that Jews and Moors, of whom very few resided in Louisiana, maintained their role in determining *limpieza de sangre* illustrates how the concept retained much of its metropolitan meaning even as that meaning was anachronistic in the colonial context.

In the minds of these petitioners, the reputation or public acknowledgement of their legitimacy, faith, social position, occupations, and nobility was perhaps as important as the veracity of these qualities. Wiltz's ancestors were praised for the "good reputation [they enjoyed] for their habits." Witness Santilly asserted that "the fathers and grandfathers of [Pedro de La Ronde], both paternal and maternal, are of noble birth and have always been held and are respected as such." Prieto y Laronde's paternal family, according to one witness, "has enjoyed a good name and has always been accepted publicly for their good qualities. . . . and held in constant and well-known esteem." As proof of the public acceptance of their purity and nobility, the witness went on to state that the Prieto home "has been visited by the most prominent people." For Prieto himself, it was not enough that his wife's parents were "known, held and respected as persons of fine and distinguished origin;" he stressed that they were also "looked up to and treated with respect."[37] As anthropologist Virginia Dominguez has argued, "social identities do not exist without public affirmation."[38] In initiating *limpieza de sangre* cases, these petitioners were attempting to codify their social status and identity within a public forum.

By embodying social qualities such as honor and occupation, faith and respectability in blood—a corporeal substance that, it was believed, was shared by members of a lineage—the petitioners and their witnesses naturalized those characteristics, made them inheritable, and, therefore, racialized them. Blood in this instance was not understood as "a body fluid but [as] a symbol of a person's whole ancestry, cultural background, and potential capabilities."[39] And without being "entirely free of all bad races" and "clean of blood, without stain or mixture," one could not possess *limpieza de sangre*. Wiltz's paternal and maternal lineages were "distinguished by [their] purity of blood from all bad races of . . . Mulatto and Indian," while Prieto y Laronde's blood was "clean and without any mixture . . . or infected by any bad race." The blood of blacks, Indians, *mulatos,* or "any other mixture" could "infect" or "stain" one's lineage, causing it to be "unclean." The notions of race expressed by these petitioners show a slippage between an older understanding of race as a particular lineage or stock (especially a noble one) and a newer one that was beginning to incorporate a modern definition of race as "physical and phenotypical difference[s]."[40] As with the other qualities testified to, it was also not good enough to be white; one had to be publicly acknowledged as possessing whiteness. The Riados, according to one witness, had been "held and respected as white persons," while the Prietos were "entirely and known to be white, of clean blood and distinguished origin."[41]

Each of these petitions was successful. La Ronde's documents were forwarded to the governor by a court official who stated he had "no reason to doubt [La Ronde's] legitimacy, cleanliness, and recommendable circumstances." When Governor Carondelet forwarded Daunoy's case onto Luis de las Casas, minister of the Indies, he requested the latter's "favorable support" in presenting the case to the king. After examining the documents and witnesses testifying to Prieto y Laronde's "legitimacy [and] cleanness of blood," Lieutenant Governor Francisco Bouligny declared, "it is evident that there exists in this young lady the well-known qualities of birth and fortune." Governor Carondelet and legal counselor Vidal agreed, decreeing that the Prieto family should be furnished with the "testimonials [they] may need for purposes advantageous to [them]."[42]

At the same time that Vidal was participating in a process that aimed at clarifying a particular racial category, he was legitimating his *quaterona* daughters, thereby "calling into question the distinctions of difference which maintained the neat boundaries of colonial rule."[43] Similarly, the children of *quaterona* Catherine Villeray and *mestiza* Clara Lopez de la Peña "passed" into the white population in as much as their baptisms were recorded in the "Book of White Persons Only" where they were not labeled with racial designations.[44] The *limpieza de sangre* petitioners, through their suits and particularly their articulations of what whiteness entailed, tried to counteract this perceived racial fluidity. Two petitioners in particular, Celeste Macarty and Adelaide d'Estrehan, may have been concerned with distinguishing their own lineages from families of color who carried the same name. One of Macarty's brothers may have had a *quaterona* daughter who received his name (an indication that the father acknowledged his child). In addition, Barthelemy, an important name in Macarty's family carried by her grandfather, father, brother, and cousin, was also the name of a free man of color while there was a free woman of color called Celeste Macarty.[45] Adelaida d'Estrehan also had a *mulata libre* namesake. To make matters more complicated, there were two Jean Baptiste Honore Destrehans in New Orleans— one was Adelaida's father, the other a *mulato libre*—and both married women named Marie Felicite.[46]

The Macarty and d'Estrehan family trees may indeed have had branches headed by women of color but, more generally, Macarty, d'Estrehan, and the other *limpieza de sangre* petitioners were expressing concern at the blurring of socioracial boundaries caused by reproductive *métissage* and the acceptance of *sang mêlé* children by their Euro-Louisianan fathers. In embodying honor, conduct, status, respectable occupations, and legitimacy in blood and in maintaining that only blood untainted by Indian or African ancestry could carry these qualities, these petitioners were articulating a vision of social order predicated on what Foucault has called a "modern, biologizing" form of racism in that it relied on both "the thematics of blood" and "the devices of sexuality."[47] This racialization of social status through the *limpieza de sangre* cases continued to influence notions of race, social order, and family status in Louisiana long after the Spanish ceded Louisiana to the French who then sold it to the United States. In an attack on the quadroon balls of New Orleans in 1825, a "Mother of a Family" wrote to the New Orleans Gazette, calling *mulata* women "Heaven's last, worst gift to white men" because they threatened "the purity of the blood of the best families [in] Louisiana."[48]

Notes

The author thanks Andy Foroughi, Robert Frame, Brett Mizelle, Matt Mulcahy, and the participants in the Early American History Workshop at the University of Minnesota for their comments and suggestions. Research was supported by an Albert J. Beveridge Grant for Research in the History of the Western Hemisphere from the American Historical Association.

1. Jack D. L. Holmes, "Do It! Don't Do It! Spanish Laws on Sex and Marriage," in *Louisiana's Legal Heritage,* ed. Edward Haas (Pensacola, Fla.: Perdido Bay Press, 1983), 19–42.

2. Including Wiltz, four of the eight cases that I found involved prospective brides of Spanish military officers. Two others involved men who wished to become priests, while another examined the family history of a young man who wished to join the Spanish Royal Guard Corps. Both the priesthood and the officer ranks of the military were among the positions of "confidence" that were reserved for those of pure blood. I have been unable to determine the impetus for the eighth and final case I have uncovered: the petitioner simply declared that it would be "advantageous" to demonstrate that he was pure of blood. The documentation for the eight *limpieza de sangre* cases are: Margarita Wiltz (1776): Archivo General de Indias, Santo Domingo, Historic New Orleans Collection (hereafter AGI, SD), legajo 2547, doc. 151, 1–23, and Spanish Judicial Records, *Louisiana Historical Quarterly* (hereafter SJR, *LHQ*) 11 (1928): 330–32; Pedro de La Ronde (1778): Despatches of the Spanish Governors of Louisiana, El Baron de Carondelet, Manuscripts Department, Howard-Tilton Memorial Library, Tulane University (hereafter Carondelet Despatches), Book 6, 245–50; Celestine Macarty: Bernardo de Gálvez to Joseph de Gálvez, May 27, 1779, Confidential Despatches of Don Bernardo de Gálvez, Manuscripts Department, Howard-Tilton Memorial Library, Tulane University, 98; Francisco Riado: New Orleans Notarial Archives (hereafter NONA), Carlos Favre Daunoy (1793): Carondelet Despatches, Book 4, 133–66; Acts of Esteban de Quiñones, March 15, 1785; Adelaida d'Estrehan (1795): AGI, SD, legajo 2588, 768–840; Martina Josefa Prieto y Laronde (1796): Carondelet Despatches, Book 6, 218–60; Joaquin de Lisa: NONA, Acts of Quiñones, August 22, 1785.

3. On these different notions of race in French thought and the transition between them, see Colette Guillaumin, "The Specific Characteristics of Racist Ideology," in her *Racism, Sexism, Power and Ideology* (London: Routledge, 1995), 40–43.

4. Michel Foucault, *The History of Sexuality,* vol. 1, *An Introduction,* trans. Robert Hurley (New York: Vintage Books, 1980), 147–48.

5. For an overview of the French and Spanish eras of Louisiana, see Joe Gray Taylor, *Louisiana: A History* (New York: W. W. Norton, 1984), 3–41.

6. Henry P. Dart, "The Place of the Civil Law in Louisiana," *Tulane Law Review* 4 (February 1930): 168.

7. On *limpieza de sangre* in Spain, see Deborah Root, "Speaking Christian: Orthodoxy and Difference in Sixteenth-Century Spain," *Representations* 23 (summer 1988): 118–34. On how the concept was transformed as it was utilized in the American colonies, see Verena Stolcke, "Conquered Women," *Report on the Americas* 24 (1991): 23–28, 39.

8. Census of New Orleans, June 1778, *Louisiana Census and Militia Lists, 1770–1789,* ed. Albert J. Robichaux (Harvey, La., 1973–74), 1:23–68; and Census of New Orleans, November 6, 1791, City Archives, Louisiana Division, New Orleans Public Library (hereafter NOPL).

9. Seed uses "racial variability" rather than "passing" to avoid the "normative connotations" of the latter: that is, passing "suggests movement in one direction, toward

'white.'" See her "Social Dimensions of Race: Mexico City, 1753," *Hispanic American Historical Review* 62 (November 1982): 591.

10. St. Louis Cathedral, Baptisms, Book B14, 1796–1802, New Orleans Archdiocesan Archives (hereafter Baptisms, Book B14), 99v, January 25, 1795; NONA, Acts of Pedesclaux, July 13, 1796; and January 21, 1797, Baptisms, Book B14, 22, Baptism of Maria del Carmen De Clouet.

11. Miró, Bando de Buen Gobierno, June 1, 1786, Records and Deliberations of the Cabildo, 1769–1803 (hereafter Cabildo Records), NOPL, Book 3, 1:107; Minter Wood, "Life in New Orleans in the Spanish Period," *LHQ* 22 (July 1939): 688; Cabildo Records, Book 4, 3:137–40, February 8, 1800; and Gilbert C. Din and John E. Harkins, *The New Orleans Cabildo: Colonial Louisiana's First City Government, 1769–1803* (Baton Rouge: Louisiana State University Press, 1996), 173–75.

12. Following Ann Stoler, I use *métissage* to refer to relationships across perceived racial boundaries rather than miscegenation, which carries negative and problematic contemporary connotations, and as a word, is anachronistic for the colonial period. See Stoler, "Sexual Affronts and Racial Frontiers: European Identities and the Cultural Politics of Exclusion in Colonial Southeast Asia," *Comparative Studies in Society and History* 34 (July 1992): 514–51.

13. Charles Gayarré, *History of Louisiana*, 4 vols., 4th ed. (New Orleans: Pelican, 1965), 3:37; and Article 6, Code Noir (1724) in *Le code noir, ou, Le calvaire de Canaan*, ed. Louis Sala-Molins (Paris: Presses Universitaires de France, 1987), 103.

14. Records of the Superior Council, *LHQ* 6 (1923): 157, November 16, 1769; and St. Louis Cathedral, Baptisms, Book B6, 1767–1771, New Orleans Archdiocesan Archives (hereafter Baptisms, Book B6), 91, October 14, 1770.

15. "Délibérations du Conseil," 1727–1902, Archives of the Ursuline Convent of New Orleans, October 31, 1797. My thanks to Dr. Charles Nolan, archivist at the New Orleans Archdiocesan Archives, for showing me this document and sharing his interpretation of it.

16. Miró, Bando de Buen Gobierno, June 1, 1786, Cabildo Records, Box 3, 1:106–7; Bishop Luis Peñalver y Cárdenas to Eugenio Llaguno y Amirola, November 1, 1795, cited in Roger Baudier, *The Catholic Church in Louisiana* (New Orleans: A. W. Hyatt, 1939), 229–30; Marques de Casa Calvo to Nicolas Maria Vilda, September 24, 1800, Cabildo Records, Book 4, 4:21; and Canella vs. Beaurepos, SJR, *LHQ* 12 (1929): 342, January 20, 1777.

17. Stolcke, "Conquered Women," 26.

18. Pierre-Clément de Laussat, *Memoirs of my Life to my Son during the Years 1803 and After* ... , trans. Agnes-Josephine Pastwa (Baton Rouge: Louisiana State University Press, 1978), 101, 16; and Bishop Luis Peñalver y Cárdenas, 1799, cited in *The Spanish Regime in Missouri*, ed. Louis Houck, 2 vols. (Chicago: R. R. Donnelley, 1909), 2:221n.

19. Mary Veronica Miceli, "The Influence of the Roman Catholic Church on Slavery in Colonial Louisiana" (Ph.D. dissertation, Tulane University, 1979), 83, 88, 92.

20. St. Louis Cathedral, Bautismos de Negros Esclavos y Mulatos, Book B8, 1777–83, New Orleans Archdiocesan Archives, 306, September 28, 1782; St. Louis Cathedral, Bautismos de Negros y Mulatos, Book B13, 1792–98, New Orleans Archdiocesan Archives (hereafter Baptisms, Book B13), 5, October 25, 1792; and Baptisms, Book B13, 68, July 15, 1793. For baptisms that record an unknown white father, see Book B13, 200, May 6, 1795; and Baptisms, Book B13, 129, May 5, 1794. For records in which the fathers are named and labeled as white, see Baptisms, Book B13, 212, June 29, 1795; and Baptisms, Book B13, 236, October 12, 1795.

21. NONA, Acts of Francisco Broutin, March 26, 1791; NONA, Acts of Broutin, March 26, 1791; NONA, Acts of Pedesclaux, February 14, 1791; and NONA, Acts of Almonester y Roxas, June 12, 1778. Between 1771 and 1803, just over a thousand slaves were manumitted. See Kimberly S. Hanger, *Bounded Lives, Bounded Places: Free Black Society in Colonial New Orleans, 1769–1803* (Durham, N.C.: Duke University Press, 1997), 31.

22. Gwendolyn Midlo Hall, "Relations raciales en Louisiane coloniale: Politique étatique et attitudes populaires," in *Colonies, Territoires, Societies l'Enjeu Français,* ed. Alain Saussol and Joseph Zitomersky (Montréal: l'Harmattan, 1996), 55.

23. SJR, *LHQ* 24 (October 1941): 1259–62, September 14, 1784. Juen did marry but had no children by this legal relationship.

24. *The Laws of Las Sietas Partidas, Which Are Still in Force in Louisiana,* trans. L. Moreau Lislet and Henry Carleton, 2 vols. (New Orleans: James McKaraher, 1820), 1:551–53.

25. Baptisms, Book B13, 23, January 24, 1793; Baptisms, Book B13, 179, February 6, 1795; and NONA, Acts of Pedesclaux, May 4, 1798.

26. Hanger, *Bounded Lives,* 55.

27. Among the petitioners' families were the widow of New Orleans' richest merchant, Chevaliers of the Order of St. Louis, architects and builders of the Ursuline Convent and the Pontalba Buildings, which line Jackson Square, court officials, militia officers, and past and future Spanish governors. The two families who did not have prominent members were those of the two men who wanted to join the priesthood, itself a path to prominence. See Stanley C. Arthur and George C. H. Kernion, *Old Families of Louisiana* (Baton Rogue, La.: Claitor's, 1971), 230–32; Grace King, *Creole Families of New Orleans* (Baton Rouge, La.: Claitor's, 1971), 313–16, 368–75; and Jay Higginbotham, *Old Mobile: Fort Louis de la Louisiane, 1702–1711* (Mobile, Ala.: Museum of the City of Mobile, 1977), 95.

28. SJR, *LHQ* 11 (1928): 330–31, February 7, 1776.

29. Stolcke, "Conquered Women," 25, 27.

30. NONA, Acts of Quiñones, March 15, 1785; and Carondelet Despatches, Book 6, 245, May 29, 1778.

31. Martin Palao to the King, May 30, 1796, Carondelet Despatches, Book 6, 219.

32. Tessie Liu, "Teaching the Differences among Women from a Historical Perspective: Rethinking Race and Gender as Social Categories," *Women's Studies International Forum* 14 (1991): 265. See also Mary Douglas, *Purity and Danger: An Analysis of the Concepts of Pollution and Taboo* (1966; reprint, London: Routledge, 1993), 125–26.

33. Ann Twinam, "Honor, Sexuality and Illegitimacy in Colonial Spanish America," in *Sexuality and Marriage in Colonial Latin America,* ed. Asunción Lavrin (Lincoln: University of Nebraska Press, 1989), 123.

34. Stolcke, "Conquered Women," 28.

35. AGI, SD, legajo 2588, 770, 1795; Carondelet Despatches, Book 4, 135, October 25, 1793; SJR, *LHQ* 11 (1928): 332, February 7, 1776; Carondelet Despatches, Book 6, 241, May 14, 1796; and NONA, Acts of Quiñones, August 22, 1785.

36. Carondelet Despatches, Book 6, 230, July 4, 1795; AGI, SD, legajo 2547, doc. 151, 332, [1776]; and NONA, Acts of Quiñones, March 15, 1785.

37. SJR, *LHQ* 11(1928): 331, 1776; Carondelet Despatches, Book 6, 247–48, May 29, 1778; Carondelet Despatches, Book 6, 241–42, May 14, 1796; and Carondelet Despatches, Book 6, 250–51, March 17, 1796.

38. Virginia R. Dominguez, *White by Definition: Social Classification in Creole Louisiana* (New Brunswick, N.J.: Rutgers University Press, 1994), 10.

39. Helen C. Rountree, *Pocahontas's People: The Powhatan Indians of Virginia through Four Centuries* (Norman: University of Oklahoma Press, 1990), 191.

40. Margo Hendricks and Patricia Parker, "Introduction," in *Women, "Race," and Writing in the Early Modern Period,* ed. Hendricks and Parker (New York: Routledge, 1994), 1–2.

41. Carondelet Despatches, Book 6, 155, October 26, 1793; Carondelet Despatches, Book 6, 234–35, July 8, 1795; AGI, SD, legajo 2547, doc. 151, 332, [1776]; and Carondelet Despatches, Book 6, 231–32, July 4, 1795; NONA, Acts of Quiñones, March 15, 1785; and Carondelet Despatches, Book 6, 237.

42. Carondelet Despatches, Book 6, 249, June 2, 1788; Carondelet to las Casas, December 15, 1793, Carondelet Despatches, Book 6, 133; Carondelet Despatches, Book 6, 242, May 18, 1796; and Francisco Bouligny to the King, May 31, 1796, Carondelet Despatches, Book 6, 219–20; and Carondelet Despatches, Book 6, 243, May 18, 1796.

43. Stoler, "Sexual Affronts and Racial Frontiers," 514.

44. On this type of "passing," see Hall, "Relations raciales en Louisiane coloniale," 58–60.

45. St. Louis Cathedral, Libro de Bautizados de Negros y Mulatos, Book 12, 1786–1792, New Orleans Archdiocesan Archives, 287–88, February 13, 1792; and *Sacramental Records of the Roman Catholic Church of the Archdiocese of New Orleans,* ed. Reverend Monsignor Earl C. Woods and Dr. Charles E. Nolan (New Orleans: Archdiocese of New Orleans, 1987) (hereafter *Sacramental Records*), 6:183, May 26, 1799.

46. *Sacramental Records,* 3:96–97, June 23, 1776; and Marriages, Book M3, 7, June 7, 1789.

47. Foucault, *The History of Sexuality,* vol. 1, 149.

48. Cited in "Mulattoes," *Niles' Weekly Register,* 3d ser., 5, no. 10 (November 5, 1825): 160.

A "*Doctrine of Signatures*"
The Epistolary Physics of Esther Burr's Journal

SUSAN M. STABILE

"Dish milk & slit milk may convey some nourishment," preached Thomas Shepherd in *The Parable of the Ten Virgins*, "but breast milk hath spirit going with it; good books may be blessed, but there is not that spirit in them as in lively dispensations of the gospels by ministers themselves."[1] Preaching, like breastfeeding, would nourish an expectant congregation with the "sincere Milk of the Word," for evangelical ministers during the Great Awakening considered themselves to be the "breasts of God."[2] Emptying their hearts of earthly concerns and desires, the congregation became vacant, receptive vessels that received God's Word as an infant receives milk. Converted saints were not only metaphorized as receptacles for spirited milk, but also were imagined as brides of Christ who would be impregnated with God's seed of grace or as nursing mothers who would suckle the unconverted.

In the eighteenth century, biological sex was understood as a fluid category indivisible into the binaries of male and female. "To be a man or a woman was to hold a social rank, a place in society, to assume a cultural role," argues historian Thomas Laqueur, "not to *be* organically one or the other of two incommensurable sexes."[3] The discourse of evangelical religion thus configured sex as a sociological rather than ontological category, where both men and women—as holy brides and mothers—were inseminated with God's seed, pregnant with His grace, delivered from sin in the moment of re-birth, engorged with milk-filled breasts, and ultimately nourished with the milk of God's Word. Spiritual conversion (awakening, purification, illumination, mortification, and union), that once rhetorically mimicked the discernible stages of pregnancy (conception, ensoulment, and birth), was collapsed into the "*absolute, immediate, instantaneous*" moment of (re)birth. Materializing the moment when Flesh became Word, images of expectant brides (at the threshold of becoming a wife), pregnant wives (awaiting a baby's birth), or nursing mothers (in the iterative gesture of spreading God's milk), gendered the conversion experience. Flesh became Word. And the Word was distinctly feminine.

The pregnant body, therefore, was a *gendered* rather than *sexed* body, for biological sex was an epiphenomenon to gender until the late eighteenth century. In what Laqueur calls the "one-sex body," there was no sharp boundary between the sexes but rather an economy of fungible fluids where blood, semen, milk, and other liquids were interchangeable, thereby representing the absence of specifically genital sex.[4] Both men and women, for example, contributed seminal fluids at the moment of conception. Whitened breast milk that mysteriously transformed from menstrual blood in the nursing mother also filled the breasts of susceptible men who had peculiarly "cold, moist, and feminine complexions." And pathological bleeding or regular bloodletting in men was likened to female menses.[5] Since biological sex did not exist as distinct ontological categories during the Great Awakening, and since the saint supposedly dissolved into God's body at the moment of re-birth, men and women experienced conversion in the same way. The only difference, therefore, was one of degree, where women described their religious revival in more sensual, emotional, and ecstatic terms. Laqueur's theory of the one-sex body thus offers a useful frame for understanding the construction of the evangelical body, where sexual difference was measured by the moderation or excesses of religious feeling.

In this chapter, I explore how the feminine images for spiritual awakening provided women with an opening, within a predominantly misogynist church discourse, for full participation in the evangelical movement. Through a close reading of Esther Edwards Burr's epistolary journal, which she kept for Sarah Prince from 1754 to 1757, I examine how the corporeal discourse of spiritual embodiment gets materialized and literalized in Burr's pregnant and nursing body. Pregnant in 1754 and again in 1756, Burr interpreted gestation as the conspicuous embodiment of God's Word. At the same time, however, she found the direct experience and responsibilities of motherhood at odds with the exalted metaphors described by the preachers. Though she practices and even exaggerates the feminine discourses of evangelicalism, Burr is troubled by the disjunction between physical and spiritual (re)birth. "In what Language shall I address you," she asks Sarah Prince, "I cant attain to what my *dear Instructris* has, yet! God of his infinite mercy grant that I may be quickned by your surprizing example." Preferring epistolary communion with Prince—who she calls the "Sister of my Heart"—to doctrinaire sermons, Burr focuses on the interrelated healing of the body and spirit during religious awakening. Because breast milk was extolled by medical discourse for its healing powers, and because letters materialized the diffusion of the ephemeral and spoken Word between spiritually awakened souls, Burr imagined her correspondence with Sarah Prince as symbiotic, for they would unbosom their "whole souls and pour them into Each other's breasts." Through correspondence, Esther Burr and Sarah Prince moved themselves from the margins of orthodox religion to the center of evangelical practices during the Great Awakening, resisting the old dictum that "your WOMEN keep silence in churches."[6]

I examine, moreover, how epistolarity—which epistolary novelist Samuel Richardson called "writing to the *moment*"—palpably captured the "private sudden sanctity" of the pregnant woman's body during conversion, where spiritual *delivery* happened "in the twinkling of an eye or a *Moment* of time."[7] Letter writing, like spiritual conversion, was private, spontaneous, and immediate: "As for coppiing [*sic*], I never do," Burr parenthetically confesses, "(I dont so much as look over what I send you. You have my thoughts just as they then happen to be)." Painting "pictures of the soul," letters "flow[ed] spontaneously from the heart," inscribing the soul's movements on paper. A reciprocal gesture between like-minded correspondents, letters reiterated the moment of sanctification: while the saint's body incorporated God's disembodied Word during conversion (Word made Flesh), letters materialized that incorporation (Flesh made Word), carrying evangelical feelings to eager recipients. Letters, therefore, spread the Word in what David Lovejoy has called "a sudden circumcision of the heart" and circulated emotions that "flow from social love, from hearts united by the same laudable ties."[8]

Spreading the Word between susceptible hearts, letters embodied newly developed configurations of sacred time and space during the Great Awakening, where worship moved out of the well-ordered and hierarchical meetinghouses into makeshift churches and open fields.[9] As George Whitefield proclaimed: "Oh, that partition-wall were broken down, and we all with one heart and one mind could glorify our common Lord and Savior Jesus Christ!" Unlike the church's partition walls that impeded the flow of spirit from soul to soul, church to church, and town to town, the saint's feminine body became the "private sudden sanctity" that would receive and circulate the Word without impediment. Writing to the "Sister of [her] Heart," Burr echoes Whitefield's image of the communal heart: "There is somthin [to] be learned go where one will if we have but an heart [to] reflect and improve."[10] Privileging emotionalism and feminine metaphors over the patriarchal authority made visible in impermeable church walls, evangelicalism became a community of language rather than of space.

As Ann Kibbey illustrates, the conversion act was a "linguistic event" in which evangelicals believed "that only spoken words, and spontaneous speech at that, could produce conversions." Written language, I would argue, materialized the ephemeral experience of rebirth that marked "the hearts, tongues, ears, and minds of a living community." Just as itinerant preachers helped spread the Word through the rhetorical "flow and circularity" among mid-Atlantic Presbyterians, New England Congregationalists and Baptists, and Southern Methodists from 1739 to the American Revolution, so the

reciprocal aesthetics of handwritten letters expressed the geographical movement of religious language. Assuring Sarah Prince that "my heart has been
at Boston with you very often," Esther Burr images letters as a metonym for
the heart: "I am thinking of you am just ready to speak as if you were
present—indeed my dear you are present—say ant your heart here—or at
least part of it."[11] Written in haste and fragmented by the journalistic style
of the entries, Esther Burr's letters thus mimicked the spontaneous and improvisational preaching during the revivals, which were consequently described in metaphors of motion, including "waves," "fires," "impulses,"
"pulsations," and "eruptions."[12]

The iterative act of letter writing constructs and endorses a theory of gender that links the self-substantiating images of epistolarity to pregnancy in
what Elaine Scarry calls the "phenomenon of emergence." Human reproduction, she argues, "entails the incorporation of God's disembodied word
into the human body. . . . iteration and repetition is the most elemental form
of substantiating the thing (existence, presence, aliveness, realness) that is repeated."[13] In this repetition, the body not only substantiates itself, but also
substantiates something beyond itself. While pregnancy exemplifies God's
presence by rehearsing the original creation, birth (or "delivery") represents
the epistolary moment that captures the instance of conversion when the soul
is materialized in palpable signs.

A perceived iteration of its mother, moreover, the newborn infant was
"stamp[ed] [with] the character of the thing imagined at the moment of conception," as the anonymous author of the popular medical treatise *Aristotle's
Master-piece* insisted. Since the brain (called the "Intelligent Principle" or
soul) was the "instrument of *conception* . . . without the intervention of matter," and since the uterus was "the brain or instrument of *conception* in Nature," the child was seen as an embodiment of the mother's mind. The suckling child continued to serve as a template for maternal sensibility after birth,
for as Scottish philosopher Lord Kames states, "[E]ven upon the breast, infants are susceptible of impressions: and the mother hath opportunities without end of instilling into them good [or bad] principles." Like letters that embody religious sensibility, babies thus carried the amniotic "watermark" of
their mothers, for "the generation of Things in Nature and the generation of
things in Art take place in the same way," wrote anatomist William Harvey.
"Both are first moved by some conceived form which is immaterial and is
produced by conception."[14] Materializing the moment of spiritual rebirth
when invisible emotions become outwardly evident, childbirth and letter writing made the soul readable.

Pregnancy, however, was understood as pathological in the eighteenth century. According to historian Susan Klepp, it was diagnosed as "lost, hidden,
obstructed, or suppressed menses" and a "coldness of the outward parts"
when "the belly waxeth flat." And too often pregnancy was misdiagnosed as
hysteria, pleurisy, rheumatism, worms, and intestinal parasites.[15] Accompa-

nied by amenorrhea (called "taking a cold"), pregnancy signaled an ob-
struction of blood (the hot humor) that needed to be purged to restore the
body's balance. The body—specifically the pregnant body—was understood
and experienced in its historical and cultural moment rather than as a tran-
scendent biological given. The intersecting discourses of humoralism, neu-
rology, and epistolarity, therefore, defined embodiment in the eighteenth century, and were imbricated in the evangelical manifestations of sensibility in
the early modern "doctrine of signatures."[16]

Based on what herbalist Nicholas Culpepper called "sympathy cures" (or
"cure by assimilate"), "the doctrine of signatures" naturalized the humoral
connections between the cosmos and the body, where plants and animals,
generated under the influence of particular planets, were accordingly marked
by natural signs indicating their medicinal use, treating like with like. "There
is a way to cure diseases sometimes by Sympathy," he argues, "and so every
planet cures his own disease as the Sun and Moon by their Herbs cure the
Eyes, Saturn the Spleen, Jupiter the Liver, Mars the Gall and diseases of
Choler, and Venus diseases in the Instruments of Generation." While the pu-
trefied flowers of St. John's Wort resembled blood and consequently healed
wounds, for example, yellow flowers such as saffron and turmeric relieved
jaundice. A physiological practice that offered a "lecture on Divinity" proving the existence of God, the doctrine of signatures reiterated the humoral
construction of the evangelical saint's fluid body, where scriptural milk was
ingested to purify the body and substantiate the moment of grace.[17]

Textualizing humoral medicine, letter writing imitated the doctrine of signatures (also called "theory of correspondence") in its curative functions. As
Esther Burr illustrates in her epistolary journal, writing letters brought "such
Corruptions to our sight as we never mistrusted we had there" by drawing
unholy humors to the paper's readable surface. Reciprocally, receiving letters "did good like a medicin," offering cordials that accordingly "cheer[ed]
the mind, strengthen[ed] the heart, and refresh[ed] the spirits thereof, being
decayed." A semiotic language of the body where signs (also called symptoms) were comprised of tangible signifiers (trembling, panting, groaning,
and fainting) that pointed toward internal conditions (temperature, humors,
blood vessels, nerves), letters created a sympathetic "theory of correspondence." "A person may tell very soon, the [tem]per of mind you was in when
you wrote such passages," remarks Esther Burr; "your *pen* describes your
Temper [ex]actly." Reading letters, therefore, was like diagnosing diseases,
where symptoms were marks "that point to something beyond itself, but
often obscurely, as some difficult pathological allegory."[18] As allegories (from
the Greek *allos,* "other" and *agoreuein,* "to speak"), women's letters materialized conversation and amplified the virtues and vices of the heart.

Mimicking the fragmentary and improvisational rhetorical style of evangelical preaching in her quickly written, colloquial journal epistles, Esther
Burr manifested the bodily effects of the spiritual affections on paper.

According to Jonathan Edwards, these signs included "trembling, groaning, being sick, crying out, panting, and fainting....they are fit and suitable figures to represent the high degree of those spiritual affections, which the Spirit of God makes use of them to represent."[19] Such symptoms of spiritual embodiment also resembled the signs of impregnation: a sudden sense of sickness or unexpected bout of shivering, for example, indicated conception had occurred, for the invisible stages of gestation taking place within the woman's interior could only be observed in its outward magnification of her physique. Esther Burr elliptically portrayed her pregnancy as *"all things considered,"* "women in my circumstances," and "with child" until she "was unexpectedly *delivered* of a Son."[20] Such euphemisms repeat the pattern of the humbled supplicant awaiting *deliverance,* which would come suddenly to the unprepared. For Burr, childbirth was analogous to the evangelical moment when Flesh became Word.

In eighteenth-century medical discourse, pregnancy was described in three stages which mimicked writing: the first stage, impregnation, represented the epistolary desire for self-expression, when the mind (metaphorically linked to the uterus) first conceived an idea.[21] The second stage, ensoulment, embodied the pregnant woman's burgeoning language, where she first felt movement (i.e., the soul's "quickening") in her "swollen belly" in the third to fifth month of pregnancy. And the final stage, birth, was the soul's emergence from the womb's darkness. The moment of *delivery* (like "writing to the moment" in letters) was rhetorically described as instantaneous. Spiritual awakening, or "the new birth," therefore imitated natural birth—"when the rational soul is first infused, the foetus immediately upon it becomes a living creature ... that before had no life." The converted mother would become, according to Jonathan Edwards, a "new creature; new, not only within, but without ... in spirit, soul and body; ... they have new hearts, and new eyes, new ears, new tongues, new hands, new feet."[22]

Aestheticized by the feminization of sensibility and the discourse of pregnancy, letter writing was considered by moralist John Bennett "an office particularly suited to the liveliness of [women's] fancy and the sensibility of [their] hearts." Women's bodies were inextricably embedded in their handwritten scripts, which were anthropomorphically called "hands." The "Italian hand," for example, particularly embodied a woman's fragile nervous system and tender sensibility, for it was considered a "tender" and "delicate" derivative of businessmen's "basic running hand." Soft, delicate, and small organs, coupled with cold, moist, and humid cellular tissues, thus granted women a neurological susceptibility to sensation. With women's distinctly refined sensibility, penmanship provided an iconic outlet for the female heart: "[O]ut of the abundance of the heart the mouth speaks," wrote Esther Burr. As "conversations upon paper between two friends at a distance," letters made permanent and material through pen and ink otherwise ephemeral speech acts. Describing her pen as a synonym for her mouth, Burr revises her earlier statement: "[O]ut of the abundance of the heart my pen has spoken." The pen, therefore, was not only an instrument of her voice, but also a metonym for it: "This *pen thinks it* has talked enough I beleive by the actions of it."[23]

As Elaine Scarry argues, a handmade artifact is a projection of the human body that contains "within its interior a material record of the nature of human sentience out of which it" was made. Alphabetic "characters" of handwritten letters manifested the moral character of the writer. In his dictionary, Samuel Johnson defined "character" as "a mark; a stamp; a representation; especially something written or inscribed; an outward or visible sign" of the invisible. Fulfilling Scarry's second characteristic of embodied artifacts, letters maintained the bodily capacities and needs (rather than concrete shapes or mechanisms of a particular body part). Esther Burr called letters the "natural breathings of the soul," as they mimicked the sympathetic nervous system where pulse and respiration were part of the "Actions and Passions almost of all the Parts of the whole Body, which belong to the involuntary Function."[24] The heart was the "seat and function of life, of heat, of spirits, of pulse and respiration ... and the seat and organ of the affections." And, its dilations and contractions could "stir and command the humors of the body." Imitating the circulation of the blood to and from the heart (which anatomist William Harvey called "the circle of perfection"), letters finally illustrate what Scarry sees as the reciprocal function of embodiment: "[T]he interchange of inside and outside surfaces requires not the literal reversal of bodily linings but the making of what is originally interior and private into something exterior and sharable."[25]

Externalizing what is originally interior and private, letters followed early modern diagnostic techniques that treated internal ailments with external cures. Without stethoscopes, thermometers, or even simple techniques of palpation, Esther Burr and her contemporaries depended on the ancient theory of humors to diagnose ailments of the body and soul. As Robert Dodsley insists in *Economy of Human Life* (1750), "sickness of the body affecteth even the soul." Because pregnancy caused a "disruption, disturbance, or imbalance of bodily humors"—particularly blood—it, too, was treated as a disease. "Heroic measures," including phlebotomy, festering (i.e., plasters and blisters), vomiting, and purging were consequently prescribed. "While vomits were more dangerous for women than men, especially such as are either with child, or subject to fits of the mother," according to herbalist Nicholas Culpepper's *Complete Herbal*, purging could draw out humors from the most remote parts of the body.[26] Mimicking menstruation (the "customary discharge"), bloodletting thus restored the sanguine humors. Because blood flowed through the heart—the locus of the spiritual affections—the absence of menstrual blood flow was both pathologically and morally suspect. And because the humors were circulated through the hollow nerves and blood vessels, tonics and cordials were accordingly ingested to stimulate or sedate the nerves. Humoral medicine thus emptied the body of excessive (called "putrid") fluids, while solidistic remedies poured fluids back into the ailing body to restore balance. Administered together, humoral and solidistic medicine comprised the "doctrine of signatures" that controlled the sympathetic nervous system.

As a "theory of correspondence," letter-writing thus offered a spiritual purge of pent-up emotions and an accompanying cordial to Esther Burr during pregnancy, nursing, and weaning: "I was quite overcome with reading the peteculars of your late Illness," she explains, "so that I was obliged to break off several times in the middest of reading *to give vent to my Passions.*" "To spill the spleen, to raise the spirits and invigorate animal Nature," replied Sarah Prince, "it exceeds the Prescriptions of the best Phisicians." The spleen was understood as a ductless organ that filters the blood and stores red blood cells "by dividing from it the dark and dreggy and melancholy Parts."[27] It refined the blood, making it "splendid, pure, and active." And it purified the heart, which was located between the brain and the liver and thus "wrought upon by reason, as well as by digestion." As the seat of the affections that "cherished life throughout the body," the heart would then circulate the elutriated blood and restore reason (i.e., the God-given faculty for knowing the truth). Since the spleen presumably lacked a natural vent for its bilious humors, doctors (like correspondents pouring out feelings) would administer purgatives to cleanse the foul humors from the body. Lacking a natural vent for religious expression, evangelical women employed letters as heroic measures.

Burr preferred letters as the superlative cordial: "O how refreshing is good news from such a friend—Tis a Cordial." She drinks Prince's words to uplift her melancholy spirit: "For my comfort and refreshment I received your No. 18....It did me good like a medicen." Letters, she believed, did her "more good than ever a Cordial did when [she] was faint." Like a physician who would utilize restorative cordials to rebalance the body's humors, Burr and Prince found the appropriate cures in their epistolary "doctrine of signatures." Letters, therefore, "cured by the assimilate": "As *Face* answers to *Face*," writes Esther Burr, "so does the *heart* of a *friend* to a *frien*d."[28]

Four months pregnant with her daughter Sally in December 1753, Burr describes herself to Sarah Prince as "more Fleshey an[d] Fresh than ever you saw me in your life." "*Carnal, fleshly, Worldly minded, and Devilish,*" Burr somatically characterizes her soul, for "what the Scripture calls carnal or fleshly, have their seat as much in the soul, as those properties that are called spiritual." Complaining that she is "confined with the Hysterick-Cholick" while pregnant with her son Aaron, suffering from "as bad a pain in [her] Head and stomach as almost ever [she] had in [her] life," Burr ultimately finds her maternal responsibilities after his birth more restrictive. For then she wrote "with the Son at the Brest," lamenting "when I had but one Child my hands were tied, but now I am tied hand and foot. (How I shall get along when I have got 1/2 dzn. or 10 children I cant devise)." To make matters worse, frequent nursing sometimes caused irritating canker sores on her breasts: "A very good layingin till about 3 weeks, then I had the Canker very bad." Seeking more time for her religious and social obligations, moreover, Burr "rode out to see if I could get a good carefull Nurse to take the Son two or three days and was succeded and have got the best Woman in Town for that purpose to late it and suckle it," only to find herself "Weaning Aaron and he makes a great Noise about it so cant add" to her journal entry. Realizing her preoccupation with maternal affairs, Burr apologizes to unmarried and childless Sarah Prince: "Theirs a Mother for you—. . . . I am affraid of giving you two large a dose of Husband and child."[29] Replete with details of pregnancy, childbirth, lactation, and weaning, Burr's epistolary journal locates the corruptions and health of her soul in her pregnant body.

Complaining about periodic feelings of barrenness, thrilled at the sensations of movement after fetal ensoulment, and awaiting the blessed moment of delivery, Esther Burr measures her own progress toward spiritual perfectibility through the stages of pregnancy. Although pregnancy was considered pathological, she welcomed it as a God-given trial, for as Reverend Benjamin Colman suggested to the female members of his congregation: "Women's natural Tenderness of Spirit and Retiredness from the Cares and Snares of the World; so more especially in your Multiplied Sorrows the curse pronounc'd upon our first Mother Eve, turned into the greatest blessing to your Soul." Being pregnant meant having the "seeds of [God's] grace in your hearts, and [the power] to bring forth the fruits of grace" to others. Pregnancy was interpreted as a God-given opportunity to display one's spiritual fortitude under physical distress, for she remarks: "I find I was not settled till I had a Child."[30]

Burr's empirical understanding of pregnancy relies on the theory of fungible fluids that governed women's bodies and letters—particularly the fluent poetics of blood and milk. Though menstruation was described as putrid blood that was sloughed off, extraneous, superfluous, foul and unclean, and though pregnant women were periodically bled to purge the retentive humor, blood ironically signified a state of life-affirming purity, for it was transformed into "seed" for reproduction. As physician Thomas Cogan suggested in the *Haven of Health*, "There is left some part of the profitable bloud" after digestion, moreover, which was "ordeyned by nature for procreation which . . . is woenderfullie conveighed and carried to the genitories, where by their proper nature that which before was plaine bloud, is now transformed and changed into seed." In this Aristotelian one-seed theory, *sperma* and *catemenia* refer to greater or lesser refinements of an ungendered blood, where the male contribution is slightly more valued than the female ejaculate. "The thicker, whiter, frothier quality of the male semen is a hint that it is more powerful, more likely to act as the efficient cause, than the thinner, less pristinely white, and more watery female ejaculate or the still red, even less concocted menstrua," according to Thomas Laqueur. "Like reproductive organs," he continues, "reproductive fluids turn out to be versions of each other; they are the biological articulation, in the language of a one-sex body, of the politics of two genders and ultimately of engendering."[31]

Milk represented God's healing Word during the Great Awakening. Just as the preacher nourished his congregation with the "sincere Milk of the Word," so a nursing mother provided nutrients to her infant. Because breast milk was associated with an elutriated state of heated blood, it was also administered to adults to soothe distempers ranging from eyesores, earaches, and gout to kidney ailments, consumption, and hysteria. Orally ingested or externally applied to the skin as part of a blister or plaster mixture, breast milk was vital to the early modern doctrine of signatures. It was given to pregnant women to alleviate the symptoms of "hysteric-cholick" ranging from a lump rising in the throat and something running up and down her legs to pains in the head, eyes, or ears. It was administered as a cordial during childbirth to induce a speedy delivery and to relieve pain. And it was imbibed after childbirth to restore the body's humors and ward off postpartum melancholy. With recurring symptoms of "hysteric-cholick" seven weeks after Aaron's birth, Burr complained: "I have got a very bad Cold and very soar Eyes which makes it very diffecult for me to write at all. Some times I am almost blind....I must lay down my pen a little while to recover my sight." Though postpartum melancholy was one "the *slow* and *lasting* Passions of women which bring on *chronical* Diseases, as we see in Grief," according to Dr. George Cheyne's *Essay on Health and Long Life* (1724), Burr believed that "*preventing* or *calming* the Passions themselves, is the Business, not of Physick, but *Virtue* and *Religion*."[32] Like nursing, religion cured the postpartum body, for breast milk was not only meliorative, but also a sign of godliness as it contained and disseminated God's spirit.

Moving from the pregnant womb to the postpartum breast, breast milk corresponded with the sympathetic nervous system. Although physicians knew that epigastric vessels going to the breast did not originate in the uterine vessels, they nonetheless linked breast milk to menstruation: "And is it not the same blood," asked one medical writer, "which, having been in the womb, is now in the breasts, whitened by the vital spirit through its natural warmth?" Considered "the common Sink of the body" that eliminated bad humors through menstruation, the uterus, according to *Aristotle's Masterpiece,* was specifically linked to the brain, liver, and heart. These organs, in turn, were responsible for the movements of the tripartite soul: natural spirits moved from the brain via the nerves; vital spirits left the heart through the arteries; and animal spirits were dispersed from the liver in the veins. Mysteriously moving from the womb to the breasts, a mother's milk followed the same "circle of perfection" that William Harvey noticed in the blood as the spirits move in a circle and communicate life, function, and consistency in the human body. Breast milk—or whitened blood stored near the heart—

was likewise "warm, perfect, vapourous, full of spirit ... and ameliorative ... [it] nourished, cherished, and quickened" other body parts through the doctrine of signatures.[33]

Although evangelical conversion required a woman to have "some sense of [her] own utter innability to do anything for [her]self and [her] whole dependence on God alone" by emptying her heart of earthly concerns and desires, a barren woman was considered incapable of receiving the seed of God's grace. Unlike the liminal states of the holy bride or pregnant wife that signified sanctification in evangelical iconography, a barren woman not only lacked the transformational power of gestation, but also its discursive correlative in language. "*Barrenness* possess me *wholy*," writes Esther Burr, "I have *nothing* to say any more than a *Dumb* Man, or an *Irrational Beast*." Because conversion depended on receiving the Scripture as restorative milk, and because Esther Burr had not yet received God's grace, she consequently experienced spiritual barrenness as linguistic lack. "But O my barrenness, unfruitfulness, under all the precious privileges I have injoied my whol Life!" she writes. "I am amazed at my barrenness under such advantages!"[34] Burr feels "dead whiles [she] lives," interpreting her barrenness as the absence of the "positive signs" of grace, for only the peace of God, the joy of believing, the light of knowledge of God's glory in Christ, and the love of God in the heart signified the presence of the divine spirit.

While skeptics claimed that evangelical sensibility degenerated into "enthusiasm"—or what Samuel Johnson called "the violence of passion," as "Sense grown diseas'd, and Reason mad"—Burr believed that the absence of ecstatic symptoms signified a diseased soul and a dead spirit. Though critics saw evangelical conversion as an infectious epidemic, Esther Burr considered it a cure to her spiritual apathy: "[B]ut I have great reason to complain of deadness and coldness under the precens of grace," she complains. "I did not feel alive in God's service. . . . But I am dead whiles I live!" "[Cold] and Dead as a stone," Esther Burr describes the state of amenhorrea before the fetus was "quickened" and before the blood was transformed into warm breast milk. Describing her spiritual progress in gestational terms, she concludes, "I am apt to think that the *indifferance* I feel ... arises from some bodily disorder, and a degree of low spiritedness."[35]

The absence of feeling and the sensation of coldness before fetal ensoulment corresponded to the regulating temperatures of the bodily humors that stimulated fecundity or sterility. While James McMath's *The Expert Midwife* (1694) contended that "*Sterility* happens likewise, from the Womans Disgust, and Satiety of the Venereal Embrace; or her dulness and insensibility therein," Nicholas Culpepper's *A Directory for Midwives* (1656) remarked that "Want of Love between man and wife, is another cause of Barrenness." Sexual desire, therefore, was understood in Galenic terms, whereby barrenness was caused by an imbalance in the body's humors (blood, phlegm, yellow bile, black bile) and its corresponding passions (sanguine, phlegmatic, choleric, melancholic). Heat and moisture prompted sensuality; coolness and dryness (called "slippery womb" in the woman) caused melancholy; blood and the sanguine complexion stirred feelings of love. Too much or too little desire affected the blood's temperature and refinement for conception to occur. Esther Burr's coldness, therefore, paralleled the misogynist theories of conception, where female orgasm was no longer requisite for impregnation after the rise of domesticity in the eighteenth century. Subsequently linked with conjugal affection and fidelity, fertilization became a "miniaturized version of monogamous marriage, where the animalcule/husband managed to get through the single opening of the egg/wife, which then closed and 'did not allow another worm to enter.' "[36] Female infertility (analogous to adultery) was considered the penalty for sexual frigidity or concupiscence. Barrenness, resulting from unholy and unnatural passions, was a sign of God's disfavor.

Remedies for infertility relied on the empiricism of the Paraclesean "doctrine of signatures," where herbal concoctions for this malady linked sexuality to the natural world: "Savin had the signature of the veins of the matrix or womb; the kernels of fistick nut the signature of testicles; the bulbous root of satyrion suggested a power to provoke lust, the lank root to abate it; cotton seeds, by their numbers, to increase the seeds of generation." Should these cures fail, aphrodisiacs were recommended. Men and women alike were given eringo (candied sea holly) and dragon's blood (resin) to warm their cool, moist humors and improve their fecundity. But if conception failed to follow copulation, the blame fell exclusively on the woman. Old wives' remedies were then recommended to her. Sitting over hot fumes of catmint, drinking concoctions of dried and powdered hare wombs, using the oil of mandrakes, and following in "the shadow of a strong lusty fruitful woman ... [would] attract the strength and fruitfulness of the other."[37]

While epigenetic notions of procreation (i.e., that all parts of the new creation developed simultaneously) dominated embryological thought until the sixteenth century and were revitalized again by the end of the eighteenth, the preformationist school (i.e., that a miniature embryonic life was already in place within the parent) prevailed during the Enlightenment.[38] Preformationists were divided between ovists (who claimed the small being existed in the mother's egg) and the animalculists (who argued it existed in the father's sperm, reducing the ovaries to the passive role of nourishing the dropped semen or denying their existence altogether): "By its very nature the uterus is the field for growing the seeds, that is to say the ova, sown upon it. Here the eggs are fostered, and here the parts of the living [foetus], when they have further unfolded, become manifest and are made strong. Yet although it has been cast off by the mother and sown, the egg is weak and powerless and so requires the energy of the semen of the male to initiate its growth." Together, the ovists and animalculists presented conception as the enlargement of what was already there. Preformationists, therefore, held that formation of each new being took place through the activities of the soul or spirit in the parent's body.

According to Preformationists, then, a mother's imagination was a potent force "which operates as a sort of seal stamping the image of the mother's fancy on the child she has conceived in the womb." Since the brain was sympathetically linked to the uterus, and because the soul was located in the brain, "conception" was both physiological and ephemeral. The child's body, like a handwritten epistle, thus materialized the mother's ineffable soul and made it readily available to scrutiny after birth. Esther Burr, for example, sees her daughter Sally as her "*own most tender self.*" Lamenting the difficulty of requisite corporal punishment for her daughter, she admits, "I confess I never had a right idea of a mothers heart as such a time before." Learning the true state of the maternal heart, Burr likewise gets a glimpse of her own soul through Sally. Concerned with the crookedness of her young daughter's neck and that "as she grows it will be a great deformity," she surmises God "forsaw that we should be two Proud of her, and so he has sent this calamaty to mortify us and her....It is best to be just as God pleases, if we could but think so all would be well."[39] Anticipating Esther's proud maternal spirit, God formed Sally accordingly.

The woman's gendered passivity and receptivity in procreation thus provided the perfect model for spiritual impregnation during the Great Awakening revivals. "I hope I felt a little more alive than I do commonly, but O my deadness!" complains Esther Burr: "See if the Lord wont [p]leas of his mercy send so[m]e quickning and inlivening word that sh[al]l awake me ou[t] of this death." Since the quickened fetus represented the promise of new life, to be pregnant meant to be full of spirit. Esther Burr, moreover, emphasized the material and immaterial contributions to embodiment in the corporeal nature of epistolarity, as she writes to Sarah Prince, "I rejoice with you my dear that you have found the Lord to be with you of a truth, and that you have experienced so much of his loving kindness to your soul, and have had his enlivneing and quickning presence." Letters approximated the moment of grace in their immediacy, and they imitated the movements of the sympathetic nervous system that spread elutriated blood to the other body parts. Linking the brain, the heart, and the uterus, women's letters thus signified the fungibility of that elutriated blood that transformed menstrua into nourishing milk. A metonym for the evangelical woman's body during sanctification, letters thus inscribed the procreative moment and the instant of ensoulment. "O Lord *quicken* me by thy unerring grace," beseeches Esther Burr. "God of his infinite mercy grant that I may be *quickned* by your surprizing example." Like a long-awaited letter from her faithful correspondent Sarah Prince that would "*quicken* [her] with God's unerring grace," Esther Burr anticipates her own rebirth, running "everytime the stage passes [her] Door, hoping for a pacquit from [her] dear Fidelia but none yet."[40]

The moment of birth was the final and complete realization of grace. Describing her delivery of Aaron, Burr laments that it had "pleased God in infinite wisdom so to order it that Mr Burr was from home....It seemd very gloomy when I found I was actually in Labour to think that I was, as it were, destitute of Earthly friends—No Mother—No Husband and none of my petecular friends that belong to this Town, they happening to be out of Town." Lonely and afraid, Burr anticipates deliverance as a humble supplicant awaiting the infusion of God's grace. Necessarily mortified, she was ready for the "New Birth," for to achieve sanctification, one must "depend wholy on God, and not on an Arm of flesh! [For] God is able to bring *sweetness* out of this exceding *bitterness*." Without her friends and family during her laying-in, Burr turned completely to God, who became a surrogate mother who was "all to me in the Hour of my distress" when she "was unexpectedly delivered of a [premature] Son." Like John Winthrop who humbled himself before God with "neither power nor will, so [he] became as a *weaned* child," and like Jonathan Edwards who preached that "the heart is not truly *wean'd* from either [sin or self-righteousness] till grace is infused," Esther Burr confesses to Sarah Prince, "I am trying to be *weaned* from you my dear, ... but for the present it seems vain—I seem more atached to [you] then ever." Rather than a concoction of breast milk administered by an attending female at childbirth, Burr thus received the "sincere Milk of God's Word," for during labour, "those words of the Psalms were [her] support and comfort thro' the whole. *They that trust in the Lord shall be as Mount Zion that cannot be mooved but abideth for ever—* and these also, *As the Mountains are found about Jerusalem so is the Lord to them that put their trust in him,* or words to that purpose."[41]

Remembering the Psalms during childbirth, Esther Burr reiterates the importance of the scriptural Word as the primary impetus for conversion during the Great Awakening.[42] Quoting liberally from Isaac Watts's *Psalms* throughout her epistolary journal, Burr ultimately appreciates their aesthetic merits in connection with pregnancy and childbirth. And she sees psalms as a poetic medium in which women excel, for her favorite female psalmist was English epistoler Elizabeth Singer Rowe.[43] The reproductive value of the psalms that multiplied and spread evangelical spirit, coupled with the feminine iconography of pregnant and nursing mothers administering the Milk of God's Word, left Burr imagining the possibility of "she [Elizabeth Rowe] and Doct Watts [getting] together and [having] one Child [so] that [we] might see what they could do." Textualizing their child as a psalm, Esther Burr celebrates the corporeality of evangelical discourse that turned Flesh into Word. By framing the new psalm in the discourse of pregnancy and the New Birth, moreover, Burr exemplifies the feminization of religion and the cultural liminality that authorized women's emergence into written language during the Great Awakening. Evangelicalism feminized the Word, for real women transformed the moment of "delivery" into the epistolary moment that was equally unmediated.

Notes

I thank my colleagues, Marian Eide and Chris Holcomb, for their generous comments on this chapter.

Born in Northampton, Massachusetts, on February 13, 1732, to Sarah Pierpont and Great Awakening revivalist Jonathan Edwards, Esther Edwards Burr descended from influential first-generation Puritan ministers Thomas Hooker and Solomon Stoddard. In 1752, she married Aaron Burr, minister and president of the Presbyterian College of New Jersey, giving birth to daughter Sally in 1754 and son Aaron (who famously shot Alexander Hamilton) in 1756. Like her father, Burr died from a smallpox inoculation in 1758.

1. Marylynn Salmon, "The Cultural Significance of Breastfeeding and Infant Care in Early Modern England and America," *Journal of Social History* (1994): 249, 253. See also Paula A. Treckel, "Breastfeeding and Maternal Sexuality in Colonial America," *Journal of Interdisciplinary History* 20 (1989): 25–51.

2. David Leverenz, *The Language of Puritan Feeling: An Exploration in Literature, Psychology, and Social History* (New Brunswick, N.J.: Rutgers University Press, 1980), 1. For an iconographical history of the feminization of Christianity, see Caroline Walker Bynum, *Holy Feast and Holy Fast: The Religious Significance of Food to Medieval Women* (Berkeley: University of California Press, 1990); and Susan Juster, *Disorderly Women: Sexual Politics and Evangelicalism in Revolutionary New England* (Ithaca, N.Y.: Cornell University Press, 1994).

3. Thomas Laqueur, *Making Sex: Body and Gender from the Greeks to Freud* (Cambridge, Mass.: Harvard University Press, 1990), 8.

4. Laqueur, *Making Sex*, 35. As he points out, however, the eighteenth century also ushered in what we know as modern sex and gender configurations, where sex was based on discernible, biological difference. The female body that was considered a lesser version of the male's in the one-sex model now became its incommensurable opposite in the two-sex model. Female organs that were seen as derivative and interior versions of the male's exterior organs now were construed to be of an entirely different nature. And physiological processes (such as menstruation and lactation) which had been imagined as part of the common economy of fluids became specific to women alone. While sexual difference within the one-sex model was completely rhetorical, dependent upon the cultural (i.e., gendered) positions and roles men and women performed in society, two sexes were invented as a new foundation of gender in the two-sex model. The language of biology, however, was inextricably embedded in the well-defined language of gender. Existing simultaneously, both models of sex were nonetheless situational, explicable only within the context of gender and power.

5. Laqueur, *Making Sex*, 103–7; Juster, *Disorderly Women*, 52.

6. Carol Karlsen and Laurie Crumpacker, eds., *The Journal of Esther Edwards Burr, 1754–1757* (New Haven, Conn.: Yale University Press, 1984), 111, 112, 307; Charles Chauncy, "Enthusiasm Described," quoted in Juster, *Disorderly Women*, 31.

7. Alexander Garden, "Regeneration and the Testimony of the Spirit," quoted in Juster, *Disorderly Women*, 28.

8. Karlsen and Crumpacker, *Journal of Esther Edwards Burr*, 61; Isabelle Howard, Countess of Carlisle (1721–1795), *Rudiments of Taste* (1789), and Letter 7 in *Lady's Pocket Library* (Philadelphia: Matthew Carey, 1797), 195–96; David Lovejoy, *Religious Enthusiasm in the New World: Heresy to Revolution* (Cambridge, Mass.: Harvard University Press, 1985), 181–82; Hugh Blair, "On Epistolary Writing," Lecture 38, *Lectures in Rhetoric and Belles Lettres*, 3 vols., 2nd ed. (London: Strahan & Cadell, 1785), 67.

9. While Juster particularly focuses on the Baptists during the Great Awakening, I find her four-pronged definition of evangelicalism as a theological position and liturgical style useful for my argument: an insistence on the primacy of the relationship of the individual to God; lay supremacy within the meetinghouse; unfettered congregational autonomy among local churches; and a language of religious pietism or emotional fervor.

10. George Whitefield, *Journals* (London: Banner of Truth Trust, 1960), 347; Karlsen and Crumpacker, *Journal of Esther Edwards Burr,* 59.

11. Ann Kibbey, *The Interpretation of Material Shapes in Puritanism: A Study of Rhetoric, Prejudice, and Violence* (New York: Cambridge University Press, 1986), 6–8; Charles Lloyd Cohen, *God's Caress: The Psychology of Puritan Religious Experience* (New York: Oxford University Press, 1986), 19, n. 37; Karlsen and Crumpacker, *Journal of Esther Edwards Burr,* 113, 240.

12. According to Jonathan Edwards: "In the month of March the people of New Hadley seemed to be *seized* with a deep concern about their salvation, and as it were at *once,* which has continued [*to spread*] in a *very great degree* ever since. About the same time there began to *appear* the like concern in the west part of Suffield, which has since *spread into all the parts of town.* It next began to appear at Sunderland, and soon became *universal, and to a very great degree.* About the same time it began to *appear* in part of Deerfield, called Green River, and since *has filled the town.* It began to *appear* also at a *part* of Hatfield, and after that the *whole town* in the second week of April seemed to be *seized* at once, and theire is a great and general concern there." Quoted in *American Literature,* ed. Elliot Emory et al. (Englewood Cliffs, N.J.: Prentice Hall, 1991), 312–13.

13. Elaine Scarry, *The Body in Pain: The Making and Unmaking of the World* (New York: Oxford University Press, 1985), 193.

14. *Aristotle's Masterpiece Completed in Two Parts* (New York: Company of Flying Stationers, 1793), 39; Lord Kames, *Six Sketches on the History of Man* (Philadelphia: R. Bell, 1776), 252–3; William Harvey, *Disputations,* quoted in Laqueur, *Making Sex,* 147. Luce Irigary argues that the amniotic fluid that protects and suspends the baby inside the mother's womb leaves a permanent "water mark" upon the child even after birth. *This Sex Which Is Not One* (Ithaca, N.Y.: Cornell University Press, 1985).

15. Susan Klepp, "Lost, Hidden, Obstructed, and Repressed: Contraceptive and Abortive Technology in the Early Delaware Valley," *Early American Technology: Making and Doing Things from the Colonial Era to 1850* (Chapel Hill: University of North Carolina Press for the Institute of Early American History and Culture, 1994), 77. Also see Susan Klepp, "Revolutionary Bodies: Women and the Fertility Transition in the Mid-Atlantic Region, 1760–1820," *Journal of American History* 85 (December 1998): 910–45. As Ilza Veith points out in *Hysteria: The History of a Disease* (Chicago: University of Chicago Press, 1965), pregnancy and hysteria—as diseases of the womb—were virtually indistinguishable ailments in the eighteenth century. See 126, 130, 132, 160–61.

16. My definition of the *lived* body follows Elizabeth Grosz's notion of "corporeal feminism" in *Volatile Bodies: Toward a Corporeal Feminism* (Bloomington: Indiana University Press, 1994). Her approach is particularly relevant to my argument since she, like early modern thinkers, resists the Western ontology that separates men and women, or the mind and body, into binaries that create a theory of gender.

17. Nicholas Culpepper, *The Complete Herbal and English Physician Enlarged* (London, 1653; reprint, Hertfordshire: Wordsworth Editions, 1995), viii; Angus McLaren, *Reproductive Rituals: The Perception of Fertility in England from the 16th to 19th Century* (New York: Methuen, 1984), 34.

18. Karlsen and Crumpacker, *Journal of Esther Edwards Burr,* 128, 189, 140. Bruce Clark and Wendell Aycock, *The Body and the Text: Comparative Essays in Literature and Medicine* (Lubbock: Texas Tech University Press, 1990), 2.

19. Jonathan Edwards, *Religious Affections,* ed. John E. Smith (New Haven, Conn.: Yale University Press, 1959), 135.

20. Although early modern folklore tried to determine the sex of the child before birth (for example, if the woman's right breast was firmer or her right eye was brighter, she was having a boy), an infant could only be adequately described after emerging from the hidden recesses of the mother's body. Contemporary theorist Julia Kristeva offers a useful frame for understanding the eighteenth-century euphemistic description of the pregnant (and fetal) body in what she calls a "poetics of invisibility" in "language that necessarily skims over from afar, allusively." Julia Kristeva, "Stabat Mater," *The Kristeva Reader,* ed. Toril Moi (New York: Columbia University Press, 1986), 162; Karlsen and Crumpacker, *Journal of Esther Edwards Burr,* 180, 188 (emphasis added), 177, 188–89.

21. In her influential essay, "The Laugh of the Medusa," theorist Hélène Cixous compares the stages of gestation with the desire to write. Located in the female body, this desire is "to live self from within, a desire for a swollen body, for language, for blood." Hélène Cixous, "The Laugh of the Medusa," in Elaine Marks and Isabelle de Courtivron, eds., *New French Feminisms* (New York: Schocken, 1980), 251. Like the early modern understanding of "conception" as an epistemological and biological power that wedded the womb and brain as organs of "generation," Cixous's theory likewise locates the creation of language in the pregnant and postpartum body.

22. In his preface to *Clarissa,* Samuel Richardson writes: "All the letters are written while the hearts of the writers must be supposed to be wholly engaged in their subjects ... with *instantaneous* descriptions and reflections." Quoted in Ian Watt, *The Rise of the Novel* (Berkeley: University of California Press, 1957), 192. Descriptions of the "New Birth" are quoted in Philip Greven, *The Protestant Temperament: Patterns of Child-Rearing, Religious Experience, and the Self in Early America* (New York: Knopf, 1977), 62.

23. Reverend John Bennett, *Letters to a Young Lady,* Letter 46, *The Lady's Pocket Library* (Philadelphia: Matthew Carey, 1797), 101. Quoted in Sylvana Tomaselli, "The Naturalized Female Intellect," *Science in Context* 5 (1992): 209–35. On Cartesianism, see Londa Schiebinger, *The Mind Has No Sex? Women and the Origins of Modern Science* (Cambridge, Mass.: Harvard University Press, 1989). For a discussion of colonial penmanship, see Tamara Thorton, *Handwriting in America: A Cultural History* (New Haven, Conn.: Yale University Press, 1996); Blair, "On Epistolary Writing," 67; Karlsen and Crumpacker, *Journal of Esther Edwards Burr,* 51, 106, 52.

24. Scarry, *The Body in Pain,* 282–85; Samuel Johnson, *A Dictionary of the English Language* (1755; reprint, London: Times Books, 1979); Karlsen and Crumpacker, *Journal of Esther Edwards Burr,* 80. Thomas Willis, *The Description and Use of the Nerves* (1681), rpt. in William Feindel, ed., *The Anatomy of the Brain and Nerves* (Montréal: McGill, 1965), 160.

25. Robert Burton, *The Anatomy of Melancholy,* trans. and ed. Floyd Dell and Paul Jordan-Smith (New York: Tudor Publishing Company, 1927), 153; Scarry, *The Body in Pain,* 284.

26. Robert Dodsley, *The Economy of Human Life* (London: R. Armstrong, 1751; reprint, Hawick: R. Armstrong, 1814), pt. 2, bk.5, 136–37; Culpepper, 583.

27. Karlsen and Crumpacker, *Journal of Esther Edwards Burr,* 212 (emphasis added), 280. Spleen reference quoted in Dustin Griffin, "Venting Spleen," *Essays in Criticism* 40 (1990): 125.

28. Karlsen and Crumpacker, *Journal of Esther Edwards Burr,* 138, 189, 55, 87.

29. Ibid., 287, 127, 181, 192, 189, 214, 258, 197.

30. Benjamin Colman in Nancy Cott, *The Bonds of Womanhood: "Women's Sphere" in New England, 1780–1835* (New Haven, Conn.: Yale University Press, 1977), 127–28; John Cotton (1655) quoted in Juster, *Disorderly Women,* 64; Karlsen and Crumpacker, *Journal of Esther Edwards Burr,* 101. See, too, 141, 155.

31. Thomas Cogan, *The Haven of Health* (London: Henric Middleton, 1584), 240; Laqueur, *Making Sex,* 38–39.

32. Salmon, "Cultural Significance of Breastfeeding," 249; Karlsen and Crumpacker, *Journal of Esther Edwards Burr,* 189; George Cheyne, *An Essay on Health and Long Life,* 8th ed. (London: Strahan and Leake, 1734), 169.

33. Treckel, "Breastfeeding and Maternal Sexuality," 26; William Harvey, *Du Mortu Cordis,* rpt. ed. Geoffrey Keynes (London: Nonesuch, 1653), 59.

34. Karlsen and Crumpacker, *Journal of Esther Edwards Burr,* 78, 81, 125, 177.

35. Evan Lloyd, *The Methodist: A Poem* (London: Printed for the author, 1766; reprint, Los Angeles: The Augustan Reprint Society, 1978), 13. Karlsen and Crumpacker, *Journal of Esther Edwards Burr,* 160, 165, 92.

36. Culpepper quoted in McLaren, *Reproductive Rituals,* 20–21. See Laqueur, *Making Sex,* 43–52, 172; and Angus McLaren, "The Pleasures of Procreation," in W. F. Bynum and Roy Porter, eds., *William Hunter and the Eighteenth-Century Medical World* (New York: Cambridge University Press, 1985), 323–41.

37. McLaren, *Reproductive Rituals,* 31–56.

38. See *Aristotle's Master-piece* in *The Works of Aristotle the Famous Philosopher* (New York: Arno Press, 1974), which had more than twenty-seven editions in colonial America before 1820. Roy Porter, "The Secrets of Generation Display'd: *Aristotle's Master-piece* in Eighteenth-Century England," *Eighteenth-Century Life* 11 (1985): 1–21; Janet Blackman, "Popular Theories of Generation: The Evolution of Aristotle's Works," in J. Woodward and D. Richards, eds., *Health Care and Popular Medicine in Nineteenth-Century England* (London: Croom Helm, 1977), 56–88; O. T. Beall, "*Aristotle's Master-piece* in America: A Landmark in the Folklore of Medicine," *William and Mary Quarterly* 20 (1963): 207–22.

39. McLaren, *Reproductive Rituals,* 50; Karlsen and Crumpacker, *Journal of Esther Edwards Burr,* 95, 133–34.

40. Karlsen and Crumpacker, *Journal of Esther Edwards Burr,* 61, 139, 66, 111, 112, 240 (emphasis added).

41. Ibid., 188–9, 137, 118, 188–89. On Burr's descriptions of the New Birth, see *Critical Essays on Jonathan Edwards,* 266. Salmon, "Cultural Significance of Breastfeeding," 253; Quoted in Conrad Cherry, "Conversion: Nature and Grace," *Critical Essays on Jonathan Edwards,* ed. William Scheick (Boston: G. K. Hall, 1980), 83.

42. For a brief description of the controversy of whether to use the Scottish Psalms or Isaac Watts's version of the Psalms in their New Light Presbyterian services, see Esther Burr's journal, 63–4 n. 30, 143 n. 9.

43. Applauding Elizabeth Rowe's contributions to epistolarity through her published letters, Burr writes: "I have been reading some of [Rowe's] Real Letters. They are very fine. I wish I could see and covers[e] with her." But she actually alludes to Rowe's famous *Letters from the Dead to the Living:* "She was, to my notion, hardly a mortal altho she did die. She seemed to live among the ded, and Angels and departed spirits" (Karlsen and Crumpacker, *Journal of Esther Edwards Burr,* 80).

III

BODIES IN PERFORMANCE: CORPOREAL MANIFESTATIONS OF IDENTITY

The Quakers Meeting, engraving by I. Bowles based on the painting by E. Van Heemskirk, Friends Historical Library of Swarthmore College.

Nursing Fathers and Brides of Christ
The Feminized Body of the Puritan Convert

Elizabeth Maddock Dillon

"Lord put these nibbles then my mouth into," wrote Edward Taylor in 1719, "And suckle me therewith I humbly pray,/Then with this milk thy Spirituall Babe I'st grow."[1] Describing himself metaphorically as an infant imbibing spiritual nourishment from God, Taylor employs surprisingly material, even anatomical terms here: suckling at the breast of God, nipples are thrust into his mouth. In another poem, however, Taylor shifts anatomical terms and describes his own breasts as dispensing milk. After first asking God to fill him with holy "perfumes" and cleanse his breasts, he then proposes to suckle others and dispense divine fluids: "Oh! let the Clouds of thy sweet Vapours rise,/And both my Mammularies Circumcise./Shall Spirits thus my Mammularies suck?/(As Witches Elves their teats)."[2] The strangeness of these images for the modern reader lies in their attribution of female anatomical characteristics to men—both to the male convert and to God—and in the explicitly physical and sexualized nature of this transgression of the physiological boundaries between sexed bodies.

Taylor's language is not unique among Puritans; while the materiality of his metaphors is a distinctive trait of his work, his meditations on the Canticles follow in the footsteps of a century of rhetoric describing the Puritan convert, both individually and collectively, as the Bride of Christ. John Cotton, for instance, preached repeatedly on the Canticles with a central focus on the Bride of Christ metaphor: "And looke what affection is between Husband and Wife, hath there been the like affection in your soules towards the Lord Jesus Christ? Have you a strong and hearty desire to meet him in the bed of loves, when ever you come to the Congregation, and desire you to have the seeds of his grace shed abroad in your hearts, and bring forth the fruits of grace to him, and desire that you may be for him, and for none other?"[3] Here the congregant becomes feminized; the bride receives the seed of Christ and becomes metaphorically impregnated by this seed. The language of this union is, much as in Taylor's case, both strikingly physical and sexual. Moreover, this imagery requires ascribing an odd morphological plasticity to the body of the male convert: it requires that the male Puritan convert discursively inhabit the shapes and forms of both male and female bodies.

The Bride of Christ image appears repeatedly in Puritan rhetoric, as does another cross-gendered image—that of "nursing fathers," usually used in reference to ministers who nourish the flock with their metaphorical milk. The Puritan rhetoric of the mutably-sexed body is striking precisely because it is so unusual in contemporary discourse, religious or otherwise. A shift in what we might call the dominant "cultural imaginary" has thus occurred such that images of men with female physical and sexual identities (breasts, invaginated bodies), which once had powerful currency, are now virtually unthinkable and incomprehensible.[4] The surprising feminization of the Puritan convert has been the subject of a great deal of critical analysis—Walter Hughes, Margaret Masson, Amanda Porterfield, and Ivy Schweitzer have all considered, often in quite opposing terms, the ways in which such language relates to Puritan notions of gender and sexuality.[5] In this essay, I am interested in pursuing the same inquiry but with a different emphasis: I am concerned with the representation of physical bodies rather than simply with gender roles. When Taylor writes, "The Soule's the Wombe. Christ is the Spermodote/And Saving Grace the seed cast thereinto,"[6] the metaphorics of conversion take insistent shape as bodily transformations. The gender-transgressing nature of these metaphors—in which a male convert describes himself as a womb receiving sperm—suggests that a far different understanding of the body is at stake in this period than that which obtains today. While current work on gender emphasizes its culturally constructed nature, much of this work nonetheless assumes that gender has historically been ideologically grounded in the static identity of the sexed body.[7] Calling into question the historical parameters of a fixedly sexed body thus calls into question, too, the very terms in which gender has been understood to be constructed in Puritan culture.

According to historians of the body such as Thomas Laqueur and Londa Schiebinger, a traditional Galenic model of sexual difference, which arrayed men and women hierarchically according to their degree of perfection, began to be replaced by a new model of binary biological difference in the eighteenth century.[8] In Laqueur's terms, the early model described the body as having one sex and many genders whereas the modern conception derives two genders from two essentially different sexes: "For thousands of years it had been a commonplace that women had the same genitals as men except that, as Nemesius, bishop of Emesa in the fourth century, put it: 'theirs are inside the body and not outside it.' Galen ... demonstrated at length that women were essentially men in whom a lack of vital heat—of perfection—had resulted in the retention, inside, of structures that in the male are visible without." On this model, then, the body is not inherently sexed: rather, the similarities between the bodies of men and women indicate a continuity of substance—a single sex that assumes a variety of forms. Yet, by the close of the eighteenth century, Laqueur argues, a binary system of sexed bodies replaces the single-sex model: "By around 1800, writers of all sorts were determined to base what they insisted were fundamental differences between the male and female sexes, and thus between man and woman, on discovering biological distinctions and to express these in a radically different rhetoric....Not only are the sexes different, but they are different in every conceivable aspect of body and soul, in every physical and moral aspect." Prior to the ascendancy of the two-sex model, then, sex did not stand as the material referent that guaranteed the truth of gender; only in the eighteenth-century did gender come to be understood as the expression of a biologically grounded identity.

Laqueur's argument suggests that premodern concepts of sex ascribed no ontological status to the sexed body. Prior to the shift to the two-sex model, "to be a man or a woman was to hold a social rank, a place in society, to assume a cultural role, not to be organically one or the other of two incommensurable sexes."[9] According to Laqueur, then, both sex *and* gender become cultural constructs or "roles," much as contemporary theorists have argued that gender itself is a culturally determined performance of identity. However, while sex may not have had an ontological status in this period, gender was not understood to be wholly without grounds as a result; rather, the grounds of gender were understood to be located elsewhere.

For the Puritans, for instance, gender was understood as grounded in the divine hierarchy of God rather than in the bodies of men and women. While the foundations of gender were not biological, gender and sex were nonetheless thoroughly fixed in a divinely ordained hierarchical order. Thus in the 1638 church trial of Anne Hutchinson, Hugh Peters contends that Hutchinson has failed to perform her gendered role: "You have stept out of your place, you have rather bine a Husband than a Wife and a preacher than a Hearer; and a magistrate than a subject."[10] While this statement from the trial is often cited as evidence of Puritan misogyny, it also indicates that Peters sees the relation of husband and wife as grounded in a fixed hierarchy that structures a series of social relations—the relation of preacher to congregant and judge to legal subject as well as husband and wife. For Peters, in other words, the relation between husband and wife is expressive of the truth of hierarchy itself rather than the truth of male and female bodies. Rather than functioning as the sign of biological sex, then, gender (as well as sex) was a sign of the order of the cosmos.

Dislodged from biological bodies, hierarchical identity was represented in the figures of sex and gender. As such, the body had a far more metaphorical status for the Puritans, and metaphors of sexed bodies emphasized relations of power more than physically grounded identities. Cotton Mather, for instance, in a 1719 sermon, shifts blithely from a series of feminizing tropes to describe man's submission to Christ to a series of masculine tropes advising husbands to exercise care over their wives. "In ONE WORD Resign they self unto Him; Resolve to be His; Engage to be For Him and not for another," urges Mather. "It is done! It is done! ... Rejoyce over her, O ye Heavens, for the Good that is done unto her," he concludes.[11] Yet he closes the sermon by urging the same men described here with the feminine pronoun to assume the masculine position of Christ toward their own wives: "Let the HUSBAND often consider; ... 'How kindly does my SAVIOUR speak unto His Church! Good words, Comfortable words!'"[12] As Mather's sermon indicates, gender was not insignificant; rather, it signified relations of authority and submission with little regard for fixed pronominal or bodily status.

Laqueur's description of the mutability of the body on the single-sex model nonetheless quite aptly describes the quality of much Puritan rhetoric of the body. "In the blood, semen, milk, and other fluids of the one-sex body," writes Laqueur, "there is no female and no sharp boundary between the sexes. Instead, a physiology of fungible fluids and corporeal flux represents in a different register the absence of specifically genital sex."[13] The flow of milk, "streames of Love,"[14] and showers of seed in these texts are indeed multidirectional and unmarked in relation to sexed bodies; as such, they have the effect of sexing and unsexing bodies at once.[15] Yet, Laqueur's description also points to one of the paradoxes of this sort of language for the understanding of gender: what does it mean to say that "there is no female" in this language? Does such a language eradicate sexual difference or does it eradicate women? More broadly, what is the relation between the one-sex body and the differentially gendered roles of Puritan society?

A series of critics have emphasized the paradoxical status of the feminized body of the male Puritan convert. While assuming a masculine role—as patriarch, as leader—within the family and society, the male convert assumes a feminine role—as receptive, sexually passive—with respect to God and Christ. Equally paradoxical, however, are the contradictory conclusions critics have deduced concerning gender roles among Puritans on the basis of this language. According to Amanda Porterfield, the language of "female piety" among Puritans emphasizes the role of women within Puritan society, and thus, despite insisting on passivity and suffering in this role, garners authority for women within the community: "[D]iscovery of the significance of female imagery in Puritan discussions of selfhood suggests that women were important participants in the Puritan movement."[16] For Porterfield, then, the feminizing language of Puritanism is one that finds a direct referent in the bodies of women in the community. Moreover, the emphasis on women's bodies in the rhetoric of conversion accrues importance to women within the culture. Margaret Masson, in contrast, reads the feminization of male converts as effecting the erasure of both sex and gender inequalities in Puritan society: "The New England Puritans ... were constrained from making a complete separation between the sexes because they used the norms of the female roles of bride and wife to describe the role of the regenerate Christian in relation to God.... Thus the Puritans would have to believe that nothing in the innate personalities of each sex prevented them, in certain specified circumstances, from adopting the behavior of the other."[17] In Masson's account, feminizing rhetoric speaks to the absence of essentialized concepts of both sex and gender. Disputing this view of the substitutability of male and female bodies for one another, Walter Hughes argues that the sexed, erotic language of the marriage covenant with Christ places the male convert in a position of "figurative homosexuality."[18] Whereas the female convert, such as Anne Bradstreet, could use her sexual relation with her husband as a model for an eroticized religious experience, Puritan men were unable to do the same without confronting unacceptable images of homosexuality. Hughes thus suggests that eroticized relations of grace were more easily accessible to Puritan women than men. However, Ivy Schweitzer argues precisely the opposite point. In a nuanced reading of Puritan semiosis, Schweitzer contends that the figurative language of a feminizing conversion must be read against (rather than together with) its literal referents. The process of conversion concerned spiritual rebirth, and thus entailed a "complete disjunction from one's human birth and life." Feminization served, then, as a masculine metaphor for absolute difference: assuming a feminized identity created a stark break with a secular, masculine identity. As such, writes Schweitzer, "identification with the characteristics of the mystical bride was, thus, significantly more disjunctive for males than for females."[19] Because this disjunction was not available to women as a metaphor of difference or rebirth, the rhetoric of feminized conversion implicitly excluded women from its purview.

The four readings of feminizing Puritan rhetoric cited here are substantially disjunctive as well: each analysis derives, from the same bodily rhetoric, a different understanding of the meaning and force of gendered identity in Puritan society. On the other hand, all of these analyses share in the methodological presupposition that a direct line can be drawn from the sexed body to a binary system of gender. It is this supposition that is indicative of a modern, rather than early- or premodern understanding of sex. If we cease to read this supposition backward in time—if we cease to take the body of the Puritan convert as the ground of Puritan ideas of gender—then the meaning of a feminizing Puritan rhetoric changes significantly. For instance, Hughes assumes that Taylor's sexualized language is obfuscating a homosexual panic. Taylor's repeated shifts in bodily figures, sexual metaphors, and sexed anatomies are read by Hughes as efforts to cover over and dispel anxiety incurred by imagining a male body (the convert) ravished by another male body (Christ): "[B]y articulating poetic bodies for both God and his own soul out of an endless variety of objects, Taylor not only overcomes his panic and awakens his desire; he ultimately blurs the distinctions of both gender and sexuality in imagining the relation between himself and God."[20] Yet, rather than read this blurring as an attempt to both enable and obscure figurations of homosexual desire, we might read this blurring and dispersal of sexuality across a multiply-sexed body as indicative of an early-modern understanding of the sexed body. Indeed, what is striking about the persistent use of the eroticized Bride of Christ tropology is the extent to which this language does not seem to induce anxiety or homosexual panic, but rather serves as a dominant, culturally accepted account of masculinity among Puritans.[21] Positing a dehiscence of the rigid correlation between sex and gender would also mean figures of female piety would not necessarily translate directly into the empowerment or disempowerment of those gendered female in the society. Thus while Schweitzer argues convincingly that sexualized rhetoric concerns the representation of difference, this difference might be understood as one that would not find its literal referent in the bodies of men and women. Rather, as a figure of difference, sexualized rhetoric might be used to articulate power differentials that did not necessarily inhere in bodies.

The contradictory readings of these critics indicate quite clearly that gender remains a vexed category for scholars of Puritan culture. The position of women in New England Puritanism has been described alternatively as one of extreme oppression and one of great opportunity.[22] However, focusing on the single-sex model of bodily identity, and thus emphasizing the mutable terms of Puritan bodily rhetoric, does not serve to resolve questions of gender identity in Puritan culture. Rather, this focus indicates the failure of the body to stand as the referent for this debate and thus tends to destabilize further our understanding of gender in this period. However, it is quite significant that the historical shift from the one-sex model of bodily identity to the two-sex model corresponds roughly to the period of Puritan cultural dominance and decline in New England. A reading of gender roles in relation to this shift suggests that elements of the instability of gender roles in this period might be understood to correspond to the shift in bodily identity over the same period. Thus while gender may not, then, be grounded in the body in Puritan rhetoric, it is, conversely, at odd moments ungrounded altogether in the shift from an older divine, hierarchical ontology to the two-sex bodily ontology of modernity.

On the cusp of the divide between modern and early-modern cultures, New England Puritanism looked forward and backward at once: ascriptive models of gender hierarchy that held women as subordinate to men went hand in hand with models of gender that implied certain forms of equality, such as the Puritan companionate marriage and the cultural emphasis on the covenant (in marriage as well as religion) itself. As John Winthrop argued in 1645, "The woman's own choice makes a man her husband; yet being so chosen, he is her lord, and she is to be subject to him, in a way of liberty, not of bondage; and a true wife accounts her subjection her honor and freedom, and would not think her condition safe and free, but in her subjection to her husband's authority."[23] Winthrop's language here emphasizes at once the woman's choice and agency as well as her submission and lack of autonomy in relation to her husband. While the Puritan ascriptive order emphasized social hierarchy grounded in divine order, Puritan theology nonetheless operated on the premise that all congregants were equally able to covenant with God in the privacy and immediacy of their own consciences. The emphasis on interiority and the unmediated relation between congregant and God potentially enabled women to speak with an authority equal to that held by men. Indeed, it is precisely the immediacy of the relation between individual and God that Anne Hutchinson deployed to assert her own religious and political authority during the Antinomian crisis. Moreover, the covenant metaphor, applied both to the relation between man and wife and the relation between convert and Christ, resonates in significant ways with social contract theory, which would later serve as the premise of eighteenth-century liberalism. Thus, as Andrew Delbanco argues, New England Puritanism looked forcefully backward to the early church for theological and political models but the use of these models propelled them perversely forward toward modernity.[24]

The shift from the one-sex to the two-sex model of bodily identity coincides with the move from a monarchical and hierarchical political order to a modern politics of natural rights, equality, and social contract in the Anglo-American world. Just as Puritan culture is itself riven by a tension between models of collective, hierarchical identity and those of individual, self-authorized identity, so too is the shift in bodily concepts marked by a fundamental change in the political orders. Indeed, as Laqueur is at pains to emphasize, the shift in the concept of the sexed body does not occur because of scientific advances in the understanding of human anatomy. Rather, under a new political order that imputes parity to all individuals as a matter of natural right, nature itself—in the form of the sexed and racialized body—begins to serve as the grounds of articulating and justifying power differentials among individuals. Differences in authority that were once sustained by divinely ordained hierarchy now begin to be sustained by biological difference. In short, once equality was posited on the transcendental level, inequality was reintroduced at the material level. As such, the two-sex model might be understood to do the work of stabilizing precisely the kinds of instability that open up with respect to gender in Puritan culture. As the individual is increasingly authorized without respect to divine hierarchy, hierarchy is reestablished elsewhere in the physical world.[25]

The shift in concepts of the body in Puritan New England is evident in a series of anatomical texts that circulated in the region from 1630 to the early 1800s. Helkiah Crooke's 1618 *Macrocosmographia*—a copy of which was most probably in the library of Anne Bradstreet[26]—describes "the Male and Female as both of one kinde [who] onely differ in certaine accidents."[27]

Crooke's claim is borne out by an anatomical diagram of the uterus and vagina that looks strikingly similar to a penis.[28] One of the two books on anatomy owned by Harvard College in 1723 was Nicholas Culpepper's 1671 translation of *A Sure Guide to the Best and Nearest Way to Physick and Chyrurgery* by Jean Riolan.[29] In this text, Riolan emphasizes the homologies between male and female genitals as well as male and female breasts:

> [The] Clitoris being the seat of Lasciviousness and Lust in Women ... imitate[s] a Mans Yard [Penis], as the Brests of Men have a resemblance to Womens Dugs.... The Ligaments of the Clitoris have Muscles fastened unto them, proceeding from the same place as those in men, and they are covered with Skin, and that Skin in the extremity or end therof is folded back, like Mans Fore-skin. Not without cause therfore is this Part called the Womans Yard or Prick.[30]

In an 1801 version of the popular, nonmedical text, *Aristotle's Master-Piece,* an argument is made that the vagina, like the penis, grows erect during intercourse: "The action and use of the neck of the womb, is the same with that of the Penis, that is erection; which is occasioned sundry ways; for First, in copulation it is erected and made straight for the passage of the Penis to the womb. Secondly, while the passage is replete with the spirits and vital blood, it becomes more straight for embracing the penis." Indeed, *Aristotle's Master-Piece* underscores the commonplace nature of the one-sex model in the commonplace form of doggerel: "Thus the women's secrets I have survey'd,/And let them see how curiously they're made,/And that, though they of different sexes be,/Yet on the whole they are the same as we./For those that have the strictest searchers been,/Find women are but men turn'd outside in:/And men if they but cast their eyes about,/May find the're women with their inside out."[31]

While *Aristotle's Master-Piece* was published well into the nineteenth century, the views contained within it began to be revised within the medical community in New England in the latter half of the eighteenth century. In his 1792 report, *The Rise, Progress, and Present State of Medicine,* Benjamin Waterhouse cites the work of Albrecht von Haller as that which radically changed the understanding of anatomy, including the "false theories of Galen."[32] Haller's textbook on reproduction begins by distinguishing the two sexes in terms of their skin, joints, flesh, muscles, breasts, bodily hair, teeth (women have less), and genitals. Moreover, far from pointing to the similarities between male and female breasts (as Riolan had done), Haller states that "the foremost of the parts in which women differ from men are the breasts, which, in women and female animals, have volume and fill up with fat and, at certain times, with milk."[33] Haller's chapter on women's breasts, which opens with this statement, extends an additional sixty-seven pages.

Successive anatomical work by John Bell, including his influential four-volume *Anatomy,* published in 1809, deploys a set of anatomical terms and drawings in which no resemblance between male and female genitalia exists. Beneath a drawing of the uterus, for instance, Bell writes, "This little drawing will better explain the figure of the womb, when dissected from the vagina and surrounding membranes, than the usual necessary reference to a bottle, a pear, or a powder-flask. As indeed, it strictly resembles no familiar object that I know."[34] The uterus thus has a strange, poetic quality and certainly bears no relation to any male organ. Bell's drawing of a vagina shows a curved cavity plumbed by the finger of a man—presumably the physician or anatomist—who seems to be tickling or probing the cervix. No longer the receptacle of the penis, the foreign territory of the vagina yields to the anatomist's skilled hand. The shift from single-sex to the two-sex model that occurred here corresponds, it should be noted, to a shift in epistemologies. From an understanding of science that lodged truth in an unseen and inscrutable divine order, the new science shifted the ground of truth to the orderly and mechanized laws of the natural world. As such, matter became the bearer of new kinds of meaning: rather than simply reflecting the truth of God, the natural world was the locus of that truth. Probing this natural order became the means of "unlocking" the secrets of the world.[35]

In religious discourse, a similar decline in the multiply- and mutably-sexed body occurs. While Jonathan Edwards, for example, continues to employ the Bride of Christ trope, he does so with less anatomical insistence than his Puritan predecessors and encounters less cultural acceptance of this rhetoric. Charles Chauncy's attack on Edwards thus begins by comparing Edwards's revival to the enthusiasm of the Antinomian faction of Anne Hutchinson. Chauncy implicitly and explicitly associates female bodies with Edwards's theology, and does so as a strategy of derogation: "The Account I have [of the revival] from one Part of the Country is,

> The Operation is principally among Women and Girls;' ... And are not these the very Persons, whose Passions according to Nature, it might be expected, would be alarmed? ... It certainly looks, as tho' the Weakness of their Nerves, and from hence their greater Liableness to be surpris'd, and overcome with Fear, was the true Account to be given of this Matter.[36]

The female body, as the locus of physical difference and disability, serves here as evidence of the weakness of the claims of Edwardsian theology. To inhabit this body is to fail to attain to the authority of eighteenth-century masculine identity. Thus, as Genevieve McCoy argues, Edwardsian religion failed in part because "it had adopted a rhetoric possessing feminine associations that contravened contemporary meanings of manhood and masculine power."[37] Inhabiting a female body, then, no longer served as a metaphor for conversion, not simply because gender roles had changed, but because inhabiting a sexed body now had far more consequences with respect to gender than it had once had.

Susan Juster compellingly traces the shift within evangelical Baptist rhetoric over the course of the eighteenth century from describing male converts as feminized "Brides of Christ" to describing them as masculine "Soldiers of Christ." While the larger American society democratized, the effect of this within the evangelical community was, Juster argues, that "a politically vigorous and socially respectable religious society needed a more masculine image, and hence we see the emergence of patriarchal language and structures in Baptist churches after 1780."[38] In a 1765 sermon delivered in Hartford by the minister Edward Dorr, *The Duty of Civil Rulers to Be Nursing Fathers to the Church of Christ,* the image of nursing fathers is invoked as a call to politicians to spiritually nurture the citizenry. However, the text of the sermon nowhere mentions sexed bodies or male breasts. Rather, Dorr describes the "nursing fathers" as soldiers and activists: "Now, civil rulers are capacitated above most other men, to do much for GOD

> ... They are armed with power and authority to suppress vice, and to encourage virtue.... And surely, this is a mighty argument, to encourage rulers to be nursing fathers to the church, that all their endeavours shall turn to a good account, to their own souls, and one day procure for them a more exceeding and eternal weight of glory.[39]

The "nursing father" in this speech has given way to an Arminian soldier who seeks to procure glory rather than suckle spiritual babes.

The term *nursing father* thus assumes a wholly vestigial form in Dorr's speech—the male nipple of this father no longer offers milk or sustenance to members of the community because doing so would comprise the masculinity and authority of the civil leaders Dorr addresses. While Jean Riolan emphasizes the obvious similarity of breasts in men and women to the extent of invoking their identity as a metaphor for similarity itself, by the eighteenth century, breasts become the sign of sexual difference between male and female bodies as well as the sign of political difference between men and women. According to Londa Schiebinger, during the French Revolution, "[T]he maternal breast became nature's sign that women belonged only in the home. Delegates to the French National Convention used the breast as a natural sign that women should be barred from citizenship and the wielding of public power."[40] Biological difference sustained political inequality in a new world order that posited the theoretical equality of all individuals. If having breasts was the sign of bodily exclusion from the public sphere, then men could ill-afford to represent their bodies as endowed with lactating "mammularies."

The ways in which the biological essentialism of the two-sex body constrains gender norms are both insidious and exhaustingly familiar. By way of contrast, however, the one-sex body does not offer a corresponding lack of constraint to women: the grounds of gender norms rest elsewhere according to the earlier model, yet these norms still have tremendous force. However, in the shift from one ontology of gender to the next, interesting and momentarily liberating dislocations do occur. Gender in Puritan culture, then, is influenced by the transition between bodily (and political) ontologies as well as an array of tensions, disruptions, and lapses occasioned by this shift. As a result of this shift, Puritan culture offered a number of potential forms of authorization for women that were briefly exploited and later eclipsed under the constraints of the two-sex ontology of gender. Mary Beth Norton, for instance, argues that the colonial model of the family as analog for the state afforded women—and particularly widows—a position of power and autonomy that was later denied them under the terms of Lockean liberal individualism.[41] Cornelia Hughes Dayton argues that New England Puritanism opened an anomalous legal space in which women's speech was far more authoritative than it was previously or would be subsequently: "Puritan jurisprudence, by encouraging lay pleading and by insisting on godly rules, created unusual opportunities for women's voices to be heard in court.... Indeed, New Haven Colony came close to establishing a single standard for men and women in the areas of sexual and moral conduct."[42] Legitimized by the pull toward individualism and equality (a single standard), and as yet not delegitimized or excluded from legal and political spaces on the basis of their breasts, wombs, or weak nerves, Puritan women—at times—achieved tremendous authority. The voices of Anne Hutchinson, Anne Bradstreet, and the girls of Salem might all be understood as occupying the anomalous space opened by the dislocations that marked the historical dominance of Puritan culture in New England.[43]

Reading the lactating and invaginated male bodies of Puritan discourse in terms of the one-sex model of bodily identity does not impute a lack of gender normativity, hierarchy, or constraint to Puritan culture. On the other hand, bringing to light the profoundly different nature of the link between biological sex and gender in this period does suggest that the "self-evident," grounding nature of contemporary biological sex for gender need not have the epistemological force it now wields.[44] In this reading of an alternative bodily discourse, moreover, we can see the dislocations that occur between gender and sex in the shift from the one-sex to the two-sex model—a shift that resonates in an array of theological, political, and legal tensions in New England Puritan culture. Reading the uneven, equivocal bodies here enables less the recovery of an idealized gender equality than a vision of possibilities opened up by a productive disequilibrium. Even as the Puritans worked to impose a stringent code of meanings to "settle" a new land, their own language and theology worked to unsettle existing meanings in instructive and potentially constructive fashions.

Notes

1. Edward Taylor, *Preparatory Meditations, 1.2, The Poems of Edward Taylor,* ed. Donald E. Stanford (New Haven, Conn.: Yale University Press, 1960), 354. Citations from the "Preparatory Meditations" are noted according to the series number and the meditation number.

2. Taylor, *Preparatory Meditations, 1.3.* The phrase "both my Mammularies Circumcise" could be glossed as "cleanse both my breasts" because "circumcise" can be used to mean "cleanse." It also, of course, refers to the cutting of the genitals, and, as such, adds another layer of sexually charged meaning to the poem.

3. John Cotton, *Christ the Fountaine of Life* (London: R. Ibbitson, 1651), 36–37. This passage is cited by Janice Knight (*Orthodoxies in Massachusetts: Rereading American Puritanism* [Cambridge, Mass.: Harvard University Press, 1994]) as exemplary of the "conjugal union with and through Christ [which] typifies the freeness of grace." Indeed, according to Knight, the passage "contains in brief the whole of [Cotton's] Cambridge theology" (116).

4. The androgyny of popular cultural icons notwithstanding, the feminization of the male body is, I would argue, now normatively understood as profoundly threatening to masculine identity. See, for instance, Stephen Jay Gould's essay, "Male Nipples and Clitoral Ripples," *Bully for Brontosaurus* (New York: Norton, 1991), 124–38, in which he states that he has received hundreds of letters from people asking him why men have nipples. Gould argues that male nipples are not the vestige of a previous adaptation, but the result of the anatomical and developmental homology between men and women—a shared morphology prior to sexual differentiation. Implicitly, Gould indicates the extent to which current readers find the existence of "female" anatomical traits such as nipples to be inexplicable and untoward on male bodies, and find the notion of a natural physical homology between men and women equally unusual. More explicitly, he argues that the understanding of a female clitoral orgasm also relies on assuming a homology between the penis and clitoris—a homology that modern culture has not been willing to assume.

5. See Walter Hughes, " 'Meat Out of the Eater': Panic and Desire in American Puritan Poetry," in Joseph A. Boone and Michael Cadden, eds., *Engendering Men* (New York: Routledge, 1990), 102–21; Margaret W. Masson, "The Typology of the Female as a Model for the Regenerate: Puritan Preaching, 1690–1730," *Signs* 2.2 (winter 1976): 304–15; Amanda Porterfield, *Female Piety in Puritan New England* (New York: Oxford University Press, 1992); and Ivy Schweitzer, *The Work of Self-Representation: Lyric Poetry in Colonial New England* (Chapel Hill: University of North Carolina Press, 1991). These works are discussed at greater length below. See in addition Philip Greven, *The Protestant Temperament: Patterns of Child-rearing, Religious Experience, and the Self in Early America* (New York: Knopf, 1977); Edmund S. Morgan, "The Puritan's Marriage with God," *South Atlantic Quarterly* 48.1 (1949): 107–12; and Janice Knight, *Orthodoxies in Massachusetts.* These works attest to the prevalence of the feminizing language of conversion in Puritan texts. While Morgan, Porterfield, and Knight focus on early New England Puritan texts, Masson argues that feminizing metaphors become more frequent in the work of third-generation Puritan ministers. Specifically, Masson discusses writings by Cotton Mather, Thomas Foxcroft, and Benjamin Colman. Porterfield, in contrast, traces the language of feminized conversion to the earlier English Puritan work of Richard Sibbes. What is significant for my purposes here, however, is both the ubiquity and sustained use of these metaphors in Puritan New England discourse from the Great Migration through the Great Awakening.

6. Taylor, *Preparatory Meditations,* 2.80.

7. I employ the terms *sex* and *gender* as they are commonly used in gender theory: sex refers to the body, whereas gender refers to cultural norms or roles. While the argument that follows concurs with theorists who have challenged the sheerly material (rather than cultural) nature of sex, for the purposes of clarity, I still rely on a distinction between the acting out of masculinity and femininity (gender) and the embodied quality of sex.

8. Thomas Laqueur, *Making Sex: Body and Gender from the Greeks to Freud* (Cambridge, Mass.: Harvard University Press, 1990); Londa Schiebinger, *The Mind Has No Sex? Women in the Origins of Modern Science* (Cambridge, Mass.: Harvard University Press, 1989), and *Nature's Body: Gender in the Making of Modern Science* (Boston: Beacon Press, 1993).

9. Laqueur, *Making Sex*, 4, 5, 8.

10. Cited in *The Antinomian Controversy, 1636–1638: A Documentary History*, ed. David A. Hall (Durham, N.C.: Duke University Press, 1990), 382–83.

11. Cotton Mather, *A Glorious Espousal* (Boston: Kneeland for Gray and Edwards, 1719), 26–28, emphases added.

12. Mather, *A Glorious Espousal*, 44.

13. Laqueur, *Making Sex*, 35.

14. Taylor, *Preparatory Meditations*, 2.12.

15. Janice Knight notes that different ministers employ sexualized rhetoric in different manners. Thomas Hooker, she argues, "often depicts the saint as masculine throughout the process [of conversion], as hammering the heart, storming the throne of God, or enjoying a husband's privilege, with Christ figured as the submissive bride: '… Hee is satisfied with her breasts at all times, and then hee comes to bee ravished with her love' " (Knight, 226, n. 30, citing Thomas Hooker, *The Soules Exaltation* [London, 1638]). This reversed rhetoric nonetheless feminizes the male body of Christ and points, again, to the "fungible" status of bodies in this rhetoric.

16. Porterfield, *Female Piety*, 11.

17. Masson, "Typology of the Female," 305. See also Jean Marie Lutes, "Negotiating Theology and Gynecology: Anne Bradstreet's Representations of the Female Body," *Signs* 22.2 (winter 1997): 309–40 for a somewhat similar claim concerning Anne Bradstreet's ability to assume a genderless identity (and thus an equality with men) within Puritan theological discourse.

18. Hughes, " 'Meat Out of the Eater,' " 103.

19. Schweitzer, *The Work of Self-Representation*, 25.

20. Hughes, " 'Meat Out of the Eater,' " 119.

21. Hughes also analyzes the diary of Michael Wigglesworth in this article, and his account of Wigglesworth's homosexual panic seems far more persuasive than his discussion of Taylor, in part because this account concerns Wigglesworth's struggles with his sexual desire for men (his students) rather than metaphorical desire for Christ.

22. For a discussion and critique of the "golden age" thesis, which argues that women had far more opportunity in colonial society than in industrialized societies, see Mary Beth Norton, "The Evolution of the White Women's Experience in Early America," *American Historical Review* 89 (June 1984): 595–601. Porterfield also gives a useful account of scholarly debates over women's status in Puritan culture, 82–87.

23. John Winthrop, *The History of New England from 1630 to 1649*, ed. Charles Savage, 2 vols. (Boston: Little, Brown, 1853), 2:281.

24. Andrew Delbanco, *The Puritan Ordeal* (Cambridge, Mass.: Harvard University Press, 1989). Delbanco speaks, for instance, of the Puritans' "flight from individualism even as they consecrated the individual in his unmediated relation to God" (22).

25. For a compelling discussion of the shift in gender identity associated with the move from a politics of divine right to a politics of social contract theory, see Carole Pateman, *The Sexual Contract* (Stanford, Calif.: Stanford University Press, 1988). While my concern here is with sex and gender, a similar shift to biologically grounded identity occurs with respect to race at the close of the eighteenth century. See Ronald Takaki, *Iron Cages: Race and Culture in Nineteenth-Century America* (New York: Knopf, 1979) for an analysis of the new "physiology" of race and its relation to republican politics. See also Londa Schiebinger, *Nature's Body: Gender in the Making of Modern Science* (Boston: Beacon Press, 1993), for a discussion of eighteenth-century transformations in concepts of race and gender.

26. Helen McMahon, "Anne Bradstreet, Jean Bertault, and Dr. Crooke," *Early American Literature* 3 (fall 1968): 118–22 argues that Bradstreet uses Crooke's theories of the humors, sometimes almost verbatim, in her poems.

27. Helkiah Crooke, *Microcosmographia, or a Description of the Body of Man, Together with Controversies Thereto Belonging* (London: W. Iaggard, 1615), 271.

28. Crooke does, however, argue against Galen's claim that woman is an imperfect version of man. However, the crux of his disagreement seems to lie less in an assertion that the bodies of women are different in kind from men's than in the assertion that women are also God's perfect creation.

29. See C. Helen Brock, "The Influence of Europe on Colonial Massachusetts Medicine," *Medicine in Colonial Massachusetts 1620–1820, Publications of the Colonial Society of Massachusetts,* vol. 57 (Boston: Colonial Society of Massachusetts, 1980), 105, for an account of the medical books owned by Harvard at this point in time.

30. Jean Riolan, *A Sure Guide to the Best and Nearest Way to Physick and Chyrurgery,* trans. Nicholas Culpepper (London: John Streater, 1671), 82.

31. *Aristotle's Master-Piece or the Secret's of Nature Displayed in the Generation of Man* (Massachusetts: Printed for the Purchasers, 1801), 21–22. Many versions of this text circulated from the mid-1600s in England through the nineteenth century in the United States. The text represents a popular form of folklore rather than medical knowledge at the time and is certainly not the work of Aristotle. The book evidently was used as a sort of sex manual by young men in Jonathan Edwards's Northampton congregation in 1744. Edwards interrogated the young men in what is called the "bad book affair." See Otho T. Beall Jr., "*Aristotle's Master Piece* in America: A Landmark in the Folklore of Medicine," *William and Mary Quarterly* 20 (1963): 207–22; and Kevin J. Hayes, *A Colonial Woman's Bookshelf* (Knoxville: University of Tennessee Press, 1996), 96. The persistence of Galenic views of the one-sex body into the early nineteenth century indicates that the shift from one view of the body to the other was far from historically discrete.

32. Benjamin Waterhouse, *The Rise, Progress, and Present State of Medicine* (Boston: Thomas and John Gleet, 1792), 24.

33. Albrecht von Haller, *La Generation* (Paris: Ventes de la Doue, 1774), 99 (my translation).

34. John Bell, *The Anatomy of the Human Body in Four Volumes,* vol. 4 (New York: Collins and Perkins, 1809), 142.

35. For an interesting account of the relation between the epistemological shift entailed by the "new science" and Puritan theology, see Michael P. Winship, "Prodigies, Puritanism, and the Perils of Natural Philosophy: The Example of Cotton Mather," *William and Mary Quarterly* 51.1 (January 1994): 92–105. Winship argues that Mather was compelled to limit his view that monstrosities were signs from God in accordance with Enlightenment views that prodigies carried no special message. See also Alice Domurant Dreger, *Hermaphrodites and the Medical Invention of Sex* (Cambridge, Mass.: Harvard University Press, 1998) who cites Rosemarie Garland Thomson's argument that in the nineteenth cen-

tury, "what was once the prodigious monster, the fanciful freak, the strange and subtle curiosity of nature, ... [became] the abnormal, the intolerable" (35).

36. Charles Chauncy, *Seasonable Thoughts on the State of Religion in New England 1743*, rept. ed. (Hicksville: Regina Press, 1975), 105. See also Amy Schrager Lang, *Prophetic Woman: Anne Hutchinson and the Problem of Dissent in the Literature of New England* (Berkeley: University of California Press, 1987), 72–106.

37. Genevieve McCoy, " 'Reason for a Hope': Evangelical Women Making Sense of Late Edwardsian Calvinism," in Stephen J. Stein, ed., *Jonathan Edwards's Writings: Text, Context, Interpretation* (Bloomington: Indiana University Press, 1996), 180.

38. Susan Juster, *Disorderly Women: Sexual Politics and Evangelicalism in Revolutionary New England* (Ithaca, N.Y.: Cornell University Press, 1994), 7.

39. Edward Dorr, *The Duty of Civil Rulers to Be Nursing Fathers to the Church of Christ* (Hartford, Conn.: Thomas Green, 1765), 21.

40. Schiebinger, *The Mind Has No Sex?* 70–71. For contemporary evidence of the relation between lactating breasts and the public sphere, see the cover illustration of the May 11, 1998, Mother's Day issue of *The New Yorker*, "Lunch Breaks," by Art Spiegelman, which depicts a construction worker on a lunch break nursing her infant. The drawing clearly plays on the presumed incompatibility of breasts and hard hats.

41. Mary Beth Norton, *Founding Mothers and Fathers: Gendered Power and the Forming of American Society* (New York: Knopf, 1996).

42. Cornelia Hughes Dayton, *Women Before the Bar: Gender, Law and Society in Connecticut, 1639–1789* (Chapel Hill: University of North Carolina Press, 1995), 10.

43. For an insightful reading of the gendering and authorization of the speech of the Salem witchcraft witnesses, see Nancy Ruttenburg, *Democratic Personality: Popular Voice and the Trial of American Authorship* (Stanford, Calif.: Stanford University Press, 1998).

44. "What does it mean," asks Judith Butler, "to have recourse to materiality, since it is clear from the start that matter has a history (indeed, more than one) and that the history of matter is in part determined by the negotiation of sexual difference." *Bodies That Matter: On the Discursive Limits of "Sex"* (New York: Routledge, 1993), 29.

Quaking in the Light

The Politics of Quaker Women's Corporeal Prophecy in the Seventeenth-Century Transatlantic World

MICHELE LISE TARTER

No one could quite comprehend what happened to Mary White after she witnessed the Quakers prophesying on the eighth of June, 1655. According to observers, Mrs. White had wanted neither to listen to Quaker preachers nor to have Quaker tracts read to her by her sister-in-law, Alice. Yet, upon beholding a Quaker Meeting for Worship at Wickham-skeyth in Suffolk, this woman first wept, then was "much troubled," and on returning to the home of her in-laws, "she spent much time in reading a book set out by the Quakers." Very shortly after, she allegedly fell into convulsive fits. At times, she would lie perfectly still, and then at other moments, in a fit of force or quaking, "three or four could scarce keep her in her bed." The final testimony given by her husband graphically accentuated the physical changes taking place in Mary: "something within her body did run up and down, and in her Fits sometime she roared like a Bull; sometime barked like a Dog, and sometime blared like a Calf, and that she did claspe her Legs about her Neck, so round as she might have been put into a Bushel." For ten days, William White scrutinized the spasmodic movements and bushel-like pose of his wife, as well as the animal sounds coming forth from her estranged mouth. He then watched her die. White and others concluded that Mary had surely been "seduced and inchanted" by that dangerous sect, the Quakers.[1]

Representing the large corpus of seventeenth-century *Anti-Quakeriana*, the story of Mary White illustrates spectators' emphasis on the physicality of Quaker worship with its fatal consequences. Indeed, the quaking body holds a most controversial and complex position in the history of this religious assembly (known formally as the Society of Friends). While Anglican and Puritan pamphleteers insisted that corporeal prophecy held no spiritual veracity at all, they nevertheless published hundreds of tracts like Mary White's that reveal their preoccupation, fascination, and even obsession with quaking. As I will discuss later in this chapter, these publications incited a tremendous wave of physical violence against Friends, indicating the subversive force outsiders perceived in the quaking bodies, which they felt compelled to mutilate and thereby disempower.

In turn, the Quakers began to catalog meticulously every single corporeal attack launched against them, compiling over forty-four manuscript folios now lodged in the Friends' British archives. Elders of Second Generation Quakerism then erased any trace of "enthusiasm," or corporeal prophecy, when they rewrote their history in the 1670's, attempting to "dignify" and save the movement in the midst of severe anti-Quaker persecutions.[2] Yet, in the obsession over, the attack on, and the excision of the quaking body from this religious history, it surfaces as a pivotal point of analysis, and one that has hardly been addressed by historians today: why was the quaking body such a threat to society at large, and even to the succeeding generations of Friends themselves?

Although Mary White never wrote her own testament of Quaker convincement,[3] there are compelling questions to ask in response to the stories that were being told about her quaking body and metamorphosed soul. Why, for example, were Friends portrayed as "seducers and inchanters"? "Inchanted," were these worshippers being drawn away from their secular roles—their wifely status, for example—and led to an alternative, more emboldened religiosity? We are informed that Mary's sister-in-law (the only other woman in this narrative) is responsible for initially introducing her to the Quakers. Is this detail intended to show how women, like stereotypical witches of the time, were most commonly blamed for seducing other women, thus linking the sisters-in-law to heresy, sexual libertinism, and ultimate moral destruction in this text? We might consider who is truly being "seduced and inchanted"—that is, mesmerized with Quakers' physical worship—when it was the pamphleteers themselves who kept returning to meetings despite their own caveats to avoid this preaching like the plague. And, finally, could this depiction of Mrs. White—as animalized and demonically possessed—rather be seen as a woman who was so deeply moved by Quaker prophesying that she subsequently experienced ecstatic, somatic responses to the message of God made manifest in the flesh?

At the time Mary lived, rumor had it that the Quakers arose from a group of women who lived beyond the sea.[4] This is not surprising, for the very corporeality of earliest Quaker prophesying instantly slated this sect as a "feminized" and deviant band of worshippers. Traditional Aristotelian dualism of Judeo-Christian ideology separated the sexes by associating men with the soul, reason, and the mind, and women with the body and emotions, ultimately marginalizing woman as "flesh" in the political and symbolic structures of church and state; moreover, it associated deviant women—and, more generally, the female body—with the biblical Eve and thus with the fall from grace, with carnality and mortification.[5] As a result, spectators derisively gave the name "Quaker" to this group in response to their alternative and quite physical form of prayer. However, First Generation Friends accepted the pejorative term as an emblem of their faith and practice, believing in the sanctity of the body-spirit connection and the affirmation of quaking as revelationary witness.

The earliest records and manuscripts of Quakers pronounced and proclaimed an embodied spirit theology; in effect, they celebrated the feminization of worship and situated women in authoritative roles as "Spiritual Mothers in Israel," bearing anew the promise of salvation for Friends as they nourished the growing religious family with the "Milk of the Word of God."[6] The act of quaking was an act laden with meaning and purpose: it was the motion of spiritual rebirth and apocalyptic delivery, both literally and metaphorically, in and through the sacralized body. While most of Quaker scholarship is based on a post-1670s revised theology that resorts to Christian dualism and a general suspicion of the flesh, there is a rising interest among Friends today to reclaim the original vision and enthusiasm of their ancestors, which have been intentionally suppressed for centuries. I posit that we must put the quaking body of Friends at the center of this recovered history, and moreover, consider the quaking phenomenon in the context of feminist theology that so poignantly reconnects the body and spirit in divine worship—a faith and practice that Quakers embraced over three hundred years ago. In returning to the foundations of this movement—and the very meaning of the body to early Friends—we can thus re-vision the dramatic transformations of thousands of women like Mary White as a wave of dynamic expression taking shape in an unparalleled women's religious movement of the seventeenth-century transatlantic world.[7]

When George Fox gathered the Society of Friends in the late 1640s, joining the most radical left-wing branch of Puritan religious practices in England, he preached that all people—despite their gender, race, age, or social status—were "one in Christ Jesus." Hundreds at a time would congregate for a Quaker Meeting for Worship, which would take place spontaneously in any number of places—on a hillside, in a barn, beside a tavern, or in the privacy of someone's home. Held at any time of day or night, meetings would last indefinitely, even up to six or eight hours, depending on how spirit "moved" among the attenders. Together, without any leading minister, Friends would wait in sacred silence to feel divine "currents" of God stirring in them, just as it had happened to the Apostles before them. As Fox cited with scriptural promise: "And it shall come to pass afterward, that I will pour out my Spirit on all flesh; your sons and your daughters shall prophesy.... Even upon the menservants and maidservants in those days, I will pour out my Spirit" (Joel 2: 28–29).[8]

In his theology of christopresentism, the leader declared that when spirit poured onto flesh, Friends returned to a prelapsarian state and experienced a concrete, substantial, and visceral convincement; indeed, they "magnified" the "indwelling Christ" and embodied perfection on earth. Such a proclamation rejected the limitations of dualism, celebrating the fusion of flesh and spirit for all humankind. In this corporeal manifestation of God, a worshipper became "celestial flesh,"[9] and anyone in this ecstatic state was thereby called to give sound or movement to such divine motion and "inward Light."

Ridding religious worship of all icons and sacraments, including the rite of communion, the Friends perceived themselves as the living texts of Christianity, the celestial flesh of a millennial world. While they honored the Bible as a holy book, they did not grant it supreme authority, trusting rather in the primitive and most pure "leadings" of God coming forth from the "living members." Friends believed themselves to be the *scriptura rediviva,* reliving apostolic narratives in and through their "heavenly flesh." Contrary to Calvinists, who located the resurrected Christ far away in a distant, spiritual heaven, Fox told his followers that the savior was with them, inhabiting every particle of their bodies. It was quaking, above all, which ushered in this revelation and celestial presence on earth: "But the time cometh that a day of Quaking shall pass over all that have not yet known Quaking," wrote Friend Dorothy White. "[T]he earth shall be terribly shaken, and not the earth onely, but the Heavens also." All should welcome this physical transformation, she announced, for it signified the very coming of Christ.[10] The body, then, became the site of divine prophecy and agency in the early Quaker movement.

Such a theology had a tremendous impact on women in England in the mid seventeenth century, as thousands from all social strata gathered to uphold and deliver this message. Due to the Puritans' derision of flesh as the locus of mortal sin and pollution, women suffered severely for being framed as the trope of body and nature: they were categorized as "weaker" or "empty" vessels in need of patriarchal guidance and control. Fox's reply to this was that the body, in its primitive Christian form, was "an earthen vessel" and not a weaker or empty one; it was a sacred entity, Friend Priscilla Cotton added, where "the treasure ... is found, that which hath been hid in ages and generations, the great mystery, *Christ in you.*" This treasure was waiting to be stirred, awakened, released, and borne anew, highlighting the Friends' ideology of immanence—salvation embodied in the "celestially fleshed Christ" of one another.[11]

The sanctity of corporeal prophecy among Quakers in many significant ways reflected the medieval tradition of *humanitas christi,* in which thirteenth-century women mystics located Christ's humanity in his physicality, so divinely borne of a woman. As Caroline Walker Bynum illustrates, these writers were empowered by the associations linking woman and flesh and the body of Christ: "Not only was Christ enfleshed with flesh from a woman; his own flesh did womanly things: it bled, it bled food and it gave birth."[12]

Women mystics thus reconnected the body and the spirit in religious experience, and their prophetic meditations are replete with ecstatic corporeal states, often likened to exclusively female experiences of pregnancy, childbirth, and nursing.

Fox's doctrine of celestial inhabitation espoused this same visceral experience of God, revealing that salvation came not despite the body but rather because of it, thus initiating a revolutionary breakthrough for women in a "world turned upside down." Rebecca Travers beckoned Friends, "[E]very one wait in the light to feel the power, and life of the Son of God manifest in your bodies"; Martha Simmonds proclaimed, "[M]ake our bodies fit for himself to dwell in." Fox himself declared, "[T]he way of Christ is found in us, God in our flesh!" Quaker men equally embraced this experience of "enthusiasm," or "divine indwelling." As William Dewsbury wrote to his religious family from York Tower's prison, "Dear and tender little Babes ... let not anything straiten you when God moves." In a letter to Friends, Thomas Willan expressed, "And I felt the presence of the Lord running through me, and shaking that which was to be shaken more than ever." Charles Marshall graphically recounted the corporeal manifestations of spirit at meetings he attended in that day: "But, ah! The seizings of soul, and prickings at heart, which attended that season! some fell on the ground, others cried out under the sense of their states, which gave experimental knowledge of what is recorded in Acts ii.37"; in another missive, he described his prophetic motion in terms of physical labor, being "made to cry like a woman in travail." While several scholars have noted the particularly "feminine" religious style of Friends, I would add to this assertion that First Generation Quakerism even more radically honored the feminized body as the very opening to God.[13]

In the Meetings for Worship, women felt sanctioned to facilitate such experiences among members, while also moving enthusiastically with "that of God" in their own bodies. As Spiritual Mothers in Israel,[14] a socioreligious position created by Fox, these women dramatically manifested "the second birth" of Christ on earth. Many reports cite that "sometimes men, but more frequently Women and Children" received the divine currents in the meetings, began to quake and thereby issued apocalyptic delivery through their bodies: they would swoon to the ground, writhe on the floor, breathe stertorously and howl in travail, push, sweat, and cry aloud; their bellies would swell "as though blown up with wind," pregnant and full; and the epiphany would come as they roared out with a voice "greater then [*sic*] the voice of a man." Seeking to know and feel God through *rachem*—in Hebrew etymology, the word for the bowels, the womb, as well as compassion and mercy—men and women Friends surrendered to the experience of the divine feminine as it rose and fell in their bodies. Such prophetic movement superseded any power language might hold. Whereas Richard Bauman writes on the ethnography of Friends' silence and "speaking in the light," I would like to emphasize the worshippers' sanctity of "quaking in the light." Indeed, silence in the Friends' meetings privileged the language of the body, allowing "the indwelling Christ" to move forth in dynamic, performative agency. As Fox pronounced, "[F]eed upon the Milk of the Word, that was before tongues."[15]

In their fluid space of worship, the possibilities of divine embodiment and expression were endless for Quakers, who also called themselves "the Children" or "Children of Light." They were encouraged to enter the infantile state, erasing "Reason" or custom and, instead, listening to the inward voice of God. In effect, Friends constructed what feminist poststructuralist Julia Kristeva terms the semiotic realm, a "feminine" space "dominated by the space of the mother's body." In this realm, Kristeva writes, the child experiences infantile drives, sensory perceptions, and polymorphous erotogenic zones, as well as permeable boundaries with others. In addition to trembling, quivering, groaning, cooing, and swelling their bellies, the Children would often lie in the fetal position on the floor, and "sometimes purge as if they had taken Physick" during meetings.[16] Such extreme release of social inhibitions illustrates their complete surrender to the semiotic fusion with the divine, nurtured by the Spiritual Mothers. Out of this space came a new relationship to language, to prophecy, and above all, to God, in and through the testament of celestial flesh. This was a radical alternative to traditional religious practices, destabilizing patriarchal authority and creating a "feminine" space—volatile, permeable, and free.

During a century when early modern Europeans were engrossed with the mysterious workings of the body—its unfolding scientific discoveries, its potential malleability, and even its material spirituality[17]—it did not take long until spectators rushed to the Friends' gatherings to behold the changing specters of these worshippers; it also did not take long for these eyewitnesses to wage a sweeping anti-Quaker campaign via the pamphleteering press. In initial attempts to undermine this assembly of believers, the writers stressed that meetings were "made up out of the dregs of the common people,"[18] thus implying the uneducated and irrational responses of these followers.

In many ways, the Friends' corporeal testimony both resisted and reinforced the claims of dualism, as their bystanders utilized quaking to depict manifestations of demonic possession and sexualized perversion. One anonymous pamphleteer thus described a meeting:

> And very observable it is ... sometimes one, sometimes more, fall into a great and dreadful shaking and trembling in their whole bodies and all of their joynts, with such risings and swellings in their bellies and bowels, sending forth shreekings, yellings, howlings and roarings, as not only affrighted the spectators, but caused the Dogs to bark, the swine to cry, and Cattle ran about, to the astonishment of all that heard them.

Associating Quaker prophecy with animalism, these tracts capitalized on the fact that the sect had arisen from a man named "Fox"; they continued, "[H]e and his whole Litter are abroad, and therefore tis fit they should be stoutly hunted." More pointedly, another pamphlet compared the early Friends to the animals of Noah's Ark, but with one flagrant distinction: "[T]he shees are far the more numerous party, and in spight of Paul's injunction, will often be holding forth to the men."[19]

Focusing upon the "shees" of this faction, pamphleteers assured their readers that Quaker women had merely fallen prey to their traditionally moist, spongy, lustful, bodily state of sin. This charge was neither new nor surprising in the early modern period, for it drew on an age-old attack linking religious dissension to sexual disorder, social deviance, and witchcraft. While overtly sexualizing Quaker women's bodies to serve the purposes of anti-Quaker propaganda, this wave of literary production aimed to fetishize them, as well; in effect, Spiritual Mothers became an object of sexual display, an enthusiastic spectacle of primitive Christianity. Warnings were issued about Quaker sexual "snares": these women allegedly left their homes by day or night to run off to "Quaker Rendezvousings," and so people were to beware "sucking in" or drinking the sect's "adulterated" wine and witnessing their "spiritual fornications." The women, in particular, were portrayed as seductive enchantresses who "propagated" false opinions and emitted unclean excretions in body and tongue. Still other publications insisted that these worshippers were merely *pretending* "extraordinary sudden extravagant Agonies, Trances, Quakings, Shakings, Raptures, Visions,"[20] and compared Quaker prophecy to the highly theatrical, ritualized practices of the Papists.

Most striking in these propagandistic tracts, however, is the nearly desperate warning that if a person views Quaker prophesying, he or she will uncontrollably follow in kind. Casting Friends' worship as spiritual theater, pamphleteers employ arguments of the Puritans' antitheatrical campaign, noting how these performances had the potential to change people merely by the act of spectatorship. At the root of this prejudice and fear was the contemporary notion that theater—and Quakerism—would "dazzle, enchant, seduce," and ultimately "effeminate" the mind. Exposed to quaking spectacles, audiences were warned that they would become the very essence of what they beheld—in a word, feminized.[21] And, it was argued, their lives were at stake for crossing such transgressive thresholds. Interestingly, pamphleteers concomitantly reinforced the theological underpinnings of Friends' worship; that is, if the divine Light resided in all human bodies, awaiting to be stirred and brought forth, there was limitless potential for any and all witnesses to be moved and transformed. To outsiders, this signified absolute chaos, and so the caveat was clear: if you are in the presence of Quaker prophesying, this, too, could happen to you, and there will be consequences to pay—losing all bodily control, you will begin to tremble, quake, gesticulate like an animal, travail like a woman, howl like a witch, and then, perhaps, die.

Portraying Quaker women as agents of contamination, pamphleteers were utilizing a strategy to control bodies that challenged the ideologies of the dominant culture. In light of anthropologist Mary Douglas's scholarship, we can see how these women were cast as virtual pollution—defined historically, Douglas reveals, as "matter out of place."[22] In the midst of Puritan and Anglican dualism, Friends presented the body as a site of sacred expression and prophetically challenged the prevalent notions of woman as inferior and the body as contaminated. While seventeenth-century Quaker tenets threatened the social stratification of Anglican and Puritan England, the institutionalized "bodyguarding" through the pamphleteering press worked to sustain and ever enforce its gender hierarchies of religious orthodoxy. Attacking with vehement rage, it instigated passionate reactions against any and all feminized, quaking bodies of God.

Women Friends, in particular, were viciously punished for their "transgressive" Quaker behavior. They were incarcerated, pelted, stoned, kicked, spit upon, verbally harassed, and locked behind a "scold's bridle," a twenty-pound headcage used to punish any seventeenth-century Englishwomen for "having too much tongue."[23] In the first two decades of Quakerism, literally thousands of these quaking women's bodies were put under the control of the British state, who then systematically abused, tortured, and reinscribed their marks of power on these radical, subversive living texts of Christianity.

With the dramatic rise of attacks on Friends, the religious sect scrupulously composed a history of their abuses; as documented in their *Book of Sufferings,* between the years 1650–89, there were 20,721 Quakers involved in legal conflicts and persecutions, and of these there were 450 deaths. Often meetings were disrupted by gangs who brutally assaulted men Friends, obscenely molested women, and most dramatically attacked pregnant Spiritual Mothers; in one incident at Horsleydown, a man struck a parturient woman "twice on the belly with his musket and once on the breast," causing her to miscarry and nearly die. The judicial system itself passed numerous conventicles and acts to control the physical actions of this religious denomination, all the while designating quaking bodies as a most threatening, anarchical force in society.[24]

Punishments against women escalated as Quakers crossed the Atlantic to deliver their message to the Bible Commonwealth of New England. Feeling divinely called to prophesy, Ann Austin, a middle-aged mother of five, and Mary Fisher, a twenty-two-year old Yorkshire maidservant, traveled to the Massachusetts Bay Colony in 1656. The Puritan leaders, deeply distressed over the rumors of Quaker women arriving in their harbor, were prepared to overcome any such "invasion," particularly by those whom they deemed to be the epitome of religious radicalism and disorderly womanhood. As soon as the boat docked, the magistrates searched it, seized the one hundred "heretical" books and tracts they found, and then insisted that these texts be burned in the marketplace. Similar to the corruption they identified in theatrical performance, Puritans transferred such lethal power to the literature of this dissenting group. From that moment forth, the authorities created laws against the "seductive and poisonous" Quaker writings, instituting heavy fines for anyone touching, possessing, dispersing, or concealing any of these tracts.[25]

Implying that Quaker bodies and texts were equally pernicious, the magistrates next seized Austin and Fisher, stripped them naked publicly, and then forced the women to undergo excruciating bodily searches for signs of witchcraft:

> not missing head nor feet, searching betwixt their toes, and amongst their hair, tewing and abusing their bodies more than modesty can mention, in so much that Anne who was a married woman, and had born 5 children said, That she had not suffered so much in the birth of them all, as she had done under their barbarous and cruel hands.

Although only midwives were allowed to conduct witchcraft searches, Austin reported that "one of them before their search was a man in a womans [*sic*] apparel,"[26] revealing the extreme and humiliating punishment these Spiritual Mothers endured as public castigation for their challenge to Puritan religious orthodoxy and its enforced gender roles.

The magistrates then imprisoned Austin and Fisher, setting up a fine of five pounds for anyone who might speak to them; to be doubly certain of keeping townspeople away from the Quaker women, the leaders also boarded up their cell window. Austin and Fisher were incarcerated under such dark, close conditions for five weeks and were deprived specifically of light and of writing materials, again reflecting the powerful connections Puritans formed between Friends' testimony in body and text. Quaker women's first encounter with the Massachusetts Bay Colony clearly indicates the challenge they posed to its leaders. One critic of this bigotry, in a tract titled *New England Judged,* asked the magistrates, "[W]hy was it that the coming of two women so shook ye, as if a formidable army had invaded your borders?"[27] "Invasion" for the Puritan leaders had become an utterly corporeal event: perceiving these female bodies as permeable and contaminating agents in the colony, they resolved to contain, tightly seal, and lock Austin and Fisher in a cell until these women could be transported out of New England.

The threat of Quaker women had everything to do with their prophetic roles as Spiritual Mothers in Israel. Recent gender studies of the Bible Commonwealth explore the empowerment and authority Puritan women derived as mothers in the community. Images of God's maternal care that were invoked in many of the ministers' sermons and tracts acknowledged this vital role women served in the colony.[28] Yet, the presence of Quaker women challenged this theological framework on many counts: to the ministers, they were reclaiming the images of mothering and the metaphors of ministry as the "Milk of the Word of God," both long appropriated by the male clergy; to the women, they were expanding the definitions of "mothering" to include the acts of preaching, speaking publicly, prophesying, traveling, and writing; and to all people, they were remonstrating the tenets of dualism by embodying the divine fusion of the body and spirit in their ecstatic demonstrations of God's presence on earth. This was perceived as nothing less than heretical and insubordinate, a vivid example of disorderly womanhood and excessive carnality gone to its extreme; above all, this was seen as a threat to male religious authority, to the institution of the family, as well as to the social and godly order of New England. Such recalcitrant bodies became the site of religious and social contestation in this dramatic history; as the consummate example of feminine evil, they too would become the bodies to bear particular punishment and symbolic, public denigration for overstepping the clearly demarcated boundaries.

Within the first year of Quaker women's arrival to the Massachusetts Bay Colony, laws were created specifically for their chastisement. On both first and second landings in the Puritan colonies, a female Friend was to be severely whipped; although these laws do not specify where on the body these lashings were to be administered, Quaker documents reveal that a woman Friend was generally stripped from the waist up and, although flogged from behind, the whip's lash often curled around her body and tore at or near her naked breasts. As Spiritual Mothers who declared that their breasts flowed with the "Milk of the Word of God," these women were in turn objectified and their breasts mutilated as penal retribution for their female sexuality, social deviance, and religious dissent. On a third appearance in the colony, a Quaker woman was to have her tongue bored with a hot iron; on a fourth, she would be hanged to death.[29]

Unmoved by these laws, women Friends continued to travel in apostolic pairs, "invading" the borders of this colony, and so many diverse female prophets came: pregnant women, elderly women, nursing mothers with their infants, crippled women, single maidservants, wealthy widows, previous Antinomian supporters, even young girls. They entered churches to interrupt ministers' sermons; they prophesied in the streets, drawing large crowds; using the body as the site of their prophetic speech acts, some dressed in sackcloth and ashes, while others "went naked as a sign," signifying the community's nakedness without the inward Light; all distributed their writings widely throughout the towns. Some women were told by constables, "I profess you must not think to make Fools of Men," and were in turn flogged vehemently for their corporeal prophecy. Others were thrown into vermin-infested dungeons, deprived of food and water for weeks at a time; regarded and treated as animals, they were told that "they should leave their carcasses behind them."[30]

Among the earliest prophets coming to Boston was Horred Gardiner, who, arriving "with her babe sucking at her breast," was immediately stripped and administered ten lashes with a threefold knotted whip of cords. As a Spiritual Mother in Israel, as a literal nursing mother, and as a living witness of

Christ manifested in the flesh, Gardiner then kneeled down saying, "The Lord forgive you; you know not what you do." Reciting the very words of Christ on the cross, she asserted both her authority as a Quaker and a woman who could witness Christ's spirit and scriptural language. After delivering her message, Gardiner and her infant were imprisoned for fourteen days. When crippled and elderly Ann Coleman, on another occasion, was flagellated for preaching publicly, her persecuting constable directed his attack with specific ferocity: "She collapsed in agony when one of the whip's knots split open her nipple, creating wounds from which some observers thought she might die." Coleman clearly recognized the importance of her corporeal testimony as a female prophet in colonial America; in a letter she wrote to George Fox in 1663, she referred to being "wipt beside stoning and kicking and striking," and still she concluded, "it hath not bin in vaine."[31]

The treatment of these women had its precedent in other displays of iconoclastic desecration committed by Puritan leaders. Having enacted truculent rampages through churches in seventeenth-century England, Puritans had deemed it appropriate to destroy any religious icons, which they asserted had no place or power in the church. However, as Ann Kibbey has shown, the very act of shattering such objects, including many beheadings of statues, implied that they perceived some form of power in them. The Puritans extended such violence to human beings in New England, Kibbey reveals, as evidenced in the Pequot genocide of 1637. I posit that the Quakers, and particularly Quaker women, were the next victims on this continuum of religious persecution, the mutilations of their bodies representing iconic destruction of their deviant practices of Christianity and womanhood. George Fox wrote to the magistrates in *A Paper to New England:* "what whipping, imprisonning, and cruel torturing of the bodyes of the people of God do you make, and have you made? what blooding of them, massacring, slaying, cutting off the ears, dismembering have you made of the servants and people of God?" Under the Puritans' "heinous yoak of Tyranny," spontaneous, arbitrary laws were continually created to destroy the Quakers, whose presence so deeply threatened the sociospiritual order of Massachusetts Bay. In *A Declaration of the Sad and Great Persecution and Martyrdom,* Friend Edward Burroughs writes that the Puritans "were so far from desiring to spare [the Quakers'] lives that they thirsted for their blood, and nothing else could satisfie them but the extinguishment of their lives by shameful torture."[32]

By 1659, John Norton, clergyman of the First Church of Boston, was commissioned by the General Court to produce a rationale for Quaker deaths, titled *The Heart of New England Rent.* Norton elaborates on the "antic and uncouth motions" of Quakers, aligning Friends with the worshipping practices of other outsiders and "evil" influences, such as the Native Americans;[33] he mocks their gestures of birthing God (their "afflictions," he writes) which most often occur in the members' bellies. The minister speaks of the fall of New England, reflecting the fall from the Garden of Eden, and associates Quakerism with disorderly womanhood—the very embodiment of Eve—which is seducing, tempting, and leading this Adamic colony into sin, mortal decay, and dissolution.

As scholars have noted, there was a lessening of the epitome of feminine evil within Puritan culture by the end of the seventeenth century, with women being viewed more positively as the helpmeets and goodwives of the Commonwealth. I would suggest that Quaker women—who were represented by Puritans as the wayward Eve, as sexualized "base quaking sluts," as witches, and as evil Mothers offering a channel for Satan—may have served as a vehicle to effect this changing status of Puritan women in the community. Standing in direct opposition to these female dissenters, the Puritan women were able to separate themselves from the very taint of Eve. A tract like Norton's was read widely throughout the colony and might have helped to influence the perceived distinction between Puritan and Quaker women. *The Heart of New England Rent,* offering a full justification for Quaker executions, was issued to every member of the Court, to townships throughout the colony, and even to London's Restoration government in 1660.[34]

When Quaker Mary Dyer was hanged at the gallows in 1660, her execution typified the apotheosis of Puritan persecution against the Friends. Convicted for disobediently, repeatedly returning to the colony as a Quaker woman, despite magistrates' warnings and laws, she stood steadfast in her challenge of Puritan injustice and rule. Dyer wrote from prison to the General Court of Boston in 1659, "Was ever the like Laws heard of among a People that profess Christ come in the flesh?" As a prophet, she warned them of their egregious wrongdoing, articulating the Puritans' irrational treatment and view of women's inferiority: "Search with the Light of Christ in ye ... which Light as you come into, and obeying what is made manifest to you therein, you will not repent, that you were kept from shedding Blood, though it were from a Woman." Mary's voice was silenced, quite literally: on her one-mile walk to the gallows, soldiers before and behind her beat drums so that no townspeople would hear her prophesying. On the ladder ascending the platform, she was asked if an Elder should pray for her, to which she replied, "Nay, first a Child, then a young man, then a strong man, before an Elder of Christ Jesus."[35] With these last words, Mary reinforced the message of the world turned upside down, honoring youth and innocence before education and social status in this Puritan colony. As a Spiritual Mother, her prophecy was complete, and she offered her body as the ultimate text—as a woman, a Quaker, and as the living Christ—sacrificed with love for the Children of Light.

The townspeople had seen many incarnations of Mary Dyer in her lifetime: once a member of the Massachusetts Bay Colony, she had been known as "the woman who had the monster," delivered of a stillborn and malformed fetus by midwife Anne Hutchinson decades earlier; she, too, had been the closest friend and Antinomian supporter of Hutchinson. Dyer then returned to the colony numerous times as a Friend, upholding the tenets of spiritual equality and prophecy. Looking up at her dead body, Magistrate Humphrey Atherton mockingly declared, "She hangs there as a flag!" Referring to her corpse as a "flag," the official was erasing her body altogether and turning Mary into a banner of Puritan supremacy and power. Through the act of execution, the leaders of the Commonwealth believed that they had succeeded in silencing and destroying such a contaminating threat to their community. It was their illusion, nonetheless, for Dyer's body became a lasting testament—the final text—of the violent, malefic[36] assaults perpetrated by the Puritan magistrates against religious dissenters. To Atherton and others, her execution was a flag of dominance; but to the rest of the world, it was an atrocity. When King Charles II learned about Dyer's corporal punishment in the colonies, he ordered that there should be no more killing of Quakers.

To the Friends, such iconoclastic treatment was another confirmation of the world gone awry and evidence of the forthcoming apocalypse, enacted in and through their celestial flesh. They found salvific meaning and ecstatic suffering in their sacrificial wounds, as Christ's own torture and mutilation was being reinvented through them. In the aftermath of these executions, the religious society created a history of martyrology, whereby the bodies of Friends remained the lasting sign of the living Christ on earth. Quaker martyrdom deeply moved the spectators of these dramatic punishments, leading to further convincements and the rapid increase of their spiritual family in New England.[37]

As the archives of this recovered history divulge, Quaker women's corporeal prophecy bore a profound testimony to the people of the seventeenth-century transatlantic world. Thousands of women's stories—ranging from Mary White's to Mary Dyer's—bring to light the politics inherent in their corporeal prophecy and spiritual force. As the *scriptura rediviva* of Mary, the Mother of God, these women proved that they were not "seduced and inchanted" at all, but rather transformed and supported by a vast network that endorsed women's preaching, prophesying, and traveling with the authority of the Word made Flesh. Despite frantic propaganda and inflamed persecutions, they persevered in their divine call as Spiritual Mothers. With the "leading" to embark on a transatlantic mission, they subsequently expanded the boundaries of gender and prophecy and ultimately transformed the cultural meanings of womanhood and motherhood on the colonial frontier. And, as foremothers, they kept returning in order to create and claim a sacred and social space for women in the making of a New England.

Notes

I thank the Society of Friends for their generous support and encouragement of my research: in particular, Pendle Hill (a Quaker study center in Pennsylvania) for their Henry

J. Cadbury Scholar-in-Residence Fellowship; the Friends' Institute, for research trips to archives in England and Philadelphia; the Friends World Committee for Consultation, for the Elizabeth Ann Bogert Grant for the Study and Practice of Christian Mysticism; and the Women's Gatherings of Philadelphia Yearly Meeting and Illinois Yearly Meeting. I also thank the librarians at the Friends House Library in London, the Friends Historical Library at Swarthmore College, and the Quaker Collection at Haverford College in Pennsylvania.

1. The comments about Mary White come from the anonymous tract, *Quakers are Inchanters and Dangerous Seducers, Appearing in Their Inchantment of One Mary White at Wickham-skeyth in Suffolk* (London: Printed by T. M. for Edward Dod, 1655), 5–6. While anti-Quaker tracts are critical of Friends' religious practices, they nevertheless provide a rich resource for reconstructing what took place at the worship gatherings. Friends themselves did not often record descriptions of their prophesyings at the meetings, whereas the spectators took copious notes in their aim to discredit the movement. The intense physicality of earliest Friends' prophecy is confirmed by numerous Quakers' manuscript letters and journals (and most notably in the writings of the founder, Fox, himself), as discussed later in this essay. Anti-Quaker paintings and sketches were also common during this time period, particularly accentuating and, in turn, caricaturizing women's corporeal prophecy (see the figure at the beginning of part 3).

2. Second Generation Quakerism, and its subsequent movement towards Quietism, resorted to quite traditional, dualistic terms of Christian theology, most evident in the foundational text of William Barclay's *Apology*. For an insightful analysis of the intentional rewriting of earliest Quaker history, see Richard Bailey's *New Light on George Fox and Early Quakerism: The Making and Unmaking of a God* (San Francisco: Mellen Research University Press, 1992). Also see Henry J. Cadbury, *George Fox's "Book of Miracles"* (Cambridge, U.K.: Cambridge University Press, 1948). Although Cadbury's book has been out of print for several decades, the Society of Friends has recently decided to re-issue it, owing to the surge of interest among members to reclaim Quakerism's long-buried history. Historians of Quakerism have often misinterpreted the earliest Friends' prophetic experiences, and this is largely due to the influences of the Second Generation of Quakers who aimed to reconstruct Quaker history by virtually excising the traces of enthusiastic and atavistic expressions among its first generation of worshippers. Phyllis Mack, for example, presents invaluable and thorough research about the lives of seventeenth-century Quaker women, but in her analysis of gender studies, she posits that these women preached as "disembodied spirits 'in the light,' not as women." She casts their prophesyings in terms of "self-annihilation," asserting that the Quaker women "transcended [their] womanhood," and finally compares them to the archetype of "the aggressive, male Old Testament hero." In such an interpretation, Mack ultimately elides the ways in which Friends were wholly in their bodies as they were filled with spirit, the one no longer separated from the other in their radicalized and feminized expression of God. See Phyllis Mack, *Visionary Women: Gender and Prophecy in Seventeenth-Century England* (Berkeley: University of California Press, 1992), 134, 173. For a Quaker woman's wonderful discussion of reclaiming the body in Friends' history and spirituality, see Sheila Ruth, *Take Back the Light: A Feminist Reclamation of Spirituality and Religion* (Lanham, Md.: Rowman & Littlefield, 1994).

3. This is the Quaker term for conversion.

4. Clarendon MS. 2624, as cited in Henry J. Cadbury, "Early Use of the Word 'Quaker,'" *Journal of the Friends Historical Society* 49 (1959): 5. For a further discussion on early Quaker women, see Christine Trevett, *Women and Quakerism in the Seventeenth Century* (York, England: Ebor Press, 1991); Margaret Hope Bacon, *Mothers of Feminism: The Story of Quaker Women in America* (San Francisco: Harper & Row, 1986); Mary Maples Dunn, "Women of Light," in Carol Ruth Berkin and Mary Beth Norton, eds.,

Women of America: A History (Boston: Houghton Mifflin Company, 1979), 115–36; Elisabeth Potts Brown and Susan Mosher Stuard, eds., *Witnesses for Change: Quaker Women over Three Centuries* (New Brunswick, N.J.: Rutgers University Press, 1989), 71–85; Cristine Levenduski, *Peculiar Power: A Quaker Woman Preacher in Eighteenth-Century America* (Washington: Smithsonian Institution Press, 1996), 1–39; Mack, *Visionary Women*; Rebecca Larson, *Daughters of Light: Quaker Women Preaching and Prophesying in the Colonies and Abroad, 1700–1775* (New York: Alfred A. Knopf, 1999); and Michele Lise Tarter, "Sites of Performance: Theorizing the History of Sexuality in the Lives and Writings of Quaker Women, 1650–1800" (Ph.D. dissertation, University of Colorado, 1993).

5. See Elizabeth V. Spelman, "Woman as Body: Ancient and Contemporary Views," in Max O. Hallman, ed., *Expanding Philosophical Horizons: A Non-Traditional Philosophy Reader* (Belmont, Calif.: Wadsworth Publishing Company, 1995), 32–45; and Mieke Bal, "Sexuality, Sin and Sorrow: The Emergence of Female Character (A Reading of Genesis 1–3)" in Susan Rubin Suleiman, ed., *The Female Body in Western Culture* (Cambridge, Mass.: Harvard University Press, 1986), 317–38.

6. This was a commonly used biblical metaphor in Anglican and Puritan literature of the seventeenth century. As Elizabeth Maddock Dillon discusses in her essay in this volume, the metaphor was quite popular among Puritan male clergy, but I suggest that Quaker women had a unique understanding and use of this phrase, reflecting their authorized roles as Spiritual Mothers and as prophets of their religious family. For a discussion of women's use of childbirth and nursing metaphors, see Susan Stanford Friedman, "Creativity and the Childbirth Metaphor: Gender Difference in Literary Discourse," in Elaine Showalter, ed., *Speaking of Gender* (New York: Routledge, 1989), 73–100.

7. Contemporary feminist theologians discuss at length the imperative of reconnecting the body and the spirit in religious practice. This, they note, will heal the destructive, misogynist fallout of dualism in Judeo-Christian religious systems. See Elizabeth A. Johnson, *She Who Is: The Mystery of God in Feminist Theological Discourse* (New York: Crossroad, 1992); Elisabeth Moltmann-Wendel, *I Am My Body: A Theology of Embodiment* (New York: Continuum, 1995); Elisabeth Schussler Fiorenza, *In Memory of Her: A Feminist Theological Reconstruction of Christian Origins* (New York: Crossroad, 1983); Rosemary Radford Ruether, *Sexism and God-Talk: Toward a Feminist Theology* (Boston: Beacon Press, 1983); and Carol Christ, *Diving Deep and Surfacing: Women Writers on Spiritual Quest* (Boston: Beacon Press, 1980).

8. For a general overview of Fox and his early preaching, see Cecil Sharman, *George Fox and the Quakers* (Richmond, Ind.: Friends United Press, 1991); Hugh Barbour and J. William Frost, *The Quakers* (New York: Greenwood Press, 1988); and Larry Ingle, *First Among Friends: George Fox and the Creation of Quakerism* (Oxford, U.K.: Oxford University Press, 1994).

9. I am indebted to Richard Bailey for the term *celestial flesh,* which he uses to describe the transformation among Friends when "spirit poured onto flesh" during their meetings and they, in turn, became the prophetic, "living Christ." Bailey's groundbreaking study re-visions Quaker history by addressing Fox's theology of christopresentism (see *New Light on George Fox and Early Quakerism*). Also see Geoffrey F. Nuttall, *Studies in Christian Enthusiasm, Illustrated from Early Quakerism* (Wallingford, Pa.: Pendle Hill Publications, 1948); I. M. Lewis, *Ecstatic Religion: A Study of Shamanism and Spirit Possession* (London: Routledge, 1989); and Clarke Garrett, *Spirit Possession and Popular Religion: From the Camisards to the Shakers* (Baltimore: Johns Hopkins University Press, 1987).

10. For a further discussion of *scriptura rediviva*—the resurrection of scripture through embodiment—among Friends, see Jackson Cope, "Seventeenth-Century Quaker Style," in

Stanley E. Fish, ed., *Seventeenth-Century Prose: Modern Essays in Criticism* (New York: Oxford University Press, 1971), 223. Quote is taken from Dorothy White, *This To Be Delivered to the Counsellors* ... (London: Printed for Thomas Simmons, 1659), 8.

11. Studies indicate that by 1660, there were as many as sixty thousand Friends, with a propensity of women members. See Mack, *Visionary Women;* Keith Thomas, "Women and Civil War Sects," *Past and Present* 13 (1958): 42–63; and Mary Maples Dunn, "Saints and Sisters," in Janet Wilson James, ed., *Women in American Religion* (Philadelphia: University of Pennsylvania Press, 1989), 71–85. Priscilla Cotton, *A Visitation of Love Unto All People* (London, 1661), 3. Also see Bailey, 227.

12. See Caroline Walker Bynum, *Fragmentation and Redemption: Essays on Gender and the Human Body* (New York: Zone Books, 1991), as well as her study of *Jesus as Mother: Studies in the Spirituality of the High Middle Ages* (Berkeley: University of California Press, 1982). Also see Margaret R. Miles, *Carnal Knowing: Female Nakedness and Religious Meaning in the Christian West* (Boston: Beacon Press, 1989). Quote is taken from Bynum's *Fragmentation and Redemption*, 101.

13. Rebecca Travers, *A Message from the Spirit of Truth Unto the Holy Seed* (London: Printed for Thomas Simmons, 1658), 4; Martha Simmonds, *Oh England thy time is come*, n.d., 4; Fox's quote is cited in Christopher Hill, *The World Turned Upside Down* (New York: Penguin, 1975), 155. William Dewsbury's epistle (10th of 12th month, 1660) is quoted in Rufus M. Jones, ed., *A Little Book of Selections from the Children of Light* (London: Headley Brothers, 1909), 20; Thomas Willan to Swarthmore Hall (1655), Swarthmore Mss. 1:255, quoted in Nuttall, *Studies in Christian Enthusiasm*, 58–59; Charles Marshall, "The Journal of that Faithful Minister of Christ Jesus, Charles Marshall," in *Friends Library*, 4:134; and *The Memory of the Righteous Revived* (1689), quoted in William C. Braithwaite, *The Beginnings of Quakerism* (Cambridge, U.K.: Cambridge University Press, 1955), 167. Michele Lise Tarter, " 'Made to Cry Like a Woman in Travail': The Construction and Performance of Quaker Masculinity in Old and New England, 1650–1800," paper delivered at Institute of Early American History and Culture conference, Boulder, Colorado, 1996. On Quakers' "feminine" religious style, see Jack Marietta, *The Reformation of American Quakerism, 1748–1783* (Philadelphia: University of Pennsylvania, 1984), 31, and Phyllis Mack, "Feminine Behavior and Radical Action," *Signs* 11 (1985–86): 457–77.

14. Some historians limit Spiritual Mothers to women who were older and held social status, but I would suggest that this stratification occurred only after the religious society was formally regulated and censored. See Hugh Barbour, "Quaker Prophetesses and Mothers in Israel," in J. William Frost and John H. Moore, eds., *Seeking the Light: Essays in Quaker History* (Wallingford, Pa.: Pendle Hill Publications, 1986), 41–60; and Mack, *Visionary Women*, 58. It is of particular note that Fox was the only "Father" of this religious family, and his wife, Margaret Fell, was called its "Nursing Mother."

15. Francis Higginson, *A Brief Relation of the Irreligion of the Northern Quakers* (London, 1653), 15; Fox's quotation, drawn from an early epistle, is cited in Cope, "Seventeenth-Century Quaker Style," 206. See Richard Bauman, "Speaking in the Light: The Role of the Quaker Minister," in Richard Bauman and Joel Sherzer, eds., *Explorations in the Ethnography of Speaking* (Cambridge, U.K.: Cambridge University Press, 1989); and also his book, *Let Your Words Be Few: Symbolism of Speaking and Silence among Seventeenth-Century Quakers* (Cambridge, U.K.: Cambridge University Press, 1983).

16. See Toril Moi, ed., *The Kristeva Reader* (New York: Columbia University Press, 1986); and Elizabeth Grosz, *Jacques Lacan: A Feminist Introduction* (London: Routledge, 1990), 151–52. Description of meeting is taken from Higginson, *A Brief Relation*, 15.

17. Many scientific tracts were issued at this time that attempted to unfold the mysteries of the body, particularly in its relation to science and spirit. See, for example, Helkiah Crooke's book, *Microcosmographia, or a Description of the Body of Man ...* (London: W. Iaggard, 1615), as well as John Bulwer's *Anthropometamorphosis: Man Transform'd* (London: Printed by William Hunt, 1653). I thank Robert Blair St. George for introducing Bulwer's text to me.

18. For an example of Friends' countenances changing during meetings, see George Fox's *Journal,* ed. John J. Nickalls (London: Religious Society of Friends, 1986), 43. Quotation is taken from Ephraim Pagitt, *Heresiography* (London: Printed for W. L., 1654), 136.

19. Anonymous, *The Quaker's Dream; or The Devil's Pilgrimmage in England* (London, 1655), 3–4; Anonymous, *The Quacking Mountebanck* (London, 1655), 4; Anonymous, *The Character of a Quaker and His True and Proper Colours...* (London, 1671), 9.

20. Anonymous, *The Quakers and Querers Cause* (London, 1653), 45; Jeremiah Ives, *The Quakers Quaking* (London, 1656), vi; William Prynne, *The Quakers Unmasked, and Clearly Detected to be but the Spawn of Romish Frogs, Jesuites, and Franciscan Freers ...* (London, 1655), 6.

21. See Huston Diehl, "Dazzling Theater: Renaissance Drama in the Age of Reform," *Journal of Medieval and Renaissance Studies* 22 (1992): 211–35; Laura Levine, *Men in Women's Clothing: Anti-theatricality and Effeminization, 1579–1642* (Cambridge, U.K.: Cambridge University Press, 1994); and Jonas Barish, *The Antitheatrical Prejudice* (Berkeley: University of California Press, 1981). I am thankful to Heather Shawn Nathans for recommending these sources on Renaissance theater to me.

22. Mary Douglas, *Purity and Danger: An Analysis of Concepts of Pollution and Taboo* (New York: Frederick A. Praeger, 1966), 40. Also see Julia Epstein and Kristina Straub, eds., *Body Guards: The Cultural Politics of Gender Ambiguity* (New York: Routledge, 1991).

23. Elaine Hobby, *The Virtue of Necessity: English Women's Writing, 1649–88* (Ann Arbor: University of Michigan Press, 1989), 39.

24. Craig W. Horle, *The Quakers and the English Legal System, 1660–1688* (Philadelphia: University of Pennsylvania Press, 1988), 102, 128. Also see Joseph Besse, *A Collection of the Sufferings of the People Called Quakers for the Testimony of a Good Conscience, from 1650–1680...,* 2 vols. (London: Luke Hinde, 1753); and Barry Reay, "Popular Hostility towards Quakers in Mid-Seventeenth-Century England," *Social History* 5 (October 1980): 387–407.

25. Humphrey Norton, *New England's Ensigne* (London: G. Calvert, 1659), 7; and Increase Mather, *An Essay for the Recording of Illustrious Providences* (Boston, 1684), 348–51. For further study on Quaker experiences in the early American colonies, see Carla Gardina Pestana, *Quakers and Baptists in Colonial Massachusetts* (Cambridge, Mass.: Cambridge University Press, 1991); Christine Leigh Heyrman, "Specters of Subversion, Societies of Friends: Dissent and the Devil in Provincial Essex County, Massachusetts," in David D. Hall, John M. Murrin, and Thad W. Tate, eds., *Saints and Revolutionaries: Essays on Early American History* (New York: W.W. Norton, 1984): 38–74; Frederick B. Tolles, *Quakers and the Atlantic Culture* (New York: Macmillan, 1960); and Lyle B. Koehler, *A Search for Power: The "Weaker Sex" in Seventeenth-Century New England* (Urbana: University of Illinois Press, 1980).

26. John Rous et al., *New England: A Degenerate Plant* (London, 1659), 7. Witchcraft searches were intended to discover "marks" of witchcraft—that is, extra teats on women's bodies, believed to be areas where Satan and his familiars could suckle. These marks could have been anything from a birthmark, a mole, a scar, a skin lesion, or even a supernumerary nipple. Between 1656 and 1664, eleven of the twenty-two witchcraft

accusations in the colonies were directed at Quaker women (no men Friends were ever accused of such a charge).

27. Rufus Jones, *The Quakers in the American Colonies* (London: MacMillan and Company, 1923), 28; George Bishop, *New England Judged By the Spirit of the Lord*, 2nd ed. (London: T. Sowle, 1703), 12.

28. See Amanda Porterfield, *Female Piety in Puritan New England* (New York: Oxford University Press, 1992); and Laurel Thatcher Ulrich, *Good Wives: Image and Reality in the Lives of Women in Northern New England, 1650–1750* (New York: Alfred A. Knopf, 1982). I am thankful to the anonymous readers of this manuscript for their insights here.

29. The Puritan authorities set up separate laws for Quaker men and women, assessing their different kinds of threats to Puritan hegemony. The first time any Quaker man came to Boston, he was to be punished by having his right ear cut off; on a second appearance, his left ear would be dismembered; on a third offense, his tongue was to be bored with a hot iron; and, on a fourth offense, he was to be hanged to death. For a thorough description of the physical persecutions, see Rous, *New England: A Degenerate Plant*, and Bishop, *New England Judged*. Also, see Pestana, *Quakers and Baptists in Colonial Massachusetts*, for an investigation of Puritan laws created specifically for Friends.

30. It should be noted that only Quaker women went naked as a sign in the early American colonies. See Kenneth Carroll, "Early Quakers and 'Going Naked as a Sign,'" *Quaker History* 67 (autumn 1978):69–87; and Norman Penney, ed., *The First Publishers of Truth* (London: Headley Brothers, 1907), 364–369. For quotations, see Bishop, *New England Judged*, 232 and Norton, *New England's Ensigne*, 70.

31. For the detailed account of Horred Gardiner, see Bishop, *New England Judged*, 52–53. On Ann Coleman, see Koehler, 255 and Swarthmoor Mss. 4:225, Friends' House Library, London. I would like to thank the Library Committee of the Britain Yearly Meeting for this reference.

32. Ann Kibbey, *The Interpretation of Material Shapes in Puritanism: A Study of Rhetoric, Prejudice, and Violence* (Cambridge, U.K.: Cambridge University Press, 1986). Fox's reference is taken from *A Paper to New England*, included in Rous, *New England: A Degenerate Plant*, 15. Also see Edward Burroughs, *A Declaration of the Sad and Great Persecution and Martyrdom of the People of God, called Quakers, in New England* (London: Printed for Robert Wilson, 1661), 14–16.

33. The use of the word *antic* offers an interesting comparison to the descriptions Puritans gave of Native Americans, as discussed in Alice Nash's essay in this volume. See John Norton, *The Heart of New-England Rent* (1659), 65–8.

34. See Koehler, *A Search for Power*, 256; Jeanette Carter Gadt, "Women and Protestant Culture: The Quaker Dissent from Puritanism" (Ph.D. dissertation, University of California, Los Angeles, 1974), 139–150; Carol F. Karlsen, *The Devil in the Shape of a Woman: Witchcraft in Colonial New England* (New York: Vintage, 1987); and Elizabeth Reis, *Damned Women: Sinners and Witches in Puritan New England* (Ithaca, N.Y.: Cornell University Press, 1997). I thank Janet Moore Lindman for her helpful comments on this point.

35. Burroughs, *A Declaration*, 26–30.

36. See Johan Winsser, "Mary Dyer and the 'Monster' Story," *Quaker History* 79 (spring 1990):20–34; and Jones, *The Quakers in the American Colonies*, 89. For a discussion of Puritan leaders' "malefic" actions, see Ann Kibbey, "Mutations of the Supernatural: Witchcraft, Remarkable Providences, and the Power of Puritan Men," *American Quarterly* 34 (summer 1982): 125–48.

37. See Carla Gardina Pestana, "The Quaker Execution as Myth and History," *The Journal of American History* 80 (September 1993): 441–69.

"Antic Deportments and Indian Postures"

Embodiment in the Seventeenth-Century Anglo-Algonquian World

ALICE NASH

William Wood's promotional tract, *New England's Prospect,* published in London in 1634, gives a charming description of the indigenous people who lived just northwest of Boston: "[T]ake them when the blood brisks in their veins, when the flesh is on their backs and the marrow in their bones, when they frolic in their antic deportments and Indian postures, and they are more amiable to behold (though only in Adam's livery) than many a compounded fantastic in the newest fashion."[1] Wood's description of Indian bodies in motion as "antic" is echoed by other seventeenth-century English writers. We might ask, what's Indian about "antic"?[2]

In this chapter, "antic" and other English representations of indigenous dance will be the point of entry for an exploration of embodiment in the seventeenth century Anglo-Algonquian world. First, we can use the information left by English writers to learn something about dance and other forms of ritual movement among eastern Algonquian peoples, producing an ethnographic breakdown of styles and occasions for dance. Second, these descriptions tell us much about the English. As Edward Said and others have noted, writings about the Other often tell us more about the seers than the seen.[3] We cannot know how Indians *felt* when they danced four hundred years ago, but we can discern much about the feelings and especially the anxieties they aroused in some English, especially the clergy. Delineating the cultural filters through which English people perceived Indians enables us to sift through their words and, with help from other kinds of ethnographic information, gain insight into why Indian dances were "antic." Finally, I will draw on theories of embodiment to consider dance and the body as sites of colonization and resistance.

European explorers witnessed Indian dances along the Atlantic coast as early as the sixteenth century. In 1534 Jacques Cartier, anchored near Chaleur Bay (New Brunswick), recorded the approach of seven canoes of Mi'kmaq, who danced and showed "many signs of joy, and of their desire to be friends." On another occasion, Cartier and his men went ashore to trade. He noted that some of the Mi'kmaq women stayed on the opposite shore where they danced and sang, "standing in the water up to their knees."[4] Although Cartier's account is not especially descriptive of the physical movements involved, his report of similar greetings on other occasions establishes that singing and dancing were an important part of the ceremony involved in meeting or leaving strangers. Samuel de Champlain made similar observations some seventy years after Cartier when he traveled from southern Maine to Cape Cod.[5]

Roger Williams reported that the Narragansett people of southern New England held feasts or dances of distinct types. He distinguished first of all between public and private events, then between ceremonies and celebrations. Ceremonies, he wrote, took place on occasions of "sicknesse, or Drouth, or Warre, or Famine"; celebrations took place during times of "caulme of Peace, Health, Plenty, Prosperity."[6] Of the latter, Williams particularly noted the winter dances, saying that "they run mad once a yeare in their kind of Christmas feasting."[7] Daniel Gookin described harvest time "dancings, and feastings, and revellings" that could last up to a week at a time. In these, the men danced singly and in the course of their turn gave away all of their possessions, "according to [their] fancy and affection." Gookin equated these giveaways with profligacy and cautioned that "much impiety is committed at such times."[8] Another example of a giveaway dance, performed by four men and four women, was described by Mary Rowlandson during her captivity among the Wampanoag in 1675. Weetamoo, a female leader, started the dance wearing "girdles of wampum from the loins upward; her arms from her elbows to her hands [were] covered with bracelets." She also wore "handfuls of necklaces about her neck and several sorts of jewels on her ears," all to be given away in a ritual that redistributed wealth among the group.[9]

Ceremonies seemed stranger than celebrations to the English, especially when conducted by *powows*, or Indian shamans. A brief digression is in order to clarify these terms. *Shaman* has become a generic word in late-twentieth-century popular culture that subsumes the diversity of spiritual and healing powers recognized among different ethnic groups across time and space.[10] *Powow* is even more problematic, having changed from a word used by a specific group to refer to a particular type of healer, what John Josselyn called a physician or "Indian priest," to a present-day term (more commonly spelled "powwow") for pan-Indian events that feature dance, music, and crafts.

Among seventeenth-century Massachusett speakers, *powow* referred specifically to one who had the power to heal or harm through spiritual means. Edward Winslow wrote, "The Powah is eager and free in speech; fierce in countenance; and joineth many antic and laborious gestures with the same, over the party diseased." Quite different abilities were attributed to *pineses,* warriors whose spirit power could make them invulnerable in battle if they only had time to prepare. Winslow also mentioned a third type of spirit power that was so rare and secret he could not determine its name.[11]

Powows and their healing ceremonies attracted particular notice from English writers. John Josselyn observed that powows placed a sick person on the ground and danced "in an Antick manner round about him, beating their naked breasts with a strong hand, and making hideous faces, sometimes calling upon the Devil for his help."[12] Indeed, Roger Williams claimed that powows cured only with the help of the Devil and that Indians knew nothing about herbal medicine.[13] It may be that curing ceremonies, being highly visible and audible, received more attention than the quiet administration of herbal medicines and poultices.[14]

Dances related to warfare seemed not only strange but also frightening to English observers, especially for captives who spent sleepless nights listening to their captors sing and dance. Sometimes the dances involved preparation for war, including divination rituals that were used to predict the likelihood of success. Before the start of King Philip's War in 1675, Peter Nunnuit, a relative of Metacomet (also known as Philip to the English), told Benjamin Church that "there would certainly be war, for Philip had held a dance of several weeks continuance, and had entertained the young men from all parts of the country." When Awashunkes, the female sachem of Saconet (present-day Little Compton, Rhode Island), had to make a decision about which side to take in the war, she called hundreds of Indians together for a great dance. Church noted that this was "the custom of that nation when they advise about momentous affairs." When he arrived at the dance, he found Awashunkes "in a foaming sweat" leading the dancers.[15] For the Indians, war dances were an occasion for honoring allies, reciting past grievances, and stirring up one's courage.

Some English captives had their worst fears confirmed as Indian dancing led to torture, although ritual torture was more systematically practiced among the Iroquois than among the eastern Algonquian speakers of New England. Cotton Mather, in his typically descriptive manner, wrote that in 1690 one Robert Rogers (better known as "Robin Pork" for his corpulence) was tortured to death by his Abenaki captors after he tried to escape. According to Mather, the Indians "made themselves a supper, singing, dancing, roaring, and uttering many signs of joy" as Rogers awaited his fate. Burning him at the stake, "they danced about him, and at every turn, they did with their knives cut collops of his flesh."[16] Mather collected horror stories from the borders of English settlement to stir up anti-Indian sentiment and justify

New England's expansionist policies, although he would have said he was putting forth evidence of God's judgment on sinners.[17]

Most descriptions of Indian dances focus on men, although women may have been present. Women's bodies in general are frustratingly absent from early accounts, except as viewed from a distance by English men. While women generally participated in group dances, there are few descriptions as graphic as those of the female leaders Awashunkes and Weetamoo noted above. Around 1690, a Narragansett woman gave a feast where she danced, gave away gifts, and took a new name for herself in an effort to rid herself of bad luck. The same year, John Gyles witnessed an example of bear cere-monialism among the Maliseet, in which an old woman and a male captive stood outside her wigwam, "shaking their hands and body as in a dance, and singing to greet the bears emerging from their winter dens."[18] It seems, then, that both men and women danced in ritual and social contexts. Gender-based proscriptions probably followed the gendered division of labor and social roles within each ethnic group. Thus, a war dance might have been limited to warriors rather than to men in a strictly biological sense. Since most women did not become warriors, a female leader such as Awashunkes stood out.[19]

One reason why some writers treated Indian dances as unfamiliar but in-teresting while others found them diabolical is that the movements and con-texts of Indian dances described by English observers varied. Different peo-ple saw different things, including dances that were healing ceremonies or divination rituals. Some of the colonists attended dances as guests at a feast, others as allies preparing for war, still others as captives unsure of their fate. Overall, these texts document a style of dancing that kept the feet closely connected to the earth, with variable movements of the upper torso, head and arms, without any swaying of the hips or sexually mimetic movements. Sometimes dancers worked themselves into a frenzy; "shouting, howling, and stamping against the ground, with many Anticke tricks and faces, making noise like so many Wolves or Devils."[20] At other times, the dancers formed a circle but stayed in one place, "or nearly so," while moving the arms and striking the ground with their feet to the accompaniment of simple chanting, a drum or a rattle.[21] Similar dances are still performed by Indians in public and private forums across the Americas. For all the distinctions that can be made between Indians across time and space, dancing is and has been an ac-tivity closely associated with Indian cultures.

The English men and women who colonized New England brought with them their own traditions of dance.[22] Even the redoubtable Increase Mather thought that "*Dancing* or *Leaping,* is a natural expression of joy: So that there is no more Sin in it, than Laughter," although he objected to what he called "promiscuous" or mixed dancing and took care to point out that the Scriptures recommend "*Gravity* and *Sobriety*" for Christians at all times. Mather had no such indulgence for what he viewed as the "*Satanical Dances*" performed by Indians, at which "by their own confessions" the Devil appeared in bodily form.[23]

But the colonists also recognized similarities between Indians and themselves, although it made them uncomfortable to do so. Puritan leaders had enough trouble trying to root out elements of English folk culture drawn from older Celtic and medieval traditions, as seen in popular religion, folk magic, and the "promiscuous dances" that Increase Mather protested. Although it is important to remember that some of these similarities were more apparent than actual, it is also true that Indian dances embodied a worldview that threatened Puritan hegemony in two ways: first, because it spoke to English customs and folk beliefs that they hoped to suppress, such as the maypoles and Morris dancing discussed below, and second, because the "energy, duration, and obvious ritual salience of these performances" dramatized the vitality of indigenous cultures in a way that challenged colonial efforts to construe them as inferior and dying-out.[24]

This is where the association between "antic" and Indian dances is most revealing. The *Oxford English Dictionary* (*OED*) defines antic as "absurd from fantastic incongruity; grotesque, bizarre, uncouthly ludicrous."[25] Of six instances where seventeenth-century New England writers used the word *antic* in relation to Indian dances, four describe a quality of movement, as in "antic deportments." Another case suggests "a performer who plays a grotesque or ludicrous part, a clown," as in "they song and danced after their manner like Anticks." Perhaps the most evocative use of the word occurs in William Wood's account of an Abenaki man who was tortured by Mohawks. Wood heard the story from the man himself, who managed to escape, but Wood put his own distinctive twist on the tale. He described the hapless victim as "hemmed in with a ring of bare-skinned Morris dancers who presented their antics before him." In this case, according to the *OED*, the word indicates "a grotesque pageant or theatrical representation." Wood deftly evoked both strangeness and spectacle. An earlier usage of "antic" in this manner appears in William Shakespeare's *Love's Labours Lost*, as "Some delightfull ostentation or show, or pageant, or anticke, or fire-works."[26] (One wonders if Wood would have worded it differently had his informant been English rather than Abenaki.)

It is worth noting that the Morris dancing referred to by Wood is an English cultural form that was highly contested in the early seventeenth century. During the sixteenth century these dances, which featured characters such as the Fool, Robin Hood (the "Lord of Misrule") and his friends, or a May Lady and Lord, frequently took place in royal or noble households or at parish fundraising events such as May games and church Ales, the latter featuring ale brewed by the church wardens. Thus, Morris dancing took place in a carnivalesque atmosphere of social inversion and alcoholic consumption with overtones of royalist and Catholic parish support that sober-minded Puritans sought to suppress, both in England and in Massachusetts Bay.[27] At the same time, other colonists inscribed these meanings onto Indians and the land, notably along the Gulf of Maine where Wabanaki leaders known to the English as Robin Hood, Dick Swash, and Jack Pudding signed deeds in the area of Merrymeeting Bay.[28] English popular culture provided a rich symbolic framework through which to interpret Indian bodies.

But *antic* is also the English version of a word first used to describe the "fantastic representations of human, animal, and floral forms, incongruously running into one another" that were found in excavating Titus's baths in late-fifteenth-century Italy. English writers called them "antic" because these images derived from ancient Rome; Italians and other Europeans described them as "grotesque," from "grotto," because the excavations opened up underground caverns.[29] In the context of an emerging discourse of English colonialism, "antic" located Indians in the ancient world, marking them as pagans and primitives, frozen in time and unworthy of the consideration due to a Christian people.[30] Simultaneously, it linked Indians to pagan English traditions such as Morris dancing and maypoles. When Thomas Morton erected a maypole at Marymount and consorted with Indian women, his peers accused him of trying to revive "the beastly practices of the mad Baccanalians."[31]

However, the use of the word *antic* also implies that these writers recognized, consciously or not, an important aspect of Indian culture—the interconnectedness of all living things—while coding it as a negative trait. It is notable that "antic" is used specifically in relation to powows in three of the six cases above. While the steps used for social dances tended to be simple, aiming at group unity rather than personal display, and steps used by hunters and warriors probably referenced hunting and warfare, powows may have used specialized movements that, by English standards, conflated the human, animal, and spirit worlds in ways that fit the *OED* definition: "grotesque, bizarre, uncouthly ludicrous." Hobbomock, the Wampanoag deity voted "most likely to be the Devil" by the English, sometimes appeared to worthy men in the shape of a man, a deer, an eagle, or, most often, a snake.[32] All of these manifestations could conceivably be represented through dance. Anyone who takes the time to observe how animals and people move, to consider the different centers of gravity, tensions, joint articulations, rhythms, and habits, can start to find that movement within their body. What one does with it, how any individual experience interprets or expresses it, is, of course, culturally and historically variable.[33]

Scattered references suggest that warriors and hunters did not simply show off their prowess when they danced. They demonstrated hunting or warrior strategies, mimicked the movement of different kinds of prey, and rehearsed unique predicaments and how the hunter or warrior responded, developing a repertoire of experience that might help someone else to survive a similar situation. Henry Grace, living as a captive among the Mi'kmaq in 1750, saw Indians "flinging themselves into different Postures, sometimes upon one

Knee, sometimes on their Elbows, and sometimes upon their Bellies, crawling along to imitate their going to kill some Centinel or wild Beast, and then suddenly jump up and dance again."[34] Skills such as "leaping and dancing" to avoid arrows when fighting on an open plain may have persisted in dance long after guns made them impractical in actual warfare.[35]

Indian dances were "antic," then, because they mixed up categories kept distinct by English sensibilities. In eastern Algonquian languages, nouns are categorized not by gender, but by qualities of being animate and inanimate—that is, into living and nonliving things.[36] What seemed antic and grotesque to English-speakers—dances that invoked relationships between human beings and animals, or human beings and the spirit world—did not cross important conceptual boundaries for the Indians.

George Lakoff and Mark Johnson, separately and together, have examined how conceptual categories are embedded in language, and how cognition and metaphor are rooted in the body. There are fundamental relationships that result from living in human bodies—what Johnson calls *image-schemata*—such as paths (the concept of going from one point to another), cycles (especially in women's bodies), and balance. While the meaning associated with these relationships may vary between cultural groups, metaphors based on embodied experience have some specific connotation in most cultures. But because they are rooted in the body, the meanings attributed to them seem to reflect objective reality or natural, timeless categories. Bodies *shape* our view of the world but also *verify* it as certain things become coded onto the body.[37] Because these codes seem "natural," it can be discomforting or frightening to encounter other people whose body codes seem undecipherable, in part because the exchange takes place at a level that cannot always be articulated. As Pierre Bourdieu has noted, ideologies are most powerful when they are unspoken, when they do not have to be put into words.[38]

One area that particularly horrified the colonists, and which is still difficult to decode, is torture as practiced by Iroquoian and eastern Algonquian peoples. Torture was not new to Europeans, of course. Elaine Scarry's analysis of torture as a power dynamic in which the torturer extends his or her self outwardly, destroying the language and selfhood of the torturee, is persuasive in a modern context.[39] But it seems clear that something else was going on when Indians tortured captives. A major consideration seems to be that it allowed people, especially women, to fulfill their obligation to avenge the dead and exorcise their grief over the death of loved ones. A brave death under torture brought spiritual power and honor to everyone involved, and rather than being deprived of language, torture victims by most accounts died singing and making jokes or noble remarks.[40] In this sense the Jesuit martyrs made a good impression on their Indian captors; physical pain as a pathway to spiritual enlightenment is one point of conjuncture between Indian and Christian religious practices. One wonders how these rituals changed when

Euro-American captives, rather than dying bravely, screamed or cried or begged for mercy.

A number of English captives carried to Canada in the mid eighteenth century reported that they were made to sing and dance before a mixed Abenaki, Iroquois, and French audience at French forts along the way, and again on entering their captors' home village. This performance, in which English men, women, and children had to dance and sing, was apparently meant to provide entertainment for the audience, at the very least, and to enhance the warriors' status. Susannah Johnson said that her captors "took great pleasure in introducing their prisoners."[41] While folklore and oral history accounts suggest that such performances offered captives an opportunity to gain status in Indian communities through a display of courage, prowess, or spiritual power,[42] English captives generally experienced these rituals as embodying a loss of social power. Nehemiah Howe was forced to dance in a circle and sing, "I don't know where I go." Titus King, a brash young man at the time of his capture, translated his song as "I'm sorry I am taken, I want to go home to see the girls." Mrs. Johnson and her six-year-old son were drilled so intensively that she still remembered the Abenaki words over forty years later. However, she primly remarked, "Whether this talk was imposed on us for their diversion, or a religious ceremonial, I cannot say, but it was very painful and offensive."[43]

Did English bodies forced into "Indian postures" become "antic"? Evidence from captivity narratives, the first "native" American literary form, suggests that this was a real possibility, either to be feared or embraced.[44] English men, women, and children who were captured by Indians during the intercolonial wars of the seventeenth and eighteenth centuries sometimes preferred to stay in Indian communities, effectively becoming Indians. While only a fraction of these captives made a permanent transition to Indian ways of life, the experience of living with Indians continued to affect those who returned to New England. Former captives appear in colonial records as interpreters, traders, and social misfits, including some of the young women who made accusations of witchcraft at Salem in 1692.[45]

When cultural identity is coded onto physical movements such as dancing or hunting, the experience of performing those movements creates a sense of order and continuity in the world—or, in the case of captives such as Susannah Johnson, disorder. This close relation between embodied experience, cultural practice, and worldview, I suggest, partly explains the persistence of Indian cultural identity in the Northeast. Hunting and fishing are not just hobbies or even sources of food, although they are important in that way. As lived practices, they affirm (and produce) a relationship to the world that continues to have meaning.

Indian bodies became part of the ongoing struggle over colonization in the Anglo-Algonquian world. Among other changes, Indians who converted to Christianity learned to sit soberly in worship instead of dancing. Colonial officials sought to regulate the external appearance of local Indians through dress codes and more intimate matters by enacting penalties for personal practices such as menstrual seclusion.[46] The interpretive frameworks available for English colonists who witnessed eastern Algonquian dances produced readings of Indian bodies in motion as pagan, unbounded, and dangerous. Rather than easing the problems of cross-cultural communication, contact had the potential to heighten English anxieties.

It is not surprising, then, that specialized dances related to hunting, warfare, divination, or curing ceremonies disappeared from view, whether they were no longer danced or whether they were simply danced away from colonizing eyes. Christian Indians may have given up those dances most closely associated with "satanical" rituals at the instigation of ministers, or of their own volition.[47] As the ecological landscape of New England changed, hunting lore once essential for survival became obsolete or hobbyist in nature, and the personal acts of skill and bravery required by old styles of warfare gave way to gun-distant killing. Yet opposition also enhanced the power of Indian dances as a site of resistance. For example, in the early eighteenth century, Abenaki people who had fled from New England to New France started practicing the Calumet Dance, a ritual they learned from other Indians, at the St. Francis mission. Their missionary, Jacques LeSueur, made every effort to suppress it. He identified the dance as both a spiritual and a political threat: spiritual, because the dancers claimed it helped them to conquer their enemies, change the weather, and chase away evil, among other things that should have been reserved for Christian prayers; political, because through this dance the Abenakis flaunted their desire to ally themselves with the Renards of the *pays d'en haut* in opposition to the French.[48] In the present day, dance continues to be a practice that asserts the ongoing presence of Indian peoples in the Northeast, as powwows proliferate in New England and across the country.

In sum, English descriptions of Indian bodies in motion enable us to learn something about the forms and occasions of eastern Algonquian dance. We see that dance played a key role in public and private life through its potential to harness and express spirit power and emotion. This same quality made it inimical to English Puritans, who rejected the worldview embodied in these dances and sought to impose order (as they understood it) on antic bodies. Whether or not dancing was central to Indian identity in the period before European contact, colonial efforts to stamp out Indian dances heightened the potential of these dances to assert, verify, and produce Indianness in the Anglo-Algonquian world.

Notes

1. William Wood, *New England's Prospect,* ed. Alden T. Vaughan (Amherst: University of Massachusetts Press, 1977 [1634]), 82. Note that "Adam's Livery" does not necessarily

mean nakedness. Daniel Gookin wrote that Indian clothing was "of the same matter as Adam's was, viz. skins of beasts, as deer, moose, beaver, otters, rackoons, foxes, and other wild creatures." See Daniel Gookin, "Historical Collections of the Indians in New England," *Massachusetts Historical Society Collections* (Boston, 1792), 1st. ser., 1:152.

2. I use the word *Indian* when making a general reference to the eastern Algonquian-speaking peoples encompassed by this study (centered on New England but stretching north to the Maritimes and south to Virginia along the eastern seaboard) because the term is contemporary to the period and appears to have been used by both English and indigenous peoples.

3. Edward W. Said, *Orientalism* (New York: Vintage Books, 1979), 20–23.

4. Ramsay Cook, intro. and ed., *The Voyages of Jacques Cartier*, trans. H. P. Biggar (Toronto: University of Toronto Press, 1993), 20, 22.

5. H. P. Biggar, ed., *The Works of Samuel de Champlain*, 6 vols. (Toronto: The Champlain Society, 1936), 1:293, 296, 323, 325, 335, 336, 338, 344, 349, 350.

6. Roger Williams, *A Key into the Language of America*, ed. John J. Teunissen and Evelyn J. Hinz (Detroit: Wayne State University Press, 1973), 191.

7. Williams, *A Key*, 192.

8. Gookin, "Historical Collections," 1:153.

9. Mary Rowlandson, *The Sovereignty and Goodness of God*, in Alden T. Vaughan and Edward W. Clark, eds., *Puritans Among the Indians: Accounts of Captivity and Redemption, 1676–1724* (Cambridge, Mass.: The Belknap Press of Harvard University Press, 1981 [1682]), 65.

10. The classic anthropological study is Mircea Eliade, *Shamanism: Archaic Techniques of Ecstasy*, trans. Willard R. Trask (Princeton, N.J.: Princeton University Press, 1964).

11. Edward Winslow, *Good News from New England*, in Edward Arber, ed., *The Story of the Pilgrim Fathers, 1606–1623 A.D.; as told by themselves, their friends, and their enemies* (Boston: Hougton, Mifflin & Co., 1897 [1624]), 583–86. The powers and function of individuals generically described as "shamans" may vary within and between ethnic groups. The Penobscot word, *mede'olinu*, refers to the sound of drumming, i.e., the hand drum used in many ceremonies. Frank G. Speck, "Penobscot Shamanism," *Memoirs of the American Anthropological Association* 6:4 (1919):240–42. The Mi'kmaq used specialized terms to differentiate types of shamanic power. A *kinap* had superhuman strength and stamina; a *nikani-kjijitekewinu* had special powers of clairvoyance and prophecy; and a *puoin* was both a shapeshifter and a healer who might choose to use those powers destructively. Ruth Holmes Whitehead, *Stories from the Six Worlds: Micmac Legends* (Halifax, N.S.: Nimbus, 1988), 8–9.

12. Paul J. Lindholdt, ed., *John Josselyn, Colonial Traveler: A Critical Edition of "Two Voyages to New-England"* (Hanover, N.H.: University Press of New England, 1988), 93–95, 96.

13. Williams, *A Key*, 245.

14. For oral traditions about herbal medicine, see William S. Simmons, *Spirit of the New England Tribes: Indian History and Folklore, 1620–1984* (Hanover, N.H.: University Press of New England, 1986), 100–105; cf. Nicholas N. Smith, "The Adoption of Medicinal Plants by the Wabanaki," in William Cowan, ed., *Papers of the Tenth Algonquian Conference* (Ottawa: Carleton University, 1979), 167–72, where Smith argues that the use of herbal medicines did not develop until after the epidemics of the early contact period.

15. Thomas Church, *The History of Philip's War* (Bowie, Md.: Heritage Books, 1989), 28, 21–22.

16. Cotton Mather, "New Assaults from the Indians," in *Puritans Among the Indians*, 138–39.

17. For further discussion of how Puritan writings demonized Indians, see Richard Slotkin, *Regeneration Through Violence: The Mythology of the American Frontier, 1600–1860* (Middletown, Conn.: Wesleyan University Press, 1973).

18. Simmons, *Spirit of the New England Tribes*, 48; John Gyles, *Memoirs of Odd Adventures, Strange Deliverances, etc.* [1736], in *Puritans Among the Indians*, 104.

19. Alice Nash, "The Abiding Frontier: Family, Gender, and Religion in Wabanaki History, 1600–1763" (Ph.D. dissertation, Columbia University, 1997), 152, 159–63, 174–78; Ann Marie Plane, "Putting a Face on Colonization: Factionalism and Gender Politics in the Life History of Awashunkes, the 'Squaw Sachem' of Saconet," in Robert S. Grumet, ed., *Northeastern Indian Lives, 1632–1816* (Amherst: University of Massachusetts Press, 1996), 140–65.

20. George Percy, "Observations Gathered Out of A Discourse of the Plantation of the Souther'ne colonie in Virginia by the English, 1606," in Edward Arber, ed., *Travels and Works of Captain John Smith* (New York: Burt Franklin, 1967), lxiv.

21. Marc Lescarbot, *The History of New France*, ed. H. P. Biggar, 3 vols. (Toronto: The Champlain Society, 1907–1914), 3:108, 183–84.

22. Kate Van Winkle Keller, "Secular Music and Dance," *Encyclopedia of the North American Colonies*, vol. 3, ed. Jacob Ernest Cooke et al. (New York: Charles Scribner's Sons, 1993), 364–69.

23. Increase Mather, "An Arrow Against Profane and Promiscuous Dancing Drawn out of the Quiver of the Scriptures" [1685], in Joseph E. Marks, *The Mathers on Dancing* (New York: Dance Horizons, 1975), 45, 31, 35, 50 (emphasis in original).

24. This quote actually comes from Jean Comaroff, *Body of Power, Spirit of Resistance: The Culture and History of a South African People* (Chicago: University of Chicago Press, 1985), 151, referring to a different colonial context. English missionaries living among the Barolong boo Ratshidi on the border of South Africa and Botswana in the nineteenth century objected to their collective song and dance. Comaroff argues that Tshidi resistance to colonialism is ongoing but coded in terms of dress, colors, spatial relations in the village, and in the use of song and dance.

25. J. A. Simpson and E. S. C. Weiner, *The Oxford English Dictionary*, 2nd ed. (Oxford: The Clarendon Press of Oxford University Press, 1989), *s.v.* antic.

26. Examples that describe a quality of movement: "[W]hen they frolic in their antic deportments" (Wood, *New England's Prospect* [1634], 82); "many antic and laborious gestures" (Winslow, *Good News* [1624], 584); "strange Antick Gestures" (Williams, *A Key* [1643], 192); and "dance in an Antick manner" (Josselyn, *Two Voyages* [1674], 96). (Note that the last three examples refer to powows.) For "they song and danced after their manner like Anticks," see William Bradford and Edward Winslow, *Mourt's Relation, or A Journal of the Plantation at Plymouth*, ed. Henry Martyn Dexter (New York: Garrett Press, 1865), 88. For "a ring of bare-skinned morris dancers who presented their antics before him," see Wood, *New England's Prospect*, 76. William Shakespeare used the phrase "or anticke, or fire-works," in *Love's Labours Lost* [1588], v.i.119.

27. John Forrest and Michael Heaney, "Charting Early Morris," *Folk Music Journal* 6:2 (1991):169–86; Keith Chandler, *"Ribbons, Bells and Squeaking Fiddles": The Social History of Morris Dancing in the English South Midlands, 1660–1900*, Publications of the Folklore Society: Tradition, 1 (London: Hisarlik Press, 1993), 9–10, 42–46, 60–61.

28. Harald E. L. Prins, "Rawandagon, Alias Robin Hood: Native 'Lord of Misrule' in the Maine Wilderness," in *Northeastern Indian Lives*, 93–115; Emerson W. Baker, " 'A Scratch with a Bear's Paw': Anglo-Indian Land Deeds in Early Maine," *Ethnohistory* 36 (1989):249–52.

29. *OED*, *s.v.* antic, grotesque; Mikhail Bakhtin, *Rabelais and His World*, trans. Hélène Iswolsky (Bloomington: Indiana University Press, 1984), 31–32. *Antic* and *antique* are

described as parallel forms in the *OED;* "antic" has always had a distinct meaning, used in English where Continentals would use "grotesque." *Grotesque* did not come into common English usage for almost a century after *antic.*

30. See Peter Hulme, "Hurricanes in the Carribees: The Constitution of the Discourse of English Colonialism," in *1642: Literature and Power in the Seventeenth Century, Proceedings of the Essex Conference on the Sociology of Literature, July, 1980,* ed. Francis Barker et al. (Essex: University of Essex, 1981), 55–83; Johannes Fabian, *Time and the Other: How Anthropology Makes Its Object* (New York: Columbia University Press, 1983).

31. Bradford and Winslow, *Mourt's Relation,* 205–6.

32. Winslow, *Good News,* 583; Josselyn, *Two Voyages,* 95.

33. My understanding of how dances could function as a teaching device for hunters and warriors is informed by the two years (1980–81) I spent studying movement at the National Shakespeare Conservatory in New York City with Peter Lobdell, who developed the stunning physical characterizations used by the actors who played horses in the Broadway version of *Equus.*

34. Henry Grace, *History of the Life and Sufferings of Henry Grace,* vol. 10, The Garland Library of Narratives of North American Captivities (New York: Garland, 1977 [1764]), 14.

35. Williams, *A Key,* 237; Gyles, *Memoirs of Odd Adventures,* 123.

36. A. Irving Hallowell, "Ojibwa Ontology, Behaviour, and World View," in Stanley Diamond, ed., *Culture in History* (New York: Columbia University Press), 24–25.

37. Mark Johnson, *The Body in the Mind: The Bodily Basis of Meaning, Imagination, and Reason* (Chicago: University of Chicago Press, 1987); George Lakoff, *Women, Fire, and Dangerous Things: What Categories Reveal about the Mind* (Chicago: University of Chicago Press, 1987).

38. Pierre Bourdieu, *Outline of a Theory of Practice,* trans. Richard Nice (1972; reprint, Cambridge, U.K.: Cambridge University Press, 1977), 188.

39. Elaine Scarry, *The Body in Pain: The Making and Unmaking of the World* (New York: Oxford University Press, 1985), 27–59.

40. Daniel K. Richter, *The Ordeal of the Longhouse: The Peoples of the Iroquois League in the Era of European Colonization* (Chapel Hill: University of North Carolina Press, 1992), 35–36, 65–71; Nash, "The Abiding Frontier," 103–4, 132, 142–43, 269–70.

41. Susannah Willard Johnson, *A Narrative of the Captivity of Mrs. Johnson, containing an Account of her Sufferings during Four Years, with the Indians and French* (Walpole, N.H.: David Carlisle, 1796), 55.

42. See, for example, the stories of early contact period warfare between the Mi'kmaq and the Kwedechk (St. Lawrence Iroquoians) in Silas T. Rand, *Legends of the Micmacs,* Wellesley Philological Publications (New York: Longmans, Green, 1994), 137–41, 169–78, 200–22.

43. Emma Lewis Coleman, *New England Captives Carried to Canada Between 1677 and 1760 During the French and Indian Wars,* 2 vols. (1926; reprint, Bowie, Md.: Heritage Books, 1989), 2:179; Titus King, *Narrative of Titus King of Northampton, Massachusetts, a Prisoner of the Indians in Canada, 1755–1758* (Hartford: Connecticut Historical Society, 1938), 9; Susannah Johnson, *A Narrative of the Captivity of Mrs. Johnson,* 54–55.

44. The classic essay on rituals of adoption is James Axtell, "The White Indians of Colonial North America," *William and Mary Quarterly* 32 (1975):55–88.

45. Nash, "The Abiding Frontier," chapter 5. One of the afflicted girls, Mercy Short, is the subject of Cotton Mather's disquisition on "A Brand pluck'd out of the Burning" in his epic *Magnalia Christi Americana* (London: T. Parkhurst, 1702). For the story of a woman who married a Mohawk man, see John Putnam Demos, *The Unredeemed Captive: A Family Story from Early America* (New York: Vintage Books, 1995).

46. James Axtell, *The Invasion Within: The Contest of Cultures in Colonial North America* (New York: Oxford University Press, 1985), 170; Thomas Shepard, "The Clear Sun-shine of the Gospel Breaking Forth Upon the Indians of New England" [1648], *Collections of the Massachusetts Historical Society*, 3rd. ser., 4 (1834):40.

47. For confessions by powows who converted to Christianity, see Simmons, *Spirit of the New England Tribes*, 41–42. For one example of how certain dances have persisted on a mission reserve, see Nicholas N. Smith, "St. Francis Indian Dances—1960," *Ethnomusicology* 6 (1962): 15–18.

48. Jacques LeSueur, *History of the Calumet and of the Dance*, vol. 12, no. 5, Contributions from the Museum of the American Indian, Heye Foundation (New York: Museum of the American Indian, Heye Foundation, 1952), 6–11. Similarly, a "trading dance" persisted in the Northeast into the twentieth century; see Frank Speck, *Penobscot Man: The Life History of a Forest Tribe in Maine* (Philadelphia: University of Philadelphia Press, 1940), 297–98; Nicholas N. Smith, "The Wabanaki Trading Dance," paper presented at the 1996 Algonquian Conference (copy in the author's possession).

The Body Baptist

Embodied Spirituality, Ritualization, and Church Discipline in Eighteenth-Century America

Janet Moore Lindman

As progeny of the English Reformation that emerged in the seventeenth century, early American Baptists strove to re-create the ethos and ambience of the New Testament church with all its rites and customs. Their desire to establish "a true church of Christ" and to be faithful to the traditions of ancient Christians demanded a high degree of piety, loyalty, and dedication. It also required adherence to a New Testament theology that placed the body at the center of Christian belief. As a site of sin and salvation, and the center of faith and unbelief, the body gauged the level of spirituality attained by the individual. This theology engulfed Baptists in layers of somatic meaning: entry into faith manifested in the body; spiritual identity was ritualized in the body; sin and falling away from faith and religious community transpired in the body.

The body as image and metaphor pervades Christian rhetoric, and corporeality is essential to the New Testament message of Christ's coming when "God was manifest in the flesh." The "enfleshment" of Christ fulfills God's plan of salvation for humanity; by taking human form, God brings redemption to the world.[1] Jesus continued the use of corporeal language to preach his message during the Last Supper when the bread became his body and the wine his blood. As a primary rite of the Christian church, the Eucharist celebrates Christ's corpus as an offering to humankind; communicants gather for a meal to eat the body of God as a testament to that sacrifice and their unity as one: "For *we being* many are one bread *and* one body" (I Cor. 10:17).

Oneness of the body—as a collective experience—is a persistent theme in Christian cosmology and is evident in the eighteenth-century concept of the Baptist church as a gathering of believers who in "all the body by joynts and bonds" are "knit together." "United together in spiritual relation with each other, as fellow members of the same body under Christ," believers became part of the visible church and thereby "limbs" of Christ's body. Early American Baptists utilized corporeal imagery to define their unity as coreligionists, which they, in turn, affirmed through faith and rite.[2]

The centrality of the body in this theology is reflected in the common Protestant phrase "holy walk and conversation," which Baptists used repeatedly. Holy walking—or to walk "the path of righteousness"—denoted faithfulness to an ideal of spiritual belief as active and embodied. Further, the use of the term *conversation* referred not only to the verbal characteristics an individual possessed but also to one's personal conduct, social reputation, and way of life generally in the eighteenth century.[3] Thus to be a good Baptist necessitated a range of physical and emotional commitments from the conviction of internal belief to the comportment of outward behavior. The sharp distinction between body and mind, belief and behavior, was blurred within Baptist cosmology, and the undifferentiated nature of the body/mind relationship was revealed in the corporeality of church ritual and discipline whereby the body became an instrument of religious faith. Such faith was more than a mental or emotional exercise to Baptists; it was a process of embodiment that encompassed all aspects of one's life.

In addition, the metaphor of the church as part of Christ's body wedded believers to a model of community that superseded all others. This drew the body and soul of the believer into both a material and spiritual realm where religious identity fused spiritual belief with bodily conduct. Baptists of eighteenth-century British North America advocated spiritual separation from the secular world by endeavoring to be "a garden enclosed, ... a spring shut up, a fountain sealed."[4] This metaphor of enclosure and demarcation bound "true believers" to associate only with others like themselves. Thus, eighteenth-century Baptists embraced the New Testament concepts of spiritual community as a corporeal entity "to unite in a complete, perfect, and glorious body in a state of eternal union and oneness with the head of Lord Christ and all his members."[5] But to create a "glorious body" of believers required surveillance by the individual and the church in both the corporeal and spiritual performance of faith. A tripartite process of conversion, ritual practice, and church discipline carried out this imperative to imprint and conserve the body Baptist.

For eighteenth-century evangelicals such as the Baptists, religious faith and practice occurred in the body.[6] Potential converts wept "bitter tears," shook uncontrollably, flailed their limbs, moaned and groaned, and dropped, sighing, onto meeting benches. Baptist sources recount gathered converts who "tremble as if in a fit of the ague," and "fall to the ground and lay still as if struck dead." Individuals, such as Samuel Harris, found themselves kneeling with their "head[s] and hands hanging down on the other side of the bench; ... as senseless as in a fit." Overcome by evangelical preaching, Philip Mulkey threw himself "to the ground expecting the fire and brimstone" and contin-ued "in this posture for some time almost dead with terror." Whether fear-ful or inert, converts ran a gamut of emotionalism from "falling down as in fits and awaking in extacies [*sic*]" to experiencing "visions and revelations," and being "melted down into tears." While attending a religious meeting, Elnathan Davis witnessed "the trembling and crying spirit" of the people present but did not believe it until the "trembling seized him also; he attempted to withdraw; but his strength failing and his understanding con-founded he, with many others, sunk to the ground."[7]

Both the evangelical message and its messenger invoked bodily movements. Baptist ministers had a reputation for their emotive style, for making "soft impressions on the heart" which induced tears in their listeners, made them "shake their very nerves," and hurled their bodies into "tumults and per-turbations." John Taylor recalled hearing Daniel Marshall preach: "Oh rocks fall on me, Oh mountains cover me from the face of him that seteth [*sic*] on the throne, and from the wrath of the Lamb, for the great day of his wrath is come, and who shall be able to stand." These words had a visceral effect on Taylor, who "felt the whole sentence dart through my whole soul, with as much sensibility as an electric shock could be felt." Lewis Craig made a similar impact on his community when, after converting to the Baptist faith, he began to preach and "many would be affected and weep, some faint, till all the neighborhood was alarmed." Even when jailed for preaching without a license, John Waller "made very serious impressions on the minds" of his listeners. Some converts claimed that a minister's penetrating stare and spiri-tual power could affect them emotionally and physically. Tilden Lane re-membered such a reaction after hearing a sermon by Shubal Stearns:

> He fixed his eyes upon me immediately, which made me feel in such a manner as I never had felt before. I turned to quit the place but could not proceed far. I walked about, sometimes catching his eyes as I walked. My uneasiness increased and became intolerable. I went up to him, thinking that a salutation and shak-ing hands would relieve me: but it happened otherwise.... When he began to preach my perturbations increased so that nature could no longer support them and I sunk to the ground.[8]

As noted here and in the sermon above by Daniel Marshall, the strength of God's message singled out individuals and physically struck them down, as the sinful literally could not stand before God's wrath and righteousness. Further, the power of the minister's gaze—to see and to survey the sinner before him—proved an impetus to conversion in the case of Tilden Lane, just as Lane's sense of being seen by another brought about his spiritual transformation.

From fervent preaching and through manifestations of the spirit, listeners became convinced of their status as damned souls. The power of the evangelical message profoundly affected potential converts and those under "soul exercise." When "very low in body," Sarah Pierce pleaded with a minister for refuge from her sins that she described "as big as mountains and as black as hell." "Can one so vile as I be pardoned?" she asked. This sense of "heavy heartedness," utter hopelessness, and eternal damnation caused confusion and even depression in some people who often went weeks "contemplating their wickedness" and searching for some sign of salvation. Converts came to their faith through visible emotional and physical struggle as the mental stress of the conviction and conversion process took its toll. After hearing a young woman describe her conversion in rapturous detail, two young women "could no longer contain [themselves] but crying out, got up and went out of the house to vent their grief."[9] That the spiritual turmoil of conversion resulted in corporeal manifestations is not surprising. Through jerks, moans, screams, and a type of spiritual/physical paralysis, converts embodied fear, sorrow, and inertia about their eternal fate that was only eradicated by the onset of conversion. After falling to the ground in a fit, Elnathan Davis "found nothing in him but dread and anxiety, bordering on horror. He continued in this situation some days" but then found joy and ease fill his soul when he experienced "relief by faith in Christ."[10]

Conversion happened in the body and changed the bodily conduct of the newly saved. Through salvation "the Lord put a new song" into the believers' mouths; what they said and how they acted would be completely altered after conversion. Having had "the Lord smite their hearts powerfully," and "brake [*sic*] in with much sweetness" upon their souls after salvation, the converted "sang and wept and smiled in tears, holding up their hands and countenances toward heaven."[11] This choreography of conversion incorporated a spectrum of bodily movements and physical behaviors that brought about radical change not only in the believers' spiritual outlook and emotional status but also in a transfigured corporeality—what they perceived as a new body.

Once individuals had related their conversion experience, the church required repositioning of their bodies for admission into membership through the enactment of ritual. Baptists assembled a repertoire of rituals with adherence to a specific corporeal style in which church rites inscribed theology on the bodies of its believers. Marking of the Baptist body began with a confession of faith—after an often laborious and physical process of finding salvation—and continued with church ritual. For Baptists, the primary rite was adult baptism by immersion. Baptism not only signified the death of the sinner but also the sinful body; to be "buried with Christ in baptism" distinguished the end of one life from the beginning of another, and the end of one body and the emergence of a new one. After passage through the "watery grave" of baptism, the true believer would be reborn to "walk in newness of life." To legitimate this rite required complete immersion of the body in water as well as its somatic expression before witnesses; equally significant, the converted body had to be seen by others undergoing spiritual transition through ritual. Daniel Fristoe oversaw such spectatorship when he administered the baptismal rite before a crowd of two thousand observers, some of whom climbed trees "Zacheus like" to get a better view of the proceedings. In addition, the celebration of baptism as a public, communal event initiated bodily performances in members and nonmembers alike. Ministers sometimes felt uncomfortable with the emotion and movement invoked by ritual practice, as Daniel Fristoe discovered after he baptized some new converts: "In going home, I turned to look at the people who remained by the water side and saw some screaming on the ground, some wringing their hands ... some praying; others cursing and swearing and exceedingly outragious [*sic*]."[12]

Eighteenth-century Baptists practiced an extensive ritual repertoire, though not all believers exercised "the nine Christian rites" at all times or in all regions of British North America.[13] Besides baptism, the other church rituals utilized by Baptists included communion, the laying on of hands, love feasts, washing the saints' feet, the kiss of charity, the right hand of fellowship, the fellowship of children (also called "dry christening"), and anointing the sick with oil. All these rites played a part in the process of marking the body Baptist, and as tactile encounters, these rituals required members to place hands on one another's bodies in spiritual expression. Also, church members often used bodily rituals in combination. For example, once converts had been baptized, they would attend church the following day when (in some congregations) the minister or elder would perform the ritual of the laying on of hands (placing his hands on the converts' heads as a sign of their entry into membership). This rite would be followed by another, "the right hand of fellowship," when the other church members would greet the converts by shaking their hands, as a sign of the members' acceptance into the church and acknowledgement of their saintly status. Similarly, at a ritual celebration like the love feast—when members gathered to eat in a private home, to sing hymns, pray, and give donations to the poor—believers practiced other rites such as washing feet and the right hand of fellowship. The mixture of food and fellowship with bodily contact increased social interaction and communion among the members at the same time it reinforced awareness of their connection to one another as part of the same spiritual family. Such physical interaction through ritual elided secular boundaries and corporeal distinctions among believers as "one body in Christ."

The regular use of church rituals preserved and enhanced the believers' spiritual status. Ritual forged a sense of identity and community among believers at the same time it maintained their separation from other religious groups and from secular society with all of its "sinful, carnal ways."[14] Ritual represents what ought to be; the Baptist ideal of sinless bodies, peaceful souls, and a religious community that is unified and contained. Ritual affirmed the saints' religious identity and animated the members' original feelings and status at the time of conversion, while simultaneously connecting them to a

larger body of believers. Evangelical Protestants such as the Baptists constructed "techniques of the body"—a whole set of movements, habits, postures, and gestures to be collectively and individually practiced on a repetitive basis.[15] The ritualization and regulation of Baptist bodies sustained
appropriate belief and behavior of church members. Through ritual, believers learned the range of motion and expression practiced in the church. Ritual
yields what Catherine Bell calls a "ritualized, social body" that has the "the
ability to deploy in the wider social context the schemes internalized in the
ritual environment." Through consistent participation in ritual, believers gain
"ritual mastery," and expertise in church ritual becomes "embodied knowing." "Embodied knowing," in turn, garnered through ritual, provides coherence of religious belief at the same time that it molds the believers' perceptions of themselves as individuals and a part of a group set apart from the
unbelieving world. As temporary and contingent, ritual requires repetition
in order to maintain spiritual identity and a sense of religious community in
a believing, ritualized body.[16]

Yet for all the fluid movement and corporeality of this religious experience,
the personal behavior of Baptists came under strict regulation by the church
during the eighteenth century.[17] Once members of the church, believers acknowledged their faith through pious speech and circumscribed demeanor
and by following the Baptist model of "holy walking and conversation." As
embodied expressions of inner faith, the personal conduct of church members
had to be consistent with Baptist theology, and church discipline enforced
bodily management among all believers. The church desired members to lead
lives of "watchfulness and prayer" and to keep order both in "their inward
and outward man according to ye Scripture." Through "holy living," believers' saintly status and internal beliefs were enacted in the body.[18] Baptists espoused a strong sense of decorum that dictated specific rules of ideal conduct
for believers which, in turn, governed all activities of daily life in order to
demonstrate restraint, piety, and meekness and "to live soberly, righteously
and godly." Members of the Shippen Township Church of Pennsylvania, for
example, made this pledge in their covenant when they stated: "[W]e take
heed to ourselves to temper our conversation and company, not to indulge in
passionate, revengeful anger, but to maintain a peaceful, quiet deportment at
home and abroad; not to allow ourselves in lascivious talking, foolish jesting,
evil speaking nor tavern haunting but to have our conversation and company
as becometh the gospel of Christ." Thus, believers' bodies manifested saintly
status in everything from speech, behavior, and social habits to daily conversations, marital relationships, and family and community life. Baptist meetings found even the minutiae of social behavior worthy of citation; members
guilty of scoffing, tattling, vanity, and even being "unsteady and useless" could
be cited for wrongdoing, according to the church.[19]

Members who appeared before the church court to explain their irregular
behavior either confessed their sin and asked forgiveness or denied the mis-

conduct and suffered admonishment, censure, or excommunication. Those who underwent censure remained members and were allowed time to reform their behavior; however, they were denied the right to take part in communion—they could not receive the body of Christ. This system of surveillance relied on eyewitness testimony from other members who investigated and reported on disorderly behavior and offered evidence of misconduct by fellow members. As part of the church covenant, members agreed to oversee each other's "walk and conversation." This obligation to cite one another was highly structured; church members had the right to "reprove one another" but not the right to "be whispering and backbiting one another." The church court deemed wrongdoing that took place in public spaces and was seen by nonbelievers to be particularly egregious. Hence, the demand for spiritual and social decorum at all times and in all contexts.

As autonomous entities, Baptist congregations operated as the highest authority over their members' conduct and used their church courts to enforce a single code of moral and social demeanor. Baptist churches wrote "gospel rules" to guard against sinful manifestations such as "fornication, covetous[ness], idolaters, railers, drunkards, whitchcraft [*sic*], hatred, variance, emulation, wrath, strife, sedition, heresies, envying members, reviling and such like."[20] The church warned its members that from these activities "many evil branches" of sin could grow to infect other members, as sin begat sin to contaminate the spiritual health of the entire church body.

The body is "a variable boundary, a surface whose permeability is politically regulated," and "a signifying practice within a cultural field," according to Judith Butler.[21] As a boundary, the body Baptist demarcated the difference between faith and unbelief, between salvation and sin, a boundary maintained and "politically regulated" by the church court. The body Baptist was both a signifier of what was sacred and orthodox in Baptist cosmology and also signified the range of somatic behavior accessible to believers. The body as decorous, sinless, and contained was central to Baptist religious belief.[22] This ideal of seamless and sinless bodies, however, confronted a reality in which impermanent and fluid bodies, with their propensity for misconduct, compelled supervision and reprimand by the church. Backsliding members perforated the boundary between sin and salvation, between the church of Christ and the degeneracy of secular society. Also, sin compromised the believer's body, a body that had been reborn and made anew through conversion and baptism; therefore, the church needed to be vigilant against conduct it defined as irregular.

Through belief, ritual, and discipline, the body Baptist was managed, molded and honed into a godly entity. The necessary ingredients for religious belief included spiritual conviction and verbal assent as well as regular participation and bodily control. Moreover, corporeal regulation inscribed the body Baptist that, in turn, constructed a discourse of an enclosed body and a concept of internalized sin whereby bodily comportment became an

outward sign of spiritual legitimacy. The Baptist body was part of an evangelical discourse—and gained its meaning through that discourse—relating
to religious propriety and social decorum in the eighteenth century. These
rules of corporeal regulation structured the dynamics of power and authority
in the church while they also held implications for notions of status, order,
and difference in the wider society.[23]

Sinful behavior easily disrupted the religious communalism of Baptist
churches, severing the spiritual link among believers. Bodily sin was both social and sexual. Social sins of the body ranged from dancing, singing secular
songs, wearing excessive dress, and the "sin of drunkenness" to verbal and
physical abuse; from fights and disputes to excessive emotionality, such as
the "sin of anger." Sexual misconduct included obvious sins such as licentiousness, illegitimacy, adultery, and fornication as well as interracial mixing
and irregular marriage practices. To maintain the faith and the community
of believers demanded the bodily management of all members. Those who
walked in sin had violated the rite of baptism and communion and, therefore, the integrity of the church body.

Sin, like salvation, entered the church through the bodies of its members.
Irregular conduct connoted not only the presence of sin, it compromised the
sanctified body of the believer at the same time it brought "disorder" into
the church and violated the bond between believers and the boundary between the church and the secular world. Ichabod Benton Halsey of Eliza-
bethtown, New Jersey, conceded this point in 1789 when he admitted to his
church that his misconduct had "disgraced the station which I professed and
have not walked as becoming a follower of Christ." Secular social behaviors
were subject to punishment because they misused the saint's body and trans-
gressed the church order for "peaceful, quiet deportment" among the
members.[24]

Social and cultural conceptions of the body that emphasized sexual and
racial differences affected the Baptist member under scrutiny for sinful behavior. Early modern society associated women with fleshiness and passions
and considered their bodies more susceptible to weakness and debility. In
medical terminology, "cold, wet humors" dominated women's bodies, while
"hot, dry humors" ruled men's bodies. Such differences in physical anatomy
translated into the validation and assignment of dichotomous social qualities to the sexes by the eighteenth century. Defined as deceptive, changeable,
and unsteady, women's bodies contrasted to the stronger, braver, and more
honorable bodies of men. This intertwining of the corporeal and metaphorical meanings of bodies continued, and with increasing medical knowledge,
various parts of the human body became gendered; the nervous system became feminized as the musculature was masculinized. Thus, women became
associated with emotionality and hysteria and continued to be considered
physically and emotionally weaker than men and therefore more liable to
succumb to outside influences.[25] In addition, black bodies were equated with

corporeality, compared to white bodies, and were sexualized as monstrous and beastly as a way to affirm racial distinctions.[26] The institution of slavery and the perpetuation of racial ideology that defined non-Europeans as inferior, savage, and uncivilized created new social meanings for bodies of color. By the eighteenth century the development of "scientific" theories to explain the origin of various races contributed to this understanding of racial difference. Contemporary scientists "naturalized" the categories of race and gender alike, with both written on the body and beneath the skin to penetrate "the entire life of the organism."[27]

Though church members of all ages, genders, and races found themselves brought before the church for misconduct, specific accusations were indicative of one's place in society. A hierarchy of body types informed Baptist conceptions of sin and disorder. As a physical demonstration, sin became gendered and racialized within the church courts. Social and sexual sin in the Baptist cosmology made the female body and the black body more liable to accusations of misconduct than the male body or white body. For example, women, both black and white, were accused of the majority of sexual sins in eighteenth-century Baptist churches, with illegitimacy overwhelmingly the fault of women.[28] In 1736, the Welsh Tract meeting in Delaware excluded Rachel Bemish from communion for being single and pregnant. Similarly, in 1797, the Shoulder's Hill Church in Virginia excommunicated both Kiziah Allmand, a white woman, and Peggy, an enslaved black woman, for "having a base begotten child." Hannah Burns found herself expelled from the Southampton Church of Pennsylvania for having a child four months after her wedding. An Isle of Wight County church in Virginia reprimanded "Great Bett" for the "sin of uncleanness" as well as not telling her husband at the time of their wedding that she was pregnant. The church court also cited women for general sexual misconduct—such as Christian, a female slave, who was barred from communion for living with a man who already had a wife. Through charges of lewdness, adultery, and illegitimacy, the church court punished female members for the sexual misuse of their bodies. Female sexuality—if not contained by parental authority, marriage, slavery, and racial barriers—was disorderly, deviant, and outside the bounds of saintly (and gendered) prescriptions.

Baptist women were not only liable to charges of sexual impropriety but also verbal misconduct. For example, church leaders brought Winifred and Susannah Pitts before them in 1778 for "speaking evil of each other." Women, who spoke in "unbecoming language," especially to male members of the church or to male relatives, were cited for disorderly conduct. Lydia Mamet of the Middletown Church of New Jersey found this out when she was chastised for making "reproachful sayings" against church members and, in particular, for sending a letter to the church that was "full of malice and scandalous language." The church soundly condemned and punished women who engaged in volatile and strident speech. For example, the Waterlick church of Virginia accused Jane Williams of the following transgressions: "speaking and writing falsely," "libeling her husband and her brother," "abusing her father-in-law by calling him a rogue hypocrite," and for "being a person of bad or immoral character, as a scold and abusive woman."[29]

The church meeting regulated the sexual activity of African-Americans, both enslaved and free. The church deemed extramarital sexual relations among African-Americans as irregular marriage practice even though they were most often the result of forced separation. Both black male and female church members found themselves cited for irregular sexuality, as did Charles, a slave and member of Shoulder's Hill Church, who was excommunicated for adultery in 1791. Some bondsmen were punished for merely attempting to engage in unsanctioned sex, as in the case of Lummers, a black Baptist, excommunicated by the church for the sin of "wanting to commit adultry" [sic]. The Raccoon Swamp Church of Virginia excommunicated a slave woman named Pegg for living with a white man as her husband "unlawfully." Milly Smith, a free woman and member of the Upper Goose Creek Church in Fauquier County, Virginia, was excommunicated for "living in fornication." The church encouraged free blacks to follow the white model of heterosexual relations, as did Benjamin and Milly Blackhead, a newly freed couple, who were strongly advised to "comply with the form of marriage" as approved by the white members.[30]

African-Americans also endured allegations related to their status in society as free or enslaved people. One of the most common charges against enslaved black Baptists was running away—that is, of stealing their own bodies. Nero, a slave in Virginia, confronted accusations not only of disobeying his master but also "threatening to leave him and to deprive him of more of his negroes and other things too devious to mention." Besides running away, slaves were brought before the church court for stealing and lying. Letty and Milly, two slave women, faced charges of theft and disobedience to their master when they stole some of his cotton. Church courts also punished black members for being bad slaves, as in the case of Jacob, who faced charges of being "a quarrelsom[e], troublesom[e], deposition" and "for depart[ing] from the truth," and Sabra, who was excommunicated in 1775 for "speaking lies."[31]

The Baptist religion repositioned the bodies of its believers for entry into a spiritual community at the same time it marked them with secular conceptions of gender and race. The surveillance of white women and African-American men and women through a system of church discipline adjudicated by white men became an intensive means of corporeal regulation which served as a vehicle of social control that reached beyond ideals of spiritual community. By modifying the Baptist body through belief, ritual performance, and church discipline, and by interweaving corporeal regulation with the dual and interactive hierarchies of gender and race, the church both challenged and affirmed existing social norms.[32]

The body Baptist set the parameters of Christian morality in which bodily performance was equated with spiritual belief and inner feeling. The body as "a variable boundary" served as a threshold between sin and salvation, between the religious community and the unbelieving world. The regulation, control, and internalization of sin accentuated the magnitude and meaning of the body to evangelical Christianity. This link between spiritual belief, moral sense, and personal behavior had been made before; however, with the Baptists the connection became more pervasive and public. The visual privileging of Baptist conversion, ritual, and discipline emphasized the significance of spectatorship in the practice of lived religion. In addition, the management of corporeal sin became a significant trope in evangelical discourse of the eighteenth century; personal piety, bodily control, and social order converged to negotiate the development of new, internalized notions of individual conduct. Further, the persistence of church discipline linked spiritual decorum to emerging concepts of difference in a changing American society. In the end, corporeal management as a religious and cultural practice in American Baptist churches enhanced the naturalization of racial and gender distinctions. Through the manifestation of an embodied faith in conversion, rite, and discipline, Baptists advocated a theology of "democratic" religion while simultaneously replicating the hierarchies of secular society.

Notes

1. In the New Testament, the Apostle Paul promulgated multiple meanings of Christian corporeality including the body of Jesus; the church as the body of Christ; the Eucharist as the body of Christ, and the body of the individual Christian believer. See Dale B. Martin, *The Corinthian Body* (New Haven, Conn.: Yale University Press, 1995) for more on New Testament meanings of the body.

2. Records of the Southampton Baptist Curch, Bucks County, Pennsylvania, Baptisms, Marriages, and Burials, 1687–1842, *Collection of the Genealogical Society of Pennsylvania*, vol. 14 (Philadelphia, 1895), 24, Historical Society of Pennsylvania (hereafter HSP).

3. This is taken from William Hubbard, *The Benefit of a Well-Ordered Conversation* (Boston, 1684), as cited in Jane Kamensky's book, *Governing the Tongue: The Politics of Speech in Early New England* (New York: Oxford University Press, 1997), 5.

4. These phrases appear in the Song of Solomon 4:12 as well as in many eighteenth-century Baptist church books such as that of the Mill Swamp Baptist Church and the Isle of Wight Baptist Church, both of Virginia. One of these phrases was also used in the title of recent book, see Jean E. Friedman, *The Enclosed Garden: Women and Community in the Evangelical South, 1830–1900* (Chapel Hill: University of North Carolina Press, 1985).

5. Minute Book of the Coan Baptist Church, 1805–23, Virginia State Library (hereafter VSL). For similar sentiments, see Records of the Southampton Baptist Church, 24, and October 2, 1785, letter, Great Valley Baptist Church to the Philadelphia Baptist Association, Church Papers, 1706–1794, Mrs. Irving F. McKesson Collection, HSP.

6. For more on Baptists in the eighteenth century, see William McLoughlin, *New England Dissent, 1630–1833: The Baptists and the Separation of Church and State* (Cambridge,

Mass.: Harvard University Press, 1971), and *Soul Liberty: The Baptists' Struggle in New England, 1630–1833* (Hanover, N.H.: University of New England Press, 1991); C. C. Goen, *Revivalism and Separation in New England, 1740–1800: Strict Congregationalists and Separate Baptists in the Great Awakening* (New Haven, Conn.: Yale University Press, 1962); Rhys Isaac, *The Transformation of Virginia, 1740–1790* (Chapel Hill: University of North Carolina Press, 1982); Richard Beeman, *The Evolution of the Southern Backcountry: A Case Study of Lunenburg, Virginia, 1746–1832* (Philadelphia: University of Pennsylvania, 1984); Carla Gardina Pestana, *Quakers and Baptists in Colonial Massachusetts* (New York: Cambridge University Press, 1991); Susan Juster, *Disorderly Women: Sexual Politics and Evangelicalism in Revolutionary New England* (Ithaca, N.Y.: Cornell University Press, 1995).

7. Morgan Edwards, *Materials Toward a History of Baptists in the Provinces of Maryland, Virginia, North Carolina, South Carolina, and Georgia,* comps. Eve B. Weeks and Mary B. Warren (Danielsville, Ga.: Heritage Books, 1984), 97; A fragment of the diary of Oliver Hart, 1754, American Baptist Historical Society (hereafter ABHS).

8. John Taylor, *Baptists on the American Frontier: A History of Ten Baptist Churches of Which the Author Has Been Alternately a Member,* ed. and intro. by Chester Raymong Young (Macon, Ga.: Mercer University Press, 1995), 20–21. Edwards, *Materials,* 57, 90 93, 97, 99, 142; Morgan Edwards, "Materials Toward a History of Baptists in Virginia, 1772" (hereafter the Furman Manuscript), bound photocopy at the Virginia Baptist Historical Society (hereafter VBHS), 58, 74.

9. William Hickman, *A Short Account of My Life and Travels, for More Than Fifty Years, A Professed Servant of Jesus Christ* (n.p., 1826), VSL; Hart diary; The diary of Henry Toler, 1783–1785, typescript, VBHS.

10. Edwards, *Materials . . . North Carolina,* 97.

11. Hart diary; Furman Manuscript, 31. Jonathan Edwards described converts as "new men" with "new hearts, and new eyes, new ears, new tongues, new hands, new feet." Cited in Philip Greven, *The Protestant Temperament: Patterns of Child-rearing, Religious Experience, and the Self in Early America* (New York: Alfred A. Knopf, 1977), 62. The bodily performance of faith was not peculiar to Baptists. The Puritans of seventeenth-century New England experienced religion in an intensely physical, even erotic, manner. What is different for Baptists in eighteenth-century America is the public nature of their bodily performances at religious meetings. Baptists meetings were held out-of-doors, on open-air stages and under groves of trees, and were attended by believers and unbelievers alike. Baptists, therefore, embodied their spiritual faith often before an unbelieving public. I would like to thank Richard Godbeer for these insights and for his commentary on an earlier draft of this paper at the American Historical Association Annual Meeting, in New York City, January 1997.

12. Morgan Edwards, the Furman Manuscript, VBHS, 30, 31.

13. For more on Baptist ritual, see Janet Moore Lindman, " 'Know How Thou Oughtest to Behave Thyself in the House of God': The Creation of Ritual Orthodoxy by Eighteenth-Century Baptists," *Mid-America: An Historical Review* 78:3 (1996): 237–57.

14. 1780 Preamble, Minute Book of the Upper King and Queen County Baptist Church, Virginia, 1774–1814,VSL.

15. Phrase taken from Marcel Mauss, cited in Peter Stallybrass, "Patriarchal Territories: The Body Enclosed," in Margaret W. Ferguson, Maureen Quilligan, and Nancy T. Vickers, eds., *Rewriting the Renaissance: The Discourses of Sexual Difference in Early Modern Europe* (Chicago: University of Chicago Press, 1986), 23.

16. Catherine Bell, *Ritual Theory, Ritual Practice* (New York: Oxford University Press, 1992), 107–9; Jonathan Z. Smith, *Imaging Religion: From Babylon to Jonestown* (Chicago: University of Chicago Press, 1982), 63–65.

17. This practice of a church court and congregational surveillance was not distinctive to Baptists; the Protestants of Calvin's Geneva, the Puritans of Massachusetts Bay, and Anglicans of England enacted similar systems to monitor sin in their communities. See Emil Oberholzer Jr., *Delinquent Saints: Disciplinary Action in the Early Congregational Church of Massachusetts* (New York: Columbia University Press, 1956); J. A. Sharpe, *Defamation and Sexual Slander in Early Modern England: The Church Courts at York,* Paper #58 (York, U.K.: The Borthwick Institute of Historical Research, 1980); and John Addy, *Sin and Society in the Seventeenth Century* (London: Routledge, 1989). E. P. Thompson points out the contrary notions of evangelical religion in regard to Methodists, who fell down in fits and expressed extreme emotions—"in an orgasm of feeling"—at religious meetings at the same time believers were required to live strict, disciplined lives of "joylessness." See E. P. Thompson, *The Making of the English Working Class* (New York: Random House, 1963), 268–69.

18. See Sermon Notes of Abel Morgan, 1743–1745, ABHS. Also see the article in this volume by Michele Lise Tarter on the Quaker conception of body and spirit as "celestial flesh."

19. American Quakers, Methodists, and Presbyterians held meetings to admonish members and published their own "book of rules" to define their standards of church discipline. 1780 Preamble, Upper King and Queen County Church, VSL; Scattered Records of the Shippen Township Baptist Church, Tioga and Potter Counties, Pennsylvania, Worden Family Papers, HSP; Sermon Notes of Abel Morgan.

20. Church clerks used physical language to describe the process of excommunication; errant members were "cut off" and "cast out" from the church. See Excommunication Papers, 1787–1847, Scotch Plains Baptist Church, Essex County, New Jersey, ABHS. "Gospel rules" taken from Records of The Welsh Tract Meeting, 1701–1838, Pencader Hundred, Newcastle County, Delaware, Delaware Historical Society (hereafter DHS).

21. Judith Butler, *Gender Trouble: Feminism and the Subversion of Identity* (New York: Routledge, 1989), 139.

22. This mirrors Bakhtin's model of the classical body as enclosed, static, and complete versus the grotesque body which is open, fluid, and porous. See Mikhail Bakhtin, *Rabelais and His World,* trans. Helene Iswolsky (Indianapolis: Indiana University Press, 1990).

23. As Stallybrass argues, "[T]he body maps out the cultural terrain and is in turn mapped out by it." "Patriarchal Territories," 138. Also see Michel Foucault, *The History of Sexuality,* vol. 1, *An Introduction,* trans. Robert Hurley (New York: Vintage Books, 1980), 154.

24. For the purposes of this paper, I am focusing on the large percentage of court cases that concerned sexual and social misconduct; members were also cited for heretical beliefs and doctrinal disputes. This assessment is based on my examination of more than sixty church books from Delaware, New Jersey, Pennsylvania, and Virginia. Excommunication Papers, Scotch Plains Baptist Church, ABHS; Minute Book of the South Quay Baptist Church, 1775–1827, Nansemond County, VSL.

25. See Ludmilla Jordanova, *Sexual Visions: Images of Gender in Science and Medicine Between the Eighteenth and Twentieth Centuries* (Madison: University of Wisconsin Press, 1989), 58; and Thomas Laqueur, *Making Sex: Body and Gender From the Greeks to Freud* (Cambridge, Mass.: Harvard University Press, 1990), 4–5, 108–109.

26. See Jennifer Morgan, " 'Some Could Suckle over Their Shoulder': Male Travelers, Female Bodies, and the Gendering of Racial Ideology, 1500–1700," *William and Mary Quarterly* 54 (January 1997): 167–92.

27. Laqueur, *Making Sex,* 155. These "natural" hierarchies of race and sex were based on cranium and pelvis size to link racial and sexual inferiority not to social causes but to "nature's truth." Therefore, systems of dominance used scientific theory to reify the

categories of race and gender. See Londa Schiebinger, *The Mind Has No Sex? Women and the Origins of Modern Science* (Cambridge, Mass.: Harvard University Press, 1989), 211–13.

28. For an alternative argument on Methodist discipline, see Cynthia Lynn Lyerly, *Methodism and the Southern Mind, 1770–1810* (New York: Oxford University Press, 1998), especially chapter 5. See Kathleen M. Brown, *Good Wives, Nasty Wenches, and Anxious Patriarchs: Gender, Race, and Power in Colonial Virginia* (Chapel Hill: University of North Carolina Press, 1996), and Cornelia Hughes Dayton, *Women Before the Bar: Gender, Law, and Society in Connecticut, 1639–1789* (Chapel Hill: University of North Carolina Press, 1995) for more on women's increasing legal and social responsibility for illegitimacy in eighteenth-century Anglo-America.

29. For more on women and speech, see Kamensky, *Governing the Tongue;* Robert Blair St. George, " 'Heated Speech' and Literacy in Seventeenth-Century New England," in David Grayson Allen and David D. Hall, eds., *Seventeenth-Century New England* (Boston: Colonial Society of Massachusetts, 1984), 275–322; Mary Beth Norton, "Gender and Defamation in Seventeenth-Century Maryland," *William and Mary Quarterly* 44 (January 1987):3–39; and Clara Ann Bowler, "Carted Whores and White Shrouded Apologies: Slander in the County Courts of Seventeenth-Century Virginia," *Virginia Magazine of History and Biography* 85 (1977):411–26. Welsh Tract Meeting, DHS; Minute Book of Shoulder's Hill Baptist Church, 1785–?, VSL; Records of the Southampton Baptist Church, GSP. See Susan Juster's work for the development of what she calls "the feminization of sin" among eighteenth-century New England Baptists. Juster, *Disorderly Women,* 169–79. Middletown Baptist Church Book, 1712–1741, ABHS; Minute Book of the Waterlick Baptist Church, 1787–1817; Minute Book of the Upper King and Queen Baptist Church, 1774–1816, VSL.

30. Shoulder's Hill Church, 1785–?,VBHS; Minute Book of the Upper Goose Creek Baptist Church, 1799–1851, VSL; Minute Book of the Racoon Swamp Baptist Church, 1772–1892, VBHS.

31. Hartwood Baptist Church, 1771–1871; South Quay Baptist Church, 1775–1827; Upper King and Queen Baptist Church, 1774–1816, VSL.

32. For the role of white men in the Baptist church, see Janet Moore Lindman, "Acting the Manly Christian: White Evangelical Masculinity in Revolutionary Virginia," *William and Mary Quarterly,* 3d ser., 57:2 (April 2000): 393–416. For more analysis of the gender and racial components of church discipline, see Janet Moore Lindman, "A World of Baptists: Gender, Race, and Religious Community in Pennsylvania and Virginia, 1689–1825" (Ph.D. dissertation, University of Minnesota, 1994), chapter 7. For nineteenth-century church courts, see Friedman, *The Enclosed Garden;* Gregory A. Wills, *Democratic Religion: Freedom, Authority, and Church Discipline in the Baptist South, 1785–1900* (New York: Oxford University Press, 1997); Randy Sparks, *On Jordan's Stormy Banks: Evangelicalism in Mississippi, 1773–1876* (Athens: University of Georgia Press, 1994); and Christopher Waldrep, " 'So Much Sin': The Decline of Religious Discipline and the 'Tidal Wave of Crime,' " *Journal of American History* 23 (1990): 535–52.

IV

BODIES IN DISCOURSE:
RACE, IDEOLOGY, AND
PUBLIC RHETORIC

Their danses which they ufe at their hyghe feastes, Theodor de Bry, *America,* part 1 (Frankfurt, 1590), plate 18, Rare Books Division, The New York Public Library, Astor, Lenox, and Tilden Foundations.

Hannah Duston's Bodies

Domestic Violence and Colonial Male Identity in
Cotton Mather's Decennium Luctuosum

TERESA A. TOULOUSE

On March 15, 1697, Hannah Duston, wife of Thomas Duston, of Haverhill, Massachusetts, was taken captive by a group of northern Abenaki Indians. Her husband escaped with seven of their children, but the Indians killed the Dustons' newborn baby and several other captives. Duston and her nurse, Mary Neff, along with Samuel Leonardson, a Worcester boy captured the year before, marched 150 miles into the wilderness toward Canada. Hearing their captors, who by this time consisted of an Indian "family" composed of two men, three women, and seven children, describe how the captives would be forced to run the gauntlet on arrival in Canada, Duston convinced Neff and Leonardson to kill them and escape. Accordingly, the three bludgeoned ten of the Indians to death and fled, Duston returning, one source suggests, to scalp their victims in order to prove the exploit and to make a plea for the bounties Massachusetts had attached to scalps. Dramatically, some two weeks after their return on April 21, Duston appeared in Cotton Mather's Second Church, perhaps invited, where he incorporated her story into the sermon he was then preaching. Mather used the Duston captivity in three different textual contexts: the sermon preached that day, "Humiliations follow'd with Deliverances"; his history of the wars of the 1690s, *Decennium Luctuosum* (1699); and finally, in his massive history of New England, *Magnalia Christi in America* (1702).

We could agree that in thus appropriating Duston's story, Cotton Mather was only repetitively demonstrating his own use of the much-discussed Puritan strategy of seizing on local specifics to make general claims about the continuing providential status of the New English body politic. Read in this light, the story of the triumph of Duston's female body over the bodies of an Indian family could be placed in a long line of sermons, poems, histories, and more recently, Mary Rowlandson's 1682 captivity narrative, in which an individual New English part could be viewed as a typological stand-in for a New English whole.

Such a reading of Mather's use of Duston's body through the traditional lens of Puritan intellectual history is only partially adequate, however. Relying on assumptions about typologically closed uses of Duston and her killings, it neglects other competing and contradictory cultural, social, and political desires figured by her own aggressive body and by those of her victims. In this chapter, Mather's history of the colonial wars of the 1690s, *Decennium Luctuosum* ("The Sorrowful Decade"), provides a crucially bounded arena for locating, separating out, and analyzing such complex desires. Analyzed in relation to this history's multiple representations of murdered bodies, it becomes clear that Duston's body does not simply or only represent the typological victory of a renewed New English social body. At one level, her triumphant female body could be used to express a return to bodily wholeness. At another level, however, read in the context of Mather's entire history, Duston's aggressive female body becomes a major sign of what has fragmented and threatened that social body in the first place. In *Decennium Luctuosum* in general and in Duston's text in particular, the murdered bodies of men, women, and children become specific sites of the colonial *male* failure to preserve the social body. The capture, torture, and murder of families—Indian and colonial alike—represented in the history underscore the lack of truly "manly" leadership, which Cotton Mather and his own third-generation cohort felt they could provide. Like other bodies presented in *Decennium Luctuosum*, Duston's body thus represents a crisis in colonial male authority as much as it typifies a providential New English victory.[1]

But the contradictory desires expressed in the text's depiction of bodies does not simply stop here. *Decennium Luctuosum* does not only call for and desire a (new) male leadership that could prevent the murder of families and thus reunite the social body. The horrific detail of its descriptions of murders and murdered victims expresses in addition a desire actively, even pleasurably, to participate in such murders. This desire suggests less a distancing from Duston's disruptive female body and its threats to the social order than it expresses a sense of identification both with its position of powerlessness and with its aggression. Just as Duston opposes her Indian family, so certain third-generation colonial sons, who feel themselves losing political and social dominance in this period, violently lash out at a New English order perceived as failing them. In *Decennium Luctuosum,* this order is most clearly represented as the patriarchal family.

Yet, if we can argue that Mather's representations of murdered bodies suggest aggressive fantasies about patriarchal Puritanism from within the Puritan elite, we also must acknowledge that these representations express a fear of such desires. Duston's murderous body as well as her murders represent, after all, a threat to the eventual status of the third-generation elite as the patriarchs who will head and control such families. To contain such murderous identifications, Mather's text must represent other fantasized solutions to murders such as Duston's. To this end, among its numerous representations of bodies, *Decennium Luctuosum* offers repeated images of a beaten and scalped victim who survives. But while this representation seems neatly to express and to solve two incompatible desires—to destroy and to save the New English family—its ultimate failure within the history's larger structure points to a different solution, one indirectly acknowledged in the history's introduction and conclusion.

Decennium Luctuosum as a whole, with the representation of Duston starkly underscoring it, limns the felt conditions of a murderous lawlessness that calls for the imposition of a new symbolic "father." This "father" is not, finally, to be internal, but external to the colonies. Only the lawful power of the English king can heal and unify a New English social body turned against itself. As this chapter suggests, however, far from offering a legitimate social or political solution to the problem of lawlessness against bodies, this equally fantasized answer only further complicates the cultural problematic expressed in *Decennium Luctuosum*'s representations of Indian and colonial bodies. For the European battles over royal legitimacy that spawned the colonial wars about which Mather writes expose far more literally than his text how brute power over bodies precedes and grounds political legitimacy rather than "legitimately" deriving from it.

Decennium Luctuosum is comprised of a collection of thirty selections called "articles." It has been read as an oddly secularized text that moves away from the standard ministerial interpretation of colonial events. Its detailing of enemy brutalities served to encourage colonial and English outrage, to justify literal and theological attacks against French and Indian (Catholics), to prove colonial New England's support for English royal policies, and less directly, to plead for English economic support of war-torn New England.[2] However, Mather's history contains an often overlooked but related desire. One of *Decennium Luctuosum*'s key purposes is to castigate certain colonial men for their lack of an appropriate defense of the colonies and for their corresponding lack of an appropriate New English "maleness." This aim becomes increasingly clear when we examine descriptions of captivity throughout the history and especially the placement of Duston's captivity towards its end.

Mather figures New England's vulnerability to external attack largely through representations of women and children physically and emotionally incapable of protecting themselves. The text demonstrates this vulnerability on at least three levels. Seven-year old Sarah Gerish, one of the first captives described, is largely teased, taunted, and insulted by her captors, but she is not killed. In contrast is the fate of the male child, James Key, whose grisly murder Mather minutely details. But Mather offers an even more shocking murder in his brief description of the pregnant Mrs. Adams, who "was with horrible Barbarity ripped up."[3] The "outraged maternity" theme here reaches its height as the text combines the murder of mothers and children in one figure.

Each of these instances signals a different degree of threat to the New English domestic body, from threat and insult, to child murder, to the figurative rape of mothers and children. The Mather text clearly aims to construct a massive disruption to New England as a whole via representations of harm to the domestic body. Representing such disruption does not simply serve to arouse outrage against external enemies. Rather, these examples of psychological and physical annihilation pointedly highlight the failure of certain New English men to preserve their own family order.[4]

That the history desires to derogate such men is underscored by its numerous representations of men's physical inefficacy. Not only are men often represented as failing at organized military engagements, they also invariably fail to thwart attacks against their families or themselves. Compassionately representing the bodily vulnerability of New English women and children, *Decennium Luctuosum* expresses little sympathy for weak men. Two instances are particularly telling: the death of Robert Rogers and the relinquishing of Fort Pemaquid.

The story of Rogers begins with a body joke: his companion escapes from the Indians "stark naught," but Rogers, "Nicknamed, Robin Pork" because of his corpulence, is taken. Attempting to escape by hiding, all too visibly, in a hollow tree, Rogers is quickly recaptured. The history details his excruciating torture and death, especially how "they did with their knives cut collops of his Flesh, from his Naked Limbs, and throw them with his Blood into his Face." The tale of the corpulent Rogers reoccurs at another level in the story of the appropriately named Colonel Pascho Chubb, who surrenders the "Brave Fort at Pemmaquid:"

> There were Ninety-Five men double-Armed, in the Fort, which might have Defended it against Nine Times as many Assailants; That a Fort now should be so basely given up! imitating the Stile of Homer and Virgil, I cannot help crying out, O merae Novanglae, necque enim Novangli! ["O mere New England women, not New England men!"].[5]

The fort at Pemaquid had been rebuilt by the recently deceased William Phips, the beleaguered New England royal governor for whom Cotton Mather had just penned a defensive biography. In surrendering it, Chubb did not simply demonstrate cowardice; he manifested blatant disloyalty to Mather's idealized representation of a more traditional New England social body under Phips. Chubb cannot escape without redress: his own bloody end comes just before the history's epilogue. Clearly, if anyone is to save New England, it may have to be New English women, not New English men, who have themselves become the "Novanglae" in need of protection.

To this end, the text often juxtaposes bloody descriptions of the destruction visited upon women and children's bodies to descriptions of female courage, ingenuity, and loyalty. There is not space to detail such instances here, but on several occasions colonial women rather than men remain to defend houses and borders. A particularly important instance of female bravery is described in the one major victory the history reports. In Wells, women provide the "Amazonian stroke" that helps save the town.[6]

Examples of female bravery thus set the stage for the appearance of the Duston captivity narrative toward the history's end, in which a woman does indeed take it upon herself to defend herself physically from the enemy. That Mather wished Duston's act to resonate for certain male colonials is borne out by his comparison of her act to that of Jael against Sisera in the Book of Judges. In chapter 4, the Israelite general Barak hesitates to fight the forces of Jabin, king of Canaan, unless the prophetess Deborah accompanies him to battle. She rebukes him for his distrust in the Lord, saying, "I will surely go with thee: notwithstanding the journey thou takest shall not be for thine honour; for the Lord shall sell Sisera into the hand of a woman"(Judges 4:9). The "woman" is Jael, the wife of Heber the Kenite, who invites Sisera, the fleeing general of Jabin's forces, into her tent. There she feeds him, lulls him to sleep, hammers a nail into his temple, and decapitates him.

Laurel Thatcher Ulrich has noted the ways in which Mather parallels Duston's aggression against her sleeping captors with that of Jael to demonstrate the similarity between the procrastination of New English male colonials and the reluctant Israelites.[7] Interpreting Duston in her role as victorious female type of all New England, however, Ulrich does not pursue the insight that her claim opens up for reading the entirety of a text like *Decennium Luctuosum*. Mather's descriptions of the brutalized bodies of family members throughout his history demonstrate how colonial men's ineptitude has led to such dreadful familial breakdown and to such corresponding gender role reversals in the first place.

For if Duston's narrative exemplifies a theme pursued throughout this history—men's physical inabilities force women bodily to defend themselves—it also reveals complicated emotions about the gendered role reversals it represents. At the text's end, Mather tries to address such reversals in two ways. First, he attempts to represent women restored to their "proper" position, and second, he represents himself as assuming the mantle of appropriate male authority. Immediately following the Duston story, Mather tells the tale of "some Women and Children [who] would needs ramble without any Guard, into the Woods to gather Strawberries."[8] Seeking to "Chastise them with a Fright," "some," clearly men, call an "Alarum"—an act that providentially frightens off several enemy Indians in the vicinity. Here the text pointedly exhibits women's foolishness rather than their heroism, and their need for a "chastisement" that alone can preserve them.

In a second attempt to contain female aggression and offer an example of loyal third-generation maleness, Mather represents himself in rhetorical battle with the Quakers, an act deemed comparable to defending New England's borders against the Indians:

> If the Indians have chosen to prey upon the Frontiers, and Out-Skirts of the Province, the Quakers have chosen the very same Frontiers, and Out-Skirts, for their more Spiritual Assaults; ... they have been Labouring incessantly, ... to Enchant and Poison the Souls of poor people, in the very places, where the Bodies and Estates of the people have presently after been devoured by the Salvages.

For Mather, Quaker danger lies not only in the analogy they provide to Indian savagery; a more pertinent threat is their defense of Indian complaints against the very rights of possession of the "Old Planters of these Colonies in their First Settlement."[9] Toward the history's end, Mather takes the role of the heroic "Minister" who valiantly exposes the moral and rhetorical stupidity of his "Quaker" opponent in order to protect the "ashes" of the "fathers." This manly colonial son will prove victorious over his opponent and, symbolically at least, preserve New England's rights of possession to the land.

Mather's "battle" with the Quakers leads into *Decennium Luctuosum*'s final article in which Cotton, like Increase Mather before him, prophesies that New England's end is near if it does not return to the fathers. Unsurprisingly, the sins calling forth such destruction involve disrespect for ministers and the "ancient" church practices granting them authority. A return to the fathers would mean a return to political as well as social power for third-generation sons like Cotton, not for those sons perceived as opposing them.

The question remains, however, of whether these additional articles, each of which seems abruptly tacked on to the history, succeed in explaining or containing the massive acts of physical destruction the text so carefully details. The excess of the history's violence against all bodies—Puritan and Indian, male and female alike—and the weakness of its attempt to contain it, raise the question of the text's desire to circumscribe the aggression it describes. If it succeeds in showing colonial men's weakness, *Decennium Luctuosum* appears to offer no compelling answer to the problem other than a much-abbreviated notion of the conventional return to the fathers. Indeed, the text's framer often seems far more attracted to the violent acts he minutely describes than he is to providing alternatives to them. Desiring to expose the problem of colonial male ineptitude, Mather's representations of bodies at the same time reveal less controllable desires and fears. Such a claim calls for a more fully contextualized reading of assertions just made about *Decennium Luctuosum* and about the part played by Hannah Duston's bodies within it.

Until 1697, New England was ravaged by ten years of intermittent wars with the French and their Indian allies. Massachusetts was concurrently rent by intense political and social infighting. Between 1686 and 1697, just before Mather published *Decennium Luctuosum,* the colony had experienced *seven* changes in government, each highly criticized by fiercely competing colonials as lacking legitimate grounds for authority. Deprived of political clout, with the erosion of local control over the Massachusetts charter and the embarrassing failures of Phips, traditional sons like Mather and his cohort also experience a loss in social and, concomitantly, religious dominance. Unable adequately to explain and contain the Salem witch crisis, they have been equally incapable of containing "threats" from other religious groups, whether from outsiders like the Quakers, or from insiders, such as Solomon Stoddard, John Leverett, and Benjamin Colman. Past jeremiads had warned of Indian wars like that with Metacomet, had seized the ideological upper hand in interpreting their meanings, and had invariably blamed the "rising generation's" apostasy for such punishments. But such ritualized warnings had clearly lost their power to construct a unified social body by the late 1690s. The competing desires expressed in *Decennium Luctuosum*'s assaults against male, female, and children's bodies should be more carefully considered both in the context of the Mather cohort's rage about its loss of control over New English self-understanding and in the context of a pervasive cultural confusion about the current lack of any identity-stabilizing representations.[10]

In *The Body in Pain,* Elaine Scarry analyzes three phenomena that structure torture: pain inflicted in ever more intense ways, pain that is objictified, and pain, finally, that is denied as pain in order that it may be read as power. Tracing the relation of torturer to tortured and the relation of both to the way physical pain dismantles a world made by language, Scarry's theory also addresses the mediated meanings torture might accrue for third parties ostensibly only describing it. In *The Name of War,* a recent study of the textual construction of "King Philip's War," Jill Lepore draws out some of the implications of Scarry's theory for a specific reading of the colonial/Indian war preceding the time period Mather describes. Lepore argues that "words and wounds ... cannot be separated, that acts of war generate acts of narration, and that both types of acts are often joined in a common purpose"—defining and maintaining a variety of "boundaries among peoples."[11]

Aspects of Scarry's and Lepore's readings are clearly pertinent to Cotton Mather's descriptions of colonial and Indian bodies, but such descriptions need to be examined not simply for what they reveal about the describer's construction of certain boundaries, but also for what they reveal about an equally violent desire to break them down. Describing tortured and murdered victims allows the Mather narrator to occupy a variety of identificatory positions vis-à-vis what is described—not merely historian, he is also victim, victimizer, sympathizer, and voyeur.

Positing that such mixed desires and feelings are expressed in *Decennium Luctuosum*'s representations of bodies helps us to understand more deeply what is at stake in the intensification and objectification of the victims Mather describes. In the case of Sarah Gerish (who was introduced earlier in this chapter), the structure and details through which her torture is displayed demonstrate the variety of ways that Mather's text takes part in what it purports merely to represent. The reader, asked to "imagine" Gerish's mental "Agonies," is enabled to do so only because of the extremely detailed picture of her "Abuse" offered by the text. But such an attempt to arouse the reader's feelings of compassion and/or outrage toward the "enemy" also reveals another, less bounded desire: the wish to torment and punish a New England child, here psychologically more than physically, through the Indians' agency. In Mather's description, Gerish is titillatingly half-stripped, but not shot; she is nearly drowned, but blamed for it herself; she is abandoned as "prey," but finally, threatened with burning at the stake, is "saved" by her master, who helped contrive the whole mental game only to "Terrifie" her. If the power that emerges from or replaces such torture would seem to accrue to Gerish's torturers, in this description, the judgment, the punishment, and the dominance seem equally to emanate from the describing text.

In comments preceding the description of the death of the child, James Key, Mather notes not only how those who were tortured were punished because they cried, but also how their compatriots who were forced to watch them could not cry lest they receive the same punishment. Here the text's obvious interest in watching someone tortured, if not literally, then descriptively, and the complicated emotions such watching arouses, becomes marked. The feeling the describer expresses seems not necessarily or only compassion, but also a kind of pleasure, but a pleasure combined with and arising out of horror at this example of a New English child's destruction. Torture moves at this point from the psychological (in Gerish) to the brutally physical, as what is being objectified—the victim's pain—is radically intensified not only by the Indian, Hopehood, who tortures the child, but also by the describer. Little James is represented as crying, exhibiting his "Natural Affections" for his parents:

> Wherefore ... this Monster Stript him Stark Naked, and lash'd both his Hands round a Tree, and Scourg'd him, so that from the Crown of his Head unto the Sole of his Foot, he was all over Bloody and Swollen; and when he was Tired with laying on his Blows, on the Forlorn Infant, he would lay him on the Ground, with Taunts remembering him of his Parents.

Later, having a "Sore Eye," the unfortunate child cries again and receives another horrific punishment only to meet his end through still another:

> laying Hold on the Head of the Child with his Left Hand, with the Thumb of his Right he forced the Ball of his Eye quite out, therewithal telling him, That

when he heard him Cry again he would Serve t'other so too, and leave him never an Eye to Weep withal. About Nine or Ten Days after ... the Child ... sat him down to rest, at which this Horrid Fellow, being provoked, he Buried the Blade of his Hatchet, in the Brains of the Child, and then chopt the Breathless Body to pieces before the rest of the Company, and threw it into the River.[12]

The sensationalism of the description is obvious: it progresses from beating, to mutilation, to total dismemberment. Although it moves from the psychological to the physical register, the description follows the same structure of intensification as Gerish's "torture." Its focus does not fall only on the child's pain but, perhaps even more significantly, on the massive rage and lethal response that his "weeping on forbidden accounts" arouses in his Master. Hopehood (Wohawa) is elsewhere described as having once been the servant of a "Christian Master," and the text represents him as possessing his own "family" as well. He is thus less culturally distant from James than Mather's readers might expect. In another context, Hopehood might even be read as any angry father "righteously" inflicting punishment on a weak son.

The text's obsession with the torturing of the New English domestic sphere both demonstrates the similarity between Gerish's psychological and James's physical abuse, and raises a series of suggestive questions. To what extent do these representations arouse emotions about Indian brutality, but also simultaneously use the Indians as agents of an anger against all New English "children" who have ignored their "fathers'" laws? To what extent does the text's emphasis on watching James be tortured as well as the warning that weeping for him will only attract equal punishment imply sadistic feelings against the New English family in addition to sympathy for James or vengefulness against the Indians? James's portrayal is only the most sustained example of numerous descriptions of children who are "brained" within and by this text.

Mather's aggression against adult male bodies in the text has been discussed, but the aggression against New English children's bodies exhibited here is in excess of the desire to expose male weakness. Given limitations of space, it remains only to suggest that this less containable aggression can also be directed against the bodies of adult women. Since the text usually represents women as saved for ransom, or as disappearing into Canada, even a brief portrait of a mother's murder is significant. The case of Mrs. Adams is thus a special one.

In the twentieth article of *Decennium Luctuosum,* Mather discusses the breakdown of the treaty of 1693 as an instance of Indian "Perfidy." Mr. Adams trusts the Indians and opens his door, only to have his wife, "then with Child ... with Horrible Barbarity ripped up."[13] Here the pregnant woman serves as a convenient symbolic marker of the breakup of the peace and the renewal of hostilities. At the same time, her death also implies her husband's stupidity in believing the Indians in the first place. If Mrs. Adams's death participates in these goals, viewed from the perspective of this analysis of other murders, her death as ripped-up mother could also suggest a wish not simply to describe her murder, but somehow to aid in it. In short, if *Decennium Luctuosum* expresses varying degrees of anger at males and at children, it also figures intense emotions about mothers.

Such descriptive murders of New English family members indicate the need to reconsider another mother's story. As we saw earlier, Duston as vengeful mother represents a unified New England victorious. At the same time, she also represents an embodied female rebuke to weak New English men. Given the descriptions just discussed, however, related but darker desires implicit in Mather's setting of Duston's story near the end of *Decennium Luctuosum* begin to suggest themselves.

Structurally, Duston's murdering of her Indian captors might simply represent an "eye for an eye" logic. As they have tortured and murdered New Englanders, so a representative New Englander, albeit a woman, now murders them. The textual descriptions of abused colonists we have examined, however, imply that while this might be true on one level, on another level Duston's aggressive female body simply continues a sadistic rage against the "family" that appears throughout Mather's history. Here it seems only more obviously justified. As in the case of Hopehood, the Indian who murdered James Key, so the Indians of Duston's narrative are represented, not as a war party, but as a family. Furthermore, as many scholars have noticed, they are set up by Mather as a religious family, even if a Catholic one, in contrast to backsliding New Englanders.

Duston's victims are thus in many ways shown as similar to New Englanders killed throughout the text: they are members of families. Considered in the wider context of the Mather text's descriptive pleasure in detailing the torture and murder of the domestic order, Duston's more apparently righteous vindication of murder seems really only a more subtle instance of a continuing desire to punish the family. Her killings, through a more justifiable displacement to an *Indian* family, simply continue *Decennium Luctuosum*'s rage against New England.

That Duston's murders could have served as a displaced version of the murder of colonials becomes plausible not only when we analyze Mather's descriptions of numerous murdered families in the text, but also when we consider a crucial extratextual event. In 1691, Hannah Duston's unmarried sister, Elizabeth Emerson, conceived twins out of wedlock, apparently in her parents' own house in Haverhill. When they were born, by all accounts, she strangled or otherwise allowed them to die of asphyxiation, and buried them in the family's back garden. Four years before he began his appropriation of Duston's murderous story, Cotton Mather preached her sister's execution sermon.

Kathleen M. Brown argues elsewhere in this collection that Elizabeth Emerson's execution and Mather's execution sermon are acts that attempt to reassert the social boundaries that her "unclean" bodily act, her fornication, has threatened. As constructed by Mather in his sermon, Elizabeth's sexual sin and her purgation become representative of those of the Puritan "body" as a whole.[14] In the context of the contradictory and competing desires that Hannah Duston and her act represent within Mather's later history, however, Elizabeth Emerson's sexual "uncleanness" becomes less resonant than her murder of her own children. Both Elizabeth Emerson and Hannah Duston murder families; both mothers threaten the domestic order from within. In the Mather history's representation of Hannah Duston's violence against an Indian family, a displacement seems to occur from Elizabeth to Hannah and from Elizabeth's murdered colonial sons to murdered Indian parents and children. Read in the light of Elizabeth's family murders, in the light of other murders described in this history, and in the light of the political and social chaos of the 1690s, *Decennium Luctuosum*'s overdetermined representation of Hannah Duston provides Mather with his most extreme means of expressing his cohort's rage against a disobedient New English domestic order and its pleasure in witnessing and vicariously participating in its destruction. If Mather's claim, in Duston's narrative, that she had come to a place where there was no law expresses his horror at New England's intersecting legal and familial breakdowns, the bloodlust of his text against all New English families equally expresses his desire for such breakdown.

In other examples, such mixed desires surface in the structure and excess of detail with which Mather intensifies and objectifies instances of aggression against the body. In the Duston narrative, they particularly express themselves in the rhythms of his prose and in the cadences of the language of the prophetess Deborah's victory chant (Judges 5:27) in which he embeds and through which he largely describes Duston's murders:

> furnishing themselves with Hatchets for the purpose, they struck such Home Blows, upon the Heads of their Sleeping Oppressors, that e'er they could any of them Struggle into any Effectual Resistance, "at the Feet" of these poor Prisoners, "they bow'd, they fell, they lay down: at their feet they bowed, they fell; where they bowed, there they fell down Dead."

The alliteration of "Hatchets," "Home-Blows," and "Heads" tells the story one way; the repetitive language of the Bible repeats the story and in its repetitions seems to prolong the murders. Mather is certainly doing far more than objectively describing the deaths of the Indian family—his narration vicariously enacts bloodshed and triumphs in its act.

Mather's defense of the context in which the murders occur expresses especially complicated feelings of justification and horror. The context that ostensibly allows for actions detailed throughout the history is finally named in the Duston narrative: "[B]eing where she had not her own life secured by any law unto her, she thought she was not forbidden by any law to take away the Life of the Murderers by whom her Child had been butchered."[15]

This explanation attempts to locate an overarching reason to justify Duston's bloodlust against the Indians and, by extension, all other forms of violence the text describes: the fact of an all-encompassing lawlessness destroying Indian and colonial alike. Another aspect of Scarry's description of the structure of torture suggests what is at stake in such an attempt. The third dimension of torture that Scarry elaborates is its transformation of the victim's pain into acceptance of the power of the torturer.[16] Such power is no longer seen in its physical dimension, however; physical pain and the breakdown and reorganization of the world it entails have now resulted in an acquiescence to the ideological rightness of the position the torturer represents. Scarry's insight demonstrates how law can paradoxically derive its justification from a power grounded in lawlessness. What Duston's bludgeoned and scalped victims reveal and what the description of tortured and murdered New Englanders throughout *Decennium Luctuosum* reveals is not that Duston has come to a place where there is not "any Law," but instead to the very source of law itself—the physical control of one body by another. Mather's descriptions of tortured New English family members express a fantasy about what aggressions can be released where there is no law; at the same time, his desire to justify and to recontain Duston's rage suggests the text's profounder knowledge that patriarchal law itself is precisely grounded in such lawless aggression against the family. In this context, Gerish's psychological torment by her master and Hopehood's "fatherly" punishment of James Key for disobeying his orders returns with disturbing clarity.[17]

But New England's patriarchal domestic order, which Mather fantasizes destroying from a current position of angry powerlessness, is also that which he depends on to renew his own desired position of cultural potency. *Decennium Luctuosum*'s feeble attempts to reconstruct gender roles and to figure true "manliness" through chastising foolish women and attacking Indianized Quakers indicate a desire to reinstate a patriarchal law that cannot be allowed to recognize its own basis in a sadistic pleasure in power over weaker bodies. Such pleasure must be ascribed to Indians, not to the "fathers" or their loyal "sons." In order to (mis)recognize this knowledge, the text must suggest that male weakness and female aggression are the real problems to be solved, not the lawless law of the fathers, which Duston's problematic act both imitates and, given her female position, rebels against. We have already examined the Mather history's representation of weak colonial men. Now, having considered the text's passionate identification with Duston's physical violence, we must also consider its fear of identification with her position.

Critics argue that Duston's story could have aroused anxiety as well as identification with her role as heroic *Judea capta*.[18] Although it seemed justified by war, even Jael's act could be viewed as problematic female aggression within the domestic sphere. In fact, if Jael's murder supported the Israelite cause, another chapter of Judges portrays a woman acting in the domestic realm who equally turns the tables on the Israelites. Delilah seduces and wins Sampson, learns the source of his bodily potency, and cuts it off (Judges 6:19–20). Mather's own allusion to the "Amazonian stroke" at Wells further implies an awareness not only that female rage can destroy the patriarchal domestic order from within, but also that women—Amazons—may function powerfully outside of it.[19] If, as we have seen, Mather's text reveals a desire for the destruction of New England exemplified in the detailed murders of families, on another level, it expresses intense fear of such destruction. *Decennium Luctuosum* wishes to torture and murder New England and at the same time to preserve its threatened domestic order; it exposes the lawless law justifying patriarchal control of weaker bodies, and, at the same time, attempts to repress this knowledge. Such contradictions, strikingly represented by the complex figure of Hannah Duston, are those that express and shape the cultural position of third-generation male elites like Cotton Mather.

Decennium Luctuosum provides two ways of dealing with the impossibly double desires it represents: the first involves its use of a body that is bludgeoned or scalped and survives; the second involves its celebration of a figure ostensibly outside the "lawless" scene, whose (re)imposition of a new law can be (mis)read as solving the impasse of mixed colonial desires.

The beaten or scalped victim who lives is described at least five times in this text. A major example is that of the Deerfield boy who lives through an "assault" in which:

> they struck an Hatchet some inches into the Scull … even so deep, that the Boy felt the Force of a Wrench used by 'em to get it out. There he lay a long while Weltring in his Blood; … considerable Quantities of his Brain came out from time to time, when they opened the Wound; yet the Lad Recovered, and is now a Living Monument of the Power and Goodness of God.[20]

Mather uses this specific case to gloat at length that there are no "mortal wounds" except those that "Providence" makes so.

Clearly, given the history's intense focus on personal agency, it seems extremely suspect to find it, near the end, abruptly offering providential justifications for why wounds kill or do not. Such claims obviously place the issue outside the physical body itself and outside the agents responsible for its destruction. A rare and extended attempt at justifying these preservations religiously indicates a fantasy at work beyond their ascription to "Providence." Specifically, the focus on colonials who are "brained," yet survive, returns attention to the dilemma just described—the text's simultaneous identification and disidentification with aggression against the New English family. In examples like this, the history attempts to solve the problem of its own violence against bodies by focusing on their "miraculous" recoveries. New England's body/bodies can be brutally punished, yet survive! This fantasy, however, is short-lived. A series of similar descriptions leads directly into the narrative of Hannah Duston, from whose bludgeonings no one recovers. Clearly, a different strategy is needed both to justify domestic aggression and to contain it.

Such a need accounts for Mather's dedicatory and concluding comments to the earl of Bellomont, who in 1697 was designated the royal governor of Massachusetts, replacing yet another disputed interim government headed by a colonial.[21] At the history's end, Mather praises King William and addresses Bellomont as the "Illustrious Image of His own Royal Virtues." Bellomont, especially lauded for his role in persuading William of Orange to overthrow the Stuart monarchy, is described as "the Greatest Person ever to set Foot on the English Continent of America." His "Conduct" as governor will impress disputatious colonials because in him meet "Virtus et Summa potestas" (virtue and highest power).[22]

Whereas such language serves as the conventional language of praise, it seems extraordinarily overblown even for a text already filled with exaggerated descriptions. Its excess suggests Mather's extreme pleasure in Bellomont's status, so close to the throne itself. The connection between such noble status and the attributes it joins together demands further attention. Nobility seems to link two terms that need not fit together— "virtue" and "highest power." Linking the two under the aegis of nobility, however, appears to solve several problems *Decennium Luctuosum* has raised. First, given the clear relation in all of the history's classical sources of virtue and *virtu,* Bellomont's nobility would seem to usher in the "manly" body the text has exposed as lacking. His nobility will thus abrogate the need for women like Duston to step out of their appropriate gender roles. In so doing, he will also symbolically solve the problem of male identification with dangerous female aggression against the patriarchal domestic order. In addition, putting "highest power" in the hands of a nobleman will implicitly resolve the problem of aggression against New England's domestic sphere by competing colonial sons. "Virtue" in the shape of a legitimate governing power will be restored by a body who legally represents the royal "father."[23]

Such, at least, is a final tentative "answer" proffered by *Decennium Luctuosum*. It is also the solution yearned for in the Book of Judges. According to the logic of Judges, Jaels would no longer be needed, Delilahs would no longer triumph, and most tellingly, the sons of the tribes of Israel would no longer rise up against each other instead of against external threats, were there only a "king in Israel." Throughout the Book of Judges runs a longing for a patriarchal king who will unify the tribes and drive out all enemies claiming possession of the land of Israel. The analogy to the colonial situation, in which third-generation sons compete for power as well as for justification of their own and their fathers' acts of Indian dispossession, seems obvious. Bellomont provides the symbolic "king in Israel" by whose authority alone aggression can be controlled, confusion dispelled, and a unified colonial (male) identity (re)stabilized (Judges 21:25).

But, as we noted earlier, there is another way to read this fantasy of stabilization in a nobility uniting "virtue" with "highest power." As the context of "King" William's own "Glorious Revolution" against the Stuarts, the corresponding colonial "revolution" against the royal governor, Edmund Andros, and the continuing wars over legitimate succession in Europe that aroused the "sorrowful decade" in New England make clear, it is not noble status that links virtue and highest power. Rather, it is power over bodies on familial, colonial, and imperial levels that determines both what is virtuous and what is noble. Once power is achieved, it constructs its own legitimacy, not vice versa. The aggressions against the domestic body described throughout *Decennium Luctuosum* and with such compelling force in Duston's narrative tell the representative story of a colonial son's desire that seeks, resists, displaces, and defers such knowledge.

Notes

1. A central assumption of this chapter is that representations of bodies should be analyzed within the specific textual contexts in which they appear. Reading their meanings in relation to a given text's other representations and their place within a particular textual economy provides a boundary for claims about the relationship between bodies and phenomena external to the text. In a larger work-in-progress on captivity, for example, I offer a reading of the uses of the Duston narrative in the sermon and the *Magnalia* that differs from that offered here. For a recent reading that shares my assumption about the relation of Duston's representation to its use within a particular structure, but focuses largely on Mather's representation of Hannah Swarton in the published sermon, see Lorrayne Carroll, " 'My Outward Man': The Curious Case of Hannah Swarton," *Early American Literature* 31 (1996): 45–73.

2. Carroll, for example, notes the text's "excessive Classicism." See " 'My Outward Man,' " 64. See also Kenneth Silverman, *The Life and Times of Cotton Mather* (New York: Harper and Rowe, 1984), 243. For varying accounts of political, social, and economic contexts in the years just preceding *Decennium Luctuosum*, see Perry Miller, *The New England Mind: From Colony to Province* (Boston: Beacon Press, 1968), 149–73; Howard Peckham, *The Colonial Wars 1689–1762* (Chicago: University of Chicago Press, 1964), 25–56; Richard Johnson, *Adjustment to Empire* (New Brunswick, N.J.: Rutgers University Press, 1981), 183–247; William Pencak, *War, Politics, and Revolution in Provincial Massachusetts* (Boston: Northeastern University Press, 1981); and Bernard Bailyn, *The New England Merchants in the Seventeenth Century* (New York: Harper and Row, 1964).

3. The text of *Decennium Luctuosum* used here is collected in Charles H. Lincoln, ed., *Narratives of the Indian Wars* (New York: Charles Scribner's Sons, 1913), 179–300. The story of Mrs. Adams occurs on 253.

4. For the structure of patriarchal family relations in New England, see Edmund S. Morgan, *The Puritan Family* (Westport, Conn.: Greenwood Press, 1966). For a study that elaborates on and dissents from Morgan, see Laurel Thatcher Ulrich, *Good Wives: Image and Reality in the Lives of Women in Northern New England 1650–1756* (New York:

Alfred Knopf, 1982). Studies specifically highlighting the anxiety and anger of colonial sons in the face of the "fathers'" literal and psychological control include: Emory Elliott, *Power and the Pulpit in Puritan New England* (Princeton, N.J.: Princeton University Press, 1975) and Philip Greven, *Four Generations: Population, Land, and Family in Colonial Andover, Massachusetts* (Ithaca, N.Y.: Cornell University Press, 1970). For a related study of how crises in political relations are imagined in terms of gender crises in the eighteenth-century South, see Kenneth Lockridge, *On the Sources of Patriarchal Rage: The Commonplace Books of William Byrd and Thomas Jefferson and the Gendering of Power in the Eighteenth Century* (New York: New York University Press, 1992). As I do here, Lockridge finds male rage to have contextually variable sources and meanings.

5. Mather, *Decennium Luctuosum*, 208, 262.

6. "The Women in the Garrison on this occasion took up the Amazonian Stroke, and not only brought Ammunition to the Men, but also with a Manly Resolution fired several Times upon the Enemy." See Mather, *Decennium Luctuosum*, 237.

7. See Ulrich, *Good Wives*, 169. This essay is indebted throughout to Ulrich's research on the Emerson and Duston families as well as to her interpretation of Hannah Duston.

8. Mather, *Decennium Luctuosum*, 266.

9. Ibid., 277–78.

10. See note 2. See also Perry Miller's chapter on the jeremiad in *The New England Mind*, 27–40; Sacvan Bercovitch, *The American Jeremiad* (Madison: University of Wisconsin Press, 1978); and Jack P. Greene, "Search for Identity: An Interpretation of the Meaning of Selected Patterns of Social Response in Eighteenth-Century America," *Journal of Social History* 3 (1970): 189–220. Note also Kathleen M. Brown's reading of these contexts in "Murderous Uncleanness," a chapter in this book. Mather published numerous jeremiads in the 1690s including, of course, his 1697 "Humiliations follow'd with Deliverances," in which he first appropriated Duston's story. In my study of late-seventeenth-century captivity, I suggest that such continual identity confusion—or phrased otherwise, multiple identifications—in fact constitutes a certain type of "Creole" male identity. The jeremiad needs reconsideration in regard to gendered as well as generational terms.

11. Elaine Scarry, *The Body in Pain* (New York: Oxford University Press, 1987), 28. Scarry's analysis, especially of mediated agency, is far richer than there is space to elaborate. See chapter 1, "The Structure of Torture," 27–59. See also Jill Lepore's very recent, *The Name of War: King Philip's War and the Origins of American Identity* (New York: Alfred Knopf, 1998), x. If, for Lepore, identity seems constituted by the creation and maintenance of literal and discursive boundaries, in my reading, it is rather a function of the play of multiple and contradictory identifications that can break down as much as, or even at the same time as, they build up such boundaries.

12. Mather, *Decennium Luctuosum*, 209–10.

13. Ibid., 253.

14. See Kathleen M. Brown's complicated argument about Elizabeth's culturally representative status in "Murderous Uncleanness."

15. Mather, *Decennium Luctuosum*, 266.

16. See Scarry, *The Body in Pain*, 56–59, where she argues that "Torture is a condensation of the act of 'overcoming' the body present in benign forms of power." In the view of power implied in Mather's text, the law grounded by such "overcoming" seems always already less than benign.

17. Michael Emerson's own excessive beating of his daughter, Elizabeth, for which he was fined by the Essex County Court in 1676, seems pertinent here as well. In spite of her sister's later ignominy, Hannah Duston named one of her daughters after her. See Ulrich,

Good Wives, 197–201. It is tempting in the context analyzed here to read Hannah's and Elizabeth's acts as both replicating and defying their father's domestic violence.

18. See Ulrich, *Good Wives,* 170, and Annette Kolodny, *The Land Before Her* (Chapel Hill: University of North Carolina Press, 1984), 22–24.

19. The history's repeated use of Classical analogies deserves further attention, especially for its implications for gender roles. For a discussion of how the notion of "Amazons" threatened Renaissance male writers, see Margaret L. King, *Women of the Renaissance* (Chicago: University of Chicago Press, 1991), 188–93.

20. Mather, *Decennium Luctuosum,* 223.

21. Bellomont, an impecunious Anglican Irishman who died in 1701, had time enough to support a colonial faction opposed to the Mathers. See Miller, *The New England Mind,* 226–68; Silverman, *The Life and Times,* 169–90; and Michael G. Hall, *The Last American Puritan: The Life of Increase Mather* (Middletown, Conn.: Wesleyan University Press, 1988), 302–10. William Stoughton was the colonial acting-governor replaced by Bellomont.

22. Mather, *Decennium Luctuosum,* 276–77. This is my translation of the Latin phrase.

23. In the equally effusive dedication, Bellomont serves as the adulated but unaware authority under whose aegis the history's aggressions can be legitimately described and justified. For a superb analysis of the symbolic father, see Slavoj Zizek, *Enjoy Your Symptom* (New York: Routledge, 1992), 149–93.

Body Language

The Body as a Source of Sameness and Difference in Eighteenth-Century American Indian Diplomacy East of the Mississippi

NANCY SHOEMAKER

In eighteenth-century North America, diplomacy did more than bring nations together for political purposes. Diplomacy also created an arena for the exchange of cultural ideas. One of the ideas most talked about at Indian councils was the body. The human body and its multiple parts—mouths, lips, eyes, ears, limbs, hearts, guts, breasts, wombs, flesh, and skin—were the basis for a host of metaphors devised by Indian and European speakers to clarify abstract points.[1] Body metaphors usually served to highlight common interests but, by the mid eighteenth century, one particular body part—skin—emerged as the primary index of difference. The shared experience of the body gave Indians and Europeans a mutually intelligible language that helped bridge the cultural divide: they understood each other's metaphors.[2] However, at the same time, the body became the means to organize new understandings of difference.

The politics and rituals of eighteenth-century Indian councils are well-trod ground or, as the historian Richard White might say, a well-trod "middle ground."[3] Scholars have been drawn to study councils because of the richness of the records, particularly Indian speeches put into writing by European functionaries—a practice cultivated most by the English. These Indian speeches give insight into the dynamics of intercultural contact in its most public guise: the council. By analyzing council ritual, White and other historians have shown how Indians and Europeans accommodated each other's cultural forms to further their own diplomatic agendas. Thus, the English or French opened councils with the Iroquois by condoling the deaths of important men and women; Indians closed councils with Europeans by drinking to the king. Europeans anticipated obedience when they addressed Indian allies as children and subjects of the great king; Indians expected protection and trade goods when they called the French their father and the English their father or brother.[4] This merging was deliberate and self-conscious, for speakers often stated which were their customs and which customs they were willing to go along with to please the other.

Rarely did eighteenth-century commentators remark on coincidences in custom and belief, for they were too busy noticing the differences. And yet, there were underlying similarities that made accommodation possible in the first place. For instance, Indians and Europeans may have differed in how they conceptualized the family, but they all had a concept of the family, which is what made kinship metaphors possible as tools for understanding the other. The body was another common aspect between contrary cultures. Whether Iroquois or Cherokee, whether English or French, everyone seems to have found body metaphors handy devices for communicating ideas to foreigners. Because council participants saw the human form as so evidently something Indians and Europeans shared, they used the body to circumnavigate a larger sphere of obscure and difficult cultural differences.

When Indians and Europeans came together in council, they already had some comparable ideas rooted in their understandings of the body's form and function. For example, the Cherokees and the English both used the metaphor of the right hand to explain political authority and diplomatic rank. Headmen of Cherokee towns each had an assistant known as his "righthand man," and when the Cherokees received visiting dignitaries from other nations, they strategized the seating arrangements because sitting on someone's right denoted a higher status than sitting on someone's left. When the Cherokees met other Indian nations and the English in council, they might disagree about what position they held in relation to other nations, but they could agree on how the seating arrangements would visibly demonstrate their relative rank.[5] Right-handedness as a metaphor for superiority was not a biologically determined universal belief, but as Robert Hertz noted for the prevalence of right-hand symbolism in religious ritual, a slight biological preference for the right hand could be elaborated into a mental construct useful for explaining status and dominance in more abstract situations.[6]

Another frequently held belief within many cultures is that the world has four directions: in English, east, west, north, and south. John Lawson, traveling among Carolina Indians in 1709, noted with amazement that his Indian guides divided up the world much the same way he did: "[T]hey have names for eight of the thirty two Points, and call the Winds by their several Names, as we do; but indeed more properly, for the North-West Wind is called the cold Wind; the North-East the wet Wind; the South the warm Wind; and so agreeably of the rest."[7] And in council, when an Iroquois speaker described a tree of peace, "the Branches of which Extended East, West, North, and South," the English shared the conceptual framework to envision such a tree.[8] The shape of the human body may be the inspiration for the four directions. The human body does not naturally have four sides, but by looking at and experiencing the human form, people could arrive at the same cultural construction and by analogy extend it to the larger world, assigning it four directions as well.

Turning to body metaphors to provide the explanation for abstract concepts is probably a universal cognitive practice, no matter the culture.[9] As they came together on the council grounds, eighteenth-century Indians and Europeans were already accustomed to building abstract meaning from the physical world. When they applied their shared metaphorical abilities to this particular cross-cultural encounter, they invested the human body with the power to explain cultural similarities and differences.

The body was, like the family, most useful as a model for articulating what it meant for nations to be allies. Thus, at a 1732 council with the English, the Six Nations (Iroquois) described their longstanding attachment to the colony of New York this way: "Corlaer [New York] is our Brother, He came to us when he was but very little, and a Child, we suckled him at our Breasts; we have nursed him & taken Care of him till he is grown up to be a Man; he is our Brother and of the same Blood. He and We have but one Ear to hear with, One Eye to see with, and one Mouth to speak with."[10] This speaker called on several analogies to explain the nature of the diplomatic tie between the Six Nations and New York. They were like a family: like brothers and, then, like mother and child. They were also like a body, and what one party observed or heard was to become known by the other. They were, in other words, united.

This particular Iroquois speaker may have picked up the phrase "we suckled him at our Breasts" from the French, for French officials frequently offered to "give suck" to Indians "to give them nourishment."[11] The image of Frenchmen nurturing Indians at their breasts probably had origins in a medieval Christian, by this time Catholic, tradition of a feminized, nurturing Jesus Christ.[12] Indian speakers more often talked about having sucked the same milk, an expression intended to invoke familial bonds. They generally did not claim the role of mother to other nations. Whoever originated the suckling-at-breast metaphor is inconsequential, however, since those who said it or heard it understood that it meant nurturing. Although the French may have intended their nurturing to include a spiritual dimension, breast milk in the language of diplomacy meant trade goods: guns, ammunition, cloth, and alcohol.[13]

As for having one eye, one ear, and one mouth, the Conestoga Indians of Pennsylvania used a similar phrase when renewing their alliance with the colony of Pennsylvania and credited the crucial wording to William Penn. In 1720, a Conestoga speaker recounted how

> when Governour Penn first held Councils with them, he promised them so much Love and Friendship that he would not call them Brothers, because Brothers

might differ, nor Children because these might offend and require Correction, but he would reckon them as one Body, one Blood, one Heart, and one Head.[14]

Three years later, Civility, speaker for the Conestogas (he may also have been the earlier speaker) paraphrased Penn a little differently:

> They remembered that William Penn did not approve of the methods of treating the Indians as Children, or Brethren by joining Hands, for in all these cases, accidents may happen to break or weaken the tyes of Friendship. But William Penn said, We must all be one half Indian & the other half English, being as one Flesh & one Blood under one Head.[15]

Besides relying on memory of the event, the Conestogas kept a written copy of the original 1701 agreement, for it was found among their papers when unruly settlers massacred the town of Conestoga in 1763.[16] According to the written account, Penn said "that they shall forever hereafter be as one head & one heart & live in true Frienship & Amity as one people."[17]

Although the written document and the Conestogas' speeches attributed the wording to Penn, Delaware Indians used a similar expression—of being one body, one heart, and one head—with Swedish colonists years before Penn planted his colony in America.[18] Because accommodating the other's cultural forms included trying to talk like the other, it is not always apparent which nation originated which metaphor, but it seems likely that Penn borrowed his phrasing from Indian diplomacy because these particular body metaphors differ from those in the New Testament, presumably a foundational text for Penn and other Quakers. In the New Testament, the mutual dependence of eyes, ears, hands, and feet models a diverse yet unified community, in which each member has a particular contribution to make. Significantly, the New Testament elevates the "head" as an especially important body part by ascribing to it authority over other "members."[19] Penn's "one head & one heart" does not imply any separation of roles or hint of hierarchy within the alliance. Moreover, the frequency of this phrasing in Indian speeches in the Northeast suggests that it originated in northeastern Indian diplomacy.[20]

By reminding the colony of Penn's promise, the Conestogas were pursuing a defined diplomatic objective. At the same time, the specific body parts mentioned in councils and their ascribed meanings established the basic elements of a shared natural history. Indian and European speakers endowed these body parts with the same functions: tongues, mouths, and lips spoke; ears listened; eyes saw; wombs and breasts gave life and sustained life; hearts were the source for the deepest feelings of sincerity, truth, and affection.[21] When doubting someone's word, speakers wondered whether they were speaking from their mouths or lips and not from their hearts.[22] Putting hands on another nation's head, gathering that nation under one's arms, keeping that nation in view under one's eyes were figurative offers of protection.[23] Having one ear, one eye, and one mouth conveyed the idea of shared interests and knowledge. To have one flesh, one blood, one heart, one head, one body expressed a desire to act in unison.[24] As the Delaware headman Teedyuscung said at a 1755 council with Pennsylvania officials, "As God has given Us, our Uncles [Six Nations], and You the English one Heart, We desire We may all act as one People, see with the same Eyes, hear with the same Ears, speak with the same Tongue, and be altogether as one Man and actuated by one Mind."[25] Although body metaphors were in a sense just the packaging for a nation's diplomatic agenda, metaphors derived from the body had the added advantage of making an alliance seem part of the natural order.

With so much of the human body apparently in common, it is especially interesting, then, that only one body part referred to differences. By the 1760s, in both the northeast and southeast, the contention that skin color obstructed unity had become commonplace in council rhetoric. At the 1763 Treaty of Augusta, the Chickasaw headman Pia Matta modified the familiar breast-suckling metaphor when he said that "he looks on the White People and them as one That they are as good Friends as if they had sucked one breast Altho his skin is not white his heart is so and as much as any White man."[26] At a 1769 council at Shamokin, the Conoy King reminded the English of the terms of their peace agreement, grounding their alliance in natural design: "Because We all came at first from one Woman, as you may easily know by this mark, 'that our little Children when born have all the same Shapes and Limbs as yours, altho' they be of a different Colour.'"[27] Missiweakiwa, speaking for the Shawnees, had made a similar remark to the English at a 1760 Conference at Fort Pitt: that when they first saw Europeans ships come to their shores, "they soon discovered they were made like themselves—but that God had made them White."[28] The general shape of the human body expressed commonalty, but the potential divisiveness of skin color had to be overcome.

Determining who first introduced this concept in council is tricky. An early instance appears in the transcript of a 1687 council between the Iroquois Confederacy and the governor of New York, at which the Iroquois appealed to the colony for help in protecting their western borders from the French and French-allied Indians. The Iroquois speaker, embracing the English king as his own, was recorded as saying, "[W]ee doe Beleive yt. our king & ye french king know onanother [one another] Verry well for they are both of one Skinn meaning they are both white Skinnd, & not brown as they [the] Indians are."[29] This speaker may have been making an observation about differences he had himself noticed in English and Iroquois skin color, or he may have, in previous conversations, heard the English describe themselves as being of white skin compared to Indians. Whatever its origin, both European and Indian speakers incorporated in their speeches the idea that skin color was the critical divide.

By the middle of the eighteenth century, remarks about differences in skin color had become entrenched in council speeches and continued in United States-Indian diplomacy after the American Revolution. In these speeches, skin color always differentiated Indians from Europeans and Europeans from Indians, never Indians from other Indians, or Europeans from other Europeans: color could ally nations together metaphorically but only if those nations were either all European or all Indian. Thus, in the mid eighteenth century, Shawnee and Iroquois ambassadors seeking allies among other Indian nations argued for common skin color as a rationale for common interests, suggesting that they "take up the Hatchet against the White People, without distinction, for all their Skin was of one Colour and the Indians of a Nother, and if the Six Nations wou'd strike the French, they wou'd strike the English."[30] Indian speakers expressed disinterest in European conflicts by saying it had nought to do with their color. They found credible rumors of English-French alliances because they "were people of your own colour."[31] And skin color served as an explanation for why Indians and Europeans differed in custom. As an Iroquois speaker explained to the English in the midst of a land dispute, "The World at the first was made on the other side of the Great water different from what it is on this side, as may be known from the different Colour of Our Skin and of Our Flesh, and that which you call Justice may not be so amongst us. You have your Laws and Customs and so have we."[32]

As land disputes heated up prior to the Seven Years War (1755–1764), Indian speakers came to rely on skin color as a divine sign that the land belonged to them and that white people were intruders on it. King Hagler's assertion that Catawba rights to land originated in "the Great man above" who had made them "of this Colour and Hue (Showing his hands & Breast)" was part of a larger argument about rights to land then circulating among eastern Indians.[33] In *A Spirited Resistance,* Gregory Dowd documented how Indian prophecies telling of separate origins gained currency in the mid eighteenth century, culminating eventually in large-scale resistance movements such as that led by the Shawnee brothers Tecumseh and Tenskwatawa in the early nineteenth century.[34]

In hindsight, it may not surprise us that speakers cast skin color as an obstacle to Indian-European alliances. However, skin color acquired this rhetorical significance amid a much more complex and ambiguous dialogue about the nature of differences. Although Europeans wrote elaborate, ethnographically thick descriptions of Indian tattoos, face paint, hairstyles, and clothing, neither Indians nor Europeans targeted these cultural influences on appearance as hindrances to uniting diverse peoples in common causes. Indeed, councils often led to a ritual exchange of clothing, a symbolic act illustrating how two nations could become "one people."[35] And in adopting war captives, the Iroquois put Indians and Europeans through the same ritual process: stripped them of their clothes and gave them a new pair of moccasins to wear.[36] Here, transfers in clothing accomplished the transformation to a new identity.

Moreover, Indians and Europeans isolated skin as especially significant out of an assortment of differences that could be classified as biological. They noticed that only Europeans or Indians of mixed descent had gray or blue eyes and that Indian men could not grow the luxurious beards sported by European men even if they tried.[37] There were also apparent biological distinctions within the categories of European and Indian. Southeastern Indians called the English "blonds" to distinguish them from the Spanish and French.[38] And European writers recorded rampant variability in the complexions of European and North American peoples, describing some Indian nations as nearly as white "as the Germans" or whiter than other Indians.[39]

As I have suggested elsewhere, Europeans' rising investment in African slavery provides some explanation for the increased emphasis on skin color in European-Indian relations.[40] In the eighteenth century, Europeans cultivated an identity as white people, as opposed to their earlier self-identification as Christian. Blacks and Indians who became Christian could not challenge a European-dominated social hierarchy if skin color instead of religious belief dictated status. Although blacks had no formal role as distinct nations in council diplomacy, Indians did interact with blacks as individuals and knew that most were held as European slaves. By the end of the eighteenth century, Indians as well as Europeans acknowledged the presence of three racial groups—codified as white, red, and black—in eastern North America.

But still there remains the question, why skin color over other bodily differences? Skin may have assumed importance because people at the time considered it the best or most visible way to discern who was who. However, in practice, skin color was not a foolproof indicator of identity. No one could count on being able to tell people apart by looking at them. Whites adopted by Indians, either through captivity or by their own choice, looked like Indians to other whites.[41] At the same time, the thorough ethnic intermixture of some communities and families confounds any attempt to categorize people by either physiology or culture.[42] And yet, despite so much ambiguity surrounding the issue of difference, the cultural exchange between Indians and Europeans led them to narrow their conceptual frame and arrive at one absolute and indelible mark of identity: skin color.

At Indian and European councils, the body became a favored vehicle for Indians and Europeans to communicate their desires, intentions, and expectations to each other. The human compulsion to analogize from the concrete to the abstract gave eighteenth-century Indians and Europeans a shared language before they even met. An ocean apart and unbeknownst to the other, they had constructed elaborate knowledge by grounding abstract ideas in the experiential basics of daily life. Applying these same methods for making meaning to cross-cultural encounters, they used the forum of the diplomatic council to build a new body of knowledge.

In this new system of knowledge, created through the exchange of cultural ideas, Indians and Europeans came to agree on essential biological similarities: the shape of the human form and the function of many bodily organs such as eyes, ears, and mouths. At the same time, they made skin color the ultimate source of their differences. However, because the biological divisions between the native people of North America and Europe were not clear-cut to begin with and became even less so with intermarriage and the incorporation of captives and other dispersed peoples, there was no perfect means to tell each other apart. In practice, skin color as a source of difference turned out to be an idea without empirical foundation. If one could become the other by simply donning clothing or similar products of culture, then all peoples east of the Mississippi knew that their differences were less than skin-deep. Language about the body was, in one sense, just talk. And yet, as relations deteriorated, as trust and friendship became harder for all nations to maintain in the face of European expansion and colonialism, skin color emerged as a powerful explanation, the natural impediment, for why Europeans and Indians constituted separate peoples.

Notes

1. Indian speakers sometimes referred to penises too, but I discuss that material elsewhere; see Nancy Shoemaker, "An Alliance Between Men: Gender Metaphors in Eighteenth-Century American Indian Diplomacy East of the Mississippi," *Ethnohistory* 46 (spring 1999): 239–63.

2. Shared ideas about the body also facilitated Christian missionary endeavors. See Jane T. Merritt, "Dreaming of the Savior's Blood: Moravians and the Indian Great Awakening in Pennsylvania," *William and Mary Quarterly* 54 (1997): 723–46, especially 741–45; Colleen Ebacher, "The Old and the New World: Incorporating American Indian Forms of Discourse and Modes of Communication into Colonial Missionary Texts," *Anthropological Linguistics* 33 (1991): 135–65.

3. Richard White, *The Middle Ground: Indians, Empires, and Republics in the Great Lakes Region, 1650–1815* (New York: Cambridge University Press, 1991). See also Francis Jennings, ed., *The History and Culture of Iroquois Diplomacy: An Interdisciplinary Guide to the Treaties of the Six Nations and Their League* (Syracuse, N.Y.: Syracuse University Press, 1985); Daniel K. Richter, *The Ordeal of the Longhouse: The Peoples of the Iroquois League in the Era of European Colonization* (Chapel Hill: University of North Carolina Press, 1992); James H. Merrell, *The Indians' New World: Catawbas and Their Neighbors from European Contact Through the Era of Removal* (Chapel Hill: University of North Carolina Press, 1989), especially chapter 4; M. Thomas Hatley, *The Dividing Paths: Cherokees and South Carolinians Through the Era of Revolution* (New York: Oxford University Press, 1993); Robert A. Williams Jr., *Linking Arms Together: American Indian Treaty Visions of Law and Peace, 1600–1800* (New York: Oxford University Press, 1997).

4. White, *Middle Ground*, 84; Mary Druke, "Linking Arms: The Structure of Iroquois Intertribal Diplomacy," in Daniel K. Richter and James H. Merrell, eds., *Beyond the Covenant Chain: The Iroquois and Their Neighbors in Indian North America, 1600–1800* (Syracuse, N.Y.: Syracuse University Press, 1987), 29–39; Patricia Galloway, "'The Chief Who Is Your Father': Choctaw and French Views of the Diplomatic Relation," in Peter H. Wood,

Gregory A. Waselkov, and M. Thomas Hatley, eds., *Powhatan's Mantle: Indians in the Colonial Southeast* (Lincoln: University of Nebraska Press, 1989), 254–78; Bruce White, " 'Give Us a Little Milk': The Social and Cultural Meanings of Gift Giving in the Lake Superior Fur Trade," *Minnesota History* 48 (1982): 60–71.

5. Eighteenth-century Cherokee political structure is described in the John Howard Payne Papers, Newberry Library, Chicago; for "righthand man," see volumes 3:58, 4:463, 4:525. "[T]he Mankiller [headman of a Cherokee town] placed the Emperor [English name for a Cherokee man who spoke for the English in council] on my left Hand and one of his principall Warriours on my right," Lt. Wall to Raymond Demere, 13 January 1757, in William L. McDowell Jr., ed., *Documents Relating to Indian Affairs, 1754–1765* (Columbia, S.C.: South Carolina Department of Archives & History, 1970), 321. At a "Generall Conference betweene the Headmen of the Cherokees and the Lower Creeke Indians in the Presence of Both Houses" in Carolina (1726–27), the Creeks, who were suing the Cherokees for peace, sat on the left hand of the council's president while the Cherokees sat on his right, C.O.5.387.245, British Public Record Office, in microfilm collection indexed in William L. Anderson and James A. Lewis, *A Guide to Cherokee Documents in Foreign Archives* (Metuchen, N.J.: Scarecrow Press, 1983), available from Western Carolina University, Cullowhee, North Carolina. For English concern over who sat on the right and left, see Peter Gordon's account of Oglethorpe's founding of Georgia, which describes how Oglethorpe sat the Yamacraw headman Tomo Chachi "upon his right hand" and later Tomo Chachi met with Oglethorpe and his aids, "Captain Scott on his right hand and Mr. Jon. Brian on his left," in E. Merton Coulter, ed., *The Journal of Peter Gordon, 1732–1735* (Athens, Ga.: University of Georgia Press, 1963), 35, 43.

6. Robert Hertz, "The Pre-eminence of the Right Hand: A Study in Religious Polarity," in Rodney Needham, ed., *Right and Left: Essays on Dual Symbolic Classification* (Chicago: University of Chicago Press, 1973), 3–31, especially 21.

7. In John Lawson, *A New Voyage to Carolina,* ed. Hugh Talmage Lefler (Chapel Hill: University of North Carolina Press, 1967), 213.

8. Teyawarunte, speaking for the Six Nations, Council at Johnson Hall (1763), in James Sullivan, Alexander C. Flick, Milton W. Hamilton, and Albert B. Corey, eds., *The Papers of Sir William Johnson,* 14 vols. (Albany: University of the State of New York, 1921–1965), 10:632.

9. George Lakoff and Mark Johnson, *Metaphors We Live By* (Chicago: University of Chicago Press, 1980); George Lakoff, *Women, Fire, and Dangerous Things: What Categories Reveal About the Mind* (Chicago: University of Chicago Press, 1987); Needham, *Right and Left;* Mary Douglas, *Natural Symbols: Explorations in Cosmology* (New York: Random House, 1970); Roy G. D'Andrade, *The Development of Cognitive Anthropology* (New York: Cambridge University Press, 1995).

10. Unnamed speaker, speaking for the Six Nations, private conference at Philadelphia (1732), in [Samuel Hazard, ed.], *Minutes of the Provincial Council of Pennsylvania,* 10 vols. (Harrisburg: Theo. Fenn and Jo. Severns, 1851–1852), 3:443.

11. Claude Charles le Roy and Bacqueville de la Potherie, "History of the Savage Peoples Who Are Allies of New France," in Emma Blair, ed., *The Indian Tribes of the Upper Mississippi Valley and Region of the Great Lakes,* 2 vols. (Cleveland: Arthur H. Clark, 1911–1912), 1:371–72. Chaussegros De Léry told a Huron man in 1754 that he would "have them drink a draught of milk from their father," in Sylvester K. Stevens and Donald H. Kent, eds., *Journal of Chaussegros De Léry* (Harrisburg: Pennsylvania Historical and Museum Commission, 1941), 50. The English eventually picked up the phrase, probably from French-allied Indians. See James Stevenson to William Johnson, 18 September 1770, in Sullivan, *Papers of Sir William Johnson,* 7:907.

12. Caroline Walker Bynum, *Jesus as Mother: Studies in the Spirituality of the High Middle Ages* (Berkeley: University of California Press, 1982) and *Fragmentation and Redemption: Essays on Gender and the Human Body in Medieval Religion* (New York: Zone Books, 1991).

13. Bruce White, "Give Us a Little Milk."

14. Unnamed speaker for Conestoga Indians, Council at the Conestoga town (1720), in Hazard, *Minutes,* 3:93.

15. Civility speaking for the Ganaweses, Conestogas, Delawares, and Shawnees living on the Susquehanna, Council at Philadelphia (1723) in Hazard, *Minutes,* 3:217.

16. John Hay to Governor of Pennsylvania, 27 December 1763, in Hazard, *Minutes,* 9:102.

17. Articles of Agreement with the Susquehanna Indians, 23 April 1701, in Mary Maples Dunn and Richard S. Dunn, eds., *The Papers of William Penn,* 5 vols. (Philadelphia: University of Pennsylvania Press, 1981–1987), 4:51.

18. Naaman, "Treaty Between the Swedes and the Indians at Tennakonck" (1654), in *Early American Indian Documents: Treaties and Laws, 1607–1789,* gen. ed. Alden T. Vaughan, *Pennsylvania and Delaware Treaties, 1629–1737,* vol. 1., ed. Donald H. Kent (Washington, D.C.: University Publications of America, 1979), 26.

19. 1 Corinthians 12:12–31; 1 Corinthians 11:3–7; and Ephesians 5:21–30. For discussion of how biblical meanings of bodily members informed seventeenth-century English culture, see Robert Blair St. George, *Conversing by Signs: Poetics of Implication in Colonial New England Culture* (Chapel Hill: University of North Carolina Press, 1998), 150–54.

20. The Six Nations also used the phrase; in 1740, they agreed to make peace with Indians to the south and west, "that we may be united as one body, one heart and one flesh," in E. B. O'Callaghan, ed., *Documents Relative to the Colonial History of the State of New York; Procured in Holland, England and France by John Romeyn Brodhead, Esq., Agent,* 15 vols. (Albany, N.Y.: Weed, Parsons, 1853–1887), 6:178.

21. "Wee profess wee will be one Heart and true to the English and to one another," according to an unnamed speaker from "upper part of the river" (1693), Hazard, *Minutes,* 1:372; Lt. Gov. Patrick Gordon told the Delawares, Five Nations, and Shawnees, Council at Philadelphia (1728) that he knew the Indians kept treaties "in their Memory & in their Hearts," in Hazard, *Minutes,* 3:316; Red Shoes (Choctaw) accused the Chickasaws of betrayal and said they had "bad hearts," as recorded in Régis du Roullet to Périer, 16 March 1731, in Dunbar Rowland and A. G. Sanders, eds., *Mississippi Provincial Archives—French Dominion,* vols. 4–5, rev. and ed. Patricia K. Galloway (Baton Rouge: Louisiana State University Press, 1984), 4:70.

22. A Ganawese Indian told Shikellamy in 1733 that "the friendship of the white People was from the Mouth only and not from the Herrt [sic]"; in Hazard, *Minutes,* 3:501; "Your speeches are then only from your mouths, and I see that your heart does not share in them," marquis de Beauharnois to Great Lakes Indians, Speeches at an Indian Council (1732), in Sylvester K. Stevens and Donald H. Kent, eds., *Wilderness Chronicles of Northwestern Pennsylvania* (Harrisburg: Pennsylvania Historical Commission, 1941), 7; "it is not from the lips that they speak to you, but from the bottom of their heart," Demoiselle, chief of the Miamis, in C. B. Galbreath, ed., *Expedition of Celoron to the Ohio Country in 1749* (Columbus, Ohio: F. J. Heer, 1921), 54. Also see the speech for the Nanticokes, Council at Philadelphia (1751), Hazard, *Minutes,* 5:544; Tokaaion, speaking for the Six Nations, Council at Easton (1758), Hazard, *Minutes,* 8:212; Torongoa, speaking for 22 French-allied nations, Council at Onondaga (1760), speech repeated by Isyonostat and recorded in "Johnson's Proceedings," in Sullivan, *Papers of Sir William Johnson,* 3:188.

23. Toanohiso, speaking for the Six Nations, Council in Ohio (1751), in Hazard, *Minutes,* 5:538–39; Scarrooyady, repeating speech made by Shawnees, meeting at Carlisle (1753), Hazard, *Minutes,* 5:676.

24. Other examples: "we are to have one eye and one ear, altho' you sometimes write to Canada, & we know nothing of ye matter," Sadeganaktie, speaking for the Iroquois, Council at Albany (1702), in O'Callaghan, *Documents Relative,* 4:993. The Nanticoke king, speaking for a coalition of Ohio Indians, said they "have but one Mouth, & speak now as one Man." Council at Philadelphia (1763), in Hazard, *Minutes,* 9:46; "As his Majesty desires so I hope we shall look with one eye, speak with one tongue and be as one people," Jud's Friend (Cherokee), Conference at Tyger River camp (1767) with Governor Tryon, in William L. Saunders, ed., *The Colonial Records of North Carolina,* 10 vols. (Raleigh, N.C.: P. M. Hale and Josephus Daniels, 1886–1890), 7:465.

25. Teedyuscung, Council at Philadelphia (1755), in Hazard, *Minutes,* 6: 363.

26. In Walter Clark, ed., *The State Records of North Carolina,* vol. 11 (Winston, N.C.: M. I. & J. C. Stewart, 1895), 183.

27. In Hazard, *Minutes,* 9:616.

28. In Sullivan, *Papers of Sir William Johnson,* 3:211. Another Great Lakes example comes from a 1770 conference at Niagara, when the Ojibwe speaker Aminabeaujeu promised the English "that altho' his Skin was Black, his heart was still good," in John Brown to Thomas Gage, 8 June 1770, in Sullivan, *Papers of Sir William Johnson,* 7:716.

29. Lawrence H. Leder, ed., *The Livingston Indian Records, 1666–1723* (Gettysburg, Pa.: Pennsylvania Historical Association, 1956), 115.

30. Hazard, *Minutes,* 7:299. The Delawares and Shawnees reminded an Indian delegation sent by the United States in the 1790s that "we whose are one colar, now have one heart and one head," in Hendrick Aupaumut, "A Short Narration of My Last Journey to the Western Contry," ed. B. H. Coates, *Memoirs of the Historical Society of Pennsylvania,* vol. 2 (Philadelphia: Carey, Lea, & Carey, 1827), 117.

31. Unnamed Shawnee speaker, meeting at Log's Town (1758), in Charles Frederick Post, "Two Journals of Western Tours," in Reuben Gold Thwaites, ed., *Early Western Travels, 1748–1765,* vol. 1 (Cleveland: Arthur H. Clark, 1904), 222.

32. Gachadow, speaking for the Six Nations, Council at Lancaster (1744), *Minutes,* 4:720. At a Council at Lancaster (1762), Thomas King, speaker for the Six Nations, explained the difficulty of returning war captives as arising from how "every one of these [Indian] Nations have different Ways"; he made no mention of skin color, but later said to the English governor, "you and the French; you are both of one Colour." The governor of Pennsylvania, pressing for the return of prisoners, then remarked that "[a]s we are of a different Colour from you, so we have different Customs." *Minutes,* 8:743, 745, 760.

33. Council at Matthew Tool's House (1754), in Saunders, *Colonial Records of North Carolina,* 5:144a.

34. Gregory Evans Dowd, *A Spirited Resistance: The North American Indian Struggle for Unity, 1745–1815* (Baltimore: Johns Hopkins University Press, 1992), 30, 44, 108.

35. Timothy J. Shannon, "Dressing for Success on the Mohawk Frontier: Hendrick, William Johnson, and the Indian Fashion," *William and Mary Quarterly* 53 (1996): 13–42.

36. John Demos, *The Unredeemed Captive: A Family Story from Early America* (New York: Random House, 1994), 147–48; June Namias, *White Captives: Gender and Ethnicity on the American Frontier* (Chapel Hill: University of North Carolina Press, 1993).

37. Iroquois Indians at Onondaga responded to an English query about whether whites had joined in an attack on the Virginia backcountry by saying that "there were not any white people in the party, but that a young fellow who is half Indian & half Christian was with them who had blue eyes which was the occasion of the mistake." In Minutes of the Proceedings of the Commissioners of Indian Affairs for New York, 2 May 1743, O'Callaghan, *Documents Relative,* 6:240; Pouchot attributed bearded Indian men to their being "mixed with European blood," in M. Pouchot, *Memoir Upon the Late War in North America, Between the French and English, 1755–60,* trans. and ed. Franklin B. Hough, 2 vols.

(Roxbury, Mass.: W. Elliot Woodward, 1866), 2:184. Pénicaut described his party of Frenchmen as "white-skinned people, some heavily bearded, some bald-headed ... different from them [Biloxi Indians], who have very tawny skin and heavy black hair which they groom very carefully." Richebourg Gaillard McWilliams, ed., *Fleur de Lys and Calumet: Being the Pénicaut Narrative of French Adventure in Louisiana* (Baton Rouge: Louisiana State University Press, 1953), 4.

38. According to a Frenchman in Louisiana, "the Indians call the English 'blond men' to distinguish them from the French and Spanish," in Seymour Feiler, ed., *Jean-Bernard Bossu's Travels in the Interior of North America, 1751–1762* (Norman: University of Oklahoma Press, 1962), 137. Catholic missionaries to Indians told them that "Judas had red hair, and that the English who have generally this kind of hair, are of his race," Pouchot, *Memoirs,* 2:223.

39. Pouchot, *Memoirs,* 2:184. The French in Louisiana thought Indian women on the upper Mississippi "whiter" than other Indians and better candidates for French intermarriage; Minutes of the Council, 1 Sept. 1716, in Dunbar Rowland and A. G. Sanders, eds., *Mississippi Provincial Archives—French Dominion,* vols. 1–3 (Jackson: Mississippi Department of Archives and History, 1927–1932), 2:218.

40. Nancy Shoemaker, "How Indians Got to Be Red," *American Historical Review* 102 (1997): 624–44.

41. Adopted Iroquois Pierre Esprit Radisson looked Iroquois to most Europeans; Francois Marbois, mystified by an Indian he met who spoke fluent French, learned he was an adopted Iroquois war captive, and then later met an Englishwoman who had escaped servitude to live with the Iroquois and now passed for Indian; see "Voyages of Pierre Esprit Radisson, 1651–1654" and the Marbois excerpt "Journey to the Oneidas, 1784," in Dean R. Snow, Charles T. Gehring, and William A. Starna, eds., *In Mohawk Country: Early Narratives about a Native People* (Syracuse, N.Y.: Syracuse University Press, 1996), 89–91, 307, 316; James Axtell further describes how Europeans could not discern white captives from Indians by their "physiognomy," in *The Invasion Within: The Contest of Cultures in Colonial North America* (New York: Oxford University Press, 1985), 308.

42. Elizabeth A. Perkins gives examples of how "[s]kin color, like dress, was not an absolute guide to a stranger's identity," in "Distinctions and Partitions Amongst Us: Identity and Interaction in the Revolutionary Ohio Valley," in Andrew R. L. Cayton and Fredrika J. Teute, eds., *Contact Points: American Frontiers from the Mohawk Valley to the Mississippi, 1750–1830* (Chapel Hill: University of North Carolina Press, 1998), 205–34, especially 218. Interpreter Andrew Montour was one example of someone whose identity was inscrutable and fluid; see James H. Merrell, " 'The Cast of his Countenance': Reading Andrew Montour," in Ronald Hoffman, Mechal Sobel, and Fredrika J. Teute, eds., *Through a Glass Darkly: Reflections on Personal Identity in Early America* (Chapel Hill: University of North Carolina Press, 1997), 13–39.

Emancipation and the Em-bodiment of "Race"

The Strange Case of the White Negroes and the Algerine Slaves

JOANNE POPE MELISH

Between the 1780s and the 1830s, the once widespread institution of slavery virtually disappeared in the New England states. Emancipation was accomplished very gradually, a process involving *post nati* statutes[1] in some states, ambiguous and contested constitutional interpretations in others, and sporadic individual manumissions and judicious disappearances everywhere. In the course of this gradual process, whites were able to map a language and a set of practices shaped in the context of slavery onto their relations with the slowly emerging population of free people of color.[2] A system of beliefs and practices rooted in relations of subordination was transformed, in freedom, to a new system of beliefs and practices focusing on the person in the body, in a discourse of inferiority. In other words, in the context of freedom, relations of subordination were naturalized, and perceived physical and cultural differences were literally em-bodied.[3]

This breakdown, so disturbing to whites, of a previously fixed and safely stable equation of "black" with "slave" took place in the larger context of post-Revolutionary instability. Ordinary citizens, wondering how Revolutionary social change might affect their heretofore secure role and status, watched a once reliable marking system for identifying persons as enslaved or free by their physical characteristics break down and become inoperative. The emergence of people of color as a categorically "free" people appeared as both a symptom and a catalyst of disorder. Males of color were becoming free men; many whites wondered, could they also become freemen? Voters? Citizens? Might women of color become free with respect to the very realm that white men had sought most anxiously to control—their sexuality? Might they become sites of ungovernable race-mixing?

Science in the late eighteenth century predicted qualitative transformation as well as physiological adaptation of humans in response to environmental change. Environmental theory explained servile demeanor, condition, and even physical attributes as environmental effects. Comte de Buffon, Samuel Stanhope Smith, and others argued that the physical characteristics of Africans were associated with their equatorial origin and would change over time to become more similar to those of the white European.[4] At the same time, antislavery advocates insisted that all of the negative social and psychological characteristics generally attributed to slaves—lack of mental acuity, laziness, dependency, and so forth—were consequences of enslavement. Emancipation and firm guidance on the part of whites would diminish, if not eradicate, those characteristics over time.

Although this argument had reassured white colonists on the eve of the Revolution as they contemplated the possibility of emancipation sometime in the future, it acquired troubling implications in the post-Revolutionary climate of anxiety over the uncertain outcome of revolutionary social change. The disassociation of "slave" and "negro" in the course of emancipation also resulted, inevitably, in the wrenching apart of the previously unchallenged correlation, "free" and "white," leaving open all possible permutations of the four terms. "White" and "slave," "negro" and "free" emerged, floating and unanchored, available as an explanatory and metaphorical language useful for investigating and describing the disruptive political, social, and perhaps biological consequences of democracy as well as emancipation.

The appearance of an extensive literature of black/white role reversal after 1780 seems clearly linked to whites' interpretation of the emergence of free people of color as a disruptive factor, somehow not merely symptomatic of but actually engendering the dis-ordering of society, with implications for the role, status, and even "nature" of white citizens. This role reversal literature constituted a medium of racializing discourse in the early Republic.

Two actual situations that engendered extraordinary interest and anxiety in this period and produced extensive literatures of role reversal were the apparent transformation of black skin into white (instances of albinism and vitiligo)[5] and the protracted captivity and enslavement of whites, especially Americans, in North Africa by the so-called Barbary states. These situations posed disturbing questions: Might the "markings" of enslaveability be mutable? Could they disappear gradually in freedom? And, on the other hand, might the relationship be inverted? Could enslavement transform whites into a servile people, as dependent and instrumental as black slaves? If so, physical characteristics might not be a reliable indicator of "aptitude," so to speak, for enslavement—or entitlement to citizenship. Underlying these questions was a profound anxiety over the manageability of revolutionary social change; the literature of role reversal posed questions about the "nature" of citizenship in terms of the "nature" of enslaveability and the permanence of its signs.

Many scholars have noted the intense public interest generated in the mid-1790s by the case of Henry Moss, an American-born man of African descent whose dark skin turned white in his early middle age. The public fascination with this and other physical anomalies might usefully be within the larger context of the Enlightenment interest in classification, observation, and experiment, and, more specifically, for analytical physiognomics—the practice of seeking systematic correspondences between the external characteristics or markings of living creatures and innate truths about their nature and condition, and classifying them according to the differences perceived. The ethnographic descriptions of American philosophers such as Samuel Stanhope Smith (1787) and leading European naturalists such as comte de Buffon (1797) classified humans by "races,"[6] following Linnaeus's 1735 model in *Systema naturae* or a subsequent alternative classification. These races were then subclassified by named groups or tribes according to differences in culture and climate, and then these differences were associated with global variations in skin color.[7]

By suggesting that explanations for previously unaccountable variety in human appearance and behavior might lie in the body's response to its environment, science seemed to hold out the possibility of rationalizing revolutionary social change. In the context of gradual emancipation and revolution, the physical transformation of a so-called "negro" into a white person or vice versa, or the birth of one to the other, demanded a scientific explanation that could also constitute a political explanation. These events raised questions about the meaning of both categories—"negro," white—and where precisely, or if, these and other categories of human identity assumed to be related to them—slave, citizen—could be located reliably in an individual human being. Such phenomena constituted sites in which environmental explanations of difference might be tested against hypothetical ones defining difference as innate and fixed, and where the validity of external, physical markers in defining essential human identity might be explored.

Moss's case was only one of more than a dozen cases of anomalies of skin color in "negroes" and in whites that were publicized and discussed between 1790 and 1810 in an attempt to explore and resolve these questions. The best known may be Jefferson's careful description in 1781 of seven cases of African albinism and one case of vitiligo.[8] Charles Willson Peale published three accounts, one in 1788 and two in 1791, of a man whose portrait he also exhibited in his museum as "James, the White Mulatto," according to Benjamin Rush.[9] Two other, similar stories, "Account of a remarkable alteration of color in a negro woman" and "Account of a white negro," were published by two physicians, James Bate and James Parsons, in 1788 and 1789, respectively. Significantly, Bate's story had originally been recounted in a private letter in 1759, which the recipient had held until the topic gained currency nearly thirty years later; Parsons's account, too, had been written much earlier, in 1765, and published more than two decades later when the subject became newsworthy.[10]

Thus, the issues of "negroes turning white" and "white negroes" had already received considerable public attention when Henry Moss became a celebrity around 1796. Moss was examined by an assortment of physicians, scientists, philanthropists, and politicians, from Benjamin Rush to Moses Brown to George Washington, and several of them published accounts of the case.[11] Public interest in Henry Moss, in turn, generated stories of other, similar cases in the popular literature and also produced lay contributions to medical periodicals. In October 1800, for example, *The Monthly Magazine and American Review* picked up an article published earlier in the year by *The Medical Repository* entitled, "Another instance of a Negro Turning White," the story of one Maurice whose "sable cloud is plainly disappearing on his shoulder."[12] A year later, *The Medical Repository* published a letter to the editors, under the headline, "ANOTHER ETHIOPIAN TURNING TO A WHITE MAN," from a Mr. A. Catlin of Lichfield, Connecticut, who reported proliferating and enlarging white spots on "Pompey, a very healthy negro," and evinced "the fullest belief that a very few years will complete the total change."[13] In 1809, the *American Magazine of Wonders* published an article largely recapitulating Jefferson's litany of known African albinos, but including an additional case of "a female of this kind born of black parents, married to an Englishman, whose children were mulattoes. The woman was exhibited as a show, but her children were the greatest curiosities."[14] (They were "curiosities" presumably because, although visibly children of color, they appeared to have two natural parents who were both white.)

Interest in Moss's case and others coincided with the gradual emancipation process in the northern states, peaking in the 1790s and dissipating by 1810. At least in part, such intense interest clearly reflected whites' anxiety about the stability of their own, as well as blacks', emerging role as citizens in the rapidly changing political and social environment of the post-Revolutionary years. While these accounts posed the possibility of radical metamorphosis, their language ultimately served to reassure white readers that even seemingly extreme types of transformation of human identity could be understood, controlled, placed within the limits of science, and finally, revealed to be superficial rather than essential.

By emphasizing the authenticity of the transformed "negro's" original blackness, the accounts secure a permanent association of a visibly altered individual with her or his former identity as a "negro."[15] Not a single account refers to a "loss of former color in a white woman," but rather to an "alteration of color in a negro woman," never to "negroid whites," but always to "white negroes," even though several of the subjects came to public attention after they had become, or were born, entirely white. These accounts seek to map the location of difference, and ultimately situate it deep within the body where heredity alone rather than skin color can provide a valid marker for it, an essence revealed only through knowledge of descent. In this way, these accounts distinguish between the appearance of individuals and their essence; these individuals are certified to be substantially "negroes," and only accidentally "white." "Race," then, could be understood as constituting an innate and permanent difference, of which skin color was one of a number of variable, and unreliable, signs.

The metaphor of mapping is extraordinarily apt for these disturbingly detached explorations of the human landscape that rendered the subjects literal objects of study. James Bate's original 1788 account of his examination of a forty-year-old cook included his observation that "her head, face, and breast, with the belly, legs, calves, and thighs, are almost wholly white, the pudenda ... , party coloured."[16] Bate was, of course, a doctor; but Moses Brown, Quaker businessman and prominent Rhode Island antislavery advocate, reported an even more intrusive examination of Henry Moss in 1803: "The white parts of his skin and especially his anus are so transparent as to show the vains [sic] as distinct, as a white mans."[17] These examinations sometimes involved subcutaneous explorations as well, here again reminiscent of the probing of the earth's surface to identify and map its inner resources. Bate reported trying to raise a blister on the cook's skin without success. Brown reported that Moss had told him of an examination by Benjamin Rush in which "the Docr apprehending he could cause his [Moss's] skin to change, he blistered him &c, but to no purpose, the black skin whereon they were put returned, til the Doc gave up further experiment." D. W.'s examination of Moss involved poking at his subject: "Upon pressing his skin with a finger, the part pressed appeared white; and on removal of the pressure, the displaced blood rushed back, suffusing the part with red, exactly as in the case of an European, in like circumstances."[18] The very nature and matter-of-fact reporting of these examinations established the intrinsic chattel nature of the subjects, despite the fact that not one was described as a slave. (Some of them may have been slaves in fact; but it was their whiteness, not their status, that generated interest in the age of emancipation, and Henry Moss, the most widely discussed, was in fact born a free man.)[19]

The last in the post-Revolutionary wave of articles on albinism and vitiligo in persons of color appeared about 1810 in *The Medical Museum* and *The American Magazine of Wonders,* two magazines devoted largely to sensational stories about freaks and curiosities. The concluding paragraph of one of these articles asserted, "These facts fully ascertain, that this [albinism] is a variety only of the Negro race."[20] The consignment of "white negroes" to the category of freaks, as opposed to products of systematic transformations that could be explained and reliably reproduced, represented a conclusion reached after more than two decades of scientific and philosophical debate—a conclusion that served political imperatives as much as it satisfied scientific ones.

Transformations of skin color (and thus, perhaps, of the "essential nature" of human beings) could occur in either direction. Speaking of abrupt changes in color, and anomalous birth coloration such as albinism, Buffon might insist that "this variation never happens but from black to white"; but his environmental theory of long-term change convinced him that "many ages might perhaps elapse before a white race would become altogether black; but there is a probability that in time a white people, transported from the north to the equator, would experience that change, especially if they were to change their manners, and to feed solely on the productions of the warm climate."[21]

But whiteness was a marker distinguishing the entitled citizen from the subordinate in republican America. Under radically different environmental conditions, enslaved in a tropical climate by a "savage" people of color, could free white Americans become slavelike? And how profound and permanent would such a change be? Was whiteness part of some kind of stable, essential nature, or did the conditions of one's existence have the power to transform the "nature" of Americans and Europeans, too, as Buffon and Smith suggested? An ongoing diplomatic crisis that coincided with the peak of the emancipation period posed these questions, and the enormous popularity of the literature it generated suggests that many Americans found them compelling.

The crisis involved the enslavement of white Americans by the North African states of Morocco, Algiers, Tunis, and Tripoli—the so-called Barbary States. The periodic seizure of American vessels by Barbary corsairs, especially those of Algiers, resulted in the capture and imprisonment of the American crew members, many of whom spent eight or more years in captivity before negotiation and payment of a ransom effected their release.[22]

The common term for the captivity in Algiers of Americans (and other Europeans as well—in 1786 there were at least 2,200 foreigners imprisoned in Algiers) was "slavery."[23] This was not a hyperbolic or allusive term: captured Europeans and Americans were sold in slave markets; they were forced to perform heavy physical labor and to beg monies from their friends and families abroad to provide anything above the barest subsistence level of food and clothing; they were regularly beaten and chained for the slightest infractions; and, because their eventual ransom was uncertain at best, unless they converted to Islam they could expect only death to liberate them from bondage.[24]

Since the 1780s, white Americans had become familiar with ethnographic descriptions of the peoples of North Africa that clearly depicted them as peoples of color.[25] When personal stories of enslavement by "tawny" Arabs and "dusky" or "swarthy" Moors of unbridled savagery began to surface in the United States, Americans were prepared to read these stories as tests of the durability of republican whiteness, in somewhat the way an earlier generation had read narratives of the captivity of colonists by native peoples as tests of the durability of Christian faith. The potential mutability of whites into slaves/people of color in Africa offered as great a symbolic challenge to the American social order as the actual mutability of blacks into free people/whites at home; both could be read symptomatically to evaluate the potential political, social, and perhaps biological consequences of democracy and emancipation.[26]

The American public was deeply interested in the fate of the American slaves in Algiers during the course of their captivity. What really seemed to seize the popular imagination were the personal narratives of the captivity experience, and literary simulations of such narratives, some in poetic and dramatic form, that appeared between 1794 and 1820.

Most accounts emphasized the brutality and inhumanity of the Algerines. Nearly every account included graphic descriptions of punishments meted out to white slaves, including being beaten repeatedly on the bottoms of the feet, burned, roasted alive, impaled, and cast over the walls to catch and dangle for days on iron hooks.[27] James Stevens said that public slaves were forced to wear an iron ring around one ankle, while private slaves sold into the country must carry burdens to market, work naked in the fields, tend cattle, drag ploughs, and "do all other kinds of the most servile drudgery." John Burnham reported forced work at trades such as sailmaking, carpentry, and smithing, and periodic labor hauling rocks from the mountains to the "mole" (breakwater protecting the harbor of Algiers), receiving for his labor "three small black loaves a day." John Foss received a "25–30 pound chain from leg to shoulder"; Robert White complained of "hellish tortures and punishments" chained to the oar of a row-galley, where he survived for four years and nine months. He reported that "others are weltering under their chains in the mines, and dragging out a miserable existence, scarce worth possessing."[28]

These reports of cruel, depraved, and bestial behavior raised serious questions for American readers: would enslavement by animal-like people degrade white American free people to a similar level? Such a transformation could seem imminent when John Burnham, commander of the ship *Hope* taken in 1793, described the housing conditions of the slaves, where "in many places of the building are Christians, monkeys, apes, and asses altogether."[29] Reduction to the condition of animals was, after all, only a metaphor, but it was the central metaphor of slavery—systematic eradication of personhood, debasement to the condition of chattel.

The narratives represented the Algerines' utterly arbitrary and despotic exercise of power as complemented by a cringing servility. Narrators blamed both extremes of Algerine behavior on their crushing oppression by the Turks. In other words, the Algerines themselves were represented as a kind of partial paradigm of environmental transformation: subjected to despotic power, the Algerines had themselves become despots; made to submit, they had become servile.[30]

If Algerine behavior, like the servile behavior of African slaves in America, could be understood as a consequence of oppression, then perhaps white Americans in slavery could become servile and even depraved as well. Many of the early narratives seemed to confirm these fears. The daily existence of the American slaves was "scarce worth possessing"; a Christian, after a long captivity, appeared "exceedingly stupid and insensible"; some "turned Turk" [adopted Islam]. In *The Algerine Captive* (1797), a fictional imitation of a captivity narrative, Royall Tyler included an incident obviously intended to dramatize just this problem of potential transformation. In it, the narrator, Dr. Updike Underhill, at the outset of his imprisonment, resists a whipping and tries to incite his fellow prisoners, long enslaved, to help him bind their overseer and escape. "But I called in vain ... I spoke to slaves, astonished at my presumption."[31]

Unlike most of the early, more "ethnographic" narratives, however, Tyler's novel proposed an answer to the transformation question. So did several other highly stylized and embellished narratives, plays, and poems that took the experiences of American slaves as their subject. This second wave of captivity-based works frankly proclaimed the triumph of republican whiteness over the enslavement experience.[32] Here, in a number of ways, the differences between Algerines/Arabs/Moors/Turks on the one hand and Europeans and Americans on the other were naturalized and embodied for the first time.

Some of these works transformed the captivity experience into highly sexualized tales of romance and rescue. Unlike the earlier narratives, in which females had virtually no role at all, many of these tales featured female characters, both Algerine and American (or sometimes British). Here, virtuous whiteness often takes the shape of a woman.[33]

For example, in Susanna Rowson's *Slaves in Algiers*, Fetnah (who is actually an English Jew but has been raised as a Moslem Algerine), favorite concubine of the Dey, learns to revere freedom and to resist both the Dey and Islam from Rebecca, a captive "from that land, where virtue in either sex is the only mark of superiority.—She was an American." Fetnah says that it was Rebecca "who nourished in my mind the love of liberty, and taught me, woman was never formed to be the abject slave of man. Nature made us equal with them, and gave us the power to render ourselves superior."[34] Rowson depicts whiteness, virtue, and republican values as innate and powerful in Rebecca, the American woman. Rebecca in turn can act as a catalyst to reawaken in Fetnah the same values that have been suppressed by sexual, political, and religious domination. Rowson seems to employ nationality and ethnicity here at least partly to suggest a kind of naturalized hierarchy of virtue and resistance to tyranny. Fetnah is unmistakably represented as white, and she is a woman, both of which endow her with an innate love of freedom. But, Rowson implies, Fetnah's English nationality leaves her more vulnerable to aristocratic domination than Rebecca's American one, just as Fetnah's Jewish ethnicity leaves her more vulnerable to the cultural snares of Islam, including sexual and religious domination, than is Rebecca the Christian. Nonetheless, whiteness and republican virtue are inborn in both these women—manifest and resistant in Rebecca, dormant but ready to be reinvigorated in Fetnah.

In these works, proud and virtuous whiteness is portrayed as triumphant over oppression and slavery because it is inborn in all whites, especially Americans. The imagery of descent, linking country and family, appears everywhere. Tyler's Dr. Underhill concludes, "I had been degraded to a slave, and was now advanced to a citizen of the freest country in the universe. I had been lost to my parent, friends, and country, and now found, in the embraces and congratulations of the former and the rights and protection of the latter." Rowson proclaims, "Nor *here* alone, Columbia's sons be free,/ *Where'er* they breath[e] there must be liberty."[35] In other words, white Americans themselves embody a liberty inherited from their mother Columbia, the personification of the American Republic.

The literatures of role reversal, then, not only posed questions about the mutability of "black/of color" and "white," "slave," and "free citizen," but, especially after 1800, they provided clear answers calculated to reassure whites. In every case, the answers challenged environmental theory itself, proposing a radically different conception of human difference: that whiteness and citizenship, savagery and servility were innate characteristics; that there was indeed a fixed and immutable human nature that was not subject to substantial change by external experience—a fixed nature to which the somatic or physiognomic could after all provide reliable clues.

The popular conclusion about the stability of whiteness paralleled the direction of scientific thought, which increasingly turned away from environmental explanations in the early nineteenth century. Now, physicians and philosophers began to offer new physical proofs of essential and permanent "racial" difference and to try to reconcile such difference with the unity of human descent. Dr. Charles White in England and Drs. John Augustine Smith and Samuel George Morton in the United States were some of the earliest of a growing body of critics of environmentalism who argued from anatomical structure and skull shape that there was a biological basis for permanent "racial" difference.[36]

Thus science affirmed what politics demanded: that the instrumentality and dependency of slaves, in fact mapped onto free people of color by the persistence of pre-Revolutionary practices during gradual emancipation, could be understood instead as characteristics innate to "negroes." People of color could never become citizens—they were not equipped by nature for the role. Similarly, republican whiteness would persist through temporary enslavement, impoverishment, and other forms of degrading experience (including post-Revolutionary social dislocation) because it, too, was an innate and "natural" quality.

The discourses of science and role reversal were mutually reinforcing. Together they located stable and virtuous republican citizenship in the essential nature of whites; at the same time, they constituted free people of color as essentially and immutably servile, "naturally" unsuitable for citizenship, and fated to remain a permanent element of disorder and a persistent obstacle for whites to ignore, overcome, or eliminate in the course of building their new Republic.

Notes

1. *Post nati* (literally, "after birth") statutes declared all children born to slaves in Connecticut and Rhode Island after March 1, 1784, to be free persons. These statutes placed such children under the authority of the owner of their mothers for a specified term, twenty-five years in Connecticut, eighteen years if female and twenty-one years if male in Rhode Island. *Post nati* statutes did not alter the status of slaves born before the effective dates of the statutes. See "An Act concerning Indian, Molatto, and Negro Servants and Slaves," January 8, 1784, *Acts and Laws of the State of Connecticut in America* (New London, 1784), 233–35; and "An Act authorizing the manumission of negroes, mulattoes, and others, and for the gradual abolition of slavery," *Records of the State of Rhode Island and Providence Plantations in New England*, ed. John Russell Bartlett, vol. 10:1784–92 (Providence: Providence Press Co., 1865), 7.

2. I use the term *whites* for those persons who were Europeans before 1776 and Euro-Americans thereafter because it was the designation most commonly used by them as well as by people of color after the Revolution, which is the focus of this paper, and because it is commonly used by scholars today. I use "people of color" in reference to "blacks" wherever the phrase will not make the sentence containing it unforgivably clumsy because slaves and their descendants throughout New England were a people of mixed African, Native American, and often white descent; I do, however, use "blacks" where it seems necessary or where I am deliberately evoking its use in the time period under discussion. Whites routinely collapsed distinctions of descent with regard to people of color by using the terms "black" and "of color" indiscriminately for all kinds of persons with some degree of African descent or native descent, although they also frequently used the terms "molatto" or "mulatto" and "mustee" to characterize persons of mixed descent as well, whether they actually were descended from native people and/or Africans or not. I do not place the terms *whites* and *blacks* in quotes, since these terms are commonly used in modern scholarship; I do not intend thereby to essentialize "whiteness" or "blackness." I do place the terms *negro, mulatto,* and *mustee* in quotes, since they are not acceptable scholarly terms today.

3. The most detailed examination of the process of emancipation is still Arthur Zilversmit, *The First Emancipation: The Abolition of Slavery in the North* (Chicago: University of Chicago Press, 1967). For a more extensive analysis of northern emancipation and "racial" production, see Joanne Pope Melish, *Disowning Slavery: Gradual Emancipation and "Race" in New England, 1780–1860* (Ithaca, N.Y.: Cornell University Press, 1998).

4. George Louis Leclerc, comte de Buffon, *Histoire Naturelle*, trans. *Barr's Buffon: Buffon's Natural History, containing A Theory of the Earth, a General History of Man . . . &c. &c. From the French With Notes By The Translator*, 10 vols. (London: H.D. Symonds, 1797), 3:324–25, 334–40, 348–52; Samuel Stanhope Smith, *An Essay on the Causes of the Variety of Complexion and Figure in the Human Species . . . ,* 2nd ed. (New-Brunswick, N.J.: J. Simpson, 1810).

5. Albinism in humans is the congenital lack of skin pigmentation or melanin, often accompanied by extreme visual sensitivity to light. Vitiligo is a rare variety of lupus characterized by the progressive loss of epidermal pigmentation.

6. It is my position that the word *race*, as used colloquially and by philosophers and naturalists in the eighteenth century to distinguish one group of humans from another on the basis of perceived physical and cultural differences, is synonymous with "category of human" and lacks ideological content. I argue in this article that one consequence of gradual emancipation in the northern United States is an anxiety over the mutability of difference, and that this anxiety is resolved in the last years of the eighteenth century and the first decade of the nineteenth by "naturalizing" difference, locating it within the body, and defining it as innate and permanent—in other words, "racializing" it (producing the ideological construct, "race"). Like David Roediger, I see this process as motivated by anxiety about the stability of whiteness; unlike him, I do not locate this process within white workers' struggle to distinguish themselves from Southern slaves, but rather within their struggle, and that of the emerging white middle class, to stabilize their role as citizen workers in opposition to "dependent and disorderly" ex-slaves emerging as a visible class in their own region. See David R. Roediger, *The Wages of Whiteness: Race and the Making of the American Working Class* (London and New York: Verso, 1991), especially 43–92.

7. A good overview of the genealogy of scientific arguments on the origin and nature of diversity of "races" is provided in William Stanton, *The Leopard's Spots: Scientific Attitudes toward Race in America 1815–59* (Chicago: The University of Chicago Press, 1960).

8. Thomas Jefferson, *Notes on the State of Virginia* (1781; reprint, New York: Harper and Row, 1964), 70–71.

9. See Charles Willison Peale, "An Account of a Person born a Negro, or a very dark Mulatto, who afterwards became white," *The New-York Magazine; or Literary Repository* 2 (November 1791): 634–35; *The Universal Asylum, and Columbian Magazine* 7 (December 1791): 409–10; and "Account of a NEGRO, or a very dark MULATTO, turning WHITE," *Massachusetts Magazine* 3:12 (December 1791): 744. Also see Benjamin Rush, "Account of Henry Moss, a White Negro," *The Philadelphia Medical and Physical Journal* 2:2 (1806): 7.

10. James Bate, "An Account of a remarkable alteration of colour in a negro woman: in a letter to the rev. mr. Alexander Williamson of Maryland, from mr. James Bate, Surgeon in that Province, 1759," *The American Museum* 4:6 (December 1788): 501–2; James Parsons, M.D., "Account of a white negro," *The American Museum* 5:2 (March 1789): 234.

11. See, for example, Benjamin Rush, "Observations intended to favour a supposition that the black Color (as it is called) of the Negroes is derived from the LEPROSY. Read at a Special Meeting July 14, 1797," *Transactions, American Philosophical Society* 4 (1799): 288–97; Moses Brown, "To all whom it may concern," 1803, Moses Brown Papers, Antislavery File, Rhode Island Historical Society; "Account of Henry Moss, a White Negro: together with Reflections on the Affection called, by Physiologists, Leucaethiopia Humana; Facts and Conjectures... ," *The Philadelphia Medical and Physical Journal* 2: 2 (1806); Smith, *An Essay on the Causes of Variety*, 52.

12. "Another instance of a Negro Turning White," *The Monthly Magazine and American Review* 3:4 (October 1800): 391–92; *The Medical Repository* 4 (1800): 199–200.

13. A. Catlin, "Another Ethiopian Turning to a White Man, *The Medical Repository* 5:1 (1801): 83–84.

14. *The American Magazine of Wonders* 1 (1809): 220.

15. D. W., "Account of a singular change of color in a negro," *The Weekly Magazine* 1 (February 24, 1798), 109; Moses Brown, "To all whom it may concern"; Buffon, *Barr's Buffon*, 324.

16. Bate, "An account of a remarkable alteration of colour," 501. An example of the shorter version, by the same author and with the same title, appeared in *New York Weekly Magazine* 2:61 (August 31, 1796): 71.

17. Moses Brown, "To all whom it may concern," 1803, Moses Brown Papers, Rhode Island Historical Society, n.p.

18. Bate, "An account of a remarkable alteration of colour," 501; Brown, "To all whom it may concern," n.p.; D. W., "Account of a singular change," 110–11.

19. William Stanton claims in *The Leopard's Spots*, 6, that Moss was born a slave in Virginia. However, both James Holt's 1798 certification that Moss had originally been "of as dark a complexion as any African" (appended to D. W., "Account of a singular change," 109) and the 1806 article by the editor of *The Philadelphia Medical and Physical Journal* entitled "Henry Moss, a White Negro," 5, detailed accounts that agree with each other, state that Moss was born free in Virginia.

20. See, for example, "Account of two Albinos," *The Medical Museum* 2 (1806): 284–86; "Account of a Negro Woman Who Became White," *The American Magazine of Wonders* 2 (1809): 312–13; "A Curious Acount of the Albino Negro," *The American Magazine of Wonders* 1 (1809): 218–20. Quotation is from this last, 220.

21. Buffon, *Barr's Buffon*, 324, 306.

22. The most recent monograph on U.S. relations with the Barbary States is Robert S. Allison, *The Crescent Obscured: The United States and the Muslim World 1776–1815* (New York: Oxford University Press, 1995).

23. The Algerines also attacked the merchant shipping of Russians, Spaniards, Neapolitans, and others. By 1786 there were about 2,200 persons in Algiers who had been captured in this way and enslaved. Michael L. S. Kitzen, *Tripoli and the United States at War: A History of American Relations with the Barbary States, 1785–1805* (Jefferson, N.C.: McFarland, 1993), 13.

24. See, for example, the treatment described in a letter to David Pearce Jr., from Samuel Calder, Slave, Algiers, December 4, 1793, *Naval Documents Related to the United States' Wars With the Barbary Powers*, vol. 1, *Naval Operations Including Diplomatic Background From 1785 through 1801* (Washington, D.C.: U.S. Navy, Office of Naval Records and Library, 1939), 57–58.

25. North Africans were not always described in the same terms as those Africans who had been brought to the United States as slaves; they were said to exhibit a range of skin colors, from "exceedingly black" and "negro colour" to "brown and tawny" to "making some approach to the European face." See Smith, *An Essay on the Causes of Variety*, 136–37. Nonetheless, virtually all commentators distinguished North Africans as peoples of color from white Europeans and Americans.

26. Robert Allison reads the ideological import of the Algerine captivity narratives as popular because they presented Americans with an analogy between American slavery and Islamic tyranny and forced them to confront slavery as the potential worm in the apple of American political liberty, 87–106. He sees the imprisonment of Americans in the Barbary States as presenting a test of the character of America and Americans in the face of severe restrictions on their liberty; absent a "racial" dimension, however, his argument does not consider the Algerine captivity as having implications for the nature of citizenship and its qualifications for American whites. See *The Crescent Obscured*, chapter 5, especially 126.

27. James W. Stevens, *An Historical and Geographical Account of Algiers* ... (Philadelphia: Hogan & M'Elroy, 1797), 161–64; Mathew Carey, *A Short Account of Algiers, Containing a Description of the Climate of that Country, of the Manners and Customs of the inhabitants* ... , (Philadelphia: J. Parker, 1794), 16–17.

28. Stevens, *An Historical and Geographical Account of Algiers,* 240, 242; *The Rural Magazine; or, Vermont Repository* (March 1795): 119, 121, 120; John Foss, *The Algerine Slaves, A Poem ... [with] A Journal, of the Captivity and Sufferings of John Foss ... ,* 2nd ed. (Newburyport: Angier March, 1798), 20–40,180–84; Robert White, "A Curious, Historical and Entertaining Narrative of the Captivity and almost unheard-of Sufferings and cruel Treatment of Mr. Robert White, Mariner," in *Bickerstaff's Boston Almanack, or Federal Calendar for 1791* (Boston: Bickerstaff, 1790), n.p.

29. *The Rural Magazine; or, Vermont Repository* (March 1795), 121.

30. See, for example, Stevens, *An Historical and Geographical Account of Algiers,* 208, for an especially clear exposition of this idea. During the late eighteenth and early nineteenth centuries, Algiers was a subordinate province of the Ottoman empire. The Dey, or governor, of Algiers was chosen by resident Turkish janissaries, members of an elite corps of the Sultan's soldiers.

31. White, "A Curious, Historical and Entertaining Narrative," n.p.; Robert Adams, *The Narrative of Robert Adams, An American Sailor ... who ... Was Detailed Three Years in Slavery by the Arabs of the Great Desert ...* (Boston: Wells and Lilly, 1817), xviii; William Ray, *Poems on Various Subjects, Religious, Moral, Sentimental and Humorous. To which is added, a brief sketch of the Author's life and of his captivity and sufferings among the Turks and barbarians of Tripoli* (Auburn: U. F. Doubleday, 1821), 235; Royall Tyler, *The Algerine Captive; or, The Life and Adventures of Dr. Updike Underhill, Six Years a Prisoner Among the Algerines* (Walpole, N.H.: David Carlisle, 1797), vol. 2, 23–24.

32. Robert Allison does not distinguish early from later narratives with respect to the responses of American captives to their captivity; he sees resistance to submission as a nearly universal position (*The Crescent Obscured,* 118, 125–126).

33. Only Stevens discussed the role and behavior of Algerine women, which he cited as evidence of Algerine depravity. He simultaneously condemned Turkish men for believing women to "have no souls" and judged Turkish women to be lascivious, indolent, and tasteless. Stevens, *An Historical and Geographical Account of Algiers,* 230, 220–22. There appears to be only one narrative in English claiming to be a factual, first-person account of a European or American woman enslaved in Algiers: Maria Martin, *History of the Captivity and Sufferings of Mrs. Maria Martin, who was Six Years a Slave in Algiers* (Boston: W. Crary, 1804). There were at least eleven editions of this narrative printed between 1806 and 1818 in the United States, attesting to its American popularity. Its authenticity is dubious, however. The content varies considerably from edition to edition; the 1810 edition gives the author's name as Lucinda Martin and may in fact be a different narrative. In all versions, the main story is a highly romanticized tale in which Englishwoman Martin virtuously chooses imprisonment and starvation over sinful sexual relations with her Turkish owner. See Allison, *The Crescent Obscured,* 79–83 and 239–40, n. 31, on the Martin narrative.

34. The Jewish ethnicity of Fetnah and her father, a merchant who brought her to Algiers in the course of his business, seems constructed at least in part to make their acceptance of Islamic practices less abhorrent to American and English readers than it might have been had they been depicted as Christians. It is Fetnah's father whose corsair actually had captured Rebecca and brought her into the Dey's household. Susanna Rowson, *Slaves in Algiers* (Philadelphia: Wrigley & Berriman, 1794), 9.

35. Tyler, *The Algerine Captive,* 226–27; Rowson, *Slaves in Algiers,* iv.

36. Charles White, *An Account of the Regular Gradation in Man, and in Different Animals and Vegetables; and from the Former to the Latter* (London: W. Johnston, 1799); John Augustine Smith, "A Lecture introductory to the Second Course of Anatomical

Instruction in the College of Physicians and Surgeons for the State of New-York ...," *New York Medical and Philosophical Journal and Review* 1 (1809): 84–96; Samuel George Morton, *Crania Americana; or, A Comparative View of the Skulls of Various Aboriginal Nations of North and South America, to which is Prefixed an Essay on The Varieties of the Human Species* (Philadelphia: J. Dobson, 1839). See Stanton, *The Leopard's Spots*, 15–44, for a discussion of the developing argument against environmentalism.

The Problematics of Absence
Looking for the Male Body in the War of 1812

Todd D. Smith

The representation of the white, male body took center stage in the discourses surrounding the War of 1812. Such a statement might not raise the attention of many, for students of history have come to expect that the male body is always key to the formation of wartime aesthetics and its accompanying commemoration. One need only think of the Revolutionary War, with the portrayal of George Washington and John Trumbull's Capitol celebrations of homosocial male body worship; the Civil War with the dead male bodies shot by Timothy O'Sullivan and spectacular Zouaves captured by Winslow Homer; and World War II with the composite imagery of soldiers raising the flag at Iwo Jima to uncover a general sense of the centrality of the male body to the presentation of war rhetoric.[1] Yet, in the case of the War of 1812, the visual commemoration that came out of the war, for the most part, presented a world that did not depend on the primacy of the imaged male body.

This chapter will explore the dynamics, concerns, and uses of the male body at the time of the war, and how such factors contributed to the production and reception of a group of paintings known as "navalscapes." This term refers to the corpus of prolific imagery produced during and immediately after the war in which two ships, each representing the fighting country, squared off against each other. Overwhelmingly presented from a standard distance and concentrated on the structure of the ships at the expense of the fighting sailors, navalscapes was a genre that specifically excluded the fighting male body as the locus of spectatorial pleasure and idealized masculine presentation. While the stakes were high for the codification of masculine (self) identity, arguably via the male body, in the aftermath of an extremely divisive war and at a time when American culture was undergoing adolescent identity crises

one after another, the exact nature of this regulatory endeavor remained unstable and transitory. In the end, the war provided instead a forum for the
demonstration of gender flux that could not have come at a more inoppor-
tune historical moment for the nascent republican enterprise.

Conceptions of the role of white men within society in the early years of
the nineteenth century relied heavily on an emerging split between the public and private, the quest for self-interest versus the maintenance of communal well-being.[2] The ideal man had emerged from the eighteenth century filled
with the notions of civic duty but increasingly consumed by the pursuit of
individual gain. The debate centered on the competing claims of self-interest,
heralded by some and feared by others, and corporate identification, likewise sought and rejected. What lay at the base of this struggle, as many historians have noted, was a fear of patriarchal hegemony, on the one hand, and
the loss of individual identity on the other. The anxieties experienced during
the early national period, according to Dana Nelson, were to have found their
resolution in a reformulation of manhood as "purified, unified, vigorous,
brotherly (and) national."[3] As Nelson points out, however, such a unified
identity was never realized nor even ever possible.

It is against such a backdrop of masculine identity formation as well as the
lingering question of access to citizenship that the War of 1812 took place.
The art created in conjunction with the war, while accentuating this tension
on one hand, partook in the furthering of the fluctuating and indecisiveness
that characterized the war efforts and outcome. In sum, American society
underwent widespread slippages and inalterable social changes during the
early republic, which coalesced into an immediate and unprecedented cultural evaluation of its past and present, and it was the art of the War of 1812
that highlighted one of the most significant issues—masculinity.

America's decision to declare war on Great Britain was premised on two
basic grievances. The curtailment of U.S. international commerce at the hands
of the British, as a result of their Order in Council of 1807, irritated many
American war hawks. With the war declaration before the public, England
agreed to rescind its Order in Council, thus nullifying, to some degree, the
American claims. The second issue, impressment, remained at center stage
throughout the war years and fueled war rhetoric. Impressment, simply
stated, was the practice of commandeering foreign vessels on the high seas
and searching all passengers for deserters from the searching navy. Such an
action proved not only highly controversial and much feared but also significantly problematic. As many sailors were not in the habit of carrying all
of their papers on their person while at sea, there was much room for mis-
impressment and misidentification. So severe was the practice that President
James Madison in his War Message of June 1, 1812, made special mention
of the activity at the outset.

In a broader sense, though, the issue of impressment addressed squarely
the concern with the rights of the state to the male body in the early years of

the republic. Couched in political terms, impressment foregrounded the society's claims on the male body both in and out of wartime and called into question the lengths to which the state could go in reclaiming and thus controlling the access to the male body and its uses. Debates raged in the United States about the practice and what it meant to the sovereignty of the new nation. The war represented, at least for some, a means of reasserting independence further from Great Britain through the possession of the male body. Any action against an individual American male body served as a synecdochical affront to the American experiment and forced a constant reassertion of American independence via the male body. Thus, the matter of the continuation of the war, in light of English appeasement early on concerning other considered belligerent actions, rested heavily on the concept of sailors' rights. While coined to express the sovereignty of the sailors over their own bodies, the phrase "sailors' rights" actually referred as much, and if not more, to the claims staked by the state to the regulation and possession of these bodies and their use in the military.

Impressment was but one aspect of a much broader debate about the male body and masculinity during and immediately after the war years. In the 1814 published account of the life of Lieutenant William Burrows (1785–1813), the relationship between the role of the male body, the war, and art was presented with remarkable clarity. The son of Lt. Colonel W. W. Burrows, first commandant of the U.S. Marine Corps, William entered the U.S. Navy in 1799, at the age of fourteen. Burrows would prove himself during the Tripolitan war, the enforcement of the U.S. embargo of 1808, and finally in his leadership on his battleship the *Enterprise* against H.M.S. *Boxer* on September 5, 1813.[4]

Although the recounting of the lieutenant's bravery was but one of many that appeared during the war years as a means of glorifying and remembering naval heroes, this particular article proved especially germane to the current discussion of the male body during the war, its necessary place in any commemoration of it, and the nature of representation in general. First of all, it was not coincidental that Burrows came from a line of accomplished military men. According to some historians, the War of 1812 provided a chance for the real sons of Revolutionary War heroes to demonstrate their own abilities in the arena of national pride and honor.[5] And while the war in all of its inconclusiveness failed to accommodate this need, the discourses around the war took every opportunity to call attention, both positively and negatively, to the plight of these real sons. Likewise, the emergence of a domineering role for women with the raising of children, especially sons, placed an even higher price on the patrilineal inheritance of military prowess. Biography after biography highlighted the exact relationship that each of the younger fighters had to their paternal compatriots and as heirs to the American Revolution. The Burrows account did not stray from this model, to be sure. What it did do, however, was concentrate

the readers' attention on the younger Burrows's adolescent pastimes as har-
bingers for future military success.

The story of young Burrows began with the extended account of his parents' view of him as lethargic. The writer stated, "In a boy so amiable, and
withal so retiring and reserved, little did his parents believe that the flame of
ambition was burning strong and intense. He would often be found musing
and solitary, as if in the acts of conversing with his own thoughts." An incident occurred that revealed to the parents and to the larger world that
Burrows did have a consuming, and even encouraging, passion: the sea. As
Burrows had undertaken drawing as a means to express himself, the parents
were shocked to find that the only subject matter that Burrows drew was
"the delineation of a ship of war." And while such a "solitary" and private
enterprise as art itself was suspect in early-nineteenth-century American culture, mainly due to its association with the feminine, in this particular case
art stood beside naval exploits as related, masculine actions.

The conclusion of the narrative, discussing the nature of Burrows's chival-
ric death on board the *Enterprise,* revisited the concern with art and war.
The writer succinctly wrote, "It is to be lamented that no likeness of this distinguished officer now exists." Regularly, each of these published stories
would have been fronted by a likeness of the featured hero. In this case, however, the desire to connect an image of a man with his accomplishments was
thwarted. This absence led the writer to continue with a statement that, I will
maintain, can speak for a more metaphorical problem at the heart of early
republic male body representation. Speaking of the missing and nonexistent
portrait, the writer contended that "the mind, in cases like the present, labors
to supply the defect, and to form for itself a sort of sensible image; for we
never read of high and illustrious actions without associating them with a
body."[6] Admittedly, in this context, the missing body belonged to the realm
of portraiture; yet, the problem of a missing male body during the crucial
moments of wartime commemoration had disastrous effects on the nature of
representation and masculinity, and likewise this problem only underscored
the slippery situation of male subjectivity in this particular, highly charged
historical moment.

The fate of the represented male body in genres other than military illustrations can lend perspective to the consequences of this absence of the male
body in the War of 1812 commemoration. In his first attempt at history painting, Samuel F. B. Morse in 1812 embraced the story of Hercules, focusing
on the portion of the narrative in which the superhero attempts to rid himself of a poisoned garment. Morse's *The Dying Hercules* was monumental,
eight by six and one-half feet. For art historians William Kloss and Paul Staiti,
the connection between Morse, Hercules, and the War of 1812 was rather
straightforward.[7] Morse received notice from his parents a mere ten days
after America declared war on Britain, while he was in London studying.
They advised their son to shy away from politics: "[B]e the artist wholly and

Samuel Finley Breese Morse, *Dying Hercules*, Yale University Art Gallery. Gift of the artist.

let politics alone." Morse responded that the war was just and expressed the hope that his Federalist father would "be neutral rather than oppose the war measure." It was indeed on the heels of these correspondences that Morse undertook work on *The Dying Hercules.*

Historians have made the strong case that an interpretation of Morse's painting relies on the association of Hercules with America, an association made specifically by Morse in a letter home and more indirectly through a reading of Morse's choice of narrative moments. Writing on July 10 to his parents, the artist remarked, "I have just heard of the unfortunate capture of the Chesapeake. Is our infant Hercules to be strangled at his birth?" Second, and speaking of the choice of subject matter, Kloss contends that "Morse must have seen America as the valiant hero who is treacherously deceived by a near relation. Hercules personifies courage and devotion to duty and has historically symbolized strong and virtuous government."[8] I do not wish to argue against these two connections and the conclusions to which they lead. What I would like to add instead is another area for consideration: the meaning and relevance of Morse's choice as it relates to the painting's embrace of the heroic male nude and its place within American culture.

Morse's father, Jedidiah, rented an exhibiting room in Boston in 1815 to show off his son's painting, *The Dying Hercules,* and possibly to welcome his son home from England. And although Morse received positive critical acclaim in London and in America for the work, the painting remained in Morse's possession until his death. The artist's inability to find a buyer for the painting might be explained as the result of the (perceived) unrefined tastes of the American art buying market more than any fault of the artist. In this case, however, a reconsideration of the subject matter might prove more illuminating, especially with regard to the work's treatment of the nude male figure. In the aftermath of a very unresolved conclusion to the war, for the Treaty of Ghent provided very little to celebrate as impressment was still in operation, the association between Hercules and America might have been too realistic a depiction for a culture coming to terms with its extremely divisive war. Hercules is presented supine, unable to wrestle the cloak of trickery from his body. He is helpless to come to terms with consequences of such deceitfulness. For all of his neoclassical and overdeveloped specular muscularity, he is powerless and sapped of his strength. One could ask in a simple fashion, "Is this the sort of imagery one wants to have associated with a problematic war effort?" In this case, the ideal symbol of strength and might—the intensely cathected male body—proves no match for the cunning and treachery of Deianeira's gift.[9] If such a representation in its embrace of neoclassical aesthetic and national pride fails to inspire, then what options were available to other artists who wished to make more concrete imagery of the war and, more importantly, how did the resulting imagery employ or reject the centrality of the male body as pictorial signpost for nationalism?

Thomas Birch, *Engagement between the Constitution and the Guerriere*, The Historical Society of Pennsylvania (accession no. 1910.12).

Within the realm of visual documentation and commemoration of the War of 1812, scenes of naval battles took priority over land encounters. Images of hand-to-hand combat or grandiloquent baroque battlefield death scenes are noticeably absent from the corpus of war imagery. Navalscapes, as indicated in Thomas Birch's *Engagement between the Constitution and the Guerriere* (1813), enjoyed such popularity, on the other hand, that the imagery made its way from paintings to prints and book illustrations and even onto Staffordshire and other English ceramics produced for an American market. Birch, in fact, is but one of numerous painters, printmakers, and artisans who specialized in such scenes of the war.[10] There is only slight variation in the design and execution of these scenes: two ships are engaged in battle. Such images required very little of the viewer, with names of the ships provided either in the title or in the caption. Details about the individual battles were well known and widely published. For most, the images provided a mere documentation that the event actually took place, this despite the fact that none of these images was based on the artist's actual presence at the sight but on journals of the ship's captain, on published reports (often the same report these images illustrated), or on conventional naval battle scene compositions. The navalscape was a genre that not only required little innovation but also actually shied away from experimentation. Then why are these works so significant in the early years of the American republic?

Some of the most profound epistemological shifts in American culture occurred during the first three decades of the nineteenth century, shifts that would radically change the nature of the American experiment. The republican subordination of individual needs to the public good of the Jeffersonian era slowly giving way and being transformed into a culture dominated by a liberal individualism; the erosion of doctrinaire Enlightenment rationalism by forces of emotion and religious evangelicalism; the emergence of a market economy that privileged achievement and speculation—all indicate a society in flux and, more important, bespeak one in which anxieties over change emerged as culturally pervasive topoi.[11]

As other historians have chronicled over the past few years, masculinity was also undergoing an anxious moment during this period. Mark Kann has recently summarized these findings in his description of the options for males, proposing four types of adult male identification: the Bachelor, the Family Man, the Better Sort, and the Heroic Man. The Bachelor was the least desirable of the group, as he represented the stymied growth from adolescence to adulthood; the second, the Family Man, "disciplined passion to fit into the role of responsible husband, father, neighbor." The Better Sort of man rose above the level of the Family Man to be able to lead others and to make laws for them. And finally, the ideal of ideals was the Heroic Man who "stood above the law and public opinion to address the exigencies of fortune but secured hegemony to ensure the consent and quiescence of most men."[12] In total, what these four types attempted to accomplish for the founders' generation was "to fend off democratic disorders by stabilizing gender relations and by promoting hegemonic norms to stigmatize disorderly men and reward stable men."[13] While Kann provides a spectrum of possibilities for the adult male, in the end the choices only further the claim that anxiety and indecisiveness reigned during the period.

Tied to the concept of anxiety in America was the fear of deceit, deception, trickery, and inauthenticity. The cultural records are full of narratives created to expose and contain incidents of such humbuggery. Debates over the most truthful representations of George Washington factored into congressional sessions; James Fenimore Cooper's 1821 novel *The Spy* essentially provided a recounting of the Major Andre spy scandal from the Revolutionary War; the national sensation of the Boorn murder case in Vermont featured con men, ghosts, and counterfeiting; and the secretive Hartford Convention of the Federalists in 1814, which called for secession in light of Democratic-Republican continuation of the war, came to be regarded as an act of high treason.[14]

In this cultural context, a connection existed between war and masculinity that centered on the key concept of authenticity.[15] As a proving ground for the sons of Revolutionary War heroes, the War of 1812 was to have provided a site from which to announce their valor, manliness, and character in the face of their real and heroic fathers' accomplishments. Yet, the claims to such a place were never realized. While Revolutionary War heroes asserted their manly independence by standing up to their British *ersatz* fathers and moved quickly as a result of their victories from boyhood to manhood, War of 1812 leaders experienced an altogether different adolescent moment. Without a clear victory and set against a divided constituency, the transition from boyhood to manhood was stunted and unsupported. The confraternity of Revolutionary heroes became a confraternity of founding fathers, whereas their analogous fraternity of fighters in the subsequent war emerged after the war as before—a band of adolescent males caught between boyhood and manhood. The brotherhood of men, which undergirds Dana Nelson's conception of white manhood in the early national period, was an attempt to provide unity to masculine identity. Nelson's ideas on fraternity can be extended into this discussion as a concept of corporate identity. At the exact moment that the debates of the self-made/individual man versus the civic/corporate man hit their most vocal note with the War of 1812 and its aftermath, the need for an association of male adulthood found its necessary corollary in the concept of authenticity (whereby adolescence was regarded as inauthenticity).

The published narrative accounts of females cross-dressing as men and entering the armed services during the War of 1812 provided but one example of the problematics of gender stabilization that accompanied the war. One of these stories, "An affective narrative of Louisa Baker," highlighted the slippage between being and appearance, foregrounding the always performative and conditional nature of gender identity.[16] As psychologists and psychohistorians have argued, war presents males with a traumatic "encounter with lack," and often a result of the war's representation is a conservative bolstering of traditional masculine qualities; yet in the case of the War of 1812, this lack, defined as a phallic insufficiency in the face of psychic and physical danger, was augmented and amplified by the myriad other masculine problematics circulating and even defining American society.[17] Tied to the operations of lack, the discourse of fraud and deception, seemingly at the core of visual representation, was reinforced in the very absence of the male body, which the most popular forms of war commemoration, the navalscapes, endorsed.

What were the expectations of and the options for an artist interested in representing the war? In a review of the third annual exhibition at the

Pennsylvania Academy of the Fine Arts published in *Port Folio* magazine in August 1813, one writer voiced the need for dramatic representation of the war. His comments on Birch's *Engagement Between the Constitution and Guerriere* struck at the heart of the matter. With an acknowledgment of the artist's execution displaying "great skill" and allowing that the "ships are painted with much truth," the reviewer contended that "we are inclined to believe that the artist has been cramped, by adhering too closely to particular descriptions. A ship is one of the most interesting and picturesque objects that can possibly be imagined; but there is a wide difference between a *picture* and a *map* of a ship." Such comments led the reviewer into a more wide-ranging indictment of the navalscape genre: "The general fault of the pictures intended to represent our naval victories is that of being too *formal* and *stiff*, and the vessels are not thrown sufficiently into perspective to appear either natural or pleasing."[18]

Desired by this reviewer and others was the very combination of baroque and romantic ideals of contrived compositions that at once glorified the events, placed them within a more complex system of meaning and interpretation, and finally forced the viewer to move beyond a basic understanding of art as illustration. For Birch and others, any tinge of the romantic, the imaginative, stood in direct opposition to their belief in the necessity for accuracy and detailing to combat accusations of untruthfulness. The shipwreck, the other formidable naval pictorial genre of the period, provided the location for the romantic consideration of the man versus nature myth, but as commemorations of a war, navalscapes needed to be easily understood; thus, there was no room for the inclusion of other battles such as those of man versus nature, as they would have only clouded the navalscape's acceptance as straightforward and real. It was not possible to jeopardize the assertions of authenticity at a time when such anxiety took center stage in American culture.

Still in search of an identifiable style as well as an approach to the appreciation of the arts, America during the early nineteenth century remained beholden to neoclassical ideals of civic virtue while embarking on a formulation of a new individualism associated with romanticism. Unfortunately for the representation of the War of 1812, the debate was still ongoing, actually dead center in its midst. So the question becomes, in a larger sense, how can a society commemorate a war during what can be called a changing of styles. Neoclassicism left most critics in America by the 1810s and 1820s with little to celebrate and support, while romanticism, for some, relied too heavily on abstracted notions of individualism and the imagination. To be sure, there were aspects of each of these approaches that appealed to painters of the war. In the case of romanticism, war would have provided an ideal source of subject matter, especially when it came to the glorification of the individual, the hero; yet in contemporary understanding of romanticism within the visual and cultural realms, such idealization was premised on the inactivity, the passiveness, and even the "to-be-looked-at-ness" of the subject. This stood in direct contrast to the need of the war machine for action-oriented works.

The War of 1812 offered two kinds of heroes—naval commanders and army generals. Account after account of the life and career of the important naval heroes appeared in the popular media. These biographies always related the naval heroes to earlier Revolutionary War heroes and made exhaustive comments on how these seamen negotiated their position of commander with the interests of the common good. In other words, in these biographies, we witness the struggle between individualism and civic duty. Likewise, these published biographies were either accompanied by appropriate navalscapes—a move that underscored the necessity of the navalscape for corroborating narrative and highlighted the struggle of individualism and common good within the image—or by portraits of the heroes. Central to many of these accounts was a gendered description of the actions of the heroes. In a July 1813 recounting of the life of William S. Bush, an author remembered the marine lieutenant as possessing "amiable and endearing manners," and displaying "correct and manly deportment."[19] Even in this brief mention, idealized masculinity finds its corporeal realization in the presentation of the body's attributes and actions. Truth and masculinity are united within a military system and linked significantly via the body.

Andrew Jackson emerged as the most celebrated of army generals; yet even in the midst of his march through the country after the war and subsequent entry into the White House in 1829, there were persistent questions—both real and philosophical—about his actions in New Orleans, with special attention devoted to his declaration and enforcement of martial law and to his assassination of some in his charge. For many in established institutional positions of power, Jackson's frontier image coupled with his populist support proved too threatening. While history has shown that the country would follow Jackson's lead and embrace the newly emergent common man myth, it was only well after Jackson himself had established his place in the White House and was criticized for his elite manners that the myth of the common man of will became pervasive.

During the heyday of the navalscapes, however, the communal good still stood beside the rights of the individual in a tenuous balance for philosophical supremacy. In many ways, these navalscapes truthfully represented this struggle, maybe even too well for their own good. The ideal art called for in the *Port Folio* review cited above would have combined dramatic conventions of battlefield combat, a victory, or at least an heroic death in pursuit of this victory with the believability of a portrait commission of the commanding general or whoever would have brought glory to the country. Underlying these sorts of scenes was an appreciation of the actions and sacrifices of the individual to the common good and the sheer force of will that brought him to that point. In the realized navalscapes, such individuality, which was at once in support of the common good but also used as an emblem for others to follow, is not present; instead, these images relied too heavily on the written texts and prior knowledge of both the events and the skillful leaders to provide the necessary complement.

Second, and as significant, navalscapes were characterized by their glorification of the technology of the ships at the expense of the human actions. Within narrative accounts of each of the numerous battles that took place on the Great Lakes and in the open seas of the Atlantic Ocean were detailed records of the size and armature of each of the frigates, brigs, and men-of-war engaged in combat. Often, in the cases of the few losses of American ships, special emphasis was directed at how the British ships might have been classified as one type of boat while in actuality they carried more weapons or men than their fraudulent designation. This tactic joined others in explaining American might and American failures on the water in terms of the technological, and not always human, prowess.

The absence of the male body and its replacement with a technological substitute—the ship—proved insufficient as a symbol of security and reassurance for the new nation. This is not to suggest, however, that the ships did not connote a masculine presence; in fact, their structure, mass, and even their designations (such as men-of-war) signified strength and valor. The war nonetheless needed a body from which to derive its national stability, an endeavor never entirely possible, but in the case of the War of 1812 never even attempted. The male body as representational phallus never materialized in the early republic, for at the very moment when its presence was most needed the shifting tides of masculine self-identity coincided with an aesthetic shifting away from the heroic male body to the inner recesses of the human psyche in the case of romanticism and to the focus on the mundane and quotidian in Jacksonian-era genre paintings.

The review of Birch's work in the *Port Folio* opened another direction for the consideration of navalscapes as indicators of a national identity. The reviewer commented that "our naval exploits are of a character so extraordinary that they have attracted the notice of all nations," and he continued, "the genius of the arts will call upon her *Trumbull* to do them justice."[20] Trumbull, of course, referred to John Trumbull, whose reputation as America's most sought-after history painter of the 1810s was well in place at the time of the review's publication. But more enlightening might have been the knowledge that Trumbull himself had served in the Revolutionary War and had made a career as the "patriot-painter" of his generation. The reference to Trumbull was telling on a number of additional counts. This was indeed an insult to Birch. The reviewer, expressing that Birch had not nor could not measure up to the accomplishments of Trumbull, proved prophetic; Trumbull was commissioned by Congress in 1817 to provide four mural panels for the new Rotunda of the rebuilt Capitol building in Washington.[21]

The destruction of Washington by the British during the War of 1812 precipitated among other things this decorative program. Writing to former president Thomas Jefferson in December 1816, Trumbull asserted his "true" place as the Revolutionary War painter by appealing to the Virginia statesman's influence in Washington through the following claim: "[F]uture artists may arise with far Superior Talents, but time has already withdrawn almost all their Models; and I who was one of the youngest Actors in the early scenes of the war, passed the Age of Sixty:—no time remains therefore for hesitation." Trumbull would go on to receive the commission for the four paintings, which were executed between 1817 and 1824. To drum up support for his efforts, the final canvases were exhibited in the Northeast; their reception proved only respectable. Additionally, Trumbull's attempts to garner subscriptions from congressmen for a series of prints after these paintings proved embarrassing, as no representative signed up.

Critic John Neal wrote of the four Trumbull pictures in the Rotunda: "I have now done with Trumbull, lamenting that a man of such strength, when young, should be, in his dotage, or, if not in his dotage, that he should be content with such labour, that the Declaration is only a respectable picture and that the 4 are among the greatest and most unaccountable failures of the age." Neal continued, "[T]he President may not be superannuated, but the pictures are"; he added that they are "valuable only as a collection of tolerably well-arranged portraits."[22] From the remainder of Neal's comments, it is obvious that what the critic sought in the type of works that Trumbull executed for the Rotunda were pictures full of action and vigor. These four images, however, failed to enliven the viewer or the critic. They were in many ways memorials to a career long past its definitive moment. Nonetheless, this commission by the United States government was key, for it not only signified a country's interest in defining its own past for national and future contemplation, a task whose goal was to bring the country back together in the wake of an extremely divisive war, but the action was significant in that it bypassed the country's most immediate nationally defining moment (the War of 1812), for an earlier and unmistakably more supportable war effort, the Revolutionary War. The inception of national identity took precedence over its mere maintenance. But, of course, with a war that resulted in little to no gains for the Americans, there was little impetus to glorify its actions.

We can return yet again to the review in *Port Folio* for more insight into the problem and the early rejection of navalscapes as national visual symbols. The reviewer wrote that "we hope to see the time when the walls of the Capitol, appropriated for our national legislature, will be decorated with representations of the victories of Hull, Decatur, Jones, Bainbridge, Pike &c., executed in a manner worthy of their actions, and of our country." He continued, "[W]e are of the opinion that the best way would be to treat the subjects in the manner that West has treated the battle of La Hogue, and to introduce portraits of the principal officers after the manner of the Death of General Wolfe, Sortie from Gibraltar, Death of Nelson."[23] Still under the guise of reviewing Birch's painting, the reviewer had cast even further dispersions on the nature of navalscapes.

With the completion of Trumbull's campaign in 1824, Congress again in 1828 went about discussing the commission of four more panel paintings for the Rotunda. And it was this debate that was the most fundamental to the appreciation of navalscapes. Bringing forward a resolution to consider the execution of a scene from the Battle of New Orleans, Representative Hamilton of South Carolina unleashed a two-day discussion on what should be done in the Rotunda. The debates included consideration of which artists should be involved; what scenes were appropriate and from what wars; whether public money should be spent on the support of the arts; and finally, whether painting was the best means to memorialize the heroes of the War of 1812. Underlying most comments was the seeming displeasure with what Trumbull had provided. Representative Randolph of Virginia offered that "he hardly ever passed through the avenue (the Rotunda) to this Hall ... without feeling ashamed of the state of the arts in this country: in his opinion the picture of the Declaration of Independence (should) be called the Shin piece for surely never was there before such a collection of legs submitted to the eyes of man."[24] So even the reification of the concept of democracy and freedom intended for Trumbull's picture was reduced, for Randolph at least, into an image about a part of a body; and by extension, we might consider Randolph's view of painting as indicating a wider search for the represented male body in early America.

The tenor of the debates indicated an unease with the options available to the legislature. The immediacy of the war and the problems with Trumbull's work might have added to the squeamish nature of the Congress. Possibly, as well, the lack of existing grand paintings from the War of 1812 on which to base their aesthetic judgments and place their hopes coupled with the folklike treatments of land battles and the problematic navalscapes reviewed here offered little comfort for the body of representatives. In the end, the Congress did decide on the program to complete the Rotunda, but it was a series of paintings based on the founding myths of the country, with Columbus, Pocahontas and the like, which caught their attention.[25] It was appropriate, indeed, that these paintings, because of the nature of the subject matter, could use grand style history painting aesthetics even when such a choice was out-of-date; the events (and not their execution) were far enough in the past that the style seemed appropriate. Unfortunately, once again, for the War of 1812, its occurrence was a little too late, or at least for the visual realm a little too immediate to warrant an eighteenth-century style. Similarly, the use of the bodies in these later mural commissions as indicators of nationalism only emphasized the essential lack found in the navalscapes.

The reality that the navalscapes depicted and even helped to create did not afford a place for the conventional symbol of military power: the male body. Without this symbol and the stability it provided, the paintings too accurately reflected the great uncertainty Americans felt about this war, an uncertainty they attempted to forget in its aftermath. The sectionalism exacerbated by the decision to go to war that threatened the unity of the country would only deepen as the century progressed. The emergence of Andrew Jackson during the 1820s as a political candidate served to reopen war wounds and call attention to the undiplomatic nature of his military service. The discussion in Congress in 1828 regarding the representation of the Battle of New Orleans might have been merely a cheap attempt by some Democratic-Republican legislators to curry the favor of Jackson as he was on the verge of being elected president. The navalscape imagery was at once popular and at the same time troubling. The decision by the U.S. Congress not to include a scene from the war laid not on the popularity or unpopularity of the war but on the inability of artists to incorporate the male body into a national discourse on masculine identity. Lieutenant Burrows, a character constructed in his biography by his love of the sea and his artistic inclination, might then be proffered as spokesperson of this failure, an irresolvable situation, but a failure nonetheless. Further, the association of trickery and deceitfulness with the massive Herculean body found a parallel in the relationship between trickery and masculinity in the war and bound these representational strategies one to another.

As there were no unproblematic heroes and thus no unproblematic real and symbolic male bodies on which to project the anxieties about what the war had wrought, commemorations of the war were at a loss; what became the standard image—navalscapes—proved inadequate in their attempt to fashion the male technological substitute into a wholly acceptable representation of masculine might. The concerns expressed by the Birch review about too perfect an image of the ships only underscored the conflicting need for imagery that was at once authentic but also which could carry the symbolic necessity of war commemoration. The war had been too indecisive to warrant a grand and national visual commemoration, yet the very proliferation of navalscape imagery in paintings, prints, and on transfer-printed ceramics demonstrated the efforts to make sense of the events. Possibly as well, by 1828, the visual commemoration of the war had been successfully relegated to the realm of the unheroic (as in the case of the prints), the souvenir (as in the case of the ceramics), and any calls for the epic treatment of the events would have been regarded as fraudulent. Further, without the symbolic, intensely cathected male body as dynamic representation of the war, such attempts at the grand image proved suspect at best and wholly inadequate at worst.

Navalscapes provide but one example of a culturally pervasive indictment of masculine identity formation during the early national period. As the most significant visual commemoration of the war efforts, these images in their varied media fail in their mission to bolster an abstracted ideal of masculinity. They fail because in a seemingly contradictory statement they are too successful; that is, they are successful in accurately reflecting and thus contributing to the uncertainty of masculine identity. As argued throughout, navalscapes appear at a moment of transition, a transition not merely in aesthetic styles and subject matter, but also a transition in the accepted presentation of the male body from an heroic body to a quotidian one. This transition finds a parallel in the movement from boyhood to male adulthood, an activity at the core of most current understandings of gender constructs for men in the period. Finally, the struggle between individual and corporate identity—such a key debate in the early national and antebellum periods—finds one of its most forceful arenas at this precise moment, and it is the overarching anxiety about this fluctuation and uncertainty that at once supports navalscapes as authentic and damns them as fraudulent.

Notes

1. There are intriguing parallels between the War of 1812 and the Vietnam War in that both were extremely divisive and failed to produce clear-cut supportable victories. Maya Lin's Vietnam Veterans Memorial, the nationally defining commemoration of the war, is noticeably devoid of the sculptured male body. It needed, according to some critics, a complement that was found in Frederick Hartt's later figural addition.

2. See, for example, E. Anthony Rotundo, *American Manhood: Transformations in Masculinity from the Revolution to the Modern Era* (New York: Basic Books, 1993), 16–25.

3. Dana D. Nelson, *National Manhood: Capitalist Citizenship and the Imagined Fraternity of White Men* (Durham, N.C.: Duke University Press, 1998), x.

4. "Life of Lt. Burrows," *Port Folio* 3:2 (February 1814): 114–26, 123.

5. See for example, Steven Watts, *The Republic Reborn: War and the Making of Liberal America, 1790–1820* (Baltimore: Johns Hopkins University Press, 1987).

6. "Lt. Burrows," 115, 126.

7. William Kloss, *Samuel F. B. Morse* (New York: Harry N. Abrams, in association with the National Museum of American Art, Smithsonian Institution, 1988), and Paul Staiti, *Samuel F. B. Morse* (New York: Cambridge University Press, 1989).

8. Kloss, *Morse*, 25, 28.

9. Hercules's death is occasioned by the actions of Deianeira. Hearing that Hercules was courting another woman, Iole, Deianeira sent Hercules a tunic that had been smeared with what Deianeira understood to be a love potion. In reality, the potion was poisonous and proved fatal for Hercules.

10. Other artists included Michele Felice Corne and John Bubier. See Richard Anthony Lewis, "Interesting Particulars and Melancholy Occurrences: Thomas Birch's Representations of the Shipping Trade, 1799–1850" (Ph.D. dissertation, Northwestern University, 1994).

11. See, for example, Watts, *Republic Reborn*; Jean Matthews, *Toward a New Society: American Thought and Culture, 1800–1830* (Boston: Twayne Publishers, 1990); Charles Sellers, *The Market Revolution: Jacksonian America, 1815–1846* (New York: Oxford Uni-

versity Press, 1991); James Roger Sharp, *American Politics in the Early Republic: The New Nation in Crisis* (New Haven, Conn.: Yale University Press, 1993); Donald Hickey, *The War of 1812: A Forgotten Conflict* (Urbana: University of Illinois Press, 1990); Daniel Feller, *The Jacksonian Promise: America, 1815–1840* (Baltimore: Johns Hopkins University Press, 1995).

12. Mark Kann, *A Republic of Men: The American Founders, Gendered Language and Patriarchal Politics* (New York: New York University Press, 1998), 155.

13. Ibid., 26.

14. Egon Verheyen, "'The Most Exact Representation of the Original': Remarks on Portraits of George Washington by Gilbert Stuart and Rembrandt Peale," *Studies in the History of Art* 20 (1989): 127–43; James Fenimore Cooper, *The Spy,* ed. James Pickering (Schenectady, N.Y.: New College and University Press, 1971); Bruce Rosenberg, *The Neutral Ground: The Andre Affair and the Background of Cooper's* The Spy (Westport, Conn.: Greenwood Press, 1994); Gerald McFarland, *The Counterfeit Man: The True Story of the Boorn-Colvin Murder Case* (Amherst: University of Massachusetts Press, 1990); John Kasson, *Rudeness and Civility: Manners in Nineteenth-Century Urban America* (New York: Hill and Wang, 1990); and Karen Halttunen, *Confidence Men and Painted Women: A Study of Middle-Class Culture in America, 1830–1870* (New Haven, Conn.: Yale University Press, 1982).

15. Norman Bryson maintains that "the male is enjoined to assume the phallic role, but the power of the phallus can never be his. The crucial result is the experience of inauthenticity within the production of the masculine, that the male can never fully achieve phallic power, however great the exertion toward that goal." Norman Bryson, "Gericault and Masculinity," in Norman Bryson and Penelope Wise, eds., *Vision and Culture: Images and Interpretations* (Hanover, N.H.: University Press of New England for Wesleyan University Press, 1994).

16. *An Affective Account of Louisa Baker* (Boston, privately printed, 1816). See also, Almira Paul, *The Surprising Adventures of Almira Paul* (Boston: Printed for M. Brewer, 1816). Daniel Cohen has read these cross-dressing accounts as representing an anxiety over the growing urban vice in Boston in the wake of the war. Daniel Cohen, "'The Female Marine' in an Era of Good Feelings: Cross-Dressing and the 'Genius' of Nathaniel Coverly, Jr.," *Proceedings of the American Antiquarian Society* 103:2 (1993):359–92. For a contemporary theoretical treatment of gender as performative, see Judith Butler, *Gender Trouble: Feminism and the Subversion of Identity* (New York: Routledge, 1990).

17. Kaja Silverman writing about this very concept argues that "[I]t is not surprising, then, that when the male subject is brought into a traumatic encounter with lack, as in the situation of war, he often experiences it as the impairment of his anatomical masculinity. What is really at issue, though, is a psychic disintegration—the disintegration, that is, of a bound and armored ego, predicated on the illusion of coherence and control." Kaja Silverman, *Male Subjectivity at the Margins* (New York: Routledge, 1992), 62.

18. "Review of the 3rd Annual Exhibition of the Columbian Society of Artists and the Pennsylvania Academy of Fine Arts," *Port Folio* 2:2, 3rd series (August 1813): 130.

19. "A Masonic Oration on the Death of Brother William S. Bush," *Port Folio* 1:6, appendix (June 1813): 4.

20. "Review," 130.

21. The four paintings are *The Surrender of Burgoyne at Saratoga, 16 October 1777* (1822); *The Surrender of Cornwallis at Yorktown, 19 October 1781* (1787–1820); *The Declaration of Independence, 4 July 1776* (1787–1819); and *The Resignation of General Washington, 23 December 1783* (1822–1824).

22. *The Autobiography of Colonel John Trumbull, Patriot-Artist, 1756–1843*, ed. Theodore Sizer (New Haven, Conn.: Yale University Press, 1953), 223–25.

23. "Review," 131.

24. *Register of Congressional Debates* (Washington, D.C.: Gales and Seaton, 1825–1837), 20th Congress, 1st Session; January 8 and 9, 1828, 929.

25. See Vivien Green Fryd, *Art and Empire: The Politics of Ethnicity in the U.S. Capitol, 1815–1860* (New Haven, Conn.: Yale University Press, 1992), 42–61.

Selected Bibliography

BOOKS

Adler, Kathleen, and Marcia Pointon, eds. 1993. *The Body Imaged: The Human Form And Visual Culture Since the Renaissance*. Cambridge, U.K.: Cambridge University Press.

Armstrong, Tim, 1998. *Modernism, Technology, and the Body: A Cultural Study*. New York: Cambridge University Press.

———, ed. 1996. *American Bodies: Cultural Histories of the Physique*. New York: New York University Press.

Baker, Lynne Rudder. 2000. *Persons and Bodies: A Constitution View*. New York: Cambridge University Press.

Bakhtin, M. M. 1968. *Rabelais and His World*. Translated by H. Iswolsky. Cambridge, Mass.: MIT Press.

Balsamo, Anne Marie. 1996. *Technologies of the Gendered Body: Reading Cyborg Women*. Durham, N.C.: Duke University Press.

Barkan, Leonard. 1975. *Nature's Work of Art: The Human Body as Image of the World*. New Haven, Conn.: Yale University Press.

Bashford, Alison. 1998. *Purity and Pollution: Gender, Embodiment and Victorian Medicine*. New York: St. Martin's Press.

Beckwith, Sarah. 1993. *Christ's Body: Identity, Culture and Society in Late Medieval Writings*. New York: Routledge.

Beizer, Janet L. 1994. *Ventriloquized Bodies: Narratives of Hysteria in Nineteenth-Century France*. Ithaca, N.Y.: Cornell University Press.

Bennett, Paula, et al., eds. 1995. *Solitary Pleasures: The Historical, Literary, and Artistic Discourses of Autoeroticism*. New York: Routledge.

Berg, Marc, and Annemarie Mol, eds. 1998. *Differences in Medicine: Unraveling Practices, Techniques, and Bodies*. Durham, N.C.: Duke University Press.

Berman, Morris. 1989. *Coming to Our Senses: Body and Spirit in the Hidden History of the West*. New York: Simon & Schuster.

Bhattacharya, Nandini. 1998. *Reading the Splendid Body: Gender and Consumerism in Eighteenth-Century British Writing on India*. Newark: University of Delaware Press.

Biller, Peter, and A. J. Minnis. 1997. *Medieval Theology and the Natural Body*. Rochester, N.Y.: York Medieval Press.

Bishop, Jonathan. 1992. *Some Bodies: The Eucharist and Its Implications*. Macon, Ga.: Mercer University Press.

Boehrer, Bruce Thomas. 1997. *The Fury of Men's Gullets: Ben Jonson and the Digestive Canal*. Philadelphia: University of Pennsylvania Press.

Bordo, Susan. 1993. *Unbearable Weight: Feminism, Western Culture, and the Body.* Berkeley: University of California Press.

Boscagli, Maurizia. 1996. *Eye on the Flesh: Fashions of Masculinity in the Early Twentieth Century.* Boulder, Colo.: Westview Press.

Bottomley, Frank. 1979. *Attitudes to the Body in Western Christendom.* London: Lepus Books.

Boucé, Paul-Gabriel, ed. 1982. *Sexuality in Eighteenth-Century Britain.* Totowa, N.J.: Barnes & Noble.

Braidotti, Rosi. 1994. *Nomadic Subjects: Embodiment and Sexual Difference in Contemporary Feminist Theory.* New York: Columbia University Press.

Brennan, Teresa. 1992. *The Interpretation of Flesh: Freud and Femininity.* New York: Routledge.

Bridgeman, Jo, and Susan Millins, eds. 1995. *Law and Body Politics: Regulating the Female Body.* Brookfield, Vt.: Dartmouth Publishing Company.

Bronfen, Elizabeth. 1992. *Over Her Dead Body: Death, Femininity, and the Aesthetic.* New York: Routledge.

Brooks, Peter. 1993. *Body Works and Objects of Desire in Modern Narrative.* Cambridge, Mass.: Harvard University Press.

Brown, Peter. 1988. *The Body and Society: Men, Women, and Sexual Renunciation in Early Christianity.* New York: Columbia University Press.

Brumberg, Joan Jacob. 1997. *Body Project: An Intimate History of American Girls.* New York: Random House.

Burbick, Joan. 1994. *Healing the Republic: The Language of Health and the Culture of Nationalism in Nineteenth-Century America.* New York: Cambridge University Press.

Burgett, Bruce. 1998. *Sentimental Bodies: Sex, Gender, and Citizenship in the Early Republic.* Princeton, N.J.: Princeton University Press.

Burney, Ian A. 2000. *Bodies of Evidence: Medicine and the Politics of the English Inquest, 1830–1926.* Baltimore: Johns Hopkins University.

Burns, E. Jane. 1993. *Bodytalk: When Women Speak in Old French Literature.* Philadelphia: University of Pennsylvania Press.

Burroughs, Catherine B., and Jeffrey David Ehrenreich, eds. 1993. *Reading the Social Body.* Iowa City: University of Iowa Press.

Burt, Richard, and John Michael Archer, eds. 1994. *Enclosure Acts: Sexuality, Property, and Culture in Early Modern England.* Ithaca, N.Y.: Cornell University Press.

Butler, Judith. 1993. *Bodies That Matter: On the Discursive Limits of "Sex."* New York: Routledge.

Bynum, Caroline Walker. 1995. *The Resurrection of the Body in Western Christianity, 200–1336.* New York: Columbia University Press.

———. 1991. *Fragmentation and Redemption: Essays on Gender and the Human Body in Medieval Religion.* New York: Zone Books.

———. 1987. *Holy Feast, Holy Fast: The Religious Significance of Food to Medieval Women.* Berkeley: University of California Press.

Bynum, W. F., and Roy Porter. 1993. *Medicine and the Five Senses.* New York: Cambridge University Press.

Cahill, Lisa Sowle, and Margaret A. Farley, eds. 1995. *Embodiment, Morality, and Medicine.* Boston: Kluwer Academic Publishers.

Chessman, Harriet Scott. 1989. *The Public Is Invited to Dance: Representation, the Body, and Dialogue in Gertrude Stein.* Stanford, Calif.: Stanford University Press.

Clarke, Bruce, and Wendell Aycock, eds. 1990. *The Body and the Text: Comparative Essays in Literature and Medicine.* Lubbock, Tex.: Texas Tech University Press.

Coakley, Sarah, ed. 1997. *Religion and the Body*. New York: Cambridge University Press.

Cohen, Margaret, and Christopher Prendergast, eds. 1995. *Spectacles of Realism: Body, Gender, Genre*. Minneapolis: University of Minnesota Press.

Comaroff, Jean. 1985. *Body of Power, Spirit of Resistance: The Culture and History of a South African People*. Chicago: University of Chicago Press.

Combs-Shilling, M. E. 1989. *Sacred Performances: Islam Sexuality and Sacrifice*. New York: Columbia University Press.

Cooey, Paula M. 1994. *Religious Imagination and the Body: A Feminist Analysis*. New York: Oxford University Press.

Cooper, Helen M., Adrienne Auslander Munich, and Susan Merrill Squier, eds. 1989. *Arms and the Woman: War, Gender, and Literary Representation*. Chapel Hill: University of North Carolina Press.

Craik, Jennifer. 1994. *The Face of Fashion: Cultural Studies in Fashion*. New York: Routledge.

Cromwell, Jason. 1999. *Transmen and FTMs: Identities, Bodies, Genders, and Sexualities*. Urbana: University of Illinois.

Cuningham, Andrew, and Roger French, eds. 1990. *The Medical Enlightenment of the Eighteenth Century*. New York: Cambridge University Press.

Daileader, Celia R. 1998. *Eroticism on the Renaissance Stage: Transcendence, Desire, and the Limits of the Visible*. New York: Cambridge University Press.

Delany, Sheila. 1998. *Impolitic Bodies: Poetry, Saints, and Society in Fifteenth-Century England: The Work of Osbern Bokenham*. New York: Oxford University Press.

Dellamora, Richard. 1990. *Masculine Desire: The Sexual Politics of Victorian Aestheticism*. Chapel Hill: University of North Carolina Press.

DeMello, Margo. 2000. *Bodies of Inscription: A Cultural History of the Modern Tattoo Community*. Durham, N.C.: Duke University Press.

D'Emilio, John, and Estelle B. Freedman. 1988. *Intimate Matters: A History of Sexuality in America*. New York: Harper & Row.

Derrick, Scott S. 1997. *Monumental Anxieties: Homoerotic Desire and Feminine Influence in Nineteenth-Century U.S. Literature*. New Brunswick, N.J.: Rutgers University Press.

Diprose, Rosalyn. 1994. *The Bodies of Women: Ethics, Embodiment, and Sexual Difference*. New York: Routledge.

——, and Robyn Ferrell, eds. 1991. *Cartographies: Poststructuralism and the Mapping of Bodies and Spaces*. Sydney: Allen & Unwin.

Douglas, Aileen. 1995. *Uneasy Sensations: Smollett and the Body*. Chicago: University of Chicago Press.

Douglas, Mary. 1996. *Natural Symbols; Explorations in Cosmology*. New York: Routledge.

——. [1966] 1992. *Purity and Danger: An Analysis of the Concepts of Pollution and Taboo*. Reprint. New York: Routledge.

Doyle, Laura Anne. 1994. *Bordering on the Body: The Racial Matrix of Modern Fiction and Culture*. New York: Oxford University Press.

Duncan, Nancy, ed. 1996. *Bodyspace: Destabilizing Geographies of Gender and Sexuality*. New York: Routledge.

Eisenstein, Zillah R. 1988. *The Female Body and the Law*. Berkeley: University of California Press.

Eisler, Riane Tennenhaus. 1995. *Sacred Pleasure: Sex, Myth, and the Politics of the Body*. San Francisco: Harper.

Elias, Norbert. 1982; 1983. *The Civilizing Process*. Translated by E. Jephcott, vols. 1 and 2. New York: Pantheon Books.

Epstein, Julia. 1995. *Altered Conditions: Disease, Medicine, and Storytelling*. New York: Routledge.

Epstein, Julia, and Kristina Straub, eds. 1991. *Body Guards: The Cultural Politics of Gender Ambiguity*. New York: Routledge.

Feher, Michel, Ramona Naddaff, and Nadia Tazi, eds. 1989. *Fragments for a History of the Human Body*. New York: Zone.

Fishburn, Katherine. 1997. *The Problem of Embodiment in Early African American Narrative*. Westport, Conn.: Greenwood Press.

Foster, Gwendolyn Audrey. 1999. *Captive Bodies: Postcolonial Subjectivity in Cinema*. Albany: State University of New York Press.

Foster, Susan Leigh, ed. 1996. *Corporealities: Dancing Knowledge, Culture and Power*. New York: Routledge.

——, ed. 1995. *Choreographing History*. Bloomington: Indiana University Press.

Foster, Thomas, Carol Siegel, and Ellen E. Berry, eds. 1996. *Bodies of Writing, Bodies in Performance*. New York: New York University Press.

Foucault, Michel. 1980. *The History of Sexuality. Vol. 1*. Translated by Robert Hurley. New York: Vintage Books.

——. 1977. *Discipline and Punish: The Birth of the Prison*. Translated by Alan Sheridan. New York: Pantheon Books.

Froula, Christine. 1996. *Modernism's Body: Sex, Culture, and Joyce*. New York: Columbia University Press.

Fudge, Erica, Ruth Gilbert, and Susan Wiseman, eds. 1999. *At the Borders of the Human: Beasts, Bodies, and Natural Philosophy in the Early Modern Period*. New York: St. Martin's Press.

Gaines, Jane, and Charlotte Herzog, eds. 1990. *Fabrications: Costume and the Female Body*. New York: Routledge.

Gallagher, Catherine, and Thomas Laqueur, eds. 1987. *The Making of the Modern Body: Sexuality and Society in the Nineteenth Century*. Berkeley: University of California Press.

Gallop, Jane. 1988. *Thinking Through the Body*. New York: Columbia University Press.

Gamman, Lorraine, and Margaret Marshment, eds. 1988. *Female Gaze: Women as Viewers of Popular Culture*. London: Women's Press.

Garb, Tamar. 1998. *Bodies of Modernity: Figure and Flesh in Fin-de-Siècle France*. New York: Thames and Hudson.

Gatens, Moira. 1996. *Imaginary Bodies: Ethics, Power, and Corporeality*. New York: Routledge.

Gent, Lucy, and Nigel Llewellyn, eds. 1990. *Renaissance Bodies: The Human Figure in English Culture, 1540–1660*. Edinburgh: Reaktion Press.

Gilbert, Pamela K. 1997. *Disease, Desire, and the Body in Victorian Women's Popular Novels: Reading, Contagion, and Transgression*. New York: Cambridge University Press.

Goldberg, Jonathan, ed. 1994. *Queering the Renaissance*. Durham, N.C.: Duke University Press.

Goldstein, Laurence, ed. 1991. *The Female Body: Figures, Styles, Speculations*. Ann Arbor: University of Michigan Press.

Grosz, Elizabeth A. 1995. *Space, Time, and Perversion: Essays on the Politics of Bodies*, New York: Routledge.

———. 1994. *Volatile Bodies: Toward a Corporeal Feminism*. Bloomington: Indiana University Press.

Hall, Donald E., ed. 1994. *Muscular Christianity: Embodying the Victorian Age*. New York: Cambridge University Press.

Hanawalt, Barbara A., and David Wallace, eds. 1996. *Bodies and Disciplines: Intersections of Literature and History in Fifteenth-Century England*. Minneapolis: University of Minnesota Press.

Harris, Jonathan Gil. 1998. *Foreign Bodies and the Body Politic: Discourses of Social Pathology in Early Modern England*. New York: Cambridge University Press.

———. 1996. *Space and Gender*. Nottingham: University of Nottingham.

———. 1995. *The Body in Medieval Art, History, and Literature*. Chicago: Loyola University of Chicago.

———. 1993. *Feminist Approaches to the Body in Medieval Literature*. Philadelphia: University of Pennsylvania Press.

Hart, Clive, and Kay Gilliland Stevenson. 1995. *Heaven and the Flesh: Imagery of Desire from the Renaissance to the Rococo*. Cambridge, U.K.: Cambridge University Press.

Hillman, David, and Carla Mazzio, eds. 1997. *The Body in Parts: Fantasies of Corporeality in Early Modern Europe*. New York: Routledge.

Hodes, Martha, ed. 1999. *Sex, Love, Race: Crossing Boundaries in North American History*. New York: New York University Press.

Hodges, Devon L. 1985. *Renaissance Fictions of Anatomy*. Amherst: University of Massachusetts Press.

Holland, Janet, and Lisa Adkins, eds. 1996. *Sex, Sensibility, and the Gendered Body*. New York: St. Martin's Press.

Hunt, Lynn, ed. 1991. *Eroticism and the Body Politic*. Baltimore: Johns Hopkins University Press.

Hurley, Kelly. 1996. *The Gothic Body: Sexuality, Materialism, and Degeneration at the Fin de Siècle*. New York: Cambridge University Press.

Jacobus, Mary, Evelyn Fox Keller, and Sally Shuttleworth, eds. 1990. *Body Politics: Women and the Discourses of Science*. New York: Routledge.

Jagger, Alison M., and Susan R. Bordo, eds. 1989. *Gender/Body/Knowledge: Feminist Reconstructions of Being and Knowing*. New Brunswick, N.J.: Rutgers University Press.

Jaouën, Françoise, and Benjamin Semple. 1994. *Corps Mystique, Corps Sacré: Textual Transfigurations of the Body from the Middle Ages to the Seventeenth Century*. New Haven, Conn.: Yale University Press.

Johnson, Mark. 1987. *The Body in the Mind: The Bodily Basis of Meaning, Imagination, and Reason*. Chicago: University of Chicago Press.

Jones, Colin, and Roy Porter. 1994. *Reassessing Foucault: Power, Medicine, and the Body*. New York: Routledge.

Jordanova, Ludmilla. 1989. *Sexual Visions: Images of Gender in Science and Medicine Between the Eighteenth and Twentieth Centuries*. Madison: University of Wisconsin Press.

Kamensky, Jane. 1997. *Governing the Tongue: The Politics of Speech in Early New England*. New York: Oxford University Press.

Kay, Sarah, and Miri Rubin, eds. 1994. *Framing Medieval Bodies*. New York: St. Martin's Press.

Kelly, Veronica, and Dorothea Von Mücke, eds. 1994. *Body and Text in the Eighteenth Century*. Stanford, Calif.: Stanford University Press.

Kibbey, Ann. 1986. *The Interpretation of Material Shapes in Puritanism: A Study of Rhetoric, Prejudice, and Violence.* New York: Cambridge University Press.

King, Lester. 1991. *Transformations in American Medicine from Benjamin Rush to William Osler.* Baltimore: Johns Hopkins University Press.

Kirk, David. 1998. *Schooling Bodies: School Practice and Public Discourse, 1880–1950.* Washington, D.C.: Leicester University Press.

Koritz, Amy. 1995. *Gendering Bodies/Performing Art: Dance and Literature in Early-Twentieth-Century British Culture.* Ann Arbor: University of Michigan Press.

Korte, Barbara. 1997. *Body Language in Literature.* Toronto: University of Toronto Press.

Kunzie, David. 1982. *Fashion and Fetishism: A Social History of the Corset, Tight-lacing, and Other Forms of Body-Sculpture in the West.* Totowa, N.J.: Rowan and Littlefield.

Lakoff, George. 1987. *Women, Fire, and Dangerous Things: What Categories Reveal about the Mind.* Chicago: University of Chicago Press.

Laqueur, Thomas. 1990. *Making Sex: Body and Gender from the Greeks to Freud.* Cambridge, Mass.: Harvard University Press.

Law, Jane Marie, ed. 1994. *Religious Reflections on the Human Body.* Bloomington: Indiana University Press.

Leahy, D. G. 1996. *Foundation: Matter the Body Itself.* Albany: State University of New York Press.

Leppert, Richard. 1993. *The Sight of Sound: Music, Representation, and the History of the Body.* Berkeley: University of California Press.

Levin, Carole, and Karen Robertson, eds. 1991. *Sexuality and Politics in Renaissance Drama.* Lewiston, N.Y.: E. Mellen Press.

Levine, Laura. 1994. *Men in Women's Clothing: Anti-theatricality and Effeminization, 1579–1642.* New York: Cambridge University Press.

Lochrie, Karma. 1991. *Margery Kempe and Translations of the Flesh.* Philadelphia: University of Pennsylvania Press.

Logan, Peter Meville. 1997. *Nerves and Narratives: A Cultural History of Hysteria in Nineteenth-Century British Prose.* Berkeley: University of California.

Lomperis, Linda, and Sarah Stanbury, eds. 1993. *Feminist Approaches to the Body in Medieval Literature.* Philadelphia: University of Pennsylvania Press.

Low, Gail Ching-Liang. 1996. *White Skins/Black Masks: Representation and Colonialism.* New York: Routledge.

MacCannell, Juliet Flower, and Laura Zakarin, eds. 1994. *Thinking Bodies.* Stanford, Calif.: Stanford University Press.

Malti, Douglas Fedwa. 1994. *Woman's Body, Woman's Word: Gender and Discourse in Arab-Islamic Writing.* Princeton, N.J.: Princeton University Press.

Marshall, Tim. 1995. *Murdering to Dissect: Grave-Robbing, Frankenstein, and Anatomy Literature.* New York: St. Martin's Press.

Marti, Kevin. 1991. *Body, Heart, and Text in the Pearl-Poet.* Lewiston, N.Y.: E. Mellen Press.

Martin, Dale. 1995. *The Corinthian Body.* New Haven, Conn.: Yale University Press.

Martin, Emily. 1987. *The Woman in the Body: A Cultural Analysis of Reproduction.* Boston: Beacon Press.

Marwick, Arthur. 1988. *Beauty in History: Society, Politics and Personal Appearance, c. 1500 to the Present.* London: Thames & Hudson.

Mascia-Lees, Frances E., and Patricia Sharpe, eds. 1992. *Tattoo, Torture, Mutilation, and Adornment: The Denaturalization of the Body in Culture and Text.* Albany: State University of New York Press.

McMullan, Gordon, ed. 1998. *Renaissance Configurations: Voices/Bodies/Spaces, 1580–1690.* New York: St. Martin's Press.

McWhorter, Ladelle. 1999. *Bodies and Pleasures: Foucault and the Politics of Sexual Normalization.* Bloomington: Indiana University Press.

Merback, Mitchell, B. 1999. *The Thief, The Cross, and the Wheel: Pain and the Spectacle of Punishment in Medieval and Renaissance Europe.* Chicago: University of Chicago.

Miller, Andrew H., and James Eli Adams, eds. 1996. *Sexualities in Victorian Britain.* Bloomington: Indiana University Press.

Moltmann-Wendel, Elisabeth. 1995. *I Am My Body: A Theology of Embodiment.* Translated by John Bowden. New York: Continuum.

Montserrat, Dominic, ed. 1998. *Changing Bodies, Changing Meanings: Studies on the Human Body in Antiquity.* London: Routledge.

Moran, Patricia L. 1996. *Word of Mouth: Body Language in Katherine Mansfield and Virginia Woolf.* Charlottesville: University Press of Virginia.

Morton, Timothy. 1994. *Shelley and the Revolution in Taste: The Body and the Natural World.* New York: Cambridge University Press.

Mueller, Monika. 1996. *This Infinite Fraternity of Feeling: Gender, Genre, and Homoerotic Crisis in Hawthorne's* The Blithedale Romance *and Melville's* Pierre. Madison, N.J.: Fairleigh Dickinson University Press.

Navarette, Susan J. 1998. *The Shape of Fear: Horror and the Fin de Siècle Culture of Decadence.* Lexington: University Press of Kentucky.

Neveldine, Robert Burns. 1998. *Bodies at Risk: Unsafe Limits in Romanticism and Postmodernism.* Albany: State University of New York Press.

Nochlin, Linda. 1994. *The Body in Pieces: The Fragment as a Metaphor of Modernity.* New York: Thames and Hudson.

Otis, Laura. 1994. *Organic Memory: History and the Body in Late Nineteenth and Early Twentieth Centuries.* Lincoln: University of Nebraska Press.

Otter, Samuel. 1999. *Melville's Anatomies.* Berkeley: University of California Press.

Outram, Dorinda. 1989. *Body and the French Revolution: Sex, Class, and Political Culture.* New Haven, Conn.: Yale University Press.

Paster, Gail. 1993. *The Body Embarrassed: Drama and Disciplines of Shame in Early Modern England.* Ithaca, N.Y.: Cornell University Press.

Petroff, Elizabeth. 1994. *Body and Soul: Essays on Medieval Women and Mysticism.* New York: Oxford University Press.

Pointon, Monica. 1990. *Naked Authority: The Body and Western Painting, 1830–1908.* New York: Cambridge University Press.

Poovey, Mary. 1995. *Making A Social Body: British Cultural Formation, 1830–1864.* Chicago: University of Chicago Press.

Porter, Roy, ed. 1995. *Medicine in the Enlightenment.* Atlanta: Rodopi.

———. 1992. *The Popularization of Medicine, 1605–1860.* New York: Routledge.

Pouchelle, Marie-Christine. 1990. *The Body and Surgery in the Middle Ages.* Translated by Rosemary Morris. New Brunswick, N.J.: Rutgers University Press.

Price, Douglas B., and Neil J. Trombly. 1978. *The Phantom Limb Phenomenon, A Medical, Folkloric, and Historical Study: Texts and Translations of Tenth- to Twentieth-Century Accounts of the Miraculous Restoration of Lost Body Parts.* Translations by Mary Chamberlain Osborne et al. Washington: Georgetown University Press.

Prosser, Diane Louise. 1995. *Transgressive Corporeality: The Body, Poststruculturalism, and the Theological Imagination.* Albany: State University New York Press.

Punter, David. 1998. *Gothic Pathologies: The Text, the Body, and the Law*. New York: St. Martin's Press.

Raschke, Carl. 1996. *Fire and Roses: Postmodernity and the Thought of the Body*. Albany: State University of New York Press.

Read, Malcolm K. 1990. *Visions in Exile: The Body in Spanish Literature and Linguistics, 1500–1800*. Philadelphia: J. Benjamin.

Reis, Elizabeth. 1997. *Damned Women: Sinners and Witches in Puritan New England*. Ithaca, N.Y.: Cornell University Press.

Richardson, John, and Alison Shaw, eds. 1998. *The Body of Quantitative Research*. Brookfield, Vt.: Ashgate.

Roberts, K. B., and J. D. W. Tomlinson. 1992. *The Fabric of the Body: European Traditions of Anatomical Illustration*. Oxford, N.Y.: Clarendon Press.

Roberts, Marie Mulvey, and Roy Porter, eds. 1993. *Literature and Medicine During the Eighteenth Century*. New York: Routledge.

Roper, Lyndal. 1994. *Oedipus and the Devil: Witchcraft, Sexuality, and Religion in Early Modern England*. New York: Routledge.

Rousseau, G. S., and Roy Porter, eds. 1988. *Sexual Underworlds of the Enlightenment*. Chapel Hill: University of North Carolina Press.

Rousselle, Aline. 1988. *Porneia: On Desire and the Body in Antiquity*. Translated by Felicia Pheasant. Cambridge, U.K.: Blackwell.

Rubin, Arnold, ed. 1988. *Marks of Civilization: Artistic Transformations of the Human Body*. Los Angeles: University of California Museum of Cultural History.

Rubinstein, Ruth P. 1995. *Dress Codes: Meanings and Messages in American Culture*. Boulder, Colo.: Westview Press.

Russo, Mary. 1995. *The Female Grotesque: Risk, Excess, and Modernity*. New York: Routledge.

Sánchez-Eppler, Karen. 1993. *Touching Liberty: Abolition, Feminism, and the Politics of the Body*. Berkeley: University of California Press.

Sawday, Jonathan. 1995. *The Body Emblazoned: Dissection and the Human Body in Renaissance Culture*. London: Routledge.

Scarry, Elaine, ed. 1988. *Literature and the Body: Essays on Populations and Persons*. Baltimore: Johns Hopkins University Press.

——. 1985. *The Body in Pain: The Making and Unmaking of the World*. New York: Oxford University Press.

Schiebinger, Londa. 1993. *Nature's Body: Gender in the Making of Modern Science*. Boston: Beacon Press.

Schoenfeldt, Michael Carl. 1999. *Bodies and Selves in Early Modern Europe: Physiology and Inwardness in Spenser, Shakespeare, Herbert and Milton*. New York: Cambridge University Press.

Scott, Sue, and David Morgan, eds. 1993. *Body Matters: Essays on the Sociology of the Body*. Washington, D.C.: Falmer Press.

Segel, Harold B. 1998. *Body Ascendant: Modernism and the Physical Imperative*. Baltimore: Johns Hopkins University Press.

Sennett, Richard. 1994. *Flesh and Stone: The Body and the City in Western Civilization*. New York: Norton & Co.

Setel, Philip. 1991. *"A Good Moral Tone": Victorian Ideals of Health and the Judgment of Persons in Nineteenth-Century Travel and Mission Accounts from East Africa*. Boston: African Studies Center, Boston University.

Shaw, Jane Alison. 1994. *The Miraculous Body and Other Rational Wonders: Religion in Enlightenment England*. Berkeley: University of California Press.

Sheets-Johnstone, Maxine. 1994. *The Roots of Power: Animate Form and Gendered Bodies.* Chicago: Open Court.

——, ed. 1992. *Giving the Body Its Due.* Albany: State University of New York Press.

Smith, Paul Julian. 1989. *The Body Hispanic: Gender and Sexuality in Spanish and Spanish American Literature.* Oxford: Clarendon Press.

Smith, Sidonie. 1993. *Subjectivity, Identity, and the Body: Women's Autobiographical Practices in the Twentieth Century.* Bloomington: Indiana University Press.

Spongberg, Mary. 1997. *Feminizing Venereal Disease: The Body of the Prostitute in Nineteenth-Century Medical Discourse.* New York: New York University Press.

Sponsler, Claire. 1997. *Drama and Resistance: Bodies, Goods, and Theatricality in Late Medieval England.* Minneapolis: University of Minnesota Press.

Stafford, Barbara Maria. 1991. *Body Criticism: Imaging the Unseen in Enlightenment Art and Medicine.* Cambridge, Mass.: MIT Press.

Stallybrass, Peter, and Allon White. 1986. *The Politics and Poetics of Transgression.* Ithaca, N.Y.: Cornell University Press.

Stearns, Peter N. 1997. *Fat History: Bodies and Beauty in the Modern West.* New York: New York University Press.

Stearns, Peter N., and Jan Lewis, eds. 1998. *An Emotional History of the United States.* New York: New York University Press.

Steward, Samuel M. 1990. *Bad Boys and Tough Tattoos: A Social History of the Tattoo with Gangs, Sailors, and Street-Corner Punks, 1950–1965.* New York: Harrington Park.

Stockton, Kathryn Bond. 1994. *God Between Their Lips: Desire between Women in Irigaray, Brontë, and Eliot.* Stanford, Calif.: Stanford University Press.

Suleiman, Susan Rubin, ed. 1986. *The Female Body in Western Culture: Contemporary Perspectives.* Cambridge, Mass.: Harvard University Press.

Tasker, Yvonne. 1993. *Spectacular Bodies: Gender, Genre, and the Action Cinema.* New York: Routledge.

Taylor, Charles. 1989. *Sources of the Self: The Making of the Modern Identity.* Cambridge, Mass.: Harvard University Press.

Teather, Elizabeth Kenworthy, ed. 1999. *Embodied Geographies: Spaces, Bodies, and Rites of Passage.* London, New York: Routledge.

Thomson, Rosemarie Garland. 1996. *Freakery: Cultural Spectacles of the Extraordinary Body.* New York University Press.

Tilly, Maureen A., and Susan A. Ross, eds. 1994. *Broken and Whole: Essays on Religion and the Body.* Lanham, Md.: University Press of America.

Tuana, Nancy. 1993. *The Less Noble Sex: Scientific, Religious, and Philosophical Conceptions of Woman's Nature.* Bloomington: Indiana University Press.

Verdery, Katherine. 1999. *The Political Lives of Dead Bodies: Reburial and Postsocialist Change.* New York: Columbia University Press.

Vrettos, Athena. 1995. *Somatic Fictions: Imaging Illness in Victorian Culture.* Stanford, Calif.: Stanford University Press.

Waterman, David F. 1999. *Disordered Bodies and Disrupted Borders: Representations of Resistance in Modern British Literature.* Landham, Md.: University Press of America.

White, Shane, and Graham White. 1998. *Stylin': African American Expressive Culture from Its Beginnings to the Zoot Suit.* Ithaca, N.Y.: Cornell University Press.

Wiegman, Robyn. 1995. *American Anatomies: Theorizing Race and Gender.* Durham, N.C.: Duke University Press.

Wilcox, Helen, ed. 1990. *The Body and the Text: Hélène Cixous—Reading and Teaching.* New York: St. Martin's Press.

Wilson, Deborah S., and Christine Moneera Laennec, eds. 1997. *Bodily Discursions: Genders, Representations, Technologies.* Albany: State University New York Press.

Wyke, Maria, ed. 1998. *Parchments of Gender: Deciphering the Bodies of Antiquity.* Oxford: Clarendon Press; New York: Oxford University Press.

Young, Katharine Galloway. 1997. *Presence in the Flesh: The Body in Medicine.* Cambridge, Mass.: Harvard University Press.

——, ed. 1993. *Bodylore.* Knoxville: University of Tennessee Press.

ARTICLES

Allen, Robert C. 1990. " 'The Leg Business': Transgression and Containment in American Burlesque." *Camera Obscura: A Journal of Feminism, Culture, and Media Studies* 23: 43–68.

Babcock, Barbara. 1994. "Pueblo Cultural Bodies." *Journal of American Folklore* 107: 40–54.

Baker, Moira P. 1991. " 'The Uncanny Stranger on Display': The Female Body in Sixteenth- and Seventeenth-Century Love Poetry." *South Atlantic Review* 56: 7–25.

Barona, Josep Luis. 1993. "The Body Republic: Social Order and Human Body in Renaissance Medical Thought." *History and Philosophy of the Life Sciences* 15: 165–80.

Barrett, Lindon. 1995. "African-American Slave Narratives: Literacy, the Body, Authority." *American Literary History* 7: 415–42.

Bennett, Paula. 1993. "Critical Clitoridectomy: Female Sexual Imagery and Feminist Psychoanalytic Theory." *Signs* 18: 235–59.

Bentley, Nancy. 1993. "White Slaves: The Mulatto Hero in Antebellum Fiction." *American Literature* 65: 501–22.

Blake, C. Fred. 1994. "Foot-binding in Neo-Confucian China and the Appropriation of Female Labor." *Signs* 19: 676–712.

Blanchard, Mary W. 1995. "Boundaries and the Victorian Body: Aesthetic Fashion in Gilded Age America." *American Historical Review* 100: 21–50.

Boehmer, Elleke. 1993. "Transfiguring: Colonial Body into Postcolonial Narrative." *Novel* 26: 268–77.

Bow, Leslie. 1991. "Hole to Whole: Feminine Subversion and Subversion of the Feminine in Cherrie Moraga's *Loving in the War Years.*" *Dispositio: Revista Americana de Estudios Comparados Culturales / American Journal of Comparative and Cultural Studies* 16: 1–12.

Brody, Jennifer DeVere. 1996. "Effaced into Flesh: Black Women's Subjectivity." In *On Your Left: Historical Materialism in the 1990s,* edited by Ann Kibbey et al., 184–205. New York: New York University Press.

Bruck, Gabriele vom. 1997. "Elusive Bodies: The Politics of Aesthetics among Yemeni Elite Women." *Signs* 23: 175–214.

Burrus, Virginia. 1994. "Word and Flesh: The Bodies and Sexuality of Ascetic Women in Christian Antiquity." *Journal of Feminist Studies in Religion* 10: 27–51.

Carpenter, Mary Wilson. 1988. " 'A bit of her flesh': Circumcision and 'The Signification of the Phallus' in *Daniel Deronda.*" *Genders* 1: 1–23.

Carpenter, William. 1991. " 'Ovals, Spheres, Ellipses, and Sundry Bulges': Alex La Guma Imagines the Human Body." *Research in African Literatures* 22: 79–98.

Chaplin, Joyce. 1997. "Natural Philosophy and an Early Racial Idiom in North America: Comparing English and Indian Bodies." *William and Mary Quarterly* 54: 229–52.

Clark, Michael. 1993. "'Like Images Made Black with the Lightning': Discourse and the Body in Colonial Witchcraft." *Eighteenth Century: Theory and Interpretation* 34: 199–220.

Cope, Kevin. 1993. "Squirrell's in the Breeches: Onanism, Diarrhea, and the Aesthetics of Antipanacreatic Discourse." *Eighteenth-Century Life* 17: 1–31.

Cowell, Andrew. 1996. "The Fall of the Oral Economy: Writing Economics on the Dead Body." *Exemplaria: A Journal of Theory in Medieval and Renaissance Studies* 8: 145–67.

Crain, Caleb. 1994. "Lovers of Human Flesh: Homosexuality and Cannibalism in Melville's Novels." *American Literature* 66: 25–53.

Cressy, David. 1990. "Death and the Social Order: The Funerary Preferences of Elizabethan Gentlemen." *Continuity and Change* 5: 99–119.

Dreger, Alice Domurat. 1995. "Doubtful Sex: The Fate of the Hermaphrodite in Victorian England." *Victorian Studies* 38: 335–70.

Drescher, Seymour. 1993. "Servile Insurrection and John Brown's Body in Europe." *Journal of American History* 80: 499–524.

Enterline, Lynn. 1994. "'Hairy on the In-Side': *The Duchess of Malfi* and the Body of Lycanthropy." *The Yale Journal of Criticism* 7: 85–129.

Farr, James. 1991. "The Pure and Disciplined Body: Hierarchy, Morality, and Symbolism in France During the Catholic Reformation." *Journal of Interdisciplinary History* 21: 391–414.

Fasick, Laura. 1992. "Sentiment, Authority, and the Female Body in the Novels of Samuel Richardson." *Essays in Literature* 19: 193–203.

Ferris, Lesley. 1992. "Absent Bodies, Dancing Bodies, Broken Dishes: Feminist Theory, Postmodernism, and the Performing Arts." *Signs* 18: 162–72.

Finch, Casey. 1991. "'Hooked and Buttoned Together': Victorian Underwear and Representations of the Female Body." *Victorian Studies* 34: 337–63.

Finke, Laurie. 1988. "Mystical Bodies and the Dialogics of Vision." *Philological Quarterly* 67: 439–50.

Flynn, Maureen. 1996. "The Spiritual Uses of Pain in Spanish Mysticism." *Journal of the American Academy of Religion* 64: 257–78.

Gilman, Sander. 1990. "The Jewish Body: A 'Footnote'." *Bulletin of the History of Medicine* 64: 588–602.

——. 1985. "Black Bodies, White Bodies: Toward an Iconography of Female Sexuality in Late Nineteenth-Century Art, Medicine, and Literature." *Critical Inquiry* 12: 204–42.

Glunz, Michael. 1995. "The Sword, the Pen, and the Phallus: Metaphors and Metonymies of Male Power and Creativity in Medieval Persian Poetry." *Edebiyat: The Journal of Middle Eastern Literatures* 6: 223–43.

Godbeer, Richard. 1995. "'Love Raptures': Marital, Romantic, and Erotic Images of Jesus Christ in Puritan New England, 1670–1730. *New England Quarterly* 68: 55–84.

Green, Susan. 1993. "Semiotic Modalities of the Female Body in Aphra Behn's *The Dutch Lover*." In *Rereading Aphra Behn: History, Theory, and Criticism,* edited by Heidi Hutner, 121–47. Charlottesville: University Press of Virginia.

Groneman, Carol. 1994. "Nymphomania: The Historical Construction of Female Sexuality." *Signs* 19: 337–67.

Haggerty, George. 1995. "Amelia's Nose: Or, Sensibility and Its Symptoms." *Eighteenth Century: Theory and Interpretation* 36: 139–56.

Hemphill, C. Dallett. 1996. "Middle Class Rising in Revolutionary America: The Evidence from Manners." *Journal of Social History* 30: 317–44.

Holsinger, Bruce Wood. 1993. "The Flesh of the Voice: Embodiment and the Homoerotics of Devotion in the Music of Hildegard of Bingen (1098–1179)." *Signs* 19: 92–125.

Howard, Leon. 1992. "Clothing as a Political Weapon in Puritan New England." *Journal of Unconventional History* 3: 25–33.

Howlett, Caroline. 1996. "Writing on the Body? Representation and Resistance in British Suffragette Accounts of Forcible Feeding." *Genders* 23: 3–41.

Hubner, Brian. 1995. "'A Race of Mules': Mixed-Bloods in Western American Fiction." *Canadian Journal of Native Studies* 15: 61–74.

Hudson, Nicholas. 1996. "From 'Nation' to 'Race': The Origin of Racial Classification in Eighteenth-century Thought." *Eighteenth-Century Studies* 29: 247–64.

Hulme, Peter. 1985. "Polytropic Man: Tropes of Sexuality and Mobility in Early Colonial Discourse." In *Europe and Its Others,* edited by Francis Barker et al., 17–32. Colchester: University of Essex.

Humphries, Jefferson. 1988. "Troping the Body: Literature and Feminism." *Diacritics* 18: 18–28.

Jagendorf, Zvi. 1990. "*Coriolanus:* Body Politic and Private Parts." *Shakespeare Quarterly* 41: 455–69.

Jankowski, Theodora A. 1989. "'As I Am Egypt's Queen': Cleopatra, Elizabeth I, and the Female Body Politic." *Assays: Critical Approaches to Medieval and Renaissance Texts* 5: 91–110.

Johnston, Georgia. 1992. "Exploring Lack and Absence in the Body/Text: Charlotte Perkins Gilman Prewriting Irigaray." *Women's Studies: An Interdisciplinary Journal* 21: 75–86.

Jones, Ann Rosalind. 1995. "Writing the Body: Toward an Understanding of l'Écriture féminine." In *The New Feminist Criticism: Essays on Women, Literature and Theory,* edited by Elaine Showalter, 361–77. New York: Pantheon.

Jordanova, Ludmilla. 1989. "Medical Meditations: Mind, Body, and the Guillotine." *History Workshop Journal* 28: 39–52.

Juster, Susan. 1993. "Body and Soul: The Modernist Impulse in American Puritanism." *Reviews in American History* 21: 19–25.

Kemeny, Annemarie. 1994. "The Female Machine in the Postmodern Circuit." In *Liminal Postmodernisms: The Postmodern, the (Post-)Colonial, and the (Post-) Feminist,* edited by Theo D'haen and Hans Bertens, 255–73. Amsterdam: Rodopi.

Klepp, Susan. 1998. "Revolutionary Bodies: Women and the Fertility Transition in the Mid-Atlantic Region, 1760–1820." *Journal of American History* 85: 910–45.

Krug, Kate. 1996. "Women Ovulate, Men Spermate: Elizabeth Blackwell as a Feminist Physiologist." *Journal of the History of Sexuality* 7: 51–72.

Lajer-Burcharth, Ewa. 1991. "David's Sabine Women: Body, Gender, and Republican Culture under the Directory." *Art History* 14: 397–430.

Lamos, Colleen. 1994. "The Postmodern Lesbian Position: On Our Backs." In *The Lesbian Postmodern,* edited by Laura Doan, 85–103. New York: Columbia University Press.

Lant, Kathleen Margaret. 1993. "The Big Strip Tease: Female Bodies and Male Power in the Poetry of Sylvia Plath." *Contemporary Literature* 34: 620–69.

Lawton, Lesley. 1994. "Margery Kempe: The Flesh, the Word and the Text." *Caliban* 31: 75–83.

Levy, Helen. 1996. "Clothes Make the Mannequin: Covering Up the Female Body in *The Sheltered Life.*" *Mississippi Quarterly: The Journal of Southern Culture* 49: 255–67.

Lincoln, Kenneth. 1989–1990. "Indians Playing Indians." *MELUS: The Journal of the Society for the Study of the Multi-Ethnic Literature of the United States* 16: 91–98.

Lo, Mun-hou. 1995. "David Leavitt and the Etiological Maternal Body." *Modern Fiction Studies* 41: 439–65.

Lochrie, Karma. 1991. "The Language of Transgression: Body, Flesh, and Word in Mystical Discourse." In *Speaking Two Languages: Traditional Disciplines and Contemporary Theory in Medieval Studies,* edited by Allen J. Frantzen. 115–40. Albany: State University of New York Press.

Lutes, Jean Marie. 1997. "Negotiating Theology and Gynecology: Anne Bradstreet's Representations of the Female Body." *Signs* 22: 309–40.

Martensen, Robert L. 1992. " 'Habit of Reason': Anatomy and Anglicanism in Restoration England." *Bulletin of the History of Medicine* 66: 511–35.

Martin, Emily. 1991. "The Egg and the Sperm: How Science Has Constructed a Romance Based on Stereotypical Male-Female Roles." *Signs* 16: 485–501.

Maus, Katherine Eisaman. 1993. "A Womb of His Own: Male Renaissance Poets in the Female Body." In *Sexuality and Gender in Early Modern Europe: Institutions, Texts, Images,* edited by James Grantham Turner, 266–88. Cambridge, U.K.: Cambridge University Press.

McCarroll, Luli. 1983. "Dissecting The Body Human: The Sexes." *Camera Obscura: A Journal of Feminism, Culture, and Media Studies* 11: 86–101.

Mechoulan, Eric. 1992. "The Embodiment of Culture: Fairy Tales of the Body in the Seventeenth and Eighteenth Centuries." *Romantic Review* 83: 427–36.

Miller, Shannon. 1996. "Consuming Mothers/Consuming Merchants: The Carnivalesque Economy of Jacobean City Comedy." *Modern Language Studies* 26: 73–97.

Nussbaum, Felicity A. 1995. "One Part of Womankind: Prostitution and Sexual Geography in *Memoirs of a Woman of Pleasure.*" *differences: A Journal of Feminist Cultural Studies* 7: 17–40.

Olson, Carl. 1986. "The Human Body as a Boundary Symbol: A Comparison of Merleau-Ponty and Dogen." *Philosophy East and West: A Quarterly of Comparative Philosophy* 36: 107–20.

Ostriker, Alicia. 1991. "A Word Made Flesh: The Bible and Revisionist Women's Poetry." *Religion and Literature* 23: 9–26.

Park, Katharine. 1995. "The Life of the Corpse: Division and Dissection in Late Medieval England." *Journal of the History of Medicine and Allied Sciences* 50: 111–32.

———. 1994. "The Criminal and the Saintly Body: Autopsy and Dissection in Renaissance Italy." *Renaissance Quarterly* 47: 1–33.

Perry, Ruth. 1992. "Colonizing the Breast: Sexuality and Maternity in Eighteenth-Century England." *Eighteenth-Century Life* 16: 185–213.

Piper, Karen. 1995. "The Signifying Corpse: Re-Reading Kristeva on Marguerite Duras." *Cultural Critique* 31: 159–77.

Pollock, Griselda. 1994. " 'With My Own Eyes': Fetishism, the Labouring Body and the Colour of Its Sex." *Art History* 17: 342–82.

Potts, Alex. 1990. "Beautiful Bodies and Dying Heroes: Images of Ideal Manhood in the French Revolution." *History Workshop Journal* 30: 1–21.

Pramaggiore, Maria T. 1992. "Resisting/Performing/Femininity: Words, Flesh, and Feminism in Karen Finley's *The Constant State of Desire.*" *Theatre Journal* 44: 269–90.

Purkiss, Diane. 1995. "Women's Stories of Witchcraft in Early Modern England: The House, The Body, The Child." *Gender & History* 7: 408–32.

Reis, Elizabeth. 1995. "The Devil, the Body, and the Feminine Soul in Puritan New England." *Journal of American History* 82: 15–36.

Reiss, Timothy J. 1996. "Denying the Body? Memory and the Dilemmas of History in Descartes." *Journal of the History of Ideas* 57: 587–607.

Rosenberg, Charles E. 1989. "Body and Mind in Nineteenth-Century Medicine: Some Clinical Origins of the Neurosis Construct." *Bulletin of the History of Medicine* 63: 185–97.

Rundblad, Georganne. 1995. "Exhuming Women's Premarket Duties in the Care of the Dead." *Gender & Society* 9: 173–92.

Rupp, Jan. 1992. "Michel Foucault, Body Politics, and the Rise and Expansion of Modern Anatomy." *Journal of Historical Sociology* 5: 31–60.

Salliant, John. 1995. "The Black Body Erotic and the Republican Body Politic, 1790–1820." *Journal of the History of Sexuality* 5: 403–28.

Saxton, Ruth. 1994. "The Female Body Veiled: From Crocus to Clitoris." In *Woolf and Lessing: Breaking the Mold,* edited by Ruth Saxton and Jean Tobin, 95–122. New York: St. Martin's.

Schlueter, June. 1992. " 'Stuffed, as They Say, with Honorable Parts': Female Breasts on The English Renaissance Stage." *The Shakespeare Yearbook* 3: 117–42.

Schramer, James, and Timothy Sweet. 1992. "Violence and Body Politic in Seventeenth-Century New England." *Arizona Quarterly: A Journal of American Literature, Culture, and Theory* 48: 1–32.

Seaton, Elizabeth. 1987. "Profaned Bodies and Purloined Looks: The Prisoner's Tattoo and the Researcher's Gaze." *Journal of Communication Inquiry* 11: 17–25.

Shelton, Robert. 1993. "The Social Text as Body: Images of Health and Disease in Three Recent Feminist Utopias." *Literature and Medicine* 12: 161–77.

Somerville, Siobhan. 1996. "Scientific Racism and the Invention of the Homosexual Body." *Journal of the History of Sexuality* 5: 243–66.

Spelman, Elizabeth. 1982. "Woman as Body: Ancient and Contemporary Views." *Feminist Studies* 8: 109–31.

Stimpson, Catharine R. 1985. "The Somagrams of Gertrude Stein." *Poetics Today* 6: 67–80.

Stone, Allucquere Rosanne. 1991. "Will the Real Body Please Stand Up? Boundary Stories about Virtual Cultures." In *Cyberspace: First Steps,* edited by Michael Benedikt, 81–118. Cambridge, Mass.: MIT Press.

Suleiman, Susan Rubin. 1985. "(Re)writing the Body: The Politics and Poetics of Female Eroticism." *Poetics Today* 6: 43–65.

Swann, Brian. 1987. " 'The Dusky Body of IT Underneath': Some Thoughts on America and Native Americans." *North Dakota Quarterly* 55: 165–87.

Valenzuela, Luisa. 1986. "The Other Face of the Phallus." In *Reinventing the Americas: Comparative Studies of Literature of the United States and Spanish America,* edited by Bell Gale Chevigny and Gari Laguardia, 242–48. New York: Cambridge University Press.

Voekel, Pamela. 1992. "Peeing on the Palace: Bodily Resistance to Bourbon Reforms in Mexico City." *Journal of Historical Sociology* 5: 183–208.

Walsh, Susan. 1993. "Bodies of Capital: *Great Expectations* and the Climacteric Economy." *Victorian Studies* 37: 73–98.

Wardley, Lynn. 1989. "Woman's Voice, Democracy's Body, and *The Bostonians.*" *ELH* 56: 639–65.

Warhol, Robyn R. 1992. "The Look, the Body, and the Heroine: A Feminist-Narratological Reading of *Persuasion.*" *Novel: A Forum on Fiction* 26: 5–19.

Weber, Harold. 1995. "Carolinean Sexuality and the Restoration Stage: Reconstructing The Royal Phallus in Sodom." In *Cultural Readings of Restoration and Eighteenth-Century English Theater,* edited by J. Douglas Canfield and Deborah C. Payne, 67–88. Athens: University of Georgia Press.

Westphal, Sarah. 1996. "Camilla: The Amazon Body in Medieval German Literature." *Exemplaria: A Journal of Theory in Medieval and Renaissance Studies* 8: 231–58.

Whitford, M. 1986. "Luce Irigaray and the Female Imaginary: Speaking as a Woman." *Radical Philosophy* 43: 3–8.

Wilson, Ann. 1989. "History and Hysteria: Writing the Body in *Portrait of Dora* and *Signs of Life.*" *Modern Drama* 32: 73–88.

Woodbridge, Linda. 1991. "Palisading the Elizabethan Body Politic." *Texas Studies in Literature and Language* 33: 327–54.

Wyatt, Jean. 1993. "Giving Body to the Word: The Maternal Symbolic in Toni Morrison's *Beloved.*" *PMLA* 108: 474–88.

Yarbro-Benjarano, Yvonne. 1995. "The Lesbian Body in Latina Cultural Production." In *Entiendes? Queer Readings, Hispanic Writings,* edited by Emilie L. Bergmann and Paul Julian Smith, 181–97. Durham, N.C.: Duke University Press.

Zerilli, Linda M. G. 1995. "The Arendtian Body." In *Feminist Interpretations of Hannah Arendt,* edited by Bonnie Honig, 167–93. University Park: Pennsylvania State University Press.

Contributors

Kathleen M. Brown is an associate professor of history at the University of Pennsylvania. She is the author of *Good Wives, Nasty Wenches, and Anxious Patriarchs: Gender, Race and Power in Colonial Virginia* (University of North Carolina Press, 1996) and several articles on early American women's history. She is the recipient of several fellowships from leading academic institutions, including the American Antiquarian Society, the Bunting Institute at Radcliffe College, and the Omohundro Institute of Early American History and Culture.

Elizabeth Maddock Dillon teaches English and American studies as an assistant professor at Yale University. She was a Mellon Postdoctoral Fellow at Cornell University for two years. She is the author of a forthcoming book from Stanford University Press entitled *The Gender of Freedom: Liberalism, Hysteria, and Dispossessive Individualism*. She has given many conference papers and has authored articles, including one in *Diacritics*.

Trudy Eden holds a J.D. from Emory University and a Ph.D. in the history of science, technology and medicine from Johns Hopkins University. Her dissertation, entitled "'Makes Like, Makes Unlike': Food, Health, and Identity in the Colonial Chesapeake," was completed in 1999. She is an assistant professor of early American history at the University of Northern Iowa and has won research fellowships from the Virginia Historical Society and the College of Physicians of Philadelphia.

Martha L. Finch received her M.A. and Ph.D. from the Department of Religious Studies at the University of California, Santa Barbara. A Pew Fellowship in Religion and American History supported her dissertation, a cultural history of the human body in early New England. She is currently a Faculty Fellow at Colby College, teaching courses in religion and American history and culture.

Janet Moore Lindman is an associate professor of history and the coordinator of the Women's Studies Program at Rowan University. She completed her dissertation, entitled "A World of Baptists: Gender, Race, and Religious

Community, 1689–1825," at the University of Minnesota. She has authored book reviews and articles, including one in the *William and Mary Quarterly*. She is the recipient of a fellowship at the McNeil Center for Early American Studies and of fellowships from the Virginia Historical Society and the John Nicholas Brown Center.

Joanne Pope Melish is an associate professor of history at the University of Kentucky. She earned her Ph.D. in American civilization at Brown University. She is the author of *Disowning Slavery: Gradual Emancipation and "Race" in New England, 1780–1860* (Cornell University Press, 1998), in addition to several conference papers and articles.

Jacquelyn C. Miller is an assistant professor of history at Seattle University. She completed her Ph.D. in early American history at Rutgers University and is the recipient of a fellowship at the McNeil Center for Early American Studies. She is the coeditor, along with Claire G. Fox and Gordon L. Miller, of *Benjamin Rush, M.D.: A Bibliographic Guide*, published by Greenwood Press. She is the author of several publications, including an article in the *Journal of Social History*.

Alice Nash is an assistant professor in the History Department at the University of Massachusetts, Amherst. She completed her dissertation, entitled "The Abiding Frontier: Family, Gender, and Religion in Wabanaki History, 1600–1763," at Columbia University. She is the author of three articles and several conference papers and the recipient of research fellowships from the American Philosophical Society, the Newberry Library, and the Massachusetts Historical Society.

Nancy Shoemaker is an associate professor at the University of Connecticut-Storrs. She is the author of *American Indian Population Recovery in the Twentieth Century* (University of New Mexico Press, 1999) and editor of *Negotiators of Change: Historical Perspectives on Native American Women* (Routledge, 1995). She has published on American Indian history in *American Historical Review, Journal of Women's History,* and other journals and has held fellowships at the Huntington Library and Newberry Library.

Todd D. Smith is the executive director of the Plains Art Museum in Fargo. He has served as curator at the Mint Museum of Art in Charlotte, North Carolina, and The Dayton Art Institute of Dayton, Ohio. He has lectured and published in the United States and Great Britain on American art, gender, and politics and is the recipient of a grant from the National Endowment for the Arts.

Jennifer M. Spear is an assistant professor of history at Dickinson College, having completed her dissertation, "Whiteness and the Purity of Blood: Race, Sexuality, and Social Order in Colonial Louisiana," in 1999 at the University of Minnesota. She has received fellowships from the Huntington Library, the John Carter Brown Library, and the American Historical Association; has presented many conference papers, including at the American Studies

Association and Omohundro Institute of Early American History and Culture annual meetings, and at the International Seminar on the History of the Atlantic World, 1500–1800; and is the author of one previous article.

Robert Blair St. George is an associate professor in the Department of History and a member of the Graduate Group in Folklore and Folklife at the University of Pennsylvania. He is the author of *Conversing by Signs: Poetics of Implication in Colonial New England Culture* (University of North Carolina Press, 1997) and editor and contributing author of *Material Life in America, 1600–1860* (Northeastern University Press, 1988), which won the 1989 Fred Kniffen Prize for the best work in material culture. He has two forthcoming publications, *The Complete Writings of Daniel Gookin* (University of Massachusetts Press) and *Possible Pasts: Becoming Colonial in Early America* (Cornell University Press).

Susan M. Stabile is an assistant professor of English at Texas A & M University. She completed her dissertation, " 'By a Female Hand': Letters, Belles Lettres, and the Philadelphian Culture of Performance, 1760–1820," at the University of Delaware. She has given many conference papers and is the recipient of fellowships from the McNeil Center for Early American Studies and the David Library of the American Revolution. She is currently working on a book project, *Beyond the Writing Closet: The Material Culture of Early American Women's Manuscripts*, as well as an anthology entitled *Female Commonplaces: An Anthology of Eighteenth-Century American Poetry*.

Michele Lise Tarter is an assistant professor of English at The College of New Jersey. She has published several articles on early American women's writings and has presented papers on her archival research at numerous national conferences. She is currently completing a book manuscript entitled *The Body as Testimony: Quaker Women's Prophesyings in Early American Culture and Text*.

Teresa A. Toulouse is an associate professor of English at Tulane University. She is the author of *The Art of Prophesying: New England Sermons and the Shaping of Belief* (University of Georgia, 1987) and is coeditor, with Andrew Delbanco, of *The Sermons of Ralph Waldo Emerson*, vol. 2 (University of Missouri Press, 1990). Two of her articles, published in *Early American Literature*, have won the R. B. Davis Award. She has written three essays on Mary Rowlandson and is completing a book on the political uses of late-seventeenth-century captivity narratives by or about New England women.

Index

Adams, John, 64, 66
Adams, Mrs., 196, 201–2
Adams, Thomas, 17
African Americans: as Baptists, 184–86;
    and black elite, 82, 95, 100; slavery and,
    96–99, 186, 217, 223, 224. *See also*
    Race; Role reversal literature
Africans, 2–3, 224, 228–29, 234 n. 25
Albinism, 224–27, 233 n. 5. *See also* Role
    reversal literature
Algerine Captive, The (Tyler), 230–31
Algiers, 228–31, 234 nn. 23, 26, 27,
    235 n. 30
Allegories, 113
Allison, Robert, 234 n. 26, 235 n. 32
Almanacs, 1, 9 n. 12
American Magazine of Wonders, 226, 227
American Philosophical Society, 65
American Revolution, 64–70, 216; mental
    disease and, 67, 69; War of 1812 and,
    237, 239, 244–45, 248
Ames, William, 47
Analogy, 217
Anarchia, 67
Anatomical texts, 135–37
Anatomy (Bell), 136–37
Anatomy, the (Man of Signs), 1–5, 9 n. 12
Animalculists, 120
Antinomians, 135, 137
Antislavery advocates, 224
Anxiety, 50–51, 244–45, 251
Argall, Samuel, 38
Aristotle's Master-Piece, 112, 118, 136,
    142 n. 31
Assimilation theory of diet, 29–37
Atherton, Humphrey, 157
Austin, Ann, 152–53
Authenticity, 244–45, 253 n. 15
Awashunkes, 165, 166
Ayres, Goodwife, 21

Bailey, Richard, 159 n. 9
Baker, Louisa, 245
Bakhtin, Mikhail, 32–33
Baptists, 138; and baptism, 180–81; black,
    184–86; and depression, 179–80; and ex-
    communication, 183, 189 n. 20; and holy
    walking, 178, 182; and oneness of body,
    177–78; and preaching, 178–79; and reg-
    ulation of body, 182–87, 189 nn. 17, 24;
    and ritual practice, 177, 180–82
Bate, James, 225–27
Bauman, Richard, 149
Beale, William, 26–27 n. 15
Bell, Catherine, 182
Bell, John, 136–37
Bellomont, earl of, 206–7, 209 nn. 21, 23
Bennett, John, 114
Berleant, Arnold, 47, 48, 57 n. 13
Biblical references, 15, 79, 149, 197, 203,
    204–7
Birch, Thomas, 243, 246, 248
Bishop, Bridget, 21, 22
Black elite, 82, 95, 100
Blacks, as term, 223, 224, 232 n. 2
Blancos, 97
Blood: pregnancy and, 113, 115, 117; as
    symbolic carrier of socioracial qualities,
    101, 103. *See also Limpieza de sangre*
    cases
Blood-letting, 61, 63, 69–71, 110
Blye, John, 22
Blye, William, 22
Body: adversity and, 50–51; Calvinist
    theology of, 46–48, 53; as decorous, 183,
    189 n. 22; domestic, 196, 203, 206;
    dynamic model of, 47; English, threats
    to, 195–96; environment and, 45–47;
    and exercise, 53, 59 n. 35; as house,
    14–21; industrious, 46, 48, 53; language
    and, 169; metaphors for, used in Indian

Body (*continued*)
councils, 212–15, 220nn. 21, 22, 221n. 24;
and miraculous recoveries, 205–6; and
ontological categories, 109, 110, 131; as
permeable, 47; planting of, 46, 51, 53–55;
providential, 82; semiotic language of,
113, 150; and textual context, 2, 193–94,
207n. 1. *See also* Embodiment; Female
body; Feminization; Gender; Male body;
Pregnancy; Regulation of body; Sexual
difference; Social body
Body in Pain, The (Scarry), 199
Body politic. *See* Social body
Book of Sufferings, 152
Book of White Persons Only, 97, 104
Boundaries, 6, 96, 104, 187; narrative and,
199–200; torture and, 199–200, 204; uncleanness as, 80, 82; women as threaten-
ing, 202–5
Boxer, H. M. S., 239
Bradford, William, 43–44, 49, 51, 53–54,
58n. 18
Bradstreet, Anne, 15, 17, 133
Breast milk imagery, 109–11, 118; Quakers
and, 150, 153–54, 159n. 6; used by Na-
tive Americans, 213, 215, 219n. 11. *See
also* Nursing fathers
Bride of Christ imagery, 8, 18, 129–30; gen-
der and, 133–34; sexed body and,
137–38. *See also* Nursing fathers
*Briefe and True Report of the New England
Land of Virginia* (Hariot), 35
Brown, John, 62–63
Brown, Kathleen M., 202–3
Brown, Mary, 22
Brown, Moses, 227
Bruce, Philip, 37
Brunhouse, Robert, 66
Bryson, Norman, 252n. 15
Buffon, comte de, 224, 225, 228
Burnham, John, 229
Burr, Esther Edwards, 110–22, 123n
Burroughs, Edward, 155
Burrows, W. W., 239
Burrows, William, 239–40
Burton, Robert, 59n. 35
Bush, William S., 247
Butler, Judith, 143n. 44, 183
Bynum, Caroline Walker, 148

Calvinist theology of body, 46–48, 53
Canella, Magdalena, 98
Canup, John, 49, 56n. 7
Captivity narratives, 91, 170, 193–209;
about Algiers, 228–31, 234nn. 23, 26,
27, 235n. 33; boundaries and, 199–200;
children in, 195–96, 200–201, 204–5;
and crisis in male authority, 194; and

threats to body politic, 194–99, 203–5;
and typological narratives, 194; and
women's bravery, 91, 197, 203; and
women's foolishness, 197–98
Cartier, Jacques, 164
Catemenia, 117
Celestial flesh, 148, 159n. 9
Champlain, Samuel de, 164
Change, 6–8, 47; diet and, 31–33, 35–36,
42n. 37; gender identity and, 135–39,
142n. 25
Charles II, 157
Chauncey, Charles, 137
Cheyne, George, 118
Children: in captivity narratives, 195–96,
200–201, 204–5; illegitimate, 83–84,
98–100; as soul of parent, 121. *See also*
Infanticide
Chimneys, 16, 19–22, 24
Choleric temperament, 36, 40n. 9
Christ, 213. *See also* Bride of Christ
imagery; Nursing fathers; Word of God
Christianity, environment and, 49–51
Christopresentism, 148, 159n. 9
Circle of perfection, 115, 118–19
Civil War imagery, 237
Cixous, Hélène, 125n. 21
Class issues, 66–71; blood-letting and,
70–71; emotionalism and, 67–68;
uncleanness and, 91–92
Clawson, Elizabeth, 21
Clothing, 86–88, 97
Code noir, 7, 97
Cogan, Thomas, 117
Cole, Eunice, 21
Cole, Sarah, 22
Coleman, Ann, 155
Columbian Exchange, 2–3
Comaroff, Jean, 173n. 24
Commodification, 45, 48, 57n. 13
Complete Herbal (Culpepper), 115
Complexion theory, 39n. 5
Conception, 112, 121
Conduct, 47, 102, 178, 206
Constitution (1787), 67, 68
Constitution, as term, 64–66, 73n. 10
Consumption metaphor, 47, 48, 54, 55, 88
Control. *See* Regulation of body
Conversation, as term, 178
Conversion: pregnancy imagery and,
109–11, 114, 119–20, 132; written lan-
guage and, 111–12
Cooper, James Fenimore, 244
Corporeal prophecy, 145–51, 157
Correspondences, 6. *See also* Doctrine of
signatures
Cotton, John, 51, 129
Cotton, Priscilla, 148

Covenant metaphor, 135
Craig, Lewis, 179
Crèvecoeur, St. John de, 54–55
Cronon, William, 48, 59 n. 31
Crooke, Helkiah, 135–36, 142 n. 28
Cry of Sodom, The (Danforth), 78, 90
Cullen, William, 62
Culpepper, Nicholas, 113, 115, 119, 136
Cushman, Robert, 51, 53

Dance, Native American, 163–64; as antic,
   163, 167–68, 170–71; as educational,
   168, 170–71, 174 n. 33; English dance
   compared to, 166–67; and *pineses,* 165;
   and *powows,* 164–65; as resistant, 164,
   167, 171; style of, 166; torture and,
   165–66, 169–70; warfare-related, 165.
   See also Native Americans
Danforth, Samuel, 78, 80, 90
Davis, Elnathan, 179, 180
Dayton, Cornelia Hughes, 139
De Bry, Thomas, 35
Decennium Luctuosum (Mather), 193–207
*Declaration of the Sad and Great Persecu-
   tion and Martyrdom, A* (Burroughs), 155
Delbanco, Andrew, 58 n. 22, 135
Demos, John, 50
Descartes, René, 4
Dewsbury, William, 149
Diet: assimilation theory of, 29–37; bodily
   changes due to, 31–33, 35–36, 42 n. 37;
   as causing savageness, 36, 37, 48–49;
   Chesapeake region foods and, 30, 33–37;
   elements and, 32–33; laws and, 37–38;
   social hierarchy of foods and, 33–35,
   38–39. *See also* Humors
Dietaries, 31, 33, 39–40 n. 6
Dillon, Elizabeth Maddock, 8, 159 n. 6
Diplomacy. *See* English-Indian diplomacy
Directory for Midwives, A (Culpepper), 119
Disease, 35; mental illness and, 67, 69; in Ply-
   mouth Colony, 44–46; uncleanness and,
   81–82; unitary theory of, 63, 64, 69–70
Doctrine of signatures, 113, 115–16, 120;
   circle of perfection and, 115, 118–19. *See
   also* Humors
Dodsley, Robert, 115
Domesticity, ideology of, 4
Donne, John, 15
Dorr, Edward, 138
Douglas, Mary, 80, 82, 87, 152
Dowd, Gregory, 216
Dualism, 146–48, 150–51, 159 n. 7
Duston, Hannah Emerson, 7, 91, 193–209;
   Emerson's execution and, 202–3;
   Mather's use of, 193–94
*Duty of Civil Rulers to Be Nursing Fathers
   to the Church of Christ, The* (Dorr), 138

Dwight, Timothy, 71
Dyer, Mary, 156–57
Dying Hercules, The (Morse), 240–42

Economy of Human Life (Dodsley), 115
Eden, Trudy, 7
Edwards, Jonathan, 114, 122, 123n,
   124 n. 12, 137, 142 n. 31
Elements, 30–33. *See also* Humors
Elias, Norbert, 32–33
Elyot, Thomas, 31
Embodiment, 45, 90, 110; evangelical reli-
   gion and, 178–82, 188 n. 11; humors
   and, 113, 124 n. 16; Quakers and,
   147–48; of subordination, 223–24,
   228–30. *See also* Body; Female body;
   Male body
Emerson, Elizabeth, 78–79, 82–84, 83–84,
   87–88, 202–3, 208–9 n. 17
Emerson, Hannah Webster, 83–84, 88
Emerson, Michael, 83, 88, 208 n. 17
Emotionalism, 179, 189 n. 17, 244; class issues, 67–68; evangelical religion and,
   111, 119–20
*Engagement between the Constitution and
   the Guerriere, The* (Birch), 243, 246
England, 195, 238–39
English, the: crops of, 37, 41 n. 28; dances
   of, 166–67; diet and, 30, 33–35, 38–39,
   41 n. 28; humors and, 31–32
English-Indian diplomacy:
   family metaphors in, 213–14; friendship
   metaphors in, 213–14; protective
   metaphors in, 214–15; and shared
   conceptual frameworks, 212–13; skin
   color metaphors in, 211, 215–18,
   221 nn. 32, 37
Enterprise, 239, 240
Environment, 6–7, 224; body's relationship
   to, 46–47; human body as, 45–46;
   humors and, 31–32, 46–48, 57 n. 16;
   morality and, 46–47, 50–51. *See also*
   Wilderness
Environmental theory, 224
Epistolarity, 111–12, 125 n. 22
Equiano, Olaudah, 3
Essay on Health and Long Life (Cheyne), 118
Eupraxia, 47, 53
Europeans, 2–3. *See also* English, the
Evangelical religion, 244; breast milk
   imagery and, 109–11, 118; congregation
   in, 109, 118, 129; conversion to, 109–12,
   114, 119–20, 132, 179–80; embodiment
   and, 178–80, 178–82, 188 n. 11;
   emotionalism and, 111, 119–20;
   feminization of Word and, 110, 122; gendered passivity of women and, 119, 121;
   pregnancy imagery in, 109–11, 114,

Evangelical religion (*continued*)
119–20, 132; techniques of the body and, 182. *See also* Baptists; Word of God
Excommunication, 183, 189 n. 20
Expert Midwife, The (McMath), 119

Family metaphors, 14–15, 202, 213–14
Farrington, John, 23
Father, symbolic, 195, 198, 201
Federalists, 244–45
Female body: and executions, 78–79, 82, 156; in Puritan language, 132–33; as symbolic of Puritan social body, 79, 82–85, 91; as unclean, 79, 85–86. *See also* Infanticide; Uncleanness
Feminization, 111; and discourse of power, 18–20; and homosexual images, 133–34; of ministers, 18, 109, 118, 129; and nursing father imagery, 128–29, 129–30, 138–39; of Puritan masculinity, 132–33, 140 n. 5; and shift in acceptance of rhetoric, 137–39, 142 n. 25; as threatening to masculinity, 133–34, 140 n. 4; of Word, 110, 122. *See also* Pregnancy imagery
Fetishized objects, 23–24
Fischler, Claude, 29
Fisher, Edward, 61
Fisher, Mary, 152–53
Fitch, Abraham, 21
Fluidity, 7, 36, 104, 109–10, 115–18, 121, 132
Fort Pemaquid, 196
Fort Pitt, 215
Fort Wilson Riot, 66
Foss, John, 229
Foucault, Michel, 96, 104
Fox, George, 147–48, 149, 155, 158 n. 1
French officials, 213
French Revolution, 65, 70, 138
Fristoe, Daniel, 181
Fungible fluids, 115–18, 121, 132

Galen, 4, 30, 32, 36, 39 n. 4, 46, 136; model of sexual difference of, 130–31
Garden imagery, 45, 51–53
Gardiner, Horred, 154–55
Gates, Thomas, 37–38
Gay, Peter, 73 n. 9
Gender, 141 n. 7; epistolary construction of, 112; European discourses of, 3–4; and hierarchical identity, 131–35; one-sex model of, 110, 123 n. 4, 130–32, 136, 138–39; and passivity, 119, 121, 132; performance of, 130–33, 138–39, 141 n. 7; shifts in understanding of, 135–39, 142 n. 25; two-sex model of, 4, 8, 131, 138–39
Gens de couleur, 100

Gerard, John, 37
Gerish, Sarah, 195, 200, 204
Glacken, Clarence J., 57 n. 16
Gookin, Daniel, 164, 172 n. 1
Gould, Stephen Jay, 140
Grace, Henry, 168–69
Great Awakening. *See* Evangelical religion
Griffitts, Samuel P., 69
Grosz, Elizabeth, 124 n. 16
Gyles, John, 166

Habitation models, 48
Hagler, King, 216
Hall, Gwendolyn Midlo, 99
Haller, Albrecht von, 136
Hammond, John, 37
Hanger, Kimberly, 100
Hariot, Thomas, 34, 35, 36
Harris, Samuel, 178
Hartford Convention, 244–45
Harvey, William, 112, 115, 118–19
Haven of Health (Cogan), 117
Hearth, 16–24; pregnancy and, 19–20; witchcraft and, 21–24
Heart imagery, 111, 115–16, 220 n. 22
Heart of New England Rent, The (Norton), 155–56
Hercules, representation of, 240–42, 251, 252 n. 9
Heroes, 240–42, 247–48, 251
Heroic measures, 115–16; blood-letting as, 61, 63, 69–71, 110; purges as, 61, 63
Hertz, Robert, 212
Hierarchical discourses, 4; and gender identity, 131–35; and racialized bodies, 185, 189 n. 27; and social hierarchy of food, 33–35, 38–39
Higginson, Francis, 48
Historical and Geographical Account of Algiers, An (Stevens), 235 nn. 28, 33
History of Sexuality, The (Foucault), 96
History of the Captivity and Sufferings of Mrs. Maria Martin, who was Six Years a Slave in Algiers (Martin), 235 nn. 33
Homosexuality, figurative, 133–34, 141 n. 21
Honor, 101–2
Hooker, Thomas, 141 n. 15
Hopewood (Wohawa), 200–202, 204
House, body as, 14–21
House of Commons, 68
Houses, 7; attacks on, by witches, 14–15, 20–22; and chimneys, 16, 19–22, 24; and countermagic against witches, 22–24; saltbox, 18–20; as spatialized domain of women, 15, 18, 20; subversion of social order and, 24–25
How, Elizabeth, 22
Hughes, Walter, 133–34, 141 n. 21

Humanitas christi, 148
Humors, 57 n. 12, 184; diet and, 31–32,
    39 n. 5, 40 nn. 9, 11; embodiment and,
    113, 124 n. 16; environment and, 31–32,
    46–48, 57 n. 16; fungible fluids and,
    115–18, 121, 132; temperaments and,
    30–32, 35–36, 40 n. 9. *See also* Doctrine
    of signatures
Hutchinson, Anne, 131, 135, 137, 156

Idleness, 53, 59 n. 35
Image-schemata, 169
Immanence, 148
Impressment, 238–39
Individualism, 141 n. 24, 244–48
Industrious body, 46, 48, 53
Infanticide, 83–84; Emerson case of, 82–84,
    86–88; and executions, 78–79, 82,
    85–86, 91; and filth-avoidance practices,
    82; legal prosecution of, 78; publications
    on, 77–79. *See also* Uncleanness
Ingestion, 47, 48
Isaac, Rhys, 46

Jackson, Andrew, 247
James I, 51
Jefferson, Thomas, 225, 249
Jews, 101, 102
Johnson, Mark, 169
Johnson, Samuel, 115, 119
Johnson, Susannah, 170
Josselyn, John, 164, 165
Juster, Susan, 124 n. 9, 138

Kames, Lord, 112
Kann, Mark, 244
Kelley, Elizabeth, 21
Key, James, 195–96, 202, 204
Keyser, Eleazar, 21–22
Kibbey, Ann, 111, 155
King Philip's War, 165, 199
Klepp, Susan, 112
Kloss, William, 240–42
Knapp, Elizabeth, 21
Knight, Janice, 141 n. 15
Kristeva, Julia, 125 n. 20, 150

Lad, Samuel, 83, 84
Lakoff, George, 169
Lane, Tilden, 179
Language, 111–13, 169. *See also* Letter
    writing
Laqueur, Thomas, 109–10, 117–18,
    123 n. 4, 130–32, 135
Lawson, John, 212
Lawson–Peebles, Robert, 73 n. 14
"Leah and Rachel" (Hammond), 37
Lemnius, Levinus, 40 n. 11

Lepore, Jill, 199, 208 n. 11
Letter writing: compared to nervous system,
    115, 121; as doctrine of signatures,
    115–16; and epistolarity, 111–12,
    125 n. 22; as heroic measure, 116; inter-
    nal conditions and, 113–14; moment of
    grace and, 121–22; penmanship and,
    114–15; pregnancy imagery linked to,
    112–14. *See also* Doctrine of signatures
Leverenz, David, 18
Limpieza de sangre cases, 7, 95–104; bap-
    tisms and, 97, 100, 104; family names
    and, 104; honor and, 101–2; occupations
    and, 95, 105 n. 2; religion and, 102; repu-
    tation and, 101–3; testimonials and,
    100–102
Linen-centered standard, 86–88
Linnaeus, 225
Lithobolia, 13
Liu, Tessie, 101
Lovejoy, David, 111
Lupton, Deborah, 29

Mack, Phyllis, 158 n. 2
Macrocosmographia (Cooke), 135–36,
    142 n. 28
Madison, James, 238
Maize, 33–34, 37, 44
Male body, 237–52; absence and, 237, 240,
    243, 245, 251; adult types of, 244;
    authenticity and, 244–45, 253 n. 15; fra-
    ternity and, 245; heroic, 247–48;
    impressment and, 238–39; individualism
    and, 244–48; masculine identity forma-
    tion and, 237–38, 245, 251–52; patrilin-
    eal inheritance of military prowess and,
    239–40; representation of, 240–42
Man of Signs (the Anatomy), 1–5, 9 n. 12
Manumission records, 99–100
Marriage: and *métissage,* 97–100,
    106 n. 12; petitions for permission,
    101–4, 107 n. 27; Puritan companionate,
    134–35
Marsh, Joseph, 21
Marshall, Charles, 149
Marshall, Daniel, 179
Martin, Lucinda, 235 n. 33
Martyrology, 157
Massachusetts Bay Colony, 51, 152–55
Massasoit, 52
Masson, Margaret, 132–33, 140 n. 5
Master, T. W., 31, 32
Materiality, 143 n. 44, 152
Mather, Cotton, 7, 17, 20, 23, 132; *Decen-*
    nium Luctuosum, 193–207; diaries of,
    90; Duston's story and, 193–94; identifi-
    catory positions of, 199–200, 208 n. 10;
    on Native Americans, 165–66; *Pillars of*

Mather, Cotton (*continued*)
Salt, 86, 91; Salem witchcraft trials and, 79, 90–91; self-perception of, 90–91; *Warnings from the Dead*, 77–92
Mather, Increase, 166–67
Mayflower, 43
McCoy, Genevieve, 137
McMath, James, 119
Medical discourse, 61–63; anatomical texts and, 135–37; medical milieu and, 62–63, 115–16; moral implications of, 64, 67–69; politics and, 64–66, 70; of pregnancy, 112–14
Medical Museum, The, 227
Medical Repository, 226
Melish, Joanne Pope, 7
Mental illness, 67, 69, 88
Mestizos, 97
Metacomet, 165
Metaphors, 7–8. *See also individual metaphors*
Métissage, 97–100, 106n. 12. *See also* Marriage
Milk imagery. *See* Breast milk imagery
Miller, Jacquelyn C., 6
Ministers, 87; disrespect for, 198, 199; feminization of, 18, 109, 118, 129; reputation of, 79, 82, 91, 199. *See also* Feminization
Miró, Governor, 97
Miscegenation, 106n. 12
Mitchell, John, 63
Montgomery, John, 70
Moors, 101, 102
Morality: environment and, 46–47, 50–51; medical discourse of, 64, 67–69; uncleanness and, 80–81
Morbid excitement, 63, 69–70
Morris dancing, 167–68
Morse, Jedediah, 240
Morse, Samuel F. B., 240–42
Morse, William, 14, 20
Morton, Samuel George, 231
Morton, Thomas, 48, 168
Moss, Henry, 225–27
Motherhood, 78, 110; in captivity narratives, 196, 201–2
Moxon, Joseph, 15
Mulatas, 99
Mulato libre, 99
Mulatos, 97
Mulkey, Philip, 178–79
Mystics, women as, 148–49

Name of War, The (Lepore), 199, 208n. 11
Narrative, boundaries and, 199–200
Native Americans, 2, 3; Abenaki people, 165, 170, 171; accommodation and, 212, 214; and adopted whites, 217, 222n. 41; Catawba people, 216; Cherokee people, 212, 219n. 5; Chickasaw people, 215; Conestoga people, 213–14; Conoy people, 215; Delaware people, 214–15; and diet, 30, 33–37; Iroquois people (Six Nations), 165, 170, 213, 215, 216; as lazy, 52, 53; Maliseet people, 166; Mi'kmaq people, 164, 168–69; Narragansett people, 164; Pequot people, 53–54, 155; Plymouth Colony and, 44; postures as "antic," 163, 167, 168, 170–71; as savage, 49, 51, 53, 55; Shawnee people, 215, 216; Wabanaki people, 168; Wampanoag people, 164, 168. *See also* Captivity narratives; Dance, Native American; English-Indian diplomacy
Navalscapes, 237, 238, 243–52; individualism in, 247–48
Neal, John, 249
Neff, Mary, 91
Negras, 99
Nelson, Dana, 238, 245
Nemesius, 130
Neoclassicism, 246
Nervous system, 62–63; letter writing compared to, 115, 121
Neve, Richard, 15
New Anatomie, A (Underwood), 16–17
New England, 7, 48–50. *See also* Diet
New England Judged, 153
New England's Prospect (Wood), 163
New Orleans: and black elite, 95, 100; hybrid legal system of, 96; and manumission, 99–100; and *métissage*, 97–100, 106n. 12; and social boundaries, 96, 100; white population of, 95–97
New Testament, 177–78, 214
Nobility, 206
Noirs, 97
North Africans, 224, 228–29, 234n. 25
Norton, John, 155–56
Norton, Mary Beth, 139
Nunnuit, Peter, 165
Nursing fathers, 129–30, 138–39, 213. *See also* Bride of Christ imagery; Feminization; Puritans
"Nutriment" (Hippocratic treatise), 30

Omnivore's paradox, 29
One-seed theory, 117–18
One-sex model, 110, 123n. 4, 130–32, 136, 138–39
Order: environment and, 45–47; physical movements and, 170; subversion of, 24–25; women as threatening, 202–5
Order in Council of 1807, 238

Ovists, 120
Oxford English Dictionary, 167
Paper to New England, A (Fox), 155
Parable of the Ten Virgins, The
 (Shepherd), 109
Parkinson, John, 37
Parsons, James, 225–26
Patuxet, 44–45
Peale, Charles Wilson, 225
Penmanship, 114–15
Penn, William, 213–14
Pennsylvania Academy of the Fine Arts, 246
Pennsylvania Constitution, 66, 70
Pequots, 53–54, 155
Performance, 6; Baptist ritual practice and,
 177, 180–82; corporeal prophecy and,
 145–51, 157; of gendered roles, 130–33,
 138–39, 141n. 7; of skills, 168–69. *See
 also* Bride of Christ imagery; Dance, Na-
 tive American; Embodiment; Feminization;
 Nursing fathers; Regulation of body
Perley, Hannah, 22
Peters, Hugh, 131
Philip III, 37
Phillips, John, 13, 20
Philosophes, 4
Phips, William, 78, 196, 199
Pillars of Salt (Mather), 86, 91
Pineses, 165
Planting of body, 46, 51, 53–55
Plymouth Colony, 43–51; illness, 44–46.
 See also Puritans
Politics, 6; elitist view of, 66–67; medical
 discourse of, 64–66, 70–71; mental dis-
 eases caused by, 67, 69; nursing father
 image and, 138; legitimacy in, 195,
 198–99, 206–7
Polygenesis, 3
Porterfield, Amanda, 132
Port Folio, 246, 247, 249–50
Possession, by witches, 14, 20, 26–27n. 15
Possession, of resources, 46, 51–54
Post nati statutes, 223, 232n. 1
Power, 2–3; feminized discourse and,
 18–20; political legitimacy and, 195, 198;
 of torturer, 199, 204, 208n. 16
Powows, 164–65
Preformationist school, 120–21
Pregnancy: barrenness and, 119–20; and
 birth as moment of grace, 110–11, 122;
 blood and, 113, 115, 117; brain-uterus
 link and, 112, 121; conception, imagination, and, 112, 121; hearth and, 19–20;
 medical discourse of, 112–14; one-seed
 theory of, 117–18; as pathological,
 112–13, 117, 118; spiritual progress and,
 117, 119, 121; stages of, 114; theories of
 procreation and, 120–21

Pregnancy imagery, 109–11, 149; letter
 writing linked to, 112–14; religious conversion and, 109–10, 114, 119–20, 132
Prince, Sarah, 110–22
Providentialism, 82, 88, 90, 205
Psalms (Watts), 122
Public versus private sphere, 238
Purges, 61, 63
Puritans, 7–8; companionate marriage of,
 134–35; crisis in male authority and,
 194–98, 206–7; gender hierarchy and,
 131–35; jurisprudence of, 139; language
 of feminization and, 132–33, 140n. 5;
 modernity and, 133–35; Quakers and,
 152–55, 198; third-generation elite of,
 194–95, 198, 205; witchcraft and, 14;
 women's voices and, 139. *See also* Feminization; Social body
Purity of blood. *See Limpieza de sangre*
 cases

Quakers, 7, 89; and anti-Quaker pamphlets,
 145–46, 150–52, 155–56, 158n. 1;
 attacks on, 152–54; and authority of
 women, 147, 149, 155; and blame of
 women, 146–47; *Book of Sufferings*, 152;
 as Children of Light, 150; and christopresentism, 148, 159n. 9; and convincement,
 146, 148, 158n. 3; and corporeal
 prophecy, 145–51, 157; and embodied
 spirit theology, 147–48; First Generation
 of, 147, 149; and Meetings for Worship,
 147, 149; and prophesying, 146, 149–50,
 154, 156, 158n. 2; and Puritans, 152–55,
 198; and quaking body, 145–50; Second
 Generation of, 146, 158n. 2; as seducers,
 145, 146, 151; and Spiritual Mothers in
 Israel, 147, 149–57, 160n. 14; and
 witchcraft, 24
Quaterons, 97, 99

Race: biological racism and, 95–96, 104;
 change metaphor and, 7–8; classification
 of, 225; and location of difference,
 226–27; Man of Signs and, 5; and melancholic temperament, 32, 35; and
 métissage, 97–100, 106n. 12; and racial
 fluidity, 104; and racialized bodies,
 184–86, 189n. 27; and racial variability,
 97; and regulation of bodies, 6–7,
 184–86; and *sangre limpia* concept,
 95–96; and skin color, 211, 215–18,
 221nn. 32, 37; social hierarchy and, 3,
 101, 103–4; uncleanness and, 91–92. *See
 also* African Americans; *Limpieza de sangre* cases; Native Americans; Role reversal literature
Rachem, 149

Randolph, William, 250
Reform efforts, 64, 65
Regulation of body, 29; by architecture, 18–20; by Baptists, 182–87, 189 nn. 17, 24; black bodies and, 184–86; control of lower classes and, 70–71; through diet, 29; masculine identity formation and, 237–38; Native Americans and, 170–71; Quaker persecutions and, 151–56; racial issues and, 6–7; social decorum and, 183–84, 187
Relation or Iournall of the beginning and proceedings of the English Plantation setled at Plimoth in New England, 43–44
Religion: *limpieza de sangre* cases and, 96, 102, 105 n. 2. *See also* Evangelical religion; Ministers
Republic, 19, 24, 62
Reputation, 79, 82, 91, 101–3
Revolutiana, 67
Richardson, Samuel, 111, 125 n. 22
Right-handedness, 212, 219 n. 5
Riolan, Jean, 136, 138
Rise, Progress, and Present State of Medicine, The (Waterhouse), 136
Ritual practice, 177, 180–82
Robin, Martin, 99
Robinson, John, 46, 47, 53, 55
Rogers, Robert, 196
Role reversal literature, 223–25; Algiers captivity as, 228–31, 234 nn. 23, 26, 27, 235 n. 33; location of difference and, 226–27, 230–31; transformation of skin and, 225–28
Romanticism, 246–47
Roper, Lyndal, 2
Rosen, George, 73 n. 13
Rotunda, 249–50
Rowe, Elizabeth Singer, 122, 126 n. 43
Rowlandson, Mary, 164, 194
Rowson, Susanna, 230–31, 235 n. 34
Rozin, Paul, 29
Rush, Benjamin, 2, 6, 225, 227; and class biases, 66–68; "Diseases of the Passions," 68; heroic therapeutics and, 61, 63; medical discourse, politics, and, 61–65; "Moral and Physical Thermometer," 69; morbid excitement theory of, 63; political influence of, 61–64; unitary theory of disease of, 63, 64, 69–70; on mental disease, 67

Safford, John, 21
Said, Edward, 163
Sailors' rights, 239
St. George, Robert Blair, 7
Saltbox houses, 18–20
Sang mêlé, 98
Sarmiento de Acuña, Diego de, 37

Scarry, Elaine, 112, 115, 169, 199, 204, 208 n. 16
Schiebinger, Londa, 130, 138
Schilling, Chris, 29
Schweitzer, Ivy, 133, 134
Scientific Revolution, 4
Scolds, 17
Scotia, Hugh, 21
Scriptura rediviva, 148, 159–60 n. 10
Seed, Patricia, 97
Self-identification, 29
Sensibility, 114–15
Seven Years War, 216
Sewall, Samuel, 17, 23
Sexual difference, 109, 141 n. 7; early modern understandings of, 133–35; Galenic model of, 130–31; one-sex model of, 110, 123 n. 4, 130–32, 136, 138–39; two-sex model of, 4, 8, 131, 138–39
Sexuality: descent lines and, 96; figurative homosexuality and, 133–34, 141 n. 21; punishment of misbehavior and, 184–86; uncleanness and, 79–80, 89–90; wilderness and, 49
Shamans, 164, 172 n. 11
Shepherd, Thomas, 109
Shoemaker, Nancy, 7–8
Silverman, Kaja, 253 n. 17
Simmonds, Martha, 149
Sin, 49–50, 79–81
Skin color: English-Indian diplomacy and, 211, 215–18, 221 nn. 32, 37; role reversal literature and, 225–28
Slavery, 96–99, 186, 217, 223–24
Slaves in Algiers (Rowson), 230–31, 235 n. 34
Smith, John, 34–37
Smith, John Augustine, 231
Smith, Samuel Stanhope, 224, 225
Smith, Sarah, 86
Social body, 2, 6, 64, 193–94; in captivity narratives, 194–99, 203–5; uncleanness of, 79–80, 82–85, 91
Social contract, 135, 142 n. 25
Social status, 102–4, 212
Society of Friends. *See* Quakers
Soul, 19, 62, 114–16, 118, 121
Spanish law, 7, 95
Spear, Jennifer M., 6–7
Sperma, 117
Spirited Resistance, A (Dowd), 216
Spiritual embodiment, 110
Spiritual Mothers in Israel, 147, 149–57, 160 n. 14
Spy, The (Cooper), 244
Spy scandals, 244
Stability, 29, 39, 135
Staiti, Paul, 240–42

Stallybrass, Peter, 2, 189n. 23
Stearns, Shubal, 179
Stevens, James W., 229, 235nn. 30, 33
Stolcke, Verena, 98, 102
Studly, Thomas, 36
Subordination: embodiment of, 223–24, 228–30; of women, 119, 121, 134–35
Sure Guide to the Best and Nearest Way to Physick and Chyrurgery, A (Riolan), 136
Surveyor's Dialogue, The, 19
Swan, Timothy, 21
Systema naturae (Linnaeus), 225

Tarter, Michele Lise, 7
Taylor, Edward, 15, 17–18, 129, 130, 133–34, 140n. 2
Taylor, John, 179
Tecumseh, 216
Teedyuscung, 215
Temperaments, 30–32, 35–36, 40n. 9
Tenskwatawa, 216
Theory of correspondence. *See* Doctrine of signatures
Thomson, Rosemarie Garland, 142–43n. 35
Threeneedles, Sarah, 86
Tisquantum (Squanto), 45, 52
Todkill, Anas, 36
Toothaker, Roger, 24
Torture, 165–66, 169–70, 229; mediated descriptions of, 199–201; and power of torturer, 199, 204, 208n. 16
Toulouse, Teresa A., 7
Transubstantiation, 29
Travers, Rebecca, 149
Treaty of Ghent, 240
Trumbull, John, 248–50
Turner, Bryan S., 45–46
Twinam, Ann, 101
Two-sex model, 4, 8, 131, 138–39
Tyler, Royall, 230–31

Ulrich, Laurel Thatcher, 197
Uncleanness, 203; animals as source of, 88–89; categories of, 80; class and, 91–92; clothing and, 86–88; Devil and, 89–90; embodied response and, 90; executions and, 85–86, 91; female body and, 79, 85–86; filth avoidance and, 81–82, 87–88; health and, 80–81, 88–89; morality and, 80–81; pollution and, 80–81, 151–52; poverty as, 89; racialized, 91–92; sexuality and, 79–80, 89–90; of social body, 79–80, 82–85, 91
Underwood, Robert, 16–17

Vidal, Nicholas Maria, 100, 104
Virginia Company, 36–37, 38

Waller, John, 179

Walton, George, 14, 20, 24
Warnings from the Dead (Mather), 77–92
War of 1812, 237–52; biographies and, 247; cross-dressing narratives and, 245; heroes and, 247; impressment and, 238–39; international commerce and, 238; visual documentation of, 243–44
Washington, George, 64, 71, 244
Waterhouse, Benjamin, 136
Watt, Isaac, 122
West, Robert, 20–21
White, Allon, 2
White, Charles, 231
White, Dorothy, 148
White, John, 35, 36
White, Mary, 145, 158n. 1
White, Richard, 211
White, Robert, 229
White, William, 145
Whitefield, George, 111
Whites, as term, 223, 224, 232n. 2
Wiegman, Robyn, 3
Wigglesworth, Michael, 141n. 21
Wilderness, 36; civilization of, 45–55; first encounters with, 43–45; garden imagery, 45, 51–53; as permeable, 47; possession of, 46, 51–54; as savage, 49, 51, 53, 55; sin and, 49–50. *See also* Environment
Willan, Thomas, 149
Willard, Samuel, 23
William of Orange, 206
Williams, Roger, 164, 165
Wilson, James, 66
Wingfield, Edward Maria, 38
Winslow, Edward, 50, 52, 165
Winter, John, 19
Winthrop, John, 51, 122, 134–35
Witch bottles, 23–24
Witchcraft, 78, 151, 170; attacks on houses and, 14–15, 20–22; countermagic against, 22–24; hearth and, 21–24; marginal status of those accused of, 13–14, 20; Mather and, 79, 90–91; possession and, 14, 20, 26–27n. 15; and property owners, 14, 20; and searches, 153, 161–62n. 26
Wolcott, Oliver, 71
Wood, William, 46, 48–49, 163, 167
Word of God: breast milk imagery and, 118, 122, 150, 153–54, 159n. 6; feminization of, 110–11, 122
Written language, 111–12

Yellow fever, 61, 63, 69–71, 72n. 5, 74n. 29

Zodiac, 1, 4–5
Zuñiga, Pedro de, 37